RECORDS OF THE
LIFE OF JESUS

RECORDS OF THE LIFE OF JESUS

Revised Standard Version

Book I: The Record of Mt-Mk-Lk
Book II: The Record of John

Henry Burton Sharman, Ph.D.

GUILD FOR PSYCHOLOGICAL STUDIES
PUBLISHING HOUSE

San Francisco

Published in the United States of America by
The Guild for Psychological Studies Publishing House
PO Box 29385
San Francisco, California 94129-0385
www.guildsf.org

Library of Congress Cataloging-in-Publication Data

Bible. N.T. Gospels. English. Revised Standard. 1990
     Records of the Life of Jesus: Revised Standard Version [as arranged by] Henry Burton Sharman.
     This edition, edited by Elizabeth Boyden Howes, substitutes the Revised Standard Version of the Gospels for the English Revised Version in H. B. Sharman's original edition.
     1. Bible. N.T. Gospels - Harmonies, English.
I. Sharman, Henry Burton. II. Howes, Elizabeth Boyden, 1907-
III. Title.
BS2560.S445   1990
226'.1 - dc20   90-47169

ISBN 978-0-917479-12-0

RECORDS OF THE LIFE OF JESUS

THE PURPOSE

The purpose of the book is to present the records of the life of Jesus in that form which will make most fully available the contributions of the several sources, both individual and collective, to an understanding of the actual career of Jesus. It has been the aim so to set forth the material as to provide primarily for an historical rather than a critical knowledge of the records. Stated in another way, the foremost intention has been to produce, in the language and in the order of the original records, a Life of Jesus. But it is thought also that, in the pursuance of that aim, the literary phenomena of the records have been so exhibited as to provide the basis for somewhat thorough critical study of the source relationships of these records.

THE METHOD

At no point throughout the work has any theory or hypothesis as to any literary or other relation of these records to one another had any part in the determination of the arrangement or the showing forth of the material. Mark is placed in the order of Mark; Luke is placed in the order of Luke, and John in its own order. In the case of Matthew only has any departure in order been made, and there for three chapters only (8-9-10) of the twenty-eight of that record. The departure made in that case was not based on any theory as to the source relations of the records, but resulted simply from the decision to conform Matthew in these chapters (8-9-10), as Matthew of itself is conformed throughout the rest of its structure, to that order of events on which Mark and Luke are in complete agreement. It will be evident, therefore, that not only has no theory of the relations of these records had any place in the work but also that the book cannot be regarded as a harmony of the records.

THE FORM

Those portions of the text that appear in roman type represent each record in its own chronological order, except that chapters 8-9-10 of Matthew, though in roman type, are not in the Matthew order,[1] but are conformed to the order of Mark-Luke. Those portions of the text that appear in italic type are not in the sequence of the records from which they come, but are placed where they stand in order that they may be studied there in relation to the record that does stand chronologically at that point. If, therefore, the reader will pass over what stands in italic type, the book may be used for the independent consecutive study of any one of the four individual records.[2]

THE FEATURES

It has been the intention throughout to show on each page all related material from all parts of the records--either by direct parallelism or by attached references to footnotes. When the related material has chronological agreement, all the reports stand in parallelism in roman type. When the relation is one of event or of thought only and not also of chronology, the report out of its own chronological order stands in parallelism in italic type, with a cross-reference to the section where it may be found in its own order and therefore in roman type. When the related material from distant places in the records has such bond with, or relationship in, those other places as cannot be properly or adequately shown by immediate parallelism, these related portions are set forth as attached footnotes. It should be true, therefore, that on any page of the book one may find the account of every occurrence within the records of those events or sayings that appear on that page--subject only to the general reservation that in the record of Matt-Mark-Luke no references forward are given to the record of John,[3] though every effort has been made to give completeness to the references that are shown throughout John to the related material in Matt-Mark-Luke.

---

1. It should be observed that even within these chapters the Matthew order of events corresponds in considerable measure to that of Mark-Luke, for example, the consecution of §§ 50-52 and of §§ 29-31.

2. In the case of the apparent (though not real) confusion in the Matthew order resulting from the conforming of Matthew 8-9-10 to the order of Mark-Luke, guidance is given by indicating in parts of Matthew the place of the succeeding portion by means of the notation (+ § 26) and the like at the end of the section, and for backward reference (§ 23 +) and the like at the head of the section.

3. The references forward from the record of Mt-Mk-Lk to the record of John are shown completely and in order on page 235.

THE SUBDIVISIONS

The subdivisions of the paragraphs, made by the simple expedient of opening the text without any change of form or order, have been determined (*a*) by what it was thought would best contribute to comparative study and to ease of cross-reference, and (*b*) by what seemed the natural subdivisions of the thought. In general, the former consideration controlled the subdivisions in Matt-Mark-Luke; while in much of John, where cross-references and comparisons are fewer, the subdivisions of paragraphs were made with the purpose of possibly facilitating at some points the grasp and memory of the complex thought.

THE ORDER

It has been believed that the clearest and soundest results could not be reached, in any serious effort to understand Jesus, by an endeavor to reconstruct the history through the direct combination of the record of Matt-Mark-Luke with the record of John. Rather it has been thought that one should first be enabled to acquire the contributions of Matt-Mark-Luke, without taking any account of the chronological or other elements of John--not necessarily because of any judgment as to the relative historical worth of these sources, but solely on the basis of the fundamental difference in the method of their approach to the theme. When one has attained some adequate knowledge of the record of Matt-Mark-Luke, the immeasurable values in the record of John will be both better understood and more justly used in coming to the fulness of the knowledge of the stature of Jesus.

Easter, 1917

INTRODUCTION TO
REVISED STANDARD VERSION

This volume of the *Records of the Life of Jesus*, according to the Revised Standard Version translation of the gospels, is a long-awaited achievement. In 1917 Dr. Henry Burton Sharman published the *Records of the Life of Jesus* in an arrangement in which the three synoptic gospels of Matthew, Mark, and Luke were placed in parallel columns *without any displacement of order* (with one minor exception). We at the Guild for Psychological Studies believe that his presentation of the parallels is still the clearest and yet most easily usable of all such gospel parallels, though others have been produced since (notably, *Gospel Parallels* by Throckmorton and *New Gospel Parallels* by Funk). This book by Dr. Sharman was based on the English Revised Version of 1881. Since that time much scholarly research has been done, thousands of manuscripts have been recovered, and many new translations have appeared, greatly advancing our knowledge.

The *Records of the Life of Jesus* was used by Dr. Sharman in seminars he conducted in Canada beginning in 1923. Among others I continued his work in California, beginning in 1934. The essence of that work is being carried on by leaders of the Guild for Psychological Studies, San Francisco and Middletown, California. The objective of this seminar approach is to discover the meaning of Jesus of Nazareth for our lives. In these seminars the desire has often been expressed for the use of a more recent translation. The present Revised Standard Version edition makes that possible.

The first step was taken by the leaders of the seminars in the Guild, especially Ruth Alura Dodd, who put the Revised Standard material in exactly the same format as found in the *Records*. This required great precision and accuracy.

A grant from an anonymous woman donor has made possible the publication. To her we offer deepest thanks for her insight into the value of this project. Heartfelt gratitude is also extended to Mary Morrison, who, for many years, has been committed to working with the *Records* and has led seminars at Pendle Hill in Wallingford, Pennsylvania. It was through her efforts that the contact was made with the donor.

The final step, then, has been the work of completing this book with some changes and additions. In this Revised Standard Version edition, references to Hebrew Scripture, not included by Dr. Sharman, and to non-canonical sources have been added. The Hebrew Scripture references are noted at the bottom of each page by *H.S. reference*. The non-canonical references are noted as *N.C. reference*. The non-canonical references are limited to the Gospel of Thomas which contains many reported sayings of Jesus, some in forms thought to be earlier than the canonical gospels. The decision to limit the non-canonical parallels was based, in part, upon the evident earliness and pristine character of some of the Gospel of Thomas sayings, as discussed by H. Koester in *The Nag Hammadi Library* (San Francisco: Harper & Row, 1977) and by A. Guillaument, et al., in *The Gospel According to Thomas* (New York: Harper & Row, 1959). We are grateful to Robert W. Funk, *New Gospel Parallels* (Philadelphia: Fortress Press, 1985 and subsequent editions by Polebridge Press, Sonoma) for his work with non-canonical sources.

While the major supervision of this project has been in my hands, there are many other individuals who have contributed time, energy and knowledge. It is not possible to list all of those who worked on the painstaking job of placing the Revised Standard material in the proper order of the *Records*. To them our gratitude is offered. I do want to recognize the contributions of a few persons. The checking on all details has been provided by John Petroni and John Williams. The re-working of references to the Hebrew Scriptures and non-canonical sources has been done by John Hitchcock, Bill Dols, Jerry Drino, Manuel Costa, John Lee, Steve Lusk, and Judith Anders-Richards. Typesetting of this arrangement proved difficult; various attempts were coordinated by Rudy Marcus; Carina Ravely computer-produced the camera-ready copy with care and enthusiasm.

Deep thanks are due to Florence Little, Librarian of the Guild, and especially to Walter Wink, who early on encouraged the undertaking of this project.

As founding leader of the Guild for Psychological Studies, I express a heartfelt hope that this edition of the *Records of the Life of Jesus* will add substantially to the field of biblical studies and will add to the possibility of understanding deeply the meaning of Jesus of Nazareth for our lives.

Four Springs, 1991   Elizabeth Boyden Howes

RECORDS OF THE LIFE OF JESUS

BOOK I: THE RECORD OF MT-MK-LK

CHAPTER I

STATEMENTS ABOUT ORIGINS

CHAPTER II

EARLY LIFE OF JOHN AND OF JESUS

CHAPTER III

ACTIVITY OF JOHN AND ITS RELATION TO JESUS

CHAPTER IV

BEGINNINGS OF THE PUBLIC ACTIVITY OF JESUS

CHAPTER V

DEVELOPMENT OF OPPOSITION TO JESUS

CHAPTER VI

DEFINITION OF STANDARDS OF RIGHTEOUSNESS BY JESUS

CHAPTER VII

CONTEMPORARY OPINIONS ABOUT THE WORTH OF JESUS

CHAPTER VIII

THE MYSTERY OF THE KINGDOM OF GOD

CHAPTER IX

THE PLACE OF FAITH IN THE WORK OF JESUS

CHAPTER X

TOUR OF THE DISCIPLES AND RESULTANT EVENTS

CHAPTER XI

DEMAND BY PHARISEES FOR CONFORMITY AND CREDENTIALS

CHAPTER XII

FORECASTS OF CONFLICT WITH THE JERUSALEM AUTHORITIES

CHAPTER XIII

DEPARTURE PROM GALILEE FOR JERUSALEM

CHAPTER XIV

CONDEMNATION FOR OPPONENTS AND CONCERN FOR DISCIPLES

CHAPTER XV

DEEP FEELING AND DIRECT TEACHING

CHAPTER XVI

MANY TRUTHS TAUGHT IN PARABLES

CHAPTER XVII

TEACHING AND JOURNEYING ON TO JERUSALEM

CHAPTER XVIII

CHALLENGE OF THE JERUSALEM LEADERS BY JESUS

CHAPTER XIX

FINAL CONTEST OF JESUS WITH THE JEWISH RULERS

CHAPTER XX

DISCOURSE IN CONDEMNATION OF SCRIBES AND PHARISEES

CHAPTER XXI

DISCOURSE ON EVENTS OF THE FUTURE

CHAPTER XXII

FINAL HOURS OF JESUS WITH HIS DISCIPLES

CHAPTER XXIII

JUDICIAL TRIALS AND CRUCIFIXION OF JESUS

CHAPTER XXIV

EVENTS SUBSEQUENT TO THE DEATH OF JESUS

BOOK II: THE RECORD OF JOHN

CHAPTER I

PROLOGUE TO THE RECORD OF JOHN

CHAPTER II

IN BETHANY BEYOND JORDAN

CHAPTER III

IN THE PROVINCE OF GALILEE

CHAPTER IV

IN JERUSALEM AT THE PASSOVER

CHAPTER V

IN THE LAND OF JUDEA

CHAPTER VI

IN THE PROVINCE OF SAMARIA

CHAPTER VII

IN THE PROVINCE OF GALILEE

CHAPTER VIII

IN JERUSALEM AT A FEAST

CHAPTER IX

ABOUT THE SEA OF GALILEE

CHAPTER X

AT THE FEAST OF TABERNACLES

CHAPTER XI

AT THE FEAST OF THE DEDICATION

CHAPTER XII

IN THE REGION OF JERUSALEM

CHAPTER XIII

CHALLENGE TO THE JERUSALEM LEADERS

CHAPTER XIV

FINAL HOURS WITH DISCIPLES

CHAPTER XV

JUDICIAL TRIALS AND CRUCIFIXION

CHAPTER XVI

SUBSEQUENT TO THE DEATH OF JESUS

BOOK I
THE RECORD OF MT-MK-LK

RECORDS OF THE LIFE OF JESUS

BOOK I

THE RECORD OF MT-MK-LK

Chapter I

STATEMENTS ABOUT ORIGINS

---

§ 1 Origin of the Records

LUKE 1:1-4

Inasmuch as many have undertaken to compile a narrative 1 of the things which have been accomplished among us, just 2 as they were delivered to us by those who from the beginning were eyewitnesses and ministers of the word, it 3 seemed good to me also, having followed all things closely for some time past, to write an orderly account for you, most excellent The-oph'ilus, that you may know the truth 4 concerning the things of which you have been informed.

§ 2 The Genealogy of Jesus

| MATT 1:1-17 | LUKE 3:23-38 |

¹The book of the ²genealogy of Jesus Christ, the son of 1 David, the son of Abraham.

Abraham was the father of Isaac, and Isaac the father of 2 Jacob, and Jacob the father of Judah and his brothers, and 3 Judah the father of Perez and Zerah by Tamar, and Perez the father of Hezron, and Hezron the father of ³Ram, and 4 ³Ram the father of Ammin'adab, and Ammin'adab the father of Nahshon, and Nahshon the father of Salmon, and 5 Salmon the father of Bo'az by Rahab, and Bo'az the father of Obed by Ruth, and Obed the father of Jesse, and Jesse 6 the father of David the king.

And David was the father of Solomon by the wife of Uri'ah, and Solomon the father of Rehobo'am, and 7 Rehobo'am the father of Abi'jah, and Abi'jah the father of ⁴Asa, and ⁴Asa the father of Jehosh'aphat, and Jehosh'aphat 8 the father of Joram, and Joram the father of Uzzi'ah, and 9 Uzzi'ah the father of Jotham, and Jotham the father of Ahaz, and Ahaz the father of Hezeki'ah, and Hezeki'ah the 10 father of Manas'seh, and Manas'seh the father of ⁵Amos, and ⁵Amos the father of Josi'ah, and Josi'ah the father of 11

Jesus, when he began his ministry, was about thirty years 23 of age, being the son (as was supposed) of Joseph, the son of Heli, the son of Matthat, the son of Levi, the son of 24 Melchi, the son of Jan'na-i, the son of Joseph, the son of 25 Mattathi'as, the son of Amos, the son of Nahum, the son of Esli, the son of Nag'ga-i, the son of Ma'ath, the son of 26 Mattathi'as, the son of Sem'e-in, the son of Josech, the son of Joda, the son of Jo-an'an, the son of Rhesa, the son of 27 Zerub'babel, the son of ⁶She-al'ti-el, the son of Neri, the 28 son of Melchi, the son of Addi, the son of Cosam, the son of Elma'dam, the son of Er, the son of Joshua, the son of 29 Elie'zer, the son of Jorim, the son of Matthat, the son of Levi, the son of Simeon, the son of Judah, the son of 30 Joseph, the son of Jonam, the son of Eli'akim, the son of 31 Me'le-a, the son of Menna, the son of Mat'tatha, the son of Nathan, the son of David, the son of Jesse, the son of 32 Obed, the son of Bo'az, the son of Sala, the son of Nahshon, the son of Ammin'adab, the son of Admin, the⁷ 33 son of ⁸Arni, the son of Hezron, the son of Perez, the son of Judah, the son of Jacob, the son of Isaac, the son of 34 Abraham, the son of Terah, the son of Nahor, the son of 35 Serug, the son of Re'u, the son of Peleg, the son of Eber,

---

1 Or *The genealogy of Jesus Christ*   2 Or *birth* as in verse 18   3 Greek *Aram*   4 Greek *Asaph*   5 Some authorities read *Amon*   6 Greek *Salathiel*   7 Many ancient authorities insert *the son of Admin: and one writes Admin* for *Amminadab*   8 Some ancient authorities write *Aram*

HS references: Mt 1:2-6 and Lk 3:31-34 = I Chronicles 2:1-15   Mt 1:3-6 and Lk 3:32-33 = Ruth 4:18-22   Mt 1:7-12 = I Chronicles 3:10-17
Mt 1:11 = II Kings 24:14 and Jeremiah 27:20   Lk 3:23-38 = Genesis 5:3-32, 11:10-26 and I Chronicles 1:1-4, 24-28 and 2:1-15
Lk 3:27 = I Chronicles 3:17

MATT 1

Jechoni'ah and his brothers, at the time of the [1]deportation to Babylon.

And after the [1]deportation to Babylon: Jechoni'ah was the 12 father of [2]She-al'ti-el, and [2]She-al'ti-el the father of Zerub'babel, and Zerub'babel the father of Abi'ud, and 13 Abi'ud the father of Eli'akim, and Eli'akim the father of Azor, and Azor the father of Zadok, and Zadok the father 14 of Achim, and Achim the father of Eli'ud, and Eli'ud the 15 father of Elea'zar, and Elea'zar the father of Matthan, and Matthan the father of Jacob, and Jacob the father of Joseph 16 the husband of Mary, of whom Jesus was born, who is called [3]Christ.

So all the generations from Abraham to David were 17 fourteen generations, and from David to the [1]deportation to Babylon fourteen generations, and from the [1]deportation to Babylon to the Christ fourteen generations.

LUKE 3

the son of Shelah, the son of Ca-i'nan, the son of 36 Arphax'ad, the son of Shem, the son of Noah, the son of Lamech, the son of Methuselah, the son of Enoch, the son 37 of Jared, the son of Maha'lale-el, the son of Cai'nan, the 38 son of Enos, the son of Seth, the son of Adam, the son of God. (§ 19)

§ 3 Forecast to the Father of John

MATTHEW

A *In the days of Herod the King, (§ 11 A) = 2:1*

D *With verse 17b, compare § 17 EF and § 41 E*

LUKE 1:5-25

A In the days of Herod, king of Judea, there was a priest 5 named Zechari'ah, of the division of Abi'jah; and he had a wife of the daughters of Aaron, and her name was Elizabeth. And they were both righteous before God, 6 walking in all the commandments and ordinances of the Lord blameless. But they had no child, because Elizabeth 7 was barren, and both [4]were advanced in years.

B Now while he was serving as priest before God when his 8 division was on duty, according to the custom of the 9 priesthood, it fell to him by lot to enter the [5]temple of the Lord and burn incense. And the whole multitude of the 10 people were praying outside at the hour of incense.

C And there appeared to him an angel of the Lord standing 11 on the right side of the altar of incense. And Zechari'ah 12 was troubled when he saw him, and fear fell upon him. But 13 the angel said to him, "Do not be afraid, Zechari'ah, for your prayer is heard, and your wife Elizabeth will bear you a son, and you shall call his name John.

D   And you will have joy and gladness,   14
    and many will rejoice at his birth;
    for he will be great before the Lord,   15
    and he shall drink no wine nor [6]strong drink,
    and he will be filled with the Holy Spirit,
    even from his mother's womb.
    And he will turn many of the sons of Israel   16

---

1 Or *removal to Babylon*   2 Greek *Salathiel*   3 Greek translation of Hebrew word "Messiah" meaning "anointed one"
4 Greek *advanced in their days*   5 Or *sanctuary*   6 Greek *sikera*

HS references: Lk 3:36-38 = I Chronicles 1:1-4   Lk 1:5 = I Chronicles 24:10   Lk 1:9 = Exodus 30:7   Lk 1:15 = Numbers 6:3 and Judges 13:4-5

LUKE 1

to the Lord their God,
and he will [1]go before him in the spirit
and power of Eli'jah,   17
to turn the hearts of the fathers to the children,
and the disobedient to the wisdom of the just,
to make ready for the Lord a people prepared."

E And Zechari'ah said to the angel, "How shall I know 18 this? For I am an old man, and my wife is [2]advanced in years." And the angel answered him, "I am Gabriel, who 19 stand in the presence of God; and I was sent to speak to you, and to bring you this good news. And behold, you 20 will be silent and unable to speak until the day that these things come to pass, because you did not believe my words, which will be fulfilled in their time."

F And the people were waiting for Zechari'ah, and they 21 wondered [3]at his delay in the [4]temple. And when he came 22 out, he could not speak to them, and they perceived that he had seen a vision in the temple; and he made signs to them and remained dumb. And when his time of service was 23 ended, he went to his home.

G After these days his wife Elizabeth conceived, and for 24 five months she hid herself, saying, "Thus the Lord has 25 done to me in the days when he looked on me, to take away my reproach among men."

§ 4 Forecast to the Mother of Jesus

MATTHEW

A *Mary had been betrothed to Joseph, (§ 6 A) = 1:18 Joseph, son of David, (§ 6 B) = 1:20*

B *She will bear a son, and you shall call his name Jesus, (§ 6 C) = 1:21*

C [8]*Where is he who has been born king of the Jews? (§ 11 B) = 2:2*

LUKE 1:26-38

A In the sixth month the angel Gabriel was sent from God 26 to a city of Galilee named Nazareth, to a virgin betrothed 27 to a man whose name was Joseph, of the house of David; and the virgin's name was Mary. And he came to her and 28 said, "Hail, [5]O favored one, the Lord is with you!"[6] But 29 she was greatly troubled at the saying, and considered in her mind what sort of greeting this might be. And the angel 30 said to her, "Do not be afraid, Mary, for you have found [7]favor with God.

B And behold, you will conceive in your womb and bear a 31 son, and you shall call his name Jesus.

C He will be great, and will be called the Son of   32
      the Most High;
   and the Lord God will give to him the throne of his
      father David,
   and he will reign over the house of   33

---

1 Some ancient authorities read *come nigh before his face*   2 Greek *advanced in her days*   3 Or *at his tarrying*   4 Or *sanctuary* 5 Or *endued with grace*   6 Many ancient authorities add *blessed* art *thou among women*: see verse 42   7 Or *grace*   8 Or *Where is the King of the Jews that is born?*

HS references: Lk 1:17 = Malachi 4:5-6   Lk 1:19 = Daniel 8:16 and 9:21   Lk 1:25 = Genesis 30:23 and Isaiah 4:1   Lk 1:31 = Isaiah 7:14   Lk 1:32-33 = II Samuel 7:12-17   Lk 1:33 = Daniel 2:44   Mt 2:2 = Numbers 24:17 and Jeremiah 23:5 and Zechariah 9:9

MATTHEW   LUKE 1

Jacob ¹for ever;
and of his kingdom there will be no end."

D *She was found to be with child of the Holy Spirit;*
(§ 6 A) = 1:18

That which is ²*conceived in her is of the Holy Spirit;*
(§ 6 B) = 1:20

D And Mary said to the angel, "How shall this be, since I 34
³have no husband?" And the angel said to her,   35
"The Holy Spirit will come upon you,
and the power of the Most High will
overshadow you;
therefore ⁴the child to be ⁵born⁶ will be
called holy,
the Son of God.

E And behold, your kinswoman Elizabeth in her old age 36
has also conceived a son; and this is the sixth month with
her who ⁷was called barren. For with God nothing will be 37
impossible." And Mary said, "Behold, I am the ⁸handmaid 38
of the Lord; let it be to me according to your word." And
the angel departed from her.

§ 5   Forecast by the Mother of John

LUKE 1:39-56

A In those days Mary arose and went with haste into the 39
hill country, to a city of Judah, and she entered the house 40
of Zechari'ah and greeted Elizabeth. And when Elizabeth 41
heard the greeting of Mary, the babe leaped in her womb;
and Elizabeth was filled with the Holy Spirit and she 42
exclaimed with a loud cry,

B "Blessed are you among women, and blessed is the fruit
of your womb! And why is this granted me, that the 43
mother of my Lord should come to me? For behold, when 44
the voice of your greeting came to my ears, the babe in my
womb leaped for joy. And blessed is she who ⁹believed that 45
there would be a fulfillment of what was spoken to her
from the Lord."

C And Mary said,   46
"My soul magnifies the Lord,
and my spirit rejoices in God my Savior,   47
for he has regarded the low estate of   48
his ¹⁰handmaiden.
For behold, henceforth all generations will
call me blessed;
for he who is mighty has done great   49
things ¹¹for me,
and holy is his name.
And his mercy is on those who fear him   50
from generation to generation.
He has shown strength with his arm,   51
he has scattered the proud ¹²in the
imagination of their hearts,

---

1 Greek *unto the ages*   2 Greek *begotten*   3 Greek *know not a man*   4 Or *the holy thing which is to be born shall be called the Son of God*
5 Or *begotten*   6 Some ancient authorities insert *of you*   7 Or *is*   8 Greek *slave*   9 Or *believed for there will be*
10 Greek *slave*   11 Greek *to me*   12 Or *by*

HS references: Lk 1:35 = Exodus 13:12   Lk 1:37 = Genesis 18:14   Lk 1:46-55 = I Samuel 2:1-10   Lk 1:47 = I Timothy 2:3; Titus 2:10; Jude 25
Lk 1:48 = I Samuel 1:11   Lk 1:50 = Psalm 103:17   Lk 1:51 = Psalm 89:10

LUKE 1

he has put down the mighty from their thrones,	52
and exalted those of low degree;	
he has filled the hungry with good things,	53
and the rich he has sent empty away.	
He has helped his servant Israel,	54
[1]in remembrance of his mercy,	
as he spoke to our fathers,	55
to Abraham and to his posterity for ever."	

D And Mary remained with her about three months, and 56 returned to her home.

§ 6 Forecast to Joseph of Nazareth

MATT 1:18-25	LUKE
A Now the [2]birth [3]of Jesus Christ took place in this way. 18 When his mother Mary had been betrothed to Joseph, before they came together she was found to be with child of the Holy Spirit; and her husband Joseph, being a just 19 man and unwilling to put her to shame, resolved to divorce her quietly.	**A** *To a virgin betrothed to a man whose name was Joseph. . . .and the virgin's name was Mary.* *(§ 4 A) = 1:27* *Mary, his betrothed. (§ 8 B) = 2:5* *Compare the passage from § 4 D under B below*
B But as he considered this, behold, an angel of the Lord 20 appeared to him in a dream, saying, "Joseph, son of David, do not fear to take Mary your wife, for that which is [4]conceived in her is of the Holy Spirit;	**B** *Joseph, of the house of David. (§ 4 A) = 1:27* *The Holy Spirit will come upon you, and the power of the Most High will overshadow you; therefore [5]the child to be [6]born[7] will be called holy, the Son of God. (§ 4 D) = 1:35*
C she will bear a son, and you shall call his name Jesus, 21 for he will save his people from their sins."	**C** *And behold, you will conceive in your womb and bear a son, and you shall call his name Jesus. (§ 4 B) = 1:31*
D All this took place to fulfil what the Lord had spoken by 22 the prophet: "Behold, a virgin shall conceive and bear a son, 23 and his name shall be called Emman'u-el" (which means, God with us).	
E When Joseph woke from sleep, he did as the angel of the 24 Lord commanded him; he took his wife, but knew her not 25 until she had borne a son; and he called his name Jesus.	**E** *And she gave birth to her first-born son. (§ 8 C) = 2:1* *He was called Jesus, the name given by the angel. (§ 10 A) = 2:21*

1 Greek *That he might remember mercy* 2 Or *genealogy: as in verse 1* 3 Some ancient authorities read *of the Christ* and some *of Jesus*
4 Greek *begotten* 5 Or *the holy thing which is to be born shall be called the Son of God* 6 Or *begotten* 7 Some ancient authorities insert *of you*

HS references: Lk 1:31 = Isaiah 7:14   Lk 1:35 = Exodus 13:12   Lk 1:52 = I Samuel 2:7-8 and Job 5:11 and 12:19   Lk 1:53 = I Samuel 2:5 and Psalm 107:9   Lk 1:54-55 = Isaiah 41:8-9   Lk 1:55 = Genesis 17:7 and Micah 7:20   Lk 2:21 = Genesis 17:12   Mt 1:23 = Isaiah 7:14

Chapter II

EARLY LIFE OF JOHN AND OF JESUS

---

§ 7 Birth of John the Baptist

MATTHEW   LUKE 1:57-80

A Now the time came for Elizabeth to be delivered, and 57 she gave birth to a son. And her neighbors and kinsfolk 58 heard that the Lord had shown great mercy to her, and they rejoiced with her. And on the eighth day they came to 59 circumcise the child;

B and they would have named him Zechari'ah after his father, but his mother said, "Not so; he shall be called 60 John." And they said to her, "None of your kindred is 61 called by this name." And they made signs to his father, 62 inquiring what he would have him called. And he asked for 63 a writing tablet, and wrote, "His name is John." And they all marveled. And immediately his mouth was opened and 64 his tongue loosed, and he spoke, blessing God.

C And fear came on all their neighbors. And all these 65 things were talked about through all the hill country of Judea; and all who heard them laid them up in their hearts, 66 saying, "What then will this child be?" For the hand of the Lord was with him.

D And his father Zechari'ah was filled with the Holy 67 Spirit, and prophesied, saying,
"Blessed be the Lord God of Israel,   68
for he has visited and redeemed his people,
and has raised up a horn of salvation for us   69
in the house of his servant David,   70
as he spoke by the mouth of his holy prophets
    from of old,
that we should be saved from our enemies,   71
and from the hand of all who hate us;
to perform the mercy promised to our fathers,   72
and to remember his holy covenant,
the oath which he swore to our father Abraham,   73
    to grant us   74
that we, being delivered from the hand of our
    enemies,
might serve him without fear,
in holiness and righteousness before him all the days   75
    of our life.

E *With verse 76 b, compare § 17 EF and § 41 E*
With verse 77 b, compare § 17 H

E And you, child, will be called the prophet of the   76
    Most High;
for you will go before the Lord to prepare his ways,
to give knowledge of salvation to his people   77
in the forgiveness of their sins,

HS references: Lk 1:59 = Genesis 17:10-13 and Leviticus 12:3   Lk 1:68 = Psalm 72:18 and 111:9   Lk 1:69 = I Samuel 2:10
Lk 1:71 = Psalm 106:10   Lk 1:72-73 = Genesis 17:7 and 22:16-18 and Leviticus 26:42 and Psalm 105:8-9 and Micah 7:20   Lk 1:76 = Malachi 4:5
Lk 1:76-77 = Malachi 3:1

LUKE 1

through the ¹tender mercy of our God,   78
²when the day ³shall dawn upon us from on high
to give light to those who sit in darkness and in the   79
     shadow of death,
to guide our feet into the way of peace."

F And the child grew and became strong in spirit, and he 80
was in the wilderness till the day of his manifestation to
Israel.

§ 8 Birth of Jesus at Bethlehem

MATTHEW

LUKE 2:1-7

A In those days a decree went out from Caesar Augustus 1
that all ⁴the world should be enrolled. This was the first 2
enrollment, when Quirin'i-us was governor of Syria. And 3
all went to be enrolled, each to his own city.

B *Jesus was born in Bethlehem of Judea (§ 11 A) = 2:1*
Mary had been betrothed to Joseph, (§ 6 A) = 1:18

B And Joseph also went up from Galilee, from the city of 4
Nazareth, to Judea, to the city of David, which is called
Bethlehem, because he was of the house and lineage of
David, to be enrolled with Mary, his betrothed, who was 5
with child.

C *But knew her not until she had borne a son;*
(§ 6 E) = 1:25

C And while they were there, the time came for her to be 6
delivered. And she gave birth to her first-born son and 7
wrapped him in swaddling cloths, and laid him in a
manger, because there was no place for them in the inn.

§ 9 Thanksgivings for the Birth of Jesus

LUKE 2:8-20

A And in that region there were shepherds out in the field, 8
keeping ⁵watch over their flock by night. And an angel of 9
the Lord appeared to them, and the glory of the Lord shone
around them, and they were filled with fear. And the angel 10
said to them, "Be not afraid; for behold, I bring you good
news of a great joy which will come to all the people; for 11
to you is born this day in the city of David a Savior, who
is ⁶Christ the Lord. And this will be a sign for you: you 12
will find a babe wrapped in swaddling cloths and lying in a
manger."

B And suddenly there was with the angel a multitude of the 13
heavenly host praising God and saying,
    "Glory to God in the highest,   14
    and on earth ⁷peace among ⁸men with whom he is
     pleased!"

C When the angels went away from them into heaven, the 15
shepherds said to one another, "Let us go over to
Bethlehem and see this ⁹thing that has happened, which the
Lord has made known to us."

---

1 Or *heart of mercy*   2 Or *Wherein*   3 Many ancient authorities read *has visited us*   4 Greek *the inhabited earth*   5 Or *night-watches*
6 Or *Anointed Lord*; or *the Anointed of the Lord*   7 Many ancient authorities read *peace, good pleasure among men*   8 Greek *men of good pleasure*
9 Or *saying*

HS references: Lk 1:78 = Malachi 4:2   Lk 1:79 = Isaiah 9:2   Lk 2:12 = Isaiah 7:14

LUKE 2

And they went with haste, and found Mary and Joseph, and 16
the babe lying in a manger.

D And when they saw it they made known the saying 17
which had been told them concerning this child; and all 18
who heard it wondered at what the shepherds told them.
But Mary kept all these things, pondering them in her 19
heart. And the shepherds returned, glorifying and praising 20
God for all they had heard and seen, as it had been told
them.

§ 10 The Dedication at Jerusalem

MATTHEW

A *And he called his name Jesus. (§ 6 E) = 1:25*

LUKE 2:21-39

A And at the end of eight days, when he was circumcised, 21
he was called Jesus, the name given by the angel before he
was conceived in the womb.

B And when the time came for their purification according 22
to the law of Moses, they brought him up to Jerusalem to
present him to the Lord (as it is written in the law of the 23
Lord, "Every male that opens the womb shall be called
holy to the Lord") and to offer a sacrifice according to 24
what is said in the law of the Lord, "a pair of turtledoves,
or two young pigeons."

C Now there was a man in Jerusalem, whose name was 25
Simeon, and this man was righteous and devout, looking
for the consolation of Israel, and the Holy Spirit was upon
him. And it had been revealed to him by the Holy Spirit 26
that he should not see death before he had seen the Lord's
Christ. And inspired by the Spirit he came into the temple; 27
and when the parents brought in the child Jesus, to do for
him according to the custom of the law, he took him up in 28
his arms and blessed God and said,

"^{1}Lord, now lettest thou thy ^{2}servant depart in peace, 29
according to thy word;
for mine eyes have seen thy salvation 30
which thou hast prepared in the presence of all 31
peoples,
a light for ^{3}reveilation to the Gentiles, 32
and for glory to thy people Israel."

And his father and his mother marveled at what was said 33
about him; and Simeon blessed them and said to Mary his 34
mother,

"Behold, this child is set for the fall and rising of
many in Israel,
and for a sign that is spoken against
(and a sword will pierce through your own soul also), 35
that thoughts out of many hearts may be revealed."

D And there was a prophetess, Anna, the daughter of 36
Phan'u-el, of the tribe of Asher; she was ^{4}of a great age,

1 Greek *Master*   2 Greek *slave*   3 Or *the unveiling of the Gentiles*   4 Greek *advanced in many days*

HS references: Lk 2:21 = Genesis 17:12 and Leviticus 12:3   Lk 2:22-24 = Leviticus 12:1-8   Lk 2:23 = Exodus 13:2, 12, 15
Lk 2:30-31 = Isaiah 52:10   Lk 2:32 = Isaiah 42:6 and 49:6   Lk 2:36 = Joshua 19:24

LUKE 2

having lived with her husband seven years from her virginity, and as a widow till she was eighty-four. She did 37 not depart from the temple, worshiping with fasting and prayer night and day. And coming up at that very hour she 38 gave thanks to God, and spoke of him to all who were looking for the redemption of Jerusalem.

E And when they had performed everything according to 39 the law of the Lord, they returned into Galilee, to their own city, Nazareth.

§ 11 Jesus as King of the Jews

MATT 2:1-12

A Now when Jesus was born in Bethlehem of Judea in the 1 days of Herod the king, behold, [1]wise men from the East came to Jerusalem,

B saying, "[2]Where is he who has been born king of the 2 Jews? For we have seen his star in the East, and have come to worship him."

C When Herod the king heard this, he was troubled, and 3 all Jerusalem with him; and assembling all the chief priests 4 and scribes of the people, he inquired of them where the Christ was to be born. They told him, "In Bethlehem of 5 Judea; for so it is written [4]by the prophet:
    'And you, O Bethlehem, in the land of Judah,   6
    are by no means least among the rulers of Judah;
    for from you shall come a ruler
    who will govern my people Israel.'"

D Then Herod summoned the [1]wise men secretly and 7 ascertained from them [5]what time the star appeared; and he 8 sent them to Bethlehem, saying, "Go and search diligently for the child, and when you have found him bring me word, that I too may come and worship him."

E When they had heard the king they went their way; and 9 lo, the star which they had seen in the East went before them, till it came to rest over the place where the child was. When they saw the star, they rejoiced exceedingly 10 with great joy; and going into the house they saw the child 11 with Mary his mother, and they fell down and worshiped him. Then, opening their treasures, they offered him gifts, gold and frankincense and myrrh.

F And being warned in a dream not to return to Herod, 12 they departed to their own country by another way.

LUKE

A *In the days of Herod, king of Judea (§ 3 A) = 1:5*
And Joseph also went up . . . to Judea . . . to Bethlehem
. . . with Mary, . . . and she gave birth to her first-born
son (§ 8 BC) = 2:4-7

B *The Lord God will give to him the throne of his*
    father David,
and he will reign over the house of Jacob [3]for ever;
and of his kingdom there will be no end"
(§ 4 C) = 1:32-33

---

1 Greek *Magi*: compare Esther 1:13 and Daniel 2:12   2 Or *Where is the King of the Jews that is born?*   3 Greek *unto the ages*   4 Or *through*
5 Or *the time of the star that appeared*

HS references: Mt 2:2 = Numbers 24:17 and Jeremiah 23:5 and Zechariah 9:9   Mt 2:6 = Micah 5:2   Lk 1:32-33 = II Samuel 7:12-17

§ 12 Roman Rule in Relation to Jesus

MATT 2:13-23

A Now when they had departed, behold, an angel of the 13
Lord appeared to Joseph in a dream and said, "Rise, take
the child and his mother, and flee to Egypt, and remain
there till I tell you; for Herod is about to search for the
child, to destroy him." And he rose and took the child and 14
his mother by night, and departed to Egypt, and remained 15
there until the death of Herod. This was to fulfil what the
Lord had spoken by the prophet, "Out of Egypt have I
called my son."

B Then Herod, when he saw that he had been tricked by 16
the ¹wise men, was in a furious rage, and he sent and killed
all the male children in Bethlehem and in all that region
who were two years old or under, according to the time
which he had ascertained from the ¹wise men. Then was 17
fulfilled what was spoken ²by the prophet Jeremiah:
> "A voice was heard in Ramah,   18
> wailing and loud lamentation,
> Rachel weeping for her children;
> she refused to be consoled,
> because they were no more."

C But when Herod died, behold, an angel of the Lord 19
appeared in a dream to Joseph in Egypt, saying, "Rise, 20
take the child and his mother, and go to the land of Israel,
for those who sought the child's life are dead." And he 21
rose and took the child and his mother, and went to the
land of Israel.

D But when he heard that Archela'us reigned over Judea in 22
place of his father Herod, he was afraid to go there, and
being warned in a dream he withdrew to the district of
Galilee. And he went and dwelt in a city called Nazareth, 23
that what was spoken ²by the prophets might be fulfilled,
"He shall be called a Nazarene."

§ 13 The Youth of John

LUKE 1:80

*And the child grew and became strong in spirit, and he was 80
in the wilderness till the day of his manifestation to Israel.
(§ 7 F)*

§ 14 The Youth of Jesus

MATT 2:22-23

*But when he heard that Archela'us reigned over Judea in 22
place of his father Herod, he was afraid to go there, and
being warned in a dream he withdrew to the district of
Galilee. And he went and dwelt in a city called Nazareth, 23
that what was spoken ²by the prophets might be fulfilled,
"He shall be called a Nazarene." (§ 12 D)*

LUKE 2:39-40

*And when they had performed everything according to the 39
law of the Lord, they returned into Galilee, to their own
city, Nazareth. (§ 10 E)*
*And the child grew and became strong, ³filled with 40
wisdom; and the favor of God was upon him.*

---

1 Greek *Magi*: compare Esther 1:13 and Daniel 2:12   2 Or *through*   3 Greek *becoming full of wisdom*

HS references: Mt 2:15 = Hosea 11:1 (cf. Exodus 4:22)   Mt 2:18 = Jeremiah 31:15   Mt 2:23 = Isaiah 11:1 (?)   Lk 2:40 = Judges 13:24 and
I Samuel 2:26

§ 15 Jesus the Youth at Jerusalem

LUKE 2:41-50

A Now his parents went to Jerusalem every year at the 41 feast of the Passover. And when he was twelve years old, 42 they went up according to custom; and when the feast was 43 ended, as they were returning, the boy Jesus stayed behind in Jerusalem. His parents did not know it, but supposing 44 him to be in the company they went a day's journey, and they sought him among their kinsfolk and acquaintances; and when they did not find him, they returned to 45 Jerusalem, seeking him.

B After three days they found him in the temple, sitting 46 among the teachers, listening to them and asking them questions; and all who heard him were amazed at his 47 understanding and his answers. And when they saw him 48 they were astonished; and his mother said to him, "¹Son, why have you treated us so? Behold, your father and I have been looking for you anxiously." And he said to them, 49 "How is it that you sought me? Did you not know that I must be ²in my Father's house?" And they did not 50 understand the saying which he spoke to them.

§ 16 Development of Jesus

LUKE 2:51-52

And he went down with them and came to Nazareth, and 51 was obedient to them; and his mother kept all these things in her heart.

And Jesus increased in wisdom and in ³stature, and in 52 ⁴favor with God and man.

---

1 Greek *Child*   2 Or *about my Father's business*: Greek *in the things of my Father*   3 Or *age*   4 Or *grace*

HS references: Lk 2:41 = Exodus 23:14-17 and Deuteronomy 16:1-8   Lk 2:52 = I Samuel 2:26

Chapter III

ACTIVITY OF JOHN AND ITS RELATION TO JESUS

§ 17 Statement of the Work of John

MATT 3:1-12	MARK 1:1-8	LUKE 3:1-20
	A The beginning of the gospel of 1 Jesus Christ, [1]the Son of God.	
		B In the fifteenth year of the reign of 1 Tibe'ri-us Caesar, Pontius Pilate being governor of Judea, and Herod being tetrarch of Galilee, and his brother Philip tetrarch of the region of Iturae'a and Trachoni'tis, and Lysa'ni-as tetrarch of Abile'ne, in the 2 high-priesthood of Annas and Ca'iaphas,
C[c] In those days came John the 1 Baptist, preaching in the wilderness of Judea, "Repent, for the kingdom of 2 heaven is at hand."	C[c] *Compare portion H below*	C[c] the word of God came to John the son of Zechari'ah in the wilderness; and he went into all the region about 3 the Jordan, preaching a baptism of repentance for the forgiveness of sins.
D For this is he who was spoken of 3 [2]by the prophet Isaiah when he said,	D As it is written [3]in Isaiah the 2 prophet,	D As it is written in the book of the 4 words of Isaiah the prophet,
E *Compare § 41 portion E*	E "Behold, I send my messenger before thy face, who shall prepare thy way;	E *Compare § 41 portion E*
F "The voice of one crying in the wilderness: Prepare the way of the Lord, make his paths straight."	F the voice of one crying in the 3 wilderness: Prepare the way of the Lord, make his paths straight--"	F "The voice of one crying in the wilderness: Prepare the way of the Lord, make his paths straight.
		G Every valley shall be filled, 5 and every mountain and hill shall be brought low, and the crooked shall be made straight, and the rough ways shall be made smooth; and all flesh shall see the 6 salvation of God."
H *Compare portion C above*	H John the baptizer appeared in the 4 wilderness, preaching a baptism of repentance for the forgiveness of sins.	H *Compare portion C above*

---

1 Some ancient authorities omit *the Son of God*   2 Or *through*   3 Some ancient authorities read *in the prophets*

HS references: Mk 1:2 = Malachi 3:1   Mt 3:3 and Mk 1:3 and Lk 3:4 = Isaiah 40:3   Lk 3:5-6 = Isaiah 40:4-5   Mt 3:2 = Daniel 2:44; 4:17; 7:22

C With the saying of John in Mt 3:2, compare the saying of Jesus in § 21 C (Mt)
C With Lk 3:3a of portion C, compare Mt 3:5b in portion J below

MATT 3	MARK 1	LUKE 3
I Now John wore a garment of 4 camel's hair, and a leather girdle around his waist; and his food was locusts and wild honey.	**I** *Compare portion K below*	
J^J Then went out to him Jerusalem 5 and all Judea and all the region about the Jordan, and they were baptized by 6 him in the river Jordan, confessing their sins.	**J**^J And there went out to him all the 5 country of Judea, and all the people of Jerusalem; and they were baptized by him in the river Jordan, confessing their sins.	
K *Compare portion I above*	**K** Now John was clothed with 6 camel's hair, and had a leather girdle around his waist, and ate locusts and wild honey.	
L But when he saw many of the 7 Pharisees and Sad'ducees coming for baptism, he said to them,		**L** He said therefore to the multitudes 7 that came out to be baptized by him,
M^M "You brood of vipers! Who warned you to flee from the wrath to come? Bear fruit that befits 8 [1]repentance, and do not presume to 9 say to yourselves, 'We have Abraham as our father'; for I tell you, God is able from these stones to raise up children to Abraham. Even now the 10 axe is laid to the root of the trees; every tree therefore that does not bear good fruit is cut down and thrown into the fire.		**M**^M "You brood of vipers! Who warned you to flee from the wrath to come? Bear fruits that befit 8 [1]repentance, and do not begin to say to yourselves, 'We have Abraham as our father'; for I tell you, God is able from these stones to raise up children to Abraham. Even now the axe is laid 9 to the root of the trees; every tree therefore that does not bear good fruit is cut down and thrown into the fire."
		N And the multitudes asked him, 10 "What then shall we do?" And he 11 answered them, "He who has two coats, let him share with him who has none; and he who has food, let him do likewise." [2]Tax collectors also 12 came to be baptized, and said to him, "Teacher, what shall we do?" And he 13 said to them, "Collect no more than is appointed you." [3]Soldiers also asked 14 him, "And we, what shall we do?" And he said to them, "Rob no one by violence or by false accusation, and be content with your wages."
		O As the people were in expectation, 15 and all men questioned in their hearts concerning John,

---

1 Or *your repentance*   2 That is *collectors or renters of Roman taxes*: and so elsewhere   3 Greek *soldiers on service*

HS references: Mt 3:4 and Mk 1:6 = II Kings 1:8 and Zechariah 13:4 and Leviticus 11:22

J With Mt 3:5b of portion J, compare Lk 3:3a in portion C above
M With the first sentence of portion M, compare § 45 N and § 132 P. With the last sentence of portion M, compare § 38 T

MATT 3	MARK 1	LUKE 3
		whether perhaps he were the Christ, John answered them all, 16
P "I baptize you [1]with water for 11 repentance, but he who is coming after me is mightier than I, whose sandals I am not [2]worthy to carry; he will baptize you [1]with the Holy Spirit and with fire.	**P** And he preached, saying, "After 7 me comes he who is mightier than I, the thong of whose sandals I am not [2]worthy to stoop down and untie. I 8 have baptized you [1]with water; but he will baptize you [1]with the Holy Spirit."	**P** "I baptize you with water; but he who is mightier than I is coming, the thong of whose sandals I am not [2]worthy to untie; he will baptize you [1]with the Holy Spirit and with fire.
Q His winnowing fork is in his hand, 12 and he will clear his threshing floor and gather his wheat into the granary, but the chaff he will burn with unquenchable fire."		**Q** His winnowing fork is in his hand, 17 to clear his threshing floor, and to gather the wheat into his granary, but the chaff he will burn with unquenchable fire."
R *Compare § 58 portion D*	**R** *Compare § 58 portion D*	**R** So, with many other exhortations, 18 he preached good news to the people. But Herod the tetrarch, who had been 19 reproved by him for Hero'di-as, his brother's wife, and for all the evil things that Herod had done, added 20 this to them all, that he shut up John in prison.

§ 18 The Baptism of Jesus by John

MATT 3:13-17	MARK 1:9-11	LUKE 3:21-22
A Then Jesus came from Galilee to 13 the Jordan to John, to be baptized by him.	**A** In those days Jesus came from 9 Nazareth of Galilee and was baptized by John [3]in the Jordan.	**A** Now when all the people were 21 baptized, and when Jesus also had been baptized
B John would have prevented him, 14 saying, "I need to be baptized by you, and do you come to me?" But Jesus 15 answered him, "Let it be so now; for thus it is fitting for us to fulfill all righteousness." Then he consented.		
C And when Jesus was baptized, he 16 went up immediately from the water, and behold, the heavens were opened [4]and he saw the Spirit of God descending [7]like a dove, and alighting on him; and lo, a voice from heaven, 17 saying,	**C** And when he came up out of the 10 water, immediately he saw the heavens [5]opened and the Spirit descending [6]upon him [7]like a dove; and a voice came from heaven, 11	**C** and was praying, the heaven was opened, and the Holy Spirit descended 22 upon him in bodily form, as a dove, and a voice came from heaven,
D[D] "[8]This is my beloved Son, with whom I am well pleased."	**D**[D] "Thou art my beloved Son; with thee I am well pleased."	**D**[D] "[9]Thou art my beloved Son; with thee I am well pleased."

---

1 Or *in* 2 Greek *sufficient* 3 Greek *into* 4 Some ancient authorities add *to him* 5 Greek *torn open*
6 Greek *into* 7 Greek *as a dove* 8 Or *This is my son; my (or the) beloved in whom I am well pleased:* 9 Some ancient authorities read: *Thou art my beloved Son; today I have begotten thee.*

HS references: Mt 3:17 and Mk 1:11 and Lk 3:22 = Psalm 2:7 and Isaiah 42:1   Mk 1:10 = Ezekiel 1:1

D Compare § 74 portion E

§ 19   The Genealogy of Jesus

MATT 1:1-17   LUKE 3:23-38

[1]The book of the [2]genealogy of Jesus Christ, the son of 1 David, the son of Abraham.

Abraham was the father of Isaac, and Isaac the father of 2 Jacob, and Jacob the father of Judah and his brothers, and 3 Judah the father of Perez and Zerah by Tamar, and Perez the father of Hezron, and Hezron the father of [3]Ram, and 4 Ram the father of Ammin'adab, and Ammin'adab the father of Nahshon, and Nahshon the father of Salmon, and Salmon 5 the father of Bo'az by Rahab, and Bo'az the father of Obed by Ruth, and Obed the father of Jesse, and Jesse the father 6 of David the king.

And David was the father of Solomon by the wife of Uri'ah, and Solomon the father of Rehobo'am, and 7 Rehobo'am the father of Abi'jah, and Abi'jah the father of [4]Asa, and [4]Asa the father of Jehosh'aphat, and 8 Jehosh'aphat the father of Joram, and Joram the father of Uzzi'ah, and Uzzi'ah the father of Jotham, and Jotham the 9 father of Ahaz, and Ahaz the father of Hezeki'ah, and 10 Hezeki'ah the father of Manas'seh, and Manas'seh the father of [5]Amos, and [5]Amos the father of Josi'ah, and 11 Josi'ah the father of Jechoni'ah and his brothers, at the time of the [6]deportation to Babylon.

And after the [6]deportation to Babylon: Jechoni'ah was the 12 father of [7]She-al'ti-el, and [7]She-al'ti-el the father of Zerub'babel, and Zerub'babel the father of Abi'ud, and 13 Abi'ud the father of Eli'akim, and Eli'akim the father of Azor, and Azor the father of Zadok, and Zadok the father of 14 Achim, and Achim the father of Eli'ud, and Eli'ud the 15 father of Elea'zar, and Elea'zar the father of Matthan, and Matthan the father of Jacob, and Jacob the father of Joseph 16 the husband of Mary, of whom Jesus was born, who is called Christ.

So all the generations from Abraham to David were 17 fourteen generations, and from David to the [6]deportation to Babylon fourteen generations, and from the [6]deportation to Babylon to the Christ fourteen generations. (§ 2)

Jesus, when he began his ministry, was about thirty years 23 of age, being the son (as was supposed) of Joseph, the son of Heli, the son of Matthat, the son of Levi, the son of 24 Melchi, the son of Jan'na-i, the son of Joseph, the son of 25 Mattathi'as, the son of Amos, the son of Nahum, the son of Esli, the son of Nag'ga-i, the son of Ma'ath, the son of 26 Mattathi'as, the son of Sem'e-in, the son of Josech, the son of Joda, the son of Jo-an'an, the son of Rhesa, the son of 27 Zerub'babel, the son of [7]She-al'ti-el, the son of Neri, the 28 son of Melchi, the son of Addi, the son of Cosam, the son of Elma'dam, the son of Er, the son of Joshua, the son of 29 Elie'zer, the son of Jorim, the son of Matthat, the son of Levi, the son of Simeon, the son of Judah, the son of 30 Joseph, the son of Jonam, the son of Eli'akim, the son of 31 Me'le-a, the son of Menna, the son of Mat'tatha, the son of Nathan, the son of David, the son of Jesse, the son of 32 Obed, the son of Bo'az, the son of Sala, the son of Nahshon, the son of Ammin'adab, the son of Admin, the 33 son of [8]Arni, the son of Hezron, the son of Perez, the son of Judah, the son of Jacob, the son of Isaac, the son of 34 Abraham, the son of Terah, the son of Nahor, the son of 35 Serug, the son of Re'u, the son of Peleg, the son of Eber, the son of Shelah, the son of Ca-i'nan, the son of 36 Arphax'ad, the son of Shem, the son of Noah, the son of Lamech, the son of Methuselah, the son of Enoch, the son 37 of Jared, the son of Maha'lale-el, the son of Ca-i'nan, the 38 son of Enos, the son of Seth, the son of Adam, the son of God.

---

1 Or *The genealogy of Jesus Christ*   2 Or *birth:* as in Mt 1:18   3 Greek *Aram*   4 Greek *Asaph*   5 Some authorities read *Amon*
6 Or *removal to Babylon*   7 Greek *Salathiel*   8 Some ancient authorities write *Aram*

HS references: Mt 1:2-6 and Lk 3:31-34 = I Chronicles 2:1-15   Mt 1:3-6 and Lk 3:32-33 = Ruth 4:18-22   Mt 1:7-12 = I Chronicles 3:10-17
Lk 3:27 = I Chronicles 3:17   Lk 3:34-36 = I Chronicles 1:24-28   Lk 3:36-38 = I Chronicles 1:1-4

§ 20 Withdrawal of Jesus to the Wilderness

MATT 4:1-11	MARK 1:12-13	LUKE 4:1-13

A Then Jesus was led up by the Spirit 1 into the wilderness to be ¹tempted by the devil. And he fasted forty days 2 and forty nights, and afterward he was hungry.

A The Spirit immediately drove him 12 out into the wilderness. And he was 13 in the wilderness forty days, ¹tempted by Satan;

A And Jesus, full of the Holy Spirit, 1 returned from the Jordan, and was led ²by the Spirit for forty days in the 2 wilderness, ¹tempted by the devil. And he ate nothing in those days; and when they were ended, he was hungry.

B And the tempter came and said to 3 him, "If you are the Son of God, command these stones to become loaves of bread." But he answered, 4 "It is written,

'Man shall not live by bread
    alone,
but by every word that proceeds
    from the mouth of God.'"

B The devil said to him, "If you are 3 the Son of God, command this stone to become ³bread." And Jesus 4 answered him, "It is written, 'Man shall not live by bread alone.'"

C Then the devil took him to the holy 5 city, and set him on the ⁴pinnacle of the temple, and said to him, "If you 6 are the Son of God, throw yourself down; for it is written,

'He will give his angels charge
    of you,'
and
'On their hands they will bear
    you up,
lest you strike your foot against
    a stone.'"

Jesus said to him, "Again it is 7 written, 'You shall not tempt the Lord your God.'"

C   *Compare portion E below*

D Again, the devil took him to a very 8 high mountain, and showed him all the kingdoms of the world and the glory of them; and he said to him, 9 "All these I will give you, if you will fall down and worship me." Then 10 Jesus said to him, "Begone, Satan! for it is written,

'You shall worship the Lord your
    God
and him only shall you serve.'"

D And the devil took him up, and 5 showed him all the kingdoms of ⁵the world in a moment of time, and said 6 to him, "To you I will give all this authority and their glory; for it has been delivered to me, and I give it to whom I will. If you, then, will 7 worship me, it shall all be yours." And Jesus answered him, "It is 8 written,

'You shall worship the Lord your
    God,
and him only shall you serve.'"

---

1 Or *tested*   2 Or *in*   3 Or *a loaf*   4 Greek *wing*   5 Greek *the inhabited earth*

HS references: Mt 4:2 and Mk 1:13 and Lk 4:2 = Exodus 34:28 and I Kings 19:8   Mt 4:4 and Lk 4:4 = Deuteronomy 8:3
Mt 4:5 = Nehemiah 11:1 and Daniel 9:24   Mt 4:6 and Lk 4:10-11 = Psalm 91:11-12   Mt 4:7 and Lk 4:12 = Deuteronomy 6:16
Mt 4:10 and Lk 4:8 = Deuteronomy 6:13

MATT 4	MARK 1	LUKE 4

E *Compare portion C above*		**E** And he took him to Jerusalem, and 9 set him on the ¹pinnacle of the temple, and said to him, "If you are the Son of God, throw yourself down from here; for it is written, 10
		    'He will give his angels charge
		      of you, to guard you,'
		and 11
		    'On their hands they will bear
		      you up,
		    lest you strike your foot against
		      a stone.'"
		And Jesus answered him, "It is said, 12 'You shall not tempt the Lord your God.'"

F Then the devil left him, 11		**F** And when the devil had ended 13 every temptation, he departed from him until an opportune time.
G and behold, angels came and ministered to him.	**G** and he was with the wild beasts; and the angels ministered to him.	

---

1 Greek *wing*

HS references: Lk 4:12 and Mt 4:7 = Deuteronomy 6:16   Mk 1:13b = Psalm 91:11-12

Chapter IV

BEGINNINGS OF THE PUBLIC ACTIVITY OF JESUS

§ 21   General Statement of the Work of Jesus

MATT 4:12-17	MARK 1:14-15	LUKE 4:14-15
A Now when he heard that John had 12 been arrested, he withdrew into Galilee;	A Now after John was arrested, Jesus 14 came into Galilee,	A And Jesus returned in the power of 14 the Spirit into Galilee,
B and leaving Nazareth he went and 13 dwelt in Caper'na-um by the sea, in the territory of Zeb'ulun and Naph'tali, that what was spoken ¹by 14 the prophet Isaiah might be fulfilled: "The land of Zeb'ulun and the 15 land of Naph'tali, ²toward the sea, across the Jordan, Galilee of the ³Gentiles-- the people who sat in darkness 16 have seen a great light, and for those who sat in the region and shadow of death light has dawned."	B *Compare § 24 portion A*	B *Compare § 24 portion A*
Cᶜ From that time Jesus began to 17 preach, saying, "Repent, for the kingdom of heaven is at hand."	Cᶜ preaching the gospel of ⁴God, and 15 saying, "The time is fulfilled, and the kingdom of God is at hand; repent, and believe in the gospel."	Cᶜ and a report concerning him went out through all the surrounding country. And he taught in their 15 synagogues, being glorified by all.

§ 22   Jesus Begins at Nazareth

MATT 13:54-58	MARK 6:1-6	LUKE 4:16-30
A *And coming to his own country he 54 taught them in their synagogue,*	A *He went away from there and came 1 to his own country; and his disciples followed him. And on the sabbath he 2 began to teach in the synagogue;*	A And he came to Nazareth, where 16 he had been brought up; and he went to the synagogue, as his custom was, on the sabbath day. And he stood up to read;
		B and there was given to him ⁵the 17 book of the prophet Isaiah. He opened the ⁶book and found the place where it was written, "The Spirit of the Lord is upon 18 me, ⁷because he has anointed me to preach good news to the poor. He has sent me to proclaim release to the captives and recovering of sight to the blind,

---

1 Or *through*   2 Greek *The way of the sea*   3 Greek *nations*: and so elsewhere   4 Some authorities add *the kingdom of*   5 Or *a roll*   6 Or *roll*
7 Or *wherefore*

HS references: Mt 4:15-16 = Isaiah 9:1-2   Lk 4:18-19 = Isaiah 61:1-2   Mt 4:17 and Mk 1:15 = Daniel 2:44; 4:17; 7:22

C With the saying of Jesus in Mt 4:17, compare the saying of John in § 17 C (Mt)

MATT 13	MARK 6	LUKE 4
		to set at liberty those who are oppressed, to proclaim the acceptable year 19 of the Lord." And he closed the ¹book, and gave it 20 back to the attendant, and sat down; and the eyes of all in the synagogue were fixed on him. And he began to 21 say to them, "Today this scripture has been fulfilled in your hearing."
C *so that they were astonished and said, "Where did this man get this wisdom and these ²mighty works? Compare portion E below*	**C** *and ³many who heard him were astonished, saying, "Where did this man get all this? What is the wisdom given to him? What ²mighty works are wrought by his hands!*	**C** ⁴And all spoke well of him, and 22 wondered at the gracious words which proceeded out of his mouth;
D *Is not this the carpenter's son? Is 55 not his mother called Mary? And are not his brothers James and Joseph and Simon and Judas? And are not all 56 his sisters with us?*	**D** *Is not this the carpenter, the son of 3 Mary and brother of James and Joses and Judas and Simon, and are not his sisters here with us?"*	**D** and they said, "Is not this Joseph's son?"
E *Where then did this man get all this?"*	**E** *Compare portion C above*	
F *And they ⁵took offense at him.* 57	**F** *And they ⁵took offense at him.*	**F** *Compare portion K below*
		G And he said to them, "Doubtless 23 you will quote to me this proverb, 'Physician, heal yourself; what we have heard you did at Caper'na-um, do here also in your own country.'"
H *But Jesus said to them, "A prophet is not without honor except in his own country and in his own house."*	**H** *And Jesus said to them, "A prophet 4 is not without honor, except in his own country, and among his own kin, and in his own house."*	**H** And he said, "Truly, I say to you, 24 no prophet is acceptable in his own country.
		I But in truth, I tell you, there were 25 many widows in Israel in the days of Eli'jah, when the heaven was shut up three years and six months, when there came a great famine over all the land; and Eli'jah was sent to none of 26 them but only to ⁶Zar'ephath, in the land of Sidon, to a woman who was a widow. And there were many lepers 27 in Israel in the time of the prophet Eli'sha; and none of them was cleansed, but only Na'aman the Syrian."

---

1 Or *roll*   2 Greek *powers*   3 Some ancient authorities insert *the*   4 Greek *And all bore witness to him*   5 Greek *were caused to stumble*
6 Greek *Sarepta*

HS references: Lk 4:25 = I Kings 17:1 and 18:1-2   Lk 4:26 = I Kings 17:8-9   Lk 4:27 = II Kings 5:1, 14

MATT 13	MARK 6	LUKE 4

J *And he did not do many* [1]*mighty* 58 *works there, because of their unbelief.* (§ 54 A-J)

J *And he could do no* [2]*mighty work* 5 *there, except that he laid his hands upon a few sick people and healed them. And he marveled because of* 6 *their unbelief.* (§ 54 A-J)

K   *Compare portion F above*

K   *Compare portion F above*

K When they heard this, all in the 28 synagogue were filled with wrath. And they rose up and put him out of 29 the city, and led him to the brow of the hill on which their city was built, that they might throw him down headlong. But passing through the 30 midst of them he went away.

§ 23 Jesus Wins Fisherman Followers

MATT 4:18-22	MARK 1:16-20	LUKE 5:1-11

A As he walked by the Sea of 18 Galilee, he saw two brothers, Simon who is called Peter and Andrew his brother, casting a net into the sea; for they were fishermen.

A And passing along by the Sea of 16 Galilee, he saw Simon and Andrew the brother of Simon casting a net in the sea; for they were fishermen.

While the people pressed upon him to 1 *hear the word of God, he was standing by the lake of Gennes'aret. And he saw two boats by the lake; but* 2 *the fishermen had gone out of them and were washing their nets. Getting* 3 *into one of the boats, which was Simon's, he asked him to put out a little from the land. And he sat down and taught the people from the boat. And when he had ceased speaking, he* 4 *said to Simon, "Put out into the deep and let down your nets for a catch." And Simon answered, "Master, we* 5 *toiled all night and took nothing! But at your word I will let down the nets." And when they had done this, they* 6 *enclosed a great shoal of fish; and as their nets were breaking, they* 7 *beckoned to their partners in the other boat to come and help them. And they came and filled both the boats, so that they began to sink. But when Simon* 8 *Peter saw it, he fell down at Jesus' knees, saying, "Depart from me, for I am a sinful man, O Lord." For he* 9 *was astonished, and all that were with him, at the catch of fish which they*

B And he said to them, "Follow me, 19 and I will make you fishers of men." Immediately they left their nets and 20 followed him.

B And Jesus said to them, "Follow 17 me and I will make you become fishers of men." And immediately 18 they left their nets and followed him.

C And going on from there he saw 21 two other brothers, [3]James the son of Zeb'edee and John his brother, in the boat with Zeb'edee their father, mending their nets,

C And going on a little farther, he 19 saw [3]James the son of Zeb'edee and John his brother, who were in their boat mending the nets.

D and he called them. Immediately 22 they left the boat and their father, and followed him.

D And immediately he called them; 20 and they left their father Zeb'edee in the boat with the hired servants, and followed him.

---

1 Greek *powers*   2 Greek *power*   3 Or *Jacob*: and so elsewhere

LUKE 5

had taken; and so also were James 10
and John, sons of Zeb'edee, who were
partners with Simon. And Jesus said
to Simon, "Do not be afraid;
henceforth you will be [1]catching men."
And when they had brought their 11
boats to land, they left everything and
followed him. (§ 27)

§ 24 Early Popular Opinions about Jesus

MATTHEW	MARK 1:21-28	LUKE 4:31-37
A *Compare § 21 portion B*	A And they went into Caper'na-um; 21	A And he went down to Caper'na-um, 31 a city of Galilee.
B *Compare § 38 portion X*	B and immediately on the sabbath he entered the synagogue and taught. And they were astonished at his 22 teaching, for he taught them as one who had authority, and not as the scribes.	B And he was teaching them on the sabbath; and they were astonished at 32 his teaching, for his word was with authority.
	C And immediately there was in their 23 synagogue a man with an unclean spirit; and he cried out, "What have 24 you to do with us, Jesus of Nazareth? Have you come to destroy us? I know who you are, the Holy One of God."	C And in the synagogue there was a 33 man who had the spirit of an unclean demon; and he cried out with a loud voice, "[2]Ah! What have you to do 34 with us, Jesus of Nazareth? Have you come to destroy us? I know who you are, the Holy One of God."
	D But Jesus rebuked [3]him, saying, 25 "Be silent, and come out of him!" And the unclean spirit, convulsing 26 him and crying with a loud voice, came out of him.	D But Jesus rebuked him, saying, "Be 35 silent, and come out of him!" And when the demon had thrown him down in the midst, he came out of him, having done him no harm.
	E And they were all amazed, so that 27 they questioned among themselves, saying, "What is this? A new teaching! With authority he commands even the unclean spirits, and they obey him."	E And they were all amazed and said 36 to one another, "What is [4]this word? For with authority and power he commands the unclean spirits, and they come out."
	F And at once his fame spread 28 everywhere throughout all the surrounding region of Galilee.	F And reports of him went out into 37 every place in the surrounding region.

§ 25 The Healing Power of Jesus

(§ 39+) MATT 8:14-17	MARK 1:29-34	LUKE 4:38-41
A And when Jesus entered Peter's 14 house,	A And immediately [5]he left the 29 synagogue, and entered the house of Simon and Andrew, with James and John.	A And he arose and left the 38 synagogue, and entered Simon's house.

---

1 Greek *taking alive*   2 Or *Let alone*   3 Or *it*   4 Or *this word, that with authority . . . come out?*   5 Some ancient authorities read *they*

MATT 8	MARK 1	LUKE 4
B he saw his mother-in-law lying sick with a fever; he touched her hand, 15	**B** Now Simon's mother-in-law lay 30 sick with a fever, and immediately they told him of her. And he came 31 and took her by the hand and lifted her up,	**B** Now Simon's mother-in-law was ill with a high fever, and they besought him for her. And he stood over her 39 and rebuked the fever,
C and the fever left her, and she rose and served him.	**C** and the fever left her; and she served them.	**C** and it left her; and immediately she rose and served them.
D That evening they brought to him 16 many who were possessed with demons;	**D** That evening, at sundown, they 32 brought to him all who were sick or possessed with demons. And the 33 whole city was gathered together about the door.	**D** Now when the sun was setting, all 40 those who had any that were sick with various diseases brought them to him;
E and he cast out the spirits with a word, and healed all who were sick.	**E** And he healed many who were sick 34 with various diseases, and cast out many demons; *Compare § 34 portion E*	**E** and he laid his hands on every one of them and healed them. And 41 demons also came out of many, crying, "You are the Son of God!"
	F and he would not permit the demons to speak, because they knew him.[1]	**F** But he rebuked them, and would not allow them to speak, because they knew that he was the Christ.
G This was to fulfil what was spoken 17 [2]by the prophet Isaiah, "He took our infirmities and bore our diseases." (+ § 50)		

§ 26 Jesus Teaches Throughout Galilee

(§ 23 +) MATT 4:23	MARK 1:35-39	LUKE 4:42-44
	A And in the morning, a great while 35 before day, he rose and went out to a lonely place, and there he prayed.	**A** And when it was day he departed 42 and went into a lonely place.
	B And Simon and those who were 36 with him pursued him, and they found 37 him and said to him, "Every one is searching for you."	**B** And the people sought him and came to him, and would have kept him from leaving them;
	C And he said to them, "Let us go on 38 to the next towns, that I may preach there also; for that is why I came out."	**C** but he said to them, "I must preach 43 the good news of the kingdom of God to the other cities also; for I was sent for this purpose."
D[D] And he went about all Galilee, 23 teaching in their synagogues and preaching the [3]gospel of the kingdom and healing every disease and every infirmity among the people. (+ § 34)	**D**[D] And he went throughout all 39 Galilee, preaching in their synagogues and casting out demons.	**D**[D] And he was preaching in the 44 synagogues of [4]Judea.

---

1 Many ancient authorities add *to be Christ*: see Lk 4:41   2 Or *through*   3 Or *good tidings*: and so elsewhere   4 Some ancient authorities read *Galilee*

HS references: Mt 8:17 = Isaiah 53:4

D With the latter half of the Matthew record, compare § 55 portion B

§ 27 Jesus Wins Fisherman Followers

MATT 4:18-22	MARK 1:16-20	LUKE 5:1-11
A *As he walked by the Sea of Galilee,* 18 *he saw two brothers, Simon who is called Peter and Andrew his brother, casting a net into the sea; for they were fishermen.*	A *And passing along by the Sea of* 16 *Galilee, he saw Simon and Andrew the brother of Simon casting a net in the sea; for they were fishermen.*	While the people pressed upon him 1 to hear the word of God, he was standing by the lake of Gennes'aret. And he saw two boats by the lake; 2 but the fishermen had gone out of them and were washing their nets. Getting into one of the boats, which 3 was Simon's, he asked him to put out a little from the land. And he sat down and taught the people from the boat. And when he had ceased 4 speaking, he said to Simon, "Put out into the deep and let down your nets for a catch." And Simon answered, 5 "Master, we toiled all night and took nothing! But at your word I will let down the nets." And when they had 6 done this, they enclosed a great shoal of fish; and as their nets were breaking, they beckoned to their 7 partners in the other boat to come and help them. And they came and filled both the boats, so that they began to sink. But when Simon Peter saw it, 8 he fell down at Jesus' knees, saying, "Depart from me, for I am a sinful man, O Lord." For he was 9 astonished, and all that were with him, at the catch of fish which they had taken; and so also were James 10 and John, sons of Zeb'edee, who were partners with Simon. And Jesus said to Simon, "Do not be afraid; henceforth you will be [2]catching men." And when they had brought 11 their boats to land, they left everything and followed him.
B *And he said to them, "Follow me,* 19 *and I will make you fishers of men." Immediately they left their nets and* 20 *followed him.*	B *And Jesus said to them, "Follow me* 17 *and I will make you become fishers of men." And immediately they left their* 18 *nets and followed him.*	
C *And going on from there he saw* 21 *two other brothers, [1]James the son of Zeb'edee and John his brother, in the boat with Zeb'edee their father, mending their nets,*	C *And going on a little farther, he* 19 *saw James the son of Zeb'edee and John his brother, who were in their boat mending the nets.*	
D *and he called them. Immediately* 22 *they left the boat and their father, and followed him. (§ 23 A-D)*	D *And immediately he called them;* 20 *and they left their father Zeb'edee in the boat with the hired servants, and followed him. (§ 23 A-D)*	

§ 28 Growth in Fame of Jesus

(§ 38 +) MATT 8:2-4	MARK 1:40-45	LUKE 5:12-16
A And behold, a leper came to him 2 and knelt before him, saying, "Lord, if you will, you can make me clean."	A And a leper came to him 40 beseeching him, and [3]kneeling said to him, "If you will, you can make me clean."	A While he was in one of the cities, 12 there came a man full of leprosy; and when he saw Jesus, he fell on his face and besought him, "Lord, if you will, you can make me clean."
B And he stretched out his hand and 3 touched him, saying, "I will; be clean." And immediately his leprosy was cleansed.	B Moved with pity, he stretched out 41 his hand and touched him, and said to him, "I will; be clean." And 42 immediately the leprosy left him, and he was made clean.	B And he stretched out his hand, and 13 touched him, saying, "I will; be clean." And immediately the leprosy left him.

---

1 Or *Jacob:* and so elsewhere   2 Greek *taking alive*   3 Some ancient authorities omit *and kneeling said to him*

MATT 8	MARK 1	LUKE 5

C And Jesus said to him, "See that 4 you say nothing to any one; but go, show yourself to the priest, and offer the gift that Moses commanded, for a proof [1]to the people." (+ § 39)

C And he sternly charged him, and 43 sent him away at once, and said to 44 him, "See that you say nothing to any one; but go, show yourself to the priest, and offer for your cleansing what Moses commanded, for a proof [1]to the people."

D But he went out and began to talk 45 freely about it, and to spread the [2]news, so that [3]Jesus could no longer openly enter [4]a town, but was out in the country; and people came to him from every quarter.

C And he charged him to tell no one; 14 but "go and show yourself to the priest, and make an offering for your cleansing, as Moses commanded, for a proof [1]to the people."

D But so much the more the report 15 went abroad concerning him; and great multitudes gathered to hear and to be healed of their infirmities. But 16 he withdrew to the wilderness and prayed.

---

1 Greek *to them*   2 Greek *word*   3 Greek *he*   4 Or *the city*

HS references: Mt 8:4 and Mk 1:44 and Lk 5:14 = Leviticus 13:49 and 14:2

Chapter V

DEVELOPMENT OF OPPOSITION TO JESUS

§ 29 Criticism of Free Forgiveness For Sin

(§ 52A +) MATT 9:2-8	MARK 2:1-12	LUKE 5:17-26
	A And when he returned to Caper'na-um after some days, it was reported that he was at home. And many were gathered together, so that there was no longer room for them, not even about the door; and he was preaching the word to them.	A On one of those days, as he was teaching, there were Pharisees and teachers of the law sitting by, who had come from every village of Galilee and Judea and from Jerusalem; and the power of the Lord was with him ¹to heal.
B And behold, they brought to him a paralytic, lying on his bed;	B And they came, bringing to him a paralytic carried by four men.	B And behold, men were bringing on a bed a man who was paralyzed, and they sought to bring him in and lay him before ²Jesus;
	C And when they could not ³get near him because of the crowd, they removed the roof above him; and when they had made an opening, they let down the pallet on which the paralytic lay.	C but finding no way to bring him in, because of the crowd, they went up on the roof and let him down with his bed through the tiles into the midst before Jesus.
D and when Jesus saw their faith he said to the paralytic, "Take heart, my ⁴son; your sins are forgiven."	D And when Jesus saw their faith, he said to the paralytic, "My ⁴son, your sins are forgiven."	D And when he saw their faith he said, "Man, your sins are forgiven you."
E And behold, some of the scribes said to themselves, "This man is blaspheming."	E Now some of the scribes were sitting there, questioning in their hearts, "Why does this man speak thus? It is blasphemy! Who can forgive sins but God alone?"	E And the scribes and the Pharisees began to question, saying, "Who is this that speaks blasphemies? Who can forgive sins but God only?"
F But Jesus, ⁵knowing their thoughts, said, "Why do you think evil in your hearts? For which is easier, to say, 'Your sins are forgiven,' or to say, 'Rise and walk'?	F And immediately Jesus, perceiving in his spirit that they thus questioned within themselves, said to them, "Why do you question thus in your hearts? Which is easier, to say to the paralytic, 'Your sins are forgiven,' or to say, 'Rise, take up your pallet and walk'?	F When Jesus perceived their questionings, he answered them, "Why do you question in your hearts? Which is easier, to say, 'Your sins are forgiven you,' or to say, 'Rise and walk'?
G But that you may know that the Son of man has authority on earth to forgive sins"--he then said to the paralytic--"Rise, take up your bed and go home."	G But that you may know that the Son of man has authority on earth to forgive sins"--he said to the paralytic--"I say to you, rise, take up your pallet and go home."	G But that you may know that the Son of man has authority on earth to forgive sins"--he said to the man who was paralyzed--"I say to you, rise, take up your bed and go home."

---

1 Greek *that he should heal*: many ancient authorities read *that he should heal them*   2 Greek *him*   3 Many ancient authorities read *bring him to him*   4 Greek *child*   5 Many ancient authorities read *seeing*

HS references: Mk 2:7 = Isaiah 43:25

MATT 9	MARK 2	LUKE 5
H And he rose and went home. When 7 the crowds saw it, they were afraid, 8 and they glorified God, who had given such authority to men.	H And he rose, and immediately took 12 up the pallet and went out before them all; so that they were all amazed and glorified God, saying, "We never saw anything like this!"	H And immediately he rose before 25 them, and took up that on which he lay, and went home, glorifying God. And amazement seized them all, and 26 they glorified God and were filled with awe, saying, "We have seen strange things today."

§ 30 Criticism for Association with Sinners

MATT 9:9-13	MARK 2:13-17	LUKE 5:27-32
	A He went out again beside the sea; 13 and all the crowd gathered about him, and he taught them.	A After this he went out, 27
B As Jesus passed on from there, he 9 saw a man called Matthew sitting at the tax office; and he said to him, "Follow me," And he rose and followed him.	B And as he passed on, he saw Levi 14 the son of Alphaeus sitting at the tax office, and he said to him, "Follow me." And he rose and followed him.	B and saw a tax collector, named Levi, sitting at the tax office; and he said to him, "Follow me." And he left 28 everything, and rose and followed him.
C And as he ¹sat at table in the 10 house, behold, many tax collectors and sinners came and sat down with Jesus and his disciples.	C And as he sat at table in his house, 15 many tax collectors² and sinners were sitting with Jesus and his disciples; for there were many who followed him.	C And Levi made him a great feast in 29 his house; and there was a large company of tax collectors and others ³sitting at table with them.
D And when the Pharisees saw this, 11 they said to his disciples, "Why does your teacher eat with tax collectors and sinners?"	D And the scribes ⁴of the Pharisees, 16 when they saw that he was eating with sinners and tax collectors, said to his disciples, "⁶Why does he eat ⁷with tax collectors and sinners?"	D And ⁵the Pharisees and their scribes 30 murmured against his disciples, saying, "Why do you eat and drink with tax collectors and sinners?"
E But when he heard it, he said, 12 "Those who are ⁸well have no need of a physician, but those who are sick.	E And when Jesus heard it, he said to 17 them, "Those who are ⁸well have no need of a physician, but those who are sick;	E And Jesus answered them, "Those 31 who are ⁸well have no need of a physician, but those who are sick;
Fᶠ Go and learn what this means, 'I 13 desire mercy, and not sacrifice.'		
G For I came not to call the righteous, but sinners."	G I came not to call the righteous, but sinners."	G I have not come to call the 32 righteous, but sinners to repentance."

§ 31 Criticism of Attitude Toward Fasting

MATT 9:14-17	MARK 2:18-22	LUKE 5:33-39
A Then the disciples of John came to 14 him, saying, "Why do we and the Pharisees fast⁹, but your disciples do not fast?"	A Now John's disciples and the 18 Pharisees were fasting; and people came and said to him, "Why do John's disciples and the disciples of	A And they said to him, "The 33 disciples of John fast often and offer prayers, and so do the disciples of

1 Greek *reclined*: and so always   2 That is, *collectors of Roman taxes*   3 Greek *reclining*   4 Some ancient authorities read *and the Pharisees*
5 Or *the Pharisees and the scribes among them*   6 Or, How is it *that he eats . . . sinners?*   7 Some ancient authorities add *and drink*   8 Greek *strong*   9 Some ancient authorities add *much or often*

HS references: Mt 9:13 = Hosea 6:6

F Compare § 32 portion E

MATT 9	MARK 2	LUKE 5
	the Pharisees fast, but your disciples do not fast?"	Pharisees, but yours eat and drink."
B And Jesus said to them, "Can the 15 wedding guests mourn as long as the bridegroom is with them? The days will come, when the bridegroom is taken away from them, and then they will fast.	B And Jesus said to them, "Can the 19 wedding guests fast while the bridegroom is with them? As long as they have the bridegroom with them, they cannot fast. The days will come, 20 when the bridegroom is taken away from them, and then they will fast in that day.	B And Jesus said to them, "Can you 34 make wedding guests fast while the bridegroom is with them? The days 35 will come, when the bridegroom is taken away from them, and then they will fast in those days."
C And no one puts a piece of 16 unshrunk cloth on an old garment, for the patch tears away from the garment, and a worse tear is made.	C No one sews a piece of unshrunk 21 cloth on an old garment; if he does, the patch tears away from it, the new from the old, and a worse tear is made.	C He told them a parable also: "No 36 one tears a piece from a new garment and puts it upon an old garment; if he does, he will tear the new, and the piece from the new will not match the old.
D Neither is new wine put into old 17 ¹wineskins; if it is, the skins burst, and the wine is spilled, and the skins are destroyed; but new wine is put into fresh wineskins, and so both are preserved." (+ § 52 B)	D And no one puts new wine into old 22 ¹wineskins; if he does, the wine will burst the skins, and the wine is lost, and so are the skins; but new wine is for fresh skins."	D And no one puts new wine into old 37 ¹wineskins; if he does, the new wine will burst the skins and it will be spilled, and the skins will be destroyed. But new wine must be put 38 into fresh wineskins.
		E And no one after drinking old wine 39 desires new; for he says, 'The old is ²good.'"

§ 32 Criticism for Working on the Sabbath

(§ 41 +) MATT 12:1-8	MARK 2:23-28	LUKE 6:1-5
A At that time Jesus went through the 1 grainfields on the sabbath; his disciples were hungry, and they began to pluck heads of grain and to eat.	A One sabbath he was going through 23 the grainfields; and as they made their way his disciples ⁴began to pluck heads of grain.	A On a ³sabbath, while he was going 1 through the grainfields, his disciples plucked and ate some heads of grain, rubbing them in their hands.
B But when the Pharisees saw it, they 2 said to him, "Look, your disciples are doing what is not lawful to do on the sabbath."	B And the Pharisees said to him, 24 "Look, why are they doing what is not lawful on the sabbath?"	B But some of the Pharisees said, 2 "Why are you doing what is not lawful to do on the sabbath?"
C He said to them, "Have you not 3 read what David did, when he was hungry, and those who were with him: how he entered the house of 4 God and ⁶ate the bread of the Presence, which it was not lawful for him to eat nor for those who were with him, but only for the priests?	C And he said to them, "Have you 25 never read what David did, when he was in need and was hungry, he and those who were with him: how he 26 entered the house of God, ⁵when Abi'athar was high priest, and ate the bread of the Presence, which it is not lawful for any but the priests to eat, and also gave it to those who were with him?"	C And Jesus answered, "Have you 3 not read what David did when he was hungry, he and those who were with him: how he entered the house of 4 God, and took and ate the bread of the Presence, which it is not lawful for any but the priests to eat, and also gave it to those with him?"

---

1 That is, *skins used as bottles*   2 Many ancient authorities read *better*   3 Many ancient authorities insert *second-first*   4 Greek *began to make their way plucking*   5 Some ancient authorities read *in the days of Abiathar the high priest*   6 Some ancient authorities read *they did eat*

HS references: Mt 12:1 and Mk 2:23 and Lk 6:1 = Deuteronomy 23:25   Mt 12:2 and Mk 2:24 and Lk 6:2 = Exodus 20:10; 23:12 and Deuteronomy 5:14   Mt 12:3-4 and Mk 2:25-26 and Lk 6:3-4 = I Samuel 21:1-6 and Leviticus 24:9   Mk 2:26 = II Samuel 8:17
NC references: Mt 9:15 and Mk 2:19-20 and Lk 5:34-35 = GT 27 and 104   Mt 9:16-17 and Mk 2:21-23 and Lk 5:36-39 = GT 47

MATT 12	MARK 2	LUKE 6
D Or have you not read in the law 5 how on the sabbath the priests in the temple profane the sabbath, and are guiltless? I tell you, ¹something 6 greater than the temple is here.		
E^E And if you had known what this 7 means, 'I desire mercy, and not sacrifice,' you would not have condemned the guiltless.		
	F And he said to them, "The sabbath 27 was made for man, not man for the sabbath;	**F** ²And he said to them, 5
G For the Son of man is lord of the 8 sabbath."	**G** so the Son of man is lord even of 28 the sabbath."	**G** "The Son of man is lord of the sabbath."

§ 33 Criticism of Healing on the Sabbath

MATT 12:9-14	MARK 3:1-6	LUKE 6:6-11
A And he went on from there, and 9 entered their synagogue. And behold, 10 there was a man with a withered hand.	**A** Again he entered the synagogue, 1 and a man was there who had a withered hand.	**A** On another sabbath, when he 6 entered the synagogue and taught, a man was there whose right hand was withered.
B And they asked him, "Is it lawful to heal on the sabbath?" so that they might accuse him.	**B** And they watched him, to see 2 whether he would heal him on the sabbath, so that they might accuse him.	**B** And the scribes and the Pharisees 7 watched him, to see whether he would heal on the sabbath, so that they might find an accusation against him.
	C And he said to the man who had 3 the withered hand, "³Come here."	**C** But he knew their thoughts, and he 8 said to the man who had the withered hand, "Come and stand here." And he rose and stood there.
D He said to them, "What man of 11 you, if he has one sheep and it falls into a pit on the sabbath, will not lay hold of it and lift it out? Of how 12 much more value is a man than a sheep!		**D** *And he said to them, "Which of* 14: *you, having an ass or an ox that has* 5 *fallen into a well, will not immediately pull him out on a sabbath day?* (§ 102 D)
E^E So it is lawful to do good on the sabbath."	**E**^E And he said to them, "Is it lawful 4 on the sabbath to do good or to do harm, to save life or to kill?" But they were silent.	**E**^E And Jesus said to them, "I ask 9 you, is it lawful on the sabbath to do good or to do harm, to save life or to destroy it?"

---

1 Or *someone greater*   2 In Codex Bezae, Lk 6:4b reads: *On the same day, seeing someone working on the sabbath, he said to him, Man, if indeed you know what you are doing, you are blessed; but if you do not know, you are cursed and a transgressor of the law.*   3 Greek *Arise into the midst*

HS references: Mt 12:5 = Numbers 28:9-10   Mt 12:7 = Hosea 6:6   Mk 2:27 = Exodus 23:12

E Compare § 30 portion F

E And Jesus spoke to the lawyers and Pharisees, saying, "Is it lawful to heal on the Sabbath, or not?" But they were silent. (§ 102 B = Lk 14:3-4)

MATT 12 | MARK 3 | LUKE 6

F Then he said to the man, "Stretch 13 out your hand." And the man stretched it out, and it was restored, whole like the other.

F And he looked around at them with 5 anger, grieved at their hardness of heart, and said to the man, "Stretch out your hand." He stretched it out, and his hand was restored.

F And he looked around on them all, 10 and said to him, "Stretch out your hand." And he did so, and his hand was restored.

G But the Pharisees went out and 14 took counsel against him, how to destroy him. (+ § 34 C)

G The Pharisees went out, and 6 immediately held counsel with the Hero'di-ans against him, how to destroy him.

G But they were filled with ¹fury and 11 discussed with one another what they might do to Jesus.

---

1 Or *foolishness*

Chapter VI

DEFINITION OF STANDARDS OF RIGHTEOUSNESS BY JESUS

§ 34 Widespread Fame of Jesus

(§ 26 +) MATT 4:24-25 (§ 33 +) MATT 12:15-21	MARK 3:7-12	LUKE
A *Compare portion C below*	**A** Jesus withdrew with his disciples to 7 the sea,	
B So his fame spread throughout all 4: Syria, and they brought him all the 24 sick, those afflicted with various diseases and pains, demoniacs, epileptics, and paralytics, and he healed them. And great crowds 25 followed him from Galilee and the Decap'olis and Jerusalem and Judea and from beyond the Jordan. (+ § 36)	**B** and a great multitude from Galilee followed; also from Judea and Jerusalem and Idume'a and from 8 beyond the Jordan and from about Tyre and Sidon a great multitude, hearing [1]all that he did, came to him.	**B** *Compare § 35 portion E*
C Jesus, aware of this, withdrew from 12: there. 15	**C** *Compare portion A above*	
D And many followed him, and he healed them all,	**D** And he told his disciples to have a 9 boat ready for him because of the crowd, lest they should crush him; for 10 he had healed many, so that all who had [2]diseases [3]pressed upon him to touch him.	**D** *Compare § 35 portion G*
	E And whenever the unclean spirits 11 beheld him, they fell down before him and cried out, "You are the Son of God."	**E** *Compare § 35 portion F* *Compare § 25 portion E*
F and ordered them not to make him 16 known.	**F** And he strictly ordered them not to 12 make him known.	

G This was to fulfil what was spoken 17 [4]by the prophet Isaiah:
    "Behold, my servant whom I 18
      have chosen,
    my beloved with whom my soul
      is well pleased.
    I will put my Spirit upon him,
    and he shall proclaim justice to
      the Gentiles.
    He will not wrangle or cry aloud, 19		

---

1 Or *all the things that he did*   2 Or *scourges*   3 Greek *fell*   4 Or *through*

HS references: Mt 12:18-21 = Isaiah 42:1-4

MATT 12

nor will any one hear his voice
   in the streets;
he will not break a bruised reed   20
   or quench a smoldering wick,
till he brings justice to
   victory;
and in his name will the Gentiles   21
   hope." (+ § 45)

§ 35 Appointment of Twelve Associates

MATT 10:1-4	MARK 3:13-19a	LUKE 6:12-19
A *Compare § 36 portion A*	**A** And he went up on the mountain, 13	**A** In these days he went out to the 12 mountain to pray; and all night he continued in prayer to God.
B *And he called to him his twelve 1 disciples and gave them authority over unclean spirits, to cast them out, and to heal every disease and every infirmity.*	**B** and called to him those whom he desired; and they came to him. And 14 he appointed twelve,[1] to be with him, and to be sent out to preach and have 15 authority to cast out demons:	**B** And when it was day, he called his 13 disciples, and chose from them twelve, whom he named apostles;
C *The names of the twelve apostles 2 are these; first, Simon, who is called Peter, and Andrew his brother; James the son of Zeb'edee, and John his brother; Philip and Bartholomew; 3 Thomas and Matthew the tax collector; James the son of Alphaeus, and Thaddaeus; Simon the 4 [3]Cananaean, and Judas Iscariot, who [5]betrayed him. (§ 56 CD)*	**C** [2]Simon whom he surnamed Peter; 16 James the son of Zeb'edee and John 17 the brother of James, whom he surnamed Bo-aner'ges, that is, sons of thunder; Andrew, and Philip, and 18 Bartholomew, and Matthew, and Thomas, and James the son of Alphaeus, and Thaddaeus, and Simon the [3]Cananaean, and Judas Iscariot, 19 who betrayed him.	**C** Simon, whom he named Peter, and 14 Andrew his brother, and James and John, and Philip, and Bartholomew, and Matthew, and Thomas, and James 15 the son of Alphaeus, and Simon who was called the Zealot, and Judas the 16 [4]son of James, and Judas Iscariot, who became a traitor.
D *Compare § 36 portion A* *Compare § 38 portion Y*		**D** And he came down with them and 17 stood on a level place,
E *Compare § 34 portion B* *Compare § 38 portion Y*	**E** *Compare § 34 portion B*	**E** with a great crowd of his disciples and a great multitude of people from all Judea and Jerusalem and the seacoast of Tyre and Sidon, who came to hear him and to be healed of their diseases;
F *Compare § 34 portion B*	**F** *Compare § 34 portion E*	**F** and those who were troubled with 18 unclean spirits were cured.
	G *Compare § 34 portion D*	**G** And all the crowd sought to touch 19 him, for power came forth from him and healed them all.

---

1 Some of the most ancient authorities add *whom also he named apostles*: See Luke 6:13   2 Some ancient authorities insert *and he appointed twelve*
3 Or *Zealot*: see Luke 6:15 and Acts 1:13   4 Or, brother: see Jude 1   5 Or *delivered him up*: and so always

§ 36 Discourse on Standards of Righteousness

(§ 34 B +) MATT 5:1-8:1   LUKE 6:20-49

A Seeing the crowds, he went up on the mountain, and 1 when he sat down his disciples came to him.

A   *Compare § 35 portion A*
       Compare § 35 portion D

B And he opened his mouth and taught them, saying: 2 "Blessed are the poor in spirit, for theirs is the kingdom 3 of heaven.

B And he lifted up his eyes on his disciples, and said: 20 "Blessed are you poor, for yours is the kingdom of God.

C [1]"Blessed are those who mourn, for they shall be 4 comforted.

C   *Compare portion F below*

D "Blessed are the meek, for they shall inherit the earth. 5

E "Blessed are those who hunger and thirst for 6 righteousness, for they shall be satisfied.

E "Blessed are you that hunger now, for you shall be 21 satisfied.

F   *Compare portion C above*

F "Blessed are you that weep now, for you shall laugh.

G "Blessed are the merciful, for they shall obtain mercy. 7 "Blessed are the pure in heart, for they shall see God. 8 "Blessed are the peacemakers, for they shall be called 9 sons of God.

H "Blessed are those who are persecuted for righteousness' 10 sake, for theirs is the kingdom of heaven.

H   *Compare portion I below*

I "Blessed are you when men revile you and persecute you 11 and utter all kinds of evil against you falsely on my account. Rejoice and be glad, for your reward is great in 12 heaven, for so men persecuted the prophets who were before you.

I "Blessed are you when men hate you, and when they 22 exclude you and revile you, and cast out your name as evil, on account of the Son of man! Rejoice in that day, and leap 23 for joy, for behold, your reward is great in heaven; for so their fathers did to the prophets.

J "But woe to you that are rich, for you have received your 24 consolation.
"Woe to you that are full now, for you shall hunger. 25
"Woe to you that laugh now, for you shall mourn and weep.
"Woe to you, when all men speak well of you, for so their 26 fathers did to the false prophets.

K "You are the salt of the earth; 13

L[L] but if salt has lost its taste, how shall its saltness be restored? It is no longer good for anything except to be thrown out and trodden under foot by men.

L[L] *"Salt is good; but if salt has lost its taste, how shall its* 14: *saltness be restored? It is fit neither for the land nor for the* 34 *dunghill; men throw it away.* (§ 104 E) 35

---

1 Some ancient authorities transpose verses 4 and 5

HS references: Mt 5:4 = Isaiah 61:2   Mt 5:5 = Psalm 37:11   Mt 5:6 = Isaiah 55:1-2   Mt 5:8 = Psalm 24:4   Mt 5:12 = II Chronicles 36:16
NC references: Mt 5:3 and Lk 6:20 = GT 54   Mt 5:6 = GT 69b   Mt 5:10 = GT 69a   Mt 5:11 = GT 68

L Salt is good; but if the salt has lost its saltness, how will you season it? Have salt in yourselves, and be at peace with one another. (§ 78 O = Mk 9:50)

MATT 5   LUKE

M "You are the light of the world.   14

N[N] A city set on a hill cannot be hid. Nor do men light a 15 lamp and put it under a bushel, but on a stand, and it gives light to all in the house.

O Let your light so shine before men, that they may see 16 your good works and give glory to your Father who is in heaven.

P "Think not that I have come to abolish the law and the 17 prophets; I have come not to abolish them but to fulfil them.

Q For truly, I say to you, till heaven and earth pass away, 18 not an iota, not a dot, will pass from the law until all is accomplished.

R Whoever then relaxes one of the least of these 19 commandments and teaches men so, shall be called least in the kingdom of heaven; but he who does them and teaches them shall be called great in the kingdom of heaven.

S For I tell you, unless your righteousness exceeds that of 20 the scribes and Pharisees, you will never enter the kingdom of heaven.

N[N] *"No one after lighting a lamp puts it in a cellar or* 11: *under a bushel, but on a stand, that those who enter may* 33 *see the light. (§ 89 A)*

Q *But it is easier for heaven and earth to pass away than* 16: *for one dot of the law to become void. (§ 107 D)*   17

§ 37 Discourse on Standards of Righteousness *(continued)*

A "You have heard that it was said to the men of old, 'You 21 shall not kill; and whoever kills shall be liable to judgment.' But I say to you that every one who is angry 22 with his brother[1] shall be liable to judgment; whoever [2]insults his brother shall be liable to the council, and whoever says, [3]'You fool!' shall be liable [4]to the [5]hell of fire. So if you are offering your gift at the altar, and there 23 remember that your brother has something against you, leave your gift there before the altar and go; first be 24 reconciled to your brother, and then come and offer your gift.

B Make friends quickly with your accuser, while you are 25 going with him to court, lest your accuser hand you over to the judge, and the judge [6]to the guard, and you be put in prison; truly, I say to you, you will never get out till you 26 have paid the last penny.

B *"As you go with your accuser before the magistrate,* 12: *make an effort to settle with him on the way, lest he drag* 58 *you to the judge, and the judge hand you over to the* [7]*officer, and the* [7]*officer put you in prison. I tell you, you* 59 *will never get out till you have paid the very last copper."* *(§ 96 C)*

---

1 Many ancient authorities insert *without cause*   2 Greek *says Raca to*, an expression of contempt   3 Or *Moreh*, a Hebrew expression of condemnation   4 Greek *unto* or *into*   5 Greek *Gehenna of fire*   6 Some ancient authorities add *deliver you*   7 Greek *exactor*

HS references: Mt 5:21 = Exodus 20:13 and Deuteronomy 5:17; also Exodus 21:12 and Leviticus 24:17 and Deuteronomy 16:18; 17:8-9
NC references: Mt 5:14b = GT 32   Mt 5:15 and Lk 8:16-17 = GT 33

N Is a lamp brought in to be put under a bushel, or under a bed, and not on a stand? (§ 47 Q = Mk 4:21)

N No one after lighting a lamp covers it with a vessel, or puts it under a bed, but puts it on a stand, that those who enter may see the light. (§ 47 Q = Lk 8:16)

MATT 5   LUKE 6

C[C] "You have heard that it was said, 'You shall not 27
commit adultery.' But I say to you that every one who 28
looks at a woman lustfully has already committed adultery
with her in his heart. If your right eye causes you to sin, 29
pluck it out and throw it away; it is better that you lose one
of your members than that your whole body be thrown into
[1]hell. And if your right hand causes you to sin, cut it off 30
and throw it away; it is better that you lose one of your
members than that your whole body go into [1]hell.

D "It was also said, 'Whoever divorces his wife, let him 31
give her a certificate of divorce.'

E[E] But I say to you that every one who divorces his wife, 32   E[E] *"Every one who divorces his wife and marries another 16:*
except on the ground of unchastity, makes her an   *commits adultery, and he who marries a woman divorced 18*
adulteress; and whoever marries a divorced woman   *from her husband commits adultery. (§ 107 E)*
commits adultery.

F "Again you have heard that it was said to the men of 33
old, 'You shall not swear falsely, but shall perform to the
Lord what you have sworn.' But I say to you, Do not 34
swear at all, either by heaven, for it is the throne of God,
or by the earth, for it is his footstool, or [2]by Jerusalem, for 35
it is the city of the great King. And do not swear by your 36
head, for you cannot make one hair white or black. [3]Let 37
what you say be simply 'Yes' or 'No'; anything more than
this comes from [4]evil.

G "You have heard that it was said, 'An eye for an eye 38
and a tooth for a tooth.'

H   *Compare portion N below*   H "But I say to you that hear, Love your enemies, do good 27
                                                          to those who hate you, bless those who curse you, pray for 28
                                                          those who abuse you.

---

1 Greek *Gehenna*   2 Or *toward*   3 Some ancient authorities read *But your speech shall be*   4 Or *the evil one* as in verse 39 and 6:13

HS references: Mt 5:27 = Exodus 20:14 and Deuteronomy 5:18   Mt 5:31-32 = Deuteronomy 24:1-4   Mt 5:33 = Leviticus 19:12 and Numbers 30:2
and Deuteronomy 23:21; also Exodus 20:7 and Deuteronomy 5:11   Mt 5:34-35a = Isaiah 66:1   Mt 5:35b = Psalm 48:2
Mt 5:38 = Exodus 21:24 and Leviticus 24:20 and Deuteronomy 19:21

C And if your hand or your foot causes you to
sin, cut it off and throw it from you; it is
better for you to enter life maimed or lame
than with two hands or two feet to be thrown
into the eternal fire. (§ 78 M = Mt 18:8-9)

C And if your hand causes you to sin, cut it
off; it is better for you to enter life maimed
than with two hands to go to hell, to the
unquenchable fire. And if your foot causes
you to sin, cut it off; it is better for you to
enter life lame than with two feet to be thrown
into hell. And if your eye causes you to sin,
pluck it out; it is better for you to enter the
kingdom of God with one eye than with two
eyes to be thrown into hell.
(§ 78 M = Mk 9:43-47)

E And I say to you: whoever divorces his
wife, except for unchastity, and marries
another, commits adultery.
(§ 115 F = Mt 19:9)

E And he said to them, "Whoever divorces his
wife and marries another, commits adultery
against her; and if she divorces her husband
and marries another, she commits adultery."
(§ 115 F = Mk 10:11-12)

MATT 5-6

I But I say to you, Do not resist [1]one who is evil. But if 39 any one strikes you on the right cheek, turn to him the other also; and if any one would sue you and take your 40 coat, let him have your cloak as well; and if any one 41 [2]forces you to go one mile, go with him two miles.

J Give to him who begs from you, and do not refuse him 42 who would borrow from you.

K　　Compare § 38 portion L

L "You have heard that it was said, 'You shall love your 43 neighbor and hate your enemy.'

M　　Compare portion Q below

N But I say to you, Love your enemies and pray for those 44 who persecute you,

O　　Compare portion J above

P so that you may be sons of your Father who is in 45 heaven; for he makes his sun rise on the evil and on the good, and sends rain on the just and on the unjust.

Q For if you love those who love you, what reward have 46 you? Do not even the [4]tax collectors do the same? And if 47 you salute only your brethren, what more are you doing than others? Do not even the Gentiles do the same?

R You, therefore, must be [5]perfect, as your heavenly 48 Father is [5]perfect.

S "Beware of practicing your piety before men in order to 6: be seen by them; for then you will have no reward from 1 your Father who is in heaven.

T "Thus, when you give alms, sound no trumpet before 2 you, as the hypocrites do in the synagogues and in the streets, that they may be praised by men. Truly, I say to you, they have received their reward. But when you give 3 alms, do not let your left hand know what your right hand is doing, so that your alms may be in secret; and your 4 Father who sees in secret will reward you.[6]

U "And when you pray, you must not be like the 5 hypocrites; for they love to stand and pray in the

LUKE 6

I To him who strikes you on the cheek, offer the other 29 also; and from him who takes away your coat do not withhold even your shirt.

J Give to every one who begs from you; and of him who 30 takes away your goods do not ask them again.

K And as you wish that men would do to you, do so to 31 them.

M "If you love those who love you, what credit is that to 32 you? For even sinners love those who love them. And if 33 you do good to those who do good to you, what credit is that to you? For even sinners do the same. And if you lend 34 to those from whom you hope to receive, what credit is that to you? Even sinners lend to sinners, to receive as much again.

N But love your enemies, and do good, 35
　　Compare portion H above

O and lend, [3]expecting nothing in return; and your reward will be great,

P and you will be sons of the Most High; for he is kind to the ungrateful and the selfish.

Q　　Compare portion M above

R Be merciful, even as your Father is merciful. 36

---

1 Or *evil*　2 Greek *impress*　3 Some ancient authorities read *despairing of no man*　4 That is, *collectors of Roman taxes*: and so elsewhere
5 Greek *complete, whole, fulfilled, all-inclusive*　6 Some ancient authorities add *openly*

HS references: Mt 5:39-42 = Proverbs 24:29　Mt 5:43a = Leviticus 19:18　Mt 5:43b = Deuteronomy 23:6 and 25:19
Mt 5:43-48 = Leviticus 19:18 and Proverbs 25:21　Mt 5:48 = Leviticus 19:2
NC references: Mt 5:42 and Lk 6:30 = GT 95　Lk 6:34-35 = GT 95

MATT 6   LUKE 6

synagogues and at the street corners, that they may be seen by men. Truly, I say to you, they have received their reward. But when you pray, go into your room and shut 6 the door and pray to your Father who is in secret; and your Father who sees in secret will reward you.

V^V "and in praying do not heap up empty phrases as the 7 Gentiles do; for they think that they will be heard for their many words. Do not be like them, for ¹your Father knows 8 what you need before you ask him.

W Pray then like this: 9   W *"When you pray, say:*   11:
    Our Father who art in heaven,   *"⁵Father, hallowed be thy name. Thy kingdom come. Give* 2b
    Hallowed be thy name.   *us each day ²our daily bread; and forgive us our sins, for 3*
    Thy kingdom come,   *we ourselves forgive every one who is indebted to us; and 4*
    Thy will be done, On earth as it is in heaven. 10 *lead us not into temptation." (§ 85 B)*
    Give us this day ²our daily bread;   11
    And forgive us our debts, As we also have forgiven 12
       our debtors;
    And lead us not into temptation, But deliver us from 13
       ³evil.⁴

X^X For if you forgive men their trespasses⁶ your heavenly 14 Father also will forgive you; but if you do not forgive men 15 their trespasses, neither will your Father forgive your trespasses.

Y "And when you fast, do not look dismal, like the 16 hypocrites, for they disfigure their faces that their fasting may be seen by men. Truly, I say to you, they have received their reward. But when you fast, anoint your head 17 and wash your face, that your fasting may not be seen by 18 men but by your Father who is in secret; and your Father who sees in secret will reward you.

§ 38 Discourse on Standards of Righteousness *(concluded)*

A "Do not lay up for yourselves treasures on earth, where 19   A *Sell your possessions, and give alms; provide yourselves* 12:
moth and ⁷rust consume and where thieves ⁸break in and   *with purses that do not grow old, with a treasure in the 33*
steal, but lay up for yourselves treasures in heaven, where 20 *heavens that does not fail, where no thief approaches and*
neither moth nor ⁷rust consumes and where thieves do not   *no moth destroys. For where your treasure is, there will 34*
break in and steal. For where your treasure is, there will 21 *your heart be also. (§ 93 I-K)*
your heart be also.

B "The eye is the lamp of the body. So, if your eye is 22   B *Your eye is the lamp of your body; when your eye is* 11:
⁹sound, your whole body will be full of light; but if your 23 *sound, your whole body is full of light; but when it is not 34*
eye is ¹⁰not sound, your whole body will be full of   *sound, your body is full of darkness. Therefore be careful 35*
darkness. If then the light in you is darkness, how great is *lest the light in you be darkness. (§ 89 BC)*
the darkness!

---

1 Some ancient authorities read *God your Father*   2 Greek *our bread for the coming day*   3 Or *the evil one*   4 Many authorities, some ancient, but with variations, add *For thine is the Kingdom, and the power, and the glory, for ever. Amen.*   ˙5 Many ancient authorities read *Our Father, which art in heaven:* see Matt 6:9   6 Some ancient authorities omit *their trespasses*   7 Or *worm*   8 Greek *dig through*   9 Greek *single*   10 Greek *evil*

HS references: Mt 6:16 = Isaiah 58:5

V With Matthew 6:8 above, compare Matthew 6:32 = Luke 12:30 in § 38 D
X And whenever you stand praying, forgive, if you have anything against any one; so that your Father also who is in heaven may forgive you your trespasses. (§ 127 E = Mk 11:25)
X So also my heavenly Father will do to every one of you, if you do not forgive your brother from your heart. (§ 78 X = Mt 18:35)

MATT 6-7   LUKE 6

C "No one can serve two masters; for either he will hate 24 the one and love the other, or he will be devoted to the one and despise the other. You cannot serve God and mammon.

D^D "Therefore I tell you, do not be anxious about your life, 25 what you shall eat or what you shall drink, nor about your body, what you shall put on. Is not life more than food, and the body more than clothing? Look at the birds of the 26 air: they neither sow nor reap nor gather into barns, and yet your heavenly Father feeds them. Are you not of more value than they? And which of you by being anxious can 27 add one cubit to his ³span of life? And why are you anxious 28 about clothing? Consider the lilies of the field, how they grow; they neither toil nor spin; yet I tell you, even 29 Solomon in all his glory was not arrayed like one of these. But if God so clothes the grass of the field, which today is 30 alive and tomorrow is thrown into the oven, will he not much more clothe you, O men of little faith? Therefore do 31 not be anxious, saying, 'What shall we eat?' or 'What shall we drink?' or 'What shall we wear?' For the Gentiles seek 32 all these things; and your heavenly Father knows that you need them all. But seek first his kingdom and his 33 righteousness, and all these things shall be yours as well.

E "Therefore do not be anxious about tomorrow, for 34 tomorrow will be anxious for itself. Let the day's own trouble be sufficient for the day.

F^F "Judge not, that you be not judged. For with the 7: judgment you pronounce you will be judged, and the 1 measure you give will be the measure you get.   2

G "Let them alone; they are blind guides. And if a blind 15: man leads a blind man, both will fall into a pit." (§ 63 J) 14

H "A disciple is not above his teacher, nor a ⁵servant above 10: his master; it is enough for the disciple to be like his 24 teacher, and the ⁵servant like his master. (§ 57 G)   25

I Why do you see the speck that is in your brother's eye, 3 but do not notice the log that is in your own eye? Or how 4 can you say to your brother, 'Let me take the speck out of your eye,' when there is the log in your own eye? You

C "No ¹servant can serve two masters; for either he will 16: hate the one and love the other, or he will be devoted to the 13 one and despise the other. You cannot serve God and mammon". (§ 107 A)

D^D "Therefore I tell you, do not be anxious about your ²life, 12: what you shall eat, nor about your body, what you shall put 22 on. For ²life is more than food, and the body more than 23 clothing. Consider the ravens; they neither sow nor reap, 24 they have neither storehouse nor barn, and yet God feeds them. Of how much more value are you than the birds! And 25 which of you by being anxious can add a cubit to his ³span of life? If then you are not able to do as small a thing as 26 that, why are you anxious about the rest? Consider the 27 lilies, how they grow; they neither toil nor spin; yet I tell you, even Solomon in all his glory was not arrayed like one of these. But if God so clothes the grass which is alive in 28 the field today and tomorrow is thrown into the oven, how much more will he clothe you, O men of little faith! And do 29 not seek what you are to eat and what you are to drink, nor be of anxious mind. For all the nations of the world seek 30 these things; and your Father knows that you need them. Instead, seek ⁴his kingdom, and these things shall be yours 31 as well.

E "Fear not, little flock, for it is your Father's good 32 pleasure to give you the kingdom. (§ 93 B-H)

F^F "Judge not, and you will not be judged; condemn not, 37 and you will not be condemned; forgive, and you will be forgiven; give, and it will be given to you; good measure, 38 pressed down, shaken together, running over, will be put into your lap. For the measure you give will be the measure you get back."

G He also told them a parable: "Can a blind man lead a 39 blind man? Will they not both fall into a pit?

H A disciple is not above his teacher, but every one when 40 he is fully taught will be like his teacher.

I Why do you see the speck that is in your brother's eye, 41 but do not notice the log that is in your own eye? Or how 42 can you say to your brother, 'Brother, let me take out the speck that is in your eye,' when you yourself do not see

---

1 Greek *household-servant*   2 Or *soul*   3 Or *stature*   4 Many ancient authorities read *the kingdom of God*   5 Greek *slave*

HS references: Mt 6:27 = Psalm 39:5   Mt 6:29 = I Kings 10:4-7
NC references: Mt 6:30-34 = GT 36   Mt 15:14 and Lk 6:39 = GT 34   Mt 7:3-5 = GT 26

D With Matthew 6:32 = Luke 12:30 above, compare Matthew 6:8 in § 37 V
F . . . the measure you give will be the measure you get, and still more will be given you. (§ 47 U = Mk 4:24)

MATT 7   LUKE 6

hypocrite, first take the log out of your own eye, and then 5
you will see clearly to take the speck out of your brother's
eye.

the log that is in your own eye? You hypocrite, first take
the log out of your own eye, and then you will see clearly
to take out the speck that is in your brother's eye.

J "Do not give dogs what is holy; and do not throw your 6
pearls before swine, lest they trample them under foot and
turn to attack you.

K "Ask, and it will be given you; seek, and you will find; 7
knock, and it will be opened to you. For every one who 8
asks receives, and he who seeks finds, and to him who
knocks it will be opened. Or what man of you, if his son 9
asks him for bread, will give him a stone? Or if he asks for 10
a fish, will give him a serpent? If you then, who are evil, 11
know how to give good gifts to your children, how much
more will your Father who is in heaven give good things to
those who ask him!

K *"And I tell you, ask, and it will be given you; seek, and* 11:
you will find; knock, and it will be opened to you. For 9
every one who asks receives, and he who seeks finds, and 10
to him who knocks it will be opened. What father among 11
you, if his son asks for [1]*a fish, will instead of a fish give*
him a serpent; or if he asks for an egg, will give him a 12
scorpion? If you then, who are evil, know how to give good 13
gifts to your children, how much more will the heavenly
Father give the Holy Spirit to those who ask him!" (§ 85 D)

L[L] So whatever you wish that men would do to you, do so 12
to them; for this is the law and the prophets.

L[L]   *Compare § 37 portion K*

M "Enter by the narrow gate; for[2] the gate is wide and the 13
way is easy, that leads to destruction, and those who enter
by it are many. [3]For the gate is narrow and the way is 14
[4]hard, that leads to life, and those who find it are few.

M   *"Strive to enter by the narrow door; for many, I tell* 13:
you, will seek to enter and will not be able." (§ 100 C)   24

N "Beware of false prophets, who come to you in sheep's 15
clothing but inwardly are ravenous wolves.

O[O]   *Compare portion S below*

O[O] "For no good tree bears bad fruit, nor again does a bad 43
tree bear good fruit;

P[P] You will know them by their fruits. Are grapes gathered 16
from thorns, or figs from thistles?

P[P] for each tree is known by its own fruit. For figs are not 44
gathered from thorns, nor are grapes picked from a
bramble bush.

Q So, every sound tree bears good fruit, but the bad tree 17
bears evil fruit.

R *For out of the abundance of the heart the mouth speaks.* 12:
The good man out of his good treasure brings forth good, 34b
and the evil man out of his evil treasure brings forth evil. 35
(§ 45 O)

R The good man out of the good treasure of his heart 45
produces good, and the evil man out of his evil treasure
produces evil; for out of the abundance of the heart his
mouth speaks.

S A sound tree cannot bear evil fruit, nor can a bad tree 18
bear good fruit.

S   *Compare portion O above*

T[T] Every tree that does not bear good fruit is cut down and 19
thrown into the fire. Thus you will know them by their 20
fruits.

---

1 Many ancient authorities add   *bread, will give him a stone*   2 Some ancient authorities read   *For wide and broad is the way that leads to*
destruction . . .   3 Many ancient authorities read *How narrow is the gate, and straitened the way, etc.*   4 Greek *straitened, constrained*

HS references: Mt 7:13-14 = Jeremiah 21:8 and Deuteronomy 30:19   Mt 7:15 = Ezekiel 22:27
NC references: Mt 7:6 = GT 93   Mt 7:7 and Lk 11:9 = GT 2, 92, 94   Mt 7:16 and Lk 6:44-45 = GT 45

L On these two commandments depend all the law and the prophets. (§ 130 N = Mt 22:40)
OP With portions of OP above, compare § 45 LM. With the first half of portion P above, compare the second half of portion T below
T For a saying by John the Baptist similar to verse 19, compare § 17 M end. With verse 20 compare portion P above.

MATT 7-8

U "Not every one who says to me, 'Lord, Lord,' shall 21 enter the kingdom of heaven, but he who does the will of my Father who is in heaven.

V On that day many will say to me, 'Lord, Lord, did we 22 not prophesy in your name, and cast out demons in your name, and do many [1]mighty works in your name?' And 23 then will I declare to them, 'I never knew you; depart from me, you evildoers.'

W "Every one then who hears these words of mine and 24 does them will be like a wise man who built his house upon the rock; and the rain fell, and the floods came, and the 25 winds blew and beat upon that house, but it did not fall, because it had been founded on the rock. And every one 26 who hears these words of mine and does not do them will be like a foolish man who built his house upon the sand; and the rain fell, and the floods came, and the winds blew 27 and beat against that house, and it fell; and great was the fall of it."

X And when Jesus finished these sayings, the crowds were 28 astonished at his teaching, for he taught them as one who 29 had authority, and not as their scribes.

Y When he came down from the mountain, great crowds 8: followed him; (+ § 28)   1

LUKE 6

U "Why do you call me 'Lord, Lord,' and not do what I 46 tell you?

V *Then you will begin to say, 'We ate and drank in your* 13: *presence, and you taught in our streets.' But he will say, 'I* 26 *tell you, I do not know where you come from; depart from* 27 *me, all you workers of iniquity!'* (§ 100 EF)

W Every one who comes to me and hears my words and 47 does them, I will show you what he is like: he is like a 48 man building a house, who dug deep, and laid the foundation upon rock; and when a flood arose, the stream broke against that house, and could not shake it,[2] because it had been well built. But he who hears and does not do 49 them is like a man who built a house on the ground without a foundation; against which the stream broke, and immediately it fell, and the ruin of that house was great."

X   *Compare § 24 portion B*

Y   *Compare § 35 portions DE*

---

1 Greek *powers*   2 Many ancient authorities read *for it had been founded upon the rock*: as in Mt 7:25

HS references: Mt 7:23 and Lk 13:27 = Psalm 6:8

Chapter VII

CONTEMPORARY OPINIONS ABOUT THE WORTH OF JESUS

§ 39 Opinion of a Roman Centurion

(§ 28 +) MATT 8:5-13   LUKE 7:1-10

A As he entered Caper'na-um, a centurion came forward to 5 him, beseeching him and saying, "Lord, my ¹servant is 6 lying paralyzed at home, in terrible distress." And he said 7 to him, "I will come and heal him."

B But the centurion answered him, "Lord, I am not 8 ³worthy to have you come under my roof; but only say ⁴the word, and my ¹servant will be healed. For I am a man⁵ 9 under authority, with soldiers under me; and I say to one, 'Go,' and he goes, and to another, 'Come,' and he comes, and to my slave, 'Do this,' and he does it."

C When Jesus heard him, he marveled, and said to those 10 who followed him, "Truly, I say to you,⁶ not even in Israel have I found such faith.

D^D I tell you, many will come from east and west and ⁷sit 11 at table with Abraham, Isaac, and Jacob in the kingdom of heaven, while the sons of the kingdom will be thrown into 12 the outer darkness; there men will weep and gnash their teeth."

E And to the centurion Jesus said, "Go; be it done for you 13 as you have believed."⁸ And the ¹servant was healed at that very moment. (+ § 25)

A After he had ended all his sayings in the hearing of the 1 people he entered Caper'na-um. Now a centurion had a 2 slave who was ²dear to him, who was sick and at the point of death. When he heard of Jesus, he sent to him elders of 3 the Jews, asking him to come and heal his slave. And when 4 they came to Jesus, they besought him earnestly, saying, "He is worthy to have you do this for him, for he loves our 5 nation, and he built us our synagogue." And Jesus went 6 with them.

B When he was not far from the house, the centurion sent friends to him, saying to him, "Lord, do not trouble yourself, for I am not ³worthy to have you come under my roof; therefore I did not presume to come to you. But ⁴say 7 the word, and let my ¹servant be healed. For I am a man 8 set under authority, with soldiers under me: and I say to one, 'Go,' and he goes; and to another, 'Come,' and he comes; and to my slave, 'Do this,' and he does it."

C When Jesus heard this he marveled at him, and turned 9 and said to the multitude that followed him, "I tell you, not even in Israel have I found such faith."

D^D *There you will weep and gnash your teeth, when you see* 13: *Abraham and Isaac and Jacob and all the prophets in the* 28 *kingdom of God and you yourselves thrust out. And men* 29 *will come from east and west, and from north and south, and ⁷sit at table in the kingdom of God.* (§ 100 G)

E And when those who had been sent returned to the 10 house, they found the slave well.

---

1 Or *boy* 2 Or *precious to him* or *honorable with him* 3 Or *sufficient* 4 Greek *with a word* 5 Some ancient authorities insert *set*: as in Luke 7:8 6 Many ancient authorities read *With no man in Israel have I found so great faith* 7 Greek *recline* 8 Some ancient authorities read *And when the centurion returned to his house in that hour he found the servant well*

HS references: Mt 8:11 and Lk 13:29 = Psalm 107:3 and Isaiah 49:12; 59:19 and Malachi 1:11

D And throw them into the furnace of fire; there men will weep and gnash their teeth. (§ 48 L = Mt 13:42)
D And throw them into the furnace of fire; there men will weep and gnash their teeth. (§ 48 Q = Mt 13:50)
D And cast him into the outer darkness; there men will weep and gnash their teeth. (§ 129 P = Mt 22:13)
D And will punish him, and put him with the hypocrites; there men will weep and gnash their teeth. (§ 136 D = Mt 24:51)
D And cast the worthless servant into the outer darkness; there men will weep and gnash their teeth. (§ 136 Q= Mt 25:30)

D And will punish him, and put him with the unfaithful. (§ 94 E = Lk 12:46)

§ 40 Opinion of the Common People

LUKE 7:11-17

¹Soon afterward he went to a city called Na'in, and his 11
disciples and a great crowd went with him. As he drew 12
near to the gate of the city, behold, a man who had died
was being carried out, the only son of his mother, and she
was a widow; and a large crowd from the city was with
her. And when the Lord saw her, he had compassion on 13
her and said to her, "Do not weep." And he came and 14
touched the bier, and the bearers stood still. And he said,
"Young man, I say to you, arise." And the dead man sat 15
up, and began to speak. And he gave him to his mother.
Fear seized them all; and they glorified God, saying, "A 16
great prophet has arisen among us!" and "God has visited
his people!" And this report concerning him spread through 17
the whole of Judea and all the surrounding country.

§ 41 Opinion of John the Baptist

(§ 57 +) MATT 11:2-30	LUKE 7:18-35

A Now when John heard in prison about the deeds of the 2
Christ, he sent word by his disciples and said to him, "Are 3
you he who is to come, or shall we look for another?"

A The disciples of John told him of all these things. And 18
John, calling to him ²two of his disciples, sent them to the 19
Lord, saying, "Are you he who is to come, or shall we
look for another?"

B And when the men had come to him, they said, "John 20
the Baptist has sent us to you, saying, 'Are you he who is
to come, or shall we look for another?'" In that hour he 21
cured many of diseases and ³plagues and evil spirits, and on
many that were blind he bestowed sight.

C And Jesus answered them, "Go and tell John what you 4
hear and see: the blind receive their sight and the lame 5
walk, lepers are cleansed and the deaf hear, and the dead
are raised up, and the poor have good news preached to
them. And blessed is he ⁴who takes no offense at me."   6

C And he answered them, "Go and tell John what you have 22
seen and heard: the blind receive their sight, the lame
walk, lepers are cleansed, and the deaf hear, the dead are
raised up, the poor have good news preached to them. And 23
blessed is he who takes no offense at me."

D As they went away, Jesus began to speak to the crowds 7
concerning John: "What did you go out into the wilderness
to behold? A reed shaken by the wind? Why then did you 8
go out? To see a man clothed in soft raiment? Behold,
those who wear soft raiment are in kings' houses. ⁵Why 9
then did you go out? To see a prophet? Yes, I tell you, and
more than a prophet.

D When the messengers of John had gone, he began to 24
speak to the crowds concerning John: "What did you go out
into the wilderness to behold? A reed shaken by the wind?
What then did you go out to see? A man clothed in soft 25
clothing? Behold, those who are gorgeously appareled and
live in luxury are in kings' courts. What then did you go 26
out to see? A prophet? Yes, I tell you, and more than a
prophet.

E^E This is he of whom it is written,   10
    'Behold, I send my messenger before thy face,
    who shall prepare thy way before thee.'
Truly, I say to you, among those born of women there has 11

E^E This is he of whom it is written,   27
    'Behold, I send my messenger before thy face,
    who shall prepare thy way before thee.'
I tell you, among those born of women none is greater than 28

---

1 Many ancient authorities read *on the next day*   2 Greek *a certain two*   3 Greek *scourges*   4 Greek *Who is not caused to stumble in me* or
who finds no obstacle in me   5 Many ancient authorities read *But what did you go out to see? A prophet?*

HS references: Lk 7:11 = I Kings 17:17-24 and II Kings 4:32-37   Mt 11:3 = Habakkuk 2:3
Mt 11:5 and Lk 7:22 = Isaiah 29:18-19 and 35:5-6 and 61:1   Mt 11:10 and Lk 7:27 = Malachi 3:1
NC references: Mt 11:7-8 and Lk 7:24-25 = GT 78   Mt 11:11 and Lk 7:28 = GT 46

E Compare the record of Mark in § 17 portion E

MATT 11

risen no one greater than John the Baptist; yet he who is [1]least in the kingdom of heaven is greater than he.

F From the days of John the Baptist until now the kingdom 12 of heaven [2]has suffered violence, and men of violence take it by force. For all the prophets and the law prophesied 13 until John;

G[G] and if you are willing to accept [3]it, he is Eli'jah who is 14 to come.

H[H] He who has ears [4]to hear, let him hear. 15

I *Jesus said to them, "Truly, I say to you, the tax collectors* 21: *and the harlots go into the kingdom of God before you. For* 31 *John came to you in the way of righteousness, and you did* 32 *not believe him, but the tax collectors and the harlots believed him; and even when you saw it, you did not afterward repent and believe him. (§ 129 B)*

J "But to what shall I compare this generation? It is like 16 children sitting in the market places and calling to their playmates,
　'We piped to you, and you did not dance; 17
　we wailed, and you did not [5]mourn.'
For John came neither eating nor drinking, and they say, 18 'He has a demon'; the Son of man came eating and 19 drinking, and they say, 'Behold, a glutton and a drunkard, a friend of tax collectors and sinners!' Yet wisdom is justified by her [7]deeds."

K Then he began to upbraid the cities where most of his 20 mighty works had been done, because they did not repent.

L　*Compare portion O below*
　Compare § 56 portion L

M "Woe to you, Chora'zin! woe to you, Beth-sa'ida! for if 21 the [8]mighty works done in you had been done in Tyre and Sidon, they would have repented long ago in sackcloth and ashes. But I tell you, it shall be more tolerable on the day 22 of judgment for Tyre and Sidon than for you. And you, 23 Caper'na-um, will you be exalted to heaven? You shall be brought down to Hades.

N For if the [8]mighty works done in you had been done in Sodom, it would have remained until this day.

LUKE 7

John; yet he who is [1]least in the kingdom of God is greater than he."

F *"The law and the prophets were until John; since then* 16: *the good news of the kingdom of God is preached, and* 16 *every one enters it violently. (§ 107 C)*

H[H] *He who has ears to hear, let him hear." (§ 104 F)* 14: 35b

I (When they heard this all the people and the tax collectors 29 justified God, having been baptized with the baptism of John; but the Pharisees and the lawyers rejected the 30 purpose of God for themselves, not having been baptized by him.)

J "To what then shall I compare the men of this 31 generation, and what are they like? They are like children 32 sitting in the market place and calling to one another,
　'We piped to you, and you did not dance;
　we wailed, and you did not weep.'
For John the Baptist has come eating no bread and drinking 33 no wine; and you say, 'He has a demon.' The Son of man 34 has come eating and drinking; and you say, 'Behold, a glutton and a drunkard, a friend of tax collectors and sinners!' Yet wisdom [6]is justified by all her children." 35

L *I tell you it shall be more tolerable on that day for* 10: *Sodom than for that town.* 12

M *"Woe to you, Chora'zin! woe to you, Beth-sa'ida! for if* 13 *the [8]mighty works done in you had been done in Tyre and Sidon, they would have repented long ago, sitting in sackcloth and ashes. But it shall be more tolerable in the* 14 *judgment for Tyre and Sidon than for you. And you,* 15 *Caper'na-um, will you be exalted to heaven? You shall be brought down to Hades. (§ 82 L-P)*

---

1 Greek *lesser*　2 Or *has been coming violently*　3 Or, him　4 Some ancient authorities omit *to hear*　5 Greek *beat the breast*　6 Or *was*
7 Many ancient authorities read *children:* as in Luke 7:35　8 Greek *powers*

HS references: Mt 11:14 = Malachi 4:5　　Mt 11:23a and Lk 10:15 = Isaiah 14:13-15　　Mt 11:23b-24 and Lk 10:12 = Genesis 19:24

G For another record of the identification of John the Baptist with Elijah by Jesus, compare § 74 K-O
H He who has ears, let him hear.　　　　　　H He who has ears to hear, let him hear.　　　　　H He who has ears to hear, let him hear.
(§ 47 F = Mt 13:9)　　　　　　　　　　　　(§ 47 F = Mk 4:9)　　　　　　　　　　　　　(§ 47 F = Lk 8:8)
H If any man has ears to hear, let him hear. (§ 47 S = Mk 4:23)
H He who has ears to hear, let him hear. (§ 48 M = Mt 13:43)

MATT 11   LUKE

O But I tell you that it shall be more tolerable on the day 24   **O**   *Compare portion L above*
of judgment for the land of Sodom than for you."
Compare § 56 portion L

P At that time Jesus declared, "I ²thank thee, Father, Lord 25   **P** *In that same hour he rejoiced ¹in the Holy Spirit and* 10:
of heaven and earth, that thou hast hidden these things from   *said, "I ²thank thee, Father, Lord of heaven and earth, that* 21
the wise and understanding and revealed them to babes;   *thou hast hidden these things from the wise and*
yea, Father, ³for such was thy gracious will.   26   *understanding and revealed them to babes; yea, Father, ³for*
   such was thy gracious will.

Q^Q All things have been delivered to me by my Father; and 27   **Q**^Q *All things have been delivered to me by my Father; and* 22
no one knows the Son except the Father, and no one knows   *no one knows who the Son is except the Father, or who the*
the Father except the Son and any one to whom the Son   *Father is except the Son and any one to whom the Son*
chooses to reveal him.   *chooses to reveal him." (§ 82 ST)*

R Come to me, all who labor and are heavy laden, and I 28
will give you rest. Take my yoke upon you, and learn from 29
me; for I am gentle and lowly in heart, and you will find
rest for your souls. For my yoke is easy, and my burden is 30
light." (+ § 32)

§ 42 Opinion of a Sinner *vs* Opinion of a Pharisee

LUKE 7:36-50

A *For an account in Matt-Mark having some elements in*   **A** One of the Pharisees asked him to eat with him, and he 36
common with the narrative here recorded by Luke, compare   went into the Pharisee's house, and took his place at table.
§ 137 B   And behold, a woman of the city, who was a sinner, when 37
   she learned that he was at table in the Pharisee's house,
   brought an alabaster flask of ointment, and standing behind 38
   him at his feet, weeping, she began to wet his feet with her
   tears, and wiped them with the hair of her head, and
   ⁴kissed his feet, and anointed them with the ointment.

   B Now when the Pharisee who had invited him saw it, he 39
   said to himself, "If this man were ⁵a prophet, he would
   have known who and what sort of woman this is who is
   touching him, for she is a sinner."

   C And Jesus answering said to him, "Simon, I have 40
   something to say to you." And he answered, "What is it,
   Teacher?" "A certain creditor had two debtors; one owed 41
   five hundred ⁶denarii, and the other fifty. When they could 42
   not pay, he forgave them both. Now which of them will
   love him more?" Simon answered, "The one, I suppose, to 43
   whom he forgave more." And he said to him, "You have
   judged rightly."

   D Then turning toward the woman he said to Simon, "Do 44
   you see this woman? I entered your house, you gave me no
   water for my feet, but she has wet my feet with her tears
   and wiped them with her hair. You gave me no kiss, but 45
   from the time I came in she has not ceased to ⁷kiss my feet.

---

1 Or *by*   2 Or *praise*   3 Or *that*   4 Greek *kissed much*   5 Some ancient authorities read *the prophet*: see John 1:21,25   6 The word in the
Greek denotes a coin worth about forty cents. A denarius was a day's wage for a laborer.   7 Greek *kiss much*

HS references: Mt 11:29 = Jeremiah 6:16
NC references: Mt 11:28-30 = GT 90

Q All authority in heaven and on earth has been given to me. (§ 151 B = Mt 28:18)

LUKE 7

You did not anoint my head with oil, but she has anointed 46 my feet with ointment. Therefore I tell you, her sins, which 47 are many, [1]are forgiven, for she loved much; but he who is forgiven little, loves little."

E And he said to her, "Your sins [1]are forgiven." Then 48 those who were at table with him began to say [2]among 49 themselves, "Who is this, who even forgives sins?" And he 50 said to the woman, "Your faith has saved you; go in peace."

§ 43 On a Tour in Galilee

LUKE 8:1-3

Soon afterward he went on through cities and villages, 1 preaching and bringing the good news of the kingdom of God. And the twelve were with him, and also some women 2 who had been healed of evil spirits and infirmities: Mary, called Mag'dalene, from whom seven demons had gone out, and Joan'na, the wife of Chu'za, Herod's steward, and 3 Susanna, and many others, who provided for [3]them out of their means.

§ 44 Opinion of the Friends of Jesus

MARK 3:19b-21

Then he went [4]home; and the crowd 19b came together again, so that they 20 could not even eat. And when his 21 family heard it, they went out to seize him, for people were saying, "He is beside himself."

§ 45 Opinion of the Religious Leaders

(§ 34 +) MATT 12:22-45	MARK 3:22-30	LUKE 11:14-32
A[A] Then a blind and dumb demoniac 22 was brought to him, and he healed him, so that the dumb man spoke and saw.		A[A] *Now he was casting out a demon 14 that was dumb; when the demon had gone out, the dumb man spoke,*
B[B] And all the people were amazed, 23 and said, "Can this be the Son of David?"		B[B] *and the people marveled.*
C[C] But when the Pharisees heard it 24 they said, "It is only [5]by Be-el'zebul, the prince of demons, that this man casts out demons."	C[C] And the scribes who came down 22 from Jerusalem said, "He is possessed by Be-el'zebul, and [5]by the prince of demons he casts out the demons."	C[C] *But some of them said, "He casts 15 out demons by Be-el'zebul, the prince of demons";*
D *Compare portion Q below*		D *while others, to test him, sought 16 from him a sign from heaven.*

---

1 Greek *have been forgiven*   2 Or *within*   3 Many ancient authorities read *him*   4 Greek *into a house*   5 Or *in*

ABC For another Matthew account covering portions ABC, compare § 53 B

MATT 12	MARK 3	LUKE 11
E Knowing their thoughts, he said to them, "Every kingdom divided against itself is laid waste, and no city or house divided against itself will stand; and if Satan casts out Satan, he is divided against himself; how then will his kingdom stand? *25 26*	**E** And he called them to him, and said to them in parables, "How can Satan cast out Satan? If a kingdom is divided against itself, that kingdom cannot stand. And if a house is divided against itself, that house will not be able to stand. And if Satan has risen up against himself and is divided, he cannot stand, but is coming to an end. *23 24 25 26*	**E** *But he, knowing their thoughts, said to them, "Every kingdom divided against itself is laid waste, [1]and a divided household falls. And if Satan also is divided against himself, how will his kingdom stand? For you say that I cast out demons [2]by Be-el'zebul.* *17 18*
F And if I cast out demons [2]by Be-el'zebul, [2]by whom do your sons cast them out? Therefore they shall be your judges. But if it is [2]by the Spirit of God that I cast out demons, then the kingdom of God has come upon you. *27 28*		**F** *And if I cast out demons [2]by Be-el'zebul, by whom do your sons cast them out? Therefore they shall be your judges. But if it is by the finger of God that I cast out demons, then the kingdom of God has come upon you.* *19 20*
G Or how can one enter a strong man's house and plunder his goods, unless he first binds the strong man? Then indeed he may plunder his house. *29*	**G** But no one can enter a strong man's house and plunder his goods, unless he first binds the strong man; then indeed he may plunder his house. *27*	**G** *When a strong man, fully armed, guards his own palace, his goods are in peace; but when one stronger than he assails him and overcomes him, he takes away his armor in which he trusted, and divides his spoil.* *21 22*
H[H] He who is not with me is against me, and he who does not gather with me scatters. *30*		**H**[H] *He who is not with me is against me, and he who does not gather with me scatters. (§ 86 A-H)* *23*
I Therefore I tell you, every sin and blasphemy will be forgiven men, but the blasphemy against the Spirit will not be forgiven. *31*	**I** "Truly, I say to you, all sins will be forgiven the sons of men, and whatever blasphemies they utter; but whoever blasphemes against the Holy Spirit [3]never has forgiveness, *28 29*	**I** *Compare portion J below*
J And whoever says a word against the Son of man will be forgiven; but whoever speaks against the Holy Spirit will not be forgiven, *32*	**J** *Compare portion I above*	**J** *And every one who speaks a word against the Son of man will be forgiven; but he who blasphemes against the Holy Spirit will not be forgiven. (§ 91 H)* *12:10*
K either in this age or in the age to come.	**K** but is guilty of an eternal sin"--for they had said, "He has an unclean spirit." *30*	
L[L] "Either make the tree good, and its fruit good; or make the tree [4]bad, and its fruit [4]bad; *33*		**L**[L] *"For no good tree bears [4]bad fruit, nor again does a [4]bad tree bear good fruit;* *6:43*

---

1 Or *and house falls upon house*   2 Or *in*   3 Some ancient authorities read *has not*   4 Or *rotten*

HS references: Mt 12:29 and Mk 3:27 = Isaiah 49:24-25
NC references: Mt 12:29 and Mk 3:27 = GT 35   Mt 12:32 and Lk 12:10 = GT 44

H With the first half of this saying, compare the last verse of § 78 portion I
L A sound tree cannot bear evil fruit. nor can a bad tree bear good   L *Luke parallel is shown above under portion L*
fruit. (§ 38 S = Mt 7:18)

MATT 12

M^M for the tree is known by its fruit.

N^N You brood of vipers! how can you 34 speak good, when you are evil?

O For out of the abundance of the heart the mouth speaks. The good 35 man out of his good treasure brings forth good, and the evil man out of his evil treasure brings forth evil.

P I tell you, on the day of judgment 36 men will render account for every careless word they utter; for by your 37 words you will be justified, and by your words you will be condemned."

Q^Q Then some of the scribes and 38 Pharisees said to him, "Teacher, we wish to see a sign from you."

R^R But he answered them, "An evil 39 and adulterous generation seeks for a sign; but no sign shall be given to it except the sign of the prophet Jonah.

S For as Jonah was three days and 40 three nights in the belly of the ¹whale, so will the Son of man be three days and three nights in the heart of the earth.

LUKE

M^M *for each tree is known by its own* 44 *fruit. For figs are not gathered from thorns, nor are grapes picked from a bramble bush.*

O *The good man out of the good* 45 *treasure of his heart produces good, and the evil man out of his evil treasure produces evil; for out of the abundance of the heart his mouth speaks. (§ 38 O-S)*

Q^Q *Compare portion D above*

LUKE 11

R^R *When the crowds were increasing,* 29 *he began to say, "This generation is an evil generation; it seeks a sign, but no sign shall be given to it except the sign of Jonah.*

S *For as Jonah became a sign to the* 30 *men of Nin'eveh, so will the Son of man be to this generation.*

---

1 Greek *sea monster*

HS references: Mt 12:39 and Lk 11:29 = Jonah 3:1-4   Mt 12:40 = Jonah 1:17
NC references: Mt 12:33-35 = GT 45

M You will know them by their fruits. Are grapes gathered   M *Luke parallel is shown above under portion M*
from thorns, or figs from thistles? (§ 38 P = Mt 7:16)
M Thus you will know them by their fruits. (§ 38 T = Mt 7:20)
N For another record of these terms as from Jesus, compare § 132 P. For the record of the use of them by John the Baptist, compare § 17 M
Q And the Pharisees and Sadducees came, and   Q The Pharisees came and began to argue
to test him they asked him to show them a   with him, seeking from him a sign from
sign from heaven.   heaven, to test him.
R He answered them, ... "An evil and   R And he sighed deeply in his spirit, and said,
adulterous generation seeks for a sign, but no   "Why does this generation seek a sign? Truly,
sign shall be given to it except the sign of   I say to you, no sign shall be given to this
Jonah". So he left them and departed.   generation". And he left them, and getting
(§ 68 A-D = Mt 16:1-4)   into the boat again he departed to the other
side. (§ 68 A-D = Mk 8:11-13)

MATT **12**

T   *Compare portion V below*

U The men of Nin'eveh will arise at 41 the judgment with this generation and condemn it; for they repented at the preaching of Jonah, and behold ¹something greater than Jonah is here.

V The queen of the South will arise at 42 the judgment with this generation and condemn it; for she came from the ends of the earth to hear the wisdom of Solomon, and behold, ¹something greater than Solomon is here.

W "When the unclean spirit has gone 43 out of a man, ²he passes through waterless places seeking rest, but ²he finds none. Then ²he says, 'I will 44 return to my house from which I came.' And when ²he comes ²he finds it empty, swept, and put in order. Then ²he goes and brings with ²him 45 seven other spirits more evil than ³himself, and they enter and dwell there; and the last state of that man becomes worse than the first.

X So shall it be also with this evil generation."

LUKE **11**

T *The queen of the South will arise at 31 the judgment with the men of this generation and condemn them; for she came from the ends of the earth to hear the wisdom of Solomon, and behold ¹something greater than Solomon is here.*

U *The men of Nin'eveh will arise at 32 the judgment with this generation and condemn it; for they repented at the preaching of Jonah, and behold ¹something greater than Jonah is here. (§ 88 A-F)*

V   *Compare portion T above*

W *"When the unclean spirit has gone 24 out of a man, ²he passes through waterless places seeking rest; and finding none ²he says, 'I will return to my house from which I came.' And 25 when ²he comes ²he finds it swept and put in order. Then ²he goes and 26 brings seven other spirits more evil than ³himself and they enter and dwell there; and the last state of that man becomes worse than the first." (§ 86 I)*

---

1 Greek *more than*   2 Or *it*   3 Or *itself*

HS references: Mt 12:41 and Lk 11:32 = Jonah 3:5-10   Mt 12:42 and Lk 11:31 = I Kings 10:1-10 and II Chronicles 9:1-12

Chapter VIII

THE MYSTERY OF THE KINGDOM OF GOD

§ 46 Basis of Real Relationship to Jesus[*]

MATT 12:46-50	MARK 3:31-35	LUKE 8:19-21
A While he was still speaking to the 46 people, behold, his mother and his brothers stood outside, asking to speak to him.	A And his mother and his brothers 31 came; and standing outside they sent to him and called him. And a crowd 32 was sitting about him;	A *Then his mother and his brothers* 19 *came to him, but they could not reach him for the crowd.*
B *See note 1 below*	B and they said to him, "Your mother and your brothers[2] are outside, asking for you."	B *And he was told, "Your mother and* 20 *your brothers are standing outside, desiring to see you."*
C But he replied to the man who told 48 him,	C And he replied, 33	C *But he said to them,* 21
D "Who is my mother, and who are my brothers?" And stretching out his 49 hand toward his disciples, he said, "Here are my mother and my brothers!	D "Who are my mother and my brothers?" And looking around on 34 those who sat about him, he said, "Here are my mother and my brothers!	
E For whoever does the will of my 50 Father in heaven is my brother, and sister, and mother."	E Whoever does the will of God is 35 my brother, and sister, and mother."	E *"My mother and my brothers are those who hear the word of God and do it." (§ 49 A-E)*

§ 47 Discourse on the Kingdom of God

MATT 13:1-53	MARK 4:1-34	LUKE 8:4-18
A That same day Jesus went out of 1 the house and sat beside the sea. And 2 great crowds gathered about him, so that he got into a boat and sat there; and the whole crowd stood on the beach. And he told them many things 3 in parables, saying:	A Again he began to teach beside the 1 sea. And a very large crowd gathered about him, so that he got into a boat and sat in it on the sea; and the whole crowd was beside the sea on the land. And he taught them many things in 2 parables, and in his teaching he said to them:	A And when a great crowd came to- 4 gether and people from town after town came to him, he said in a parable: *Compare § 27 verses 1-3*
B "A sower went out to sow. And as 4 he sowed, some seeds fell along the path, and the birds came and devoured them.	B "Listen! A sower went out to sow. 3 And as he sowed, some seed fell 4 along the path, and the birds came and devoured it.	B "A sower went out to sow his seed; 5 and as he sowed, some fell along the path, and was trodden under foot, and the birds of the air devoured it.
C Other seeds fell on rocky ground, 5 where they had not much soil, and immediately they sprang up, since they had no depth of soil, but when 6 the sun rose they were scorched; and since they had no root they withered away.	C Other seed fell on rocky ground, 5 where it had not much soil, and immediately it sprang up, since it had no depth of soil; and when the sun rose 6 it was scorched, and since it had no root it withered away.	C And some fell on the rock; and as 6 it grew up, it withered away, because it had no moisture.

1 Some ancient authorities add verse 47: *Some one told him, "Your mother and your brothers are standing outside, asking to speak to you."*
2 Some ancient authorities add *and your sisters*

HS references: Mt 12:46-50 and Mk 3:31-35 and Lk 8:19-21 = Zechariah 13:3
NC references: Mt 12:46-50 and Mk 3:31-35 and Lk 8:19-21 = GT 99

[*] With these accounts compare the record in § 87

MATT 13	MARK 4	LUKE 8
D Other seeds fell upon thorns, and 7 the thorns grew up and choked them.	**D** Other seed fell among thorns and 7 the thorns grew up and choked it, and it yielded no grain.	**D** And some fell among thorns; and 7 the thorns grew with it and choked it.
E Other seeds fell on good soil and 8 brought forth grain, some a hundredfold, some sixty, some thirty.	**E** And other seeds fell into good soil 8 and brought forth grain, growing up and increasing and yielding thirtyfold and sixtyfold and a hundredfold."	**E** And some fell into good soil and 8 grew, and yielded a hundredfold."
F[F] He who has ears,[1] let him hear." 9	**F**[F] And he said, "He who has ears to 9 hear, let him hear."	**F**[F] As he said this, he called out, "He who has ears to hear, let him hear."
G Then the disciples came and said to 10 him, "Why do you speak to them in parables?" And he answered them, 11 "To you it has been given to know the secrets of the kingdom of heaven, but to them it has not been given.	**G** And when he was alone, those who 10 were about him with the twelve asked him concerning the parables. And he 11 said to them, "To you has been given the secret of the kingdom of God, but for those outside everything is in parables;	**G** And when his disciples asked him 9 what this parable meant, he said, "To 10 you it has been given to know the secrets of the kingdom of God; but for others they are in parables,
H For to him who has will more be 12 given, and he will have abundance; but from him who has not, even what he has will be taken away.	**H** *Compare portion V below*	**H** *Compare portion V below*
I This is why I speak to them in par- 13 ables, because seeing they do not see, and hearing they do not hear, nor do they understand.	**I** so that they may indeed see but not 12 perceive, and may indeed hear but not understand;	**I** so that seeing they may not see, and hearing they may not understand.
J With them indeed is fulfilled the 14 prophecy of Isaiah which says:	**J** lest they should turn again, and be forgiven."	
'You shall indeed hear but never understand, and you shall indeed see but never perceive. For this people's heart has grown 15 dull, and their ears are heavy of hearing, and their eyes they have closed, lest they should perceive with their eyes, and hear with their ears, and understand with their heart, and turn for me to heal them.'		

---

1   Some ancient authorities add here, and in verse 43, *to hear*: as in Mark 4:9 and Luke 8:8

HS references: Mt 13:13-15 and Mk 4:12 and Lk 8:10 = Isaiah 6:9-10; Jeremiah 5:21; Ezekiel 12:2
NC references: Mt 13:3-8 and Mk 4:2-8 and Lk 8:4-8 = GT 9   Mt 13:12 = GT 41

F He who has ears to hear, let him hear.
(§ 41 H = Mt 11:15)
F Compare portion S below and § 48 M

                               F He who has ears to hear, let him hear.
                               (§ 104 F = Lk 14:35)

MATT 13	MARK 4	LUKE 8
K But blessed are your eyes, for they 16 see, and your ears, for they hear. Truly, I say to you, many prophets 17 and righteous men longed to see what you see, and did not see it, and to hear what you hear, and did not hear it.		**K** *"Blessed are the eyes which see* 10: *what you see! For I tell you that many* 23 *prophets and kings desired to see* 24 *what you see, and did not see it, and to hear what you hear, and did not hear it." (§ 82 U)*
L "Hear then the parable of the 18 sower.	**L** And he said to them, "Do you not 13 understand this parable? How then will you understand all the parables?	**L** Now the parable is this: 11
M When any one hears the word of 19 the kingdom and does not understand it, the evil one comes and snatches away what is sown in his heart; this is what was sown along the path.	**M** The sower sows the word. And 14 these are the ones along the path, 15 where the word is sown; when they hear, Satan immediately comes and takes away the word which is sown in them.	**M** The seed is the word of God. The 12 ones along the path are those who have heard; then the devil comes and takes away the word from their hearts, that they may not believe and be saved.
N As for what was sown on rocky 20 ground, this is he who hears the word and immediately receives it with joy; yet he has no root in himself, but 21 endures for a while, and when tribulation or persecution arises on account of the word, immediately he [1]falls away.	**N** And these in like manner are the 16 ones sown upon rocky ground, who, when they hear the word, immediately receive it with joy; and they have no 17 root in themselves, but endure for a while; then, when tribulation or persecution arises on account of the word, immediately they [2]fall away.	**N** And the ones on the rock are those 13 who, when they hear the word, receive it with joy; but these have no root, they believe for a while and in time of temptation fall away.
O As for what was sown among 22 thorns, this is he who hears the word, but the cares of the [3]world and the delight in riches choke the word, and it proves unfruitful.	**O** And others are the ones sown 18 among thorns; they are those who hear the word, but the cares of the 19 [3]world, and the delight in riches, and the desire for other things, enter in and choke the word, and it proves unfruitful.	**O** And as for what fell among the 14 thorns, they are those who hear, but as they go on their way they are choked by the cares and riches and pleasures of life, and their fruit does not mature.
P As for what was sown on good 23 soil, this is he who hears the word and understands it; he indeed bears fruit, and yields, in one case a hundredfold, in another sixty, and in another thirty."	**P** But those that were sown upon the 20 good soil are the ones who hear the word and accept it and bear fruit, thirtyfold and sixtyfold and a hundredfold."	**P** And as for that in the good soil, 15 they are those who, hearing the word, hold it fast in an honest and good heart, and bring forth fruit with patience.
	Q[Q] And he said to them, "Is a lamp 21 brought in to be put under a bushel, or under a bed, and not on a stand?	**Q**[Q] "No one after lighting a lamp 16 covers it with a vessel, or puts it under a bed, but puts it on a stand, that those who enter may see the light.
	R[R] For there is nothing hid, except to 22 be made manifest; nor is anything secret, except to come to light.	**R**[R] For nothing is hid that shall not be 17 made manifest, nor anything secret that shall not be known and come to light.

---

1 Greek *stumbles*   2 Greek *stumble*   3 Or *age*

NC references: Mk 4:21-22 and Lk 8:16-17 = GT 33   Mk 4:22 and Lk 8:17 = GT 5,6

Q Nor do men light a lamp and put it under a bushel, but on a stand, and it gives light to all in the house. (§ 36 N = Mt 5:15)
R For nothing is covered that will not be revealed, or hidden that will not be known. (§ 57 H = Mt 10:26)

Q No one after lighting a lamp puts it in a cellar or under a bushel, but on a stand, that those who enter may see the light. (§ 89 A = Lk 11:33)
R Nothing is covered up that will not be revealed, or hidden that will not be known. (§ 91 C = Lk 12:2)

MATT 13	MARK 4	LUKE 8
	S^s If any man has ears to hear, let 23 him hear."	
	T And he said to them, "Take heed 24 what you hear;	T Take heed then how you hear; 18
	U^U the measure you give will be the measure you get, and still more will be given you.	
V^v *Compare portion H above*	V^v For to him who has will more be 25 given; and from him who has not, even what he has will be taken away."	V^v for to him who has will more be given, and from him who has not, even what he¹ thinks that he has will be taken away."

§ 48   Discourse on the Kingdom of God *(concluded)*

A Another parable he put before 24 them, saying, "The kingdom of heaven may be compared to a man who sowed good seed in his field; but 25 while men were sleeping, his enemy came and sowed weeds among the wheat, and went away. So when the 26 plants came up and bore grain, then the weeds appeared also.

B And the ²servants of the house- 27 holder came and said to him, 'Sir, did you not sow good seed in your field? How then has it weeds?' He said to 28 them, '³An enemy has done this.' The ²servants said to him, 'Then do you want us to go and gather them?' But 29 he said, 'No; lest in gathering the weeds you root up the wheat along with them. Let both grow together 30 until the harvest;

C and at harvest time I will tell the reapers, Gather the weeds first and bind them in bundles to be burned, but gather the wheat into my barn.'"

D And he said, "The kingdom of God 26 is as if a man should scatter seed upon the ground, and should sleep 27 and rise night and day, and the seed

---

1 Or *seems to have*   2 Or *slaves*   3 Greek *A man* that is *an enemy*

NC references: Mk 4:25 and Lk 8:18 = GT 41   Mt 13:24-30 = GT 57

S Compare portion F above and attached references
U And the measure you give will be the measure you get.
(§ 38 F = Mt 7:2)
V For to every one who has will more be given, and he will have abundance; but from him who has not, even what he has will be taken away. (§ 136 P = Mt 25:29)

U For the measure you give will be the measure you get back.
(§ 38 F = Lk 6:38)
V I tell you, that to every one who has will more be given; but from him who has not, even what he has will be taken away.
(§ 123 J = Lk 19:26)

MATT 13	MARK 4	LUKE

MARK 4

should sprout and grow, he knows not how. The earth [1]produces of itself, 28 first the blade, then the ear, then the full grain in the ear. But when the 29 grain [2]is ripe, at once he [3]puts in the sickle, because the harvest has come."

MATT 13

E Another parable he put before 31 them, saying, "The kingdom of heaven is like a grain of mustard seed which a man took and sowed in his field; it is the smallest of all seeds, 32 but when it has grown it is the greatest of shrubs and becomes a tree, so that the birds of the air come and make nests in its branches."

MARK 4

E And he said, "With what can we 30 compare the kingdom of God, or what parable shall we use for it? [4]It is like 31 a grain of mustard seed, which, when sown upon the ground, is the smallest of all the seeds on earth; yet when it 32 is sown it grows up and becomes the greatest of all shrubs, and puts forth large branches, so that the birds of the air can make nests in its shade."

LUKE

E *He said therefore, "What is the* 13: *kingdom of God like? And to what* 18 *shall I compare it? It is like a grain* 19 *of mustard seed which a man took and sowed in his garden; and it grew and became a tree, and the birds of the air made nests in its branches."*

MATT 13

F He told them another parable. "The 33 kingdom of heaven is like leaven which a woman took and hid in three [5]measures of flour, till it was all leavened."

LUKE

F *And again he said, "To what shall I* 20 *compare the kingdom of God? It is* 21 *like leaven which a woman took and hid in three [5]measures of flour, till it was all leavened." (§ 99 AB)*

MATT 13

G All this Jesus said to the crowds in 34 parables; indeed he said nothing to them without a parable.

MARK 4

G With many such parables he spoke 33 the word to them, as they were able to hear it; he did not speak to them 34 without a parable,

H but privately to his own disciples he explained everything.

MATT 13

I This was to fulfil what was spoken 35 [6]by the prophet:[7]

"I will open my mouth in parables,
I will utter what has been hidden since the foundation [8]of the world."

J Then he left the crowds and went 36 into the house. And his disciples came to him, saying, "Explain to us the parable of the weeds of the field."

K He answered, "He who sows the 37 good seed is the Son of man; the field 38 is the world, and the good seed means the sons of the kingdom; the weeds are the sons of the evil one, and the 39 enemy who sowed them is the devil;

---

1 Or *bears fruit*   2 Or *allows*   3 Or *sends forth*   4 Greek *As*   5 The word in the Greek denotes the Hebrew seah, a measure containing nearly a peck and a half   6 Or *through*   7 Some ancient authorities add *Isaiah*   8 Many ancient authorities omit *of the world*

HS references: Mk 4:29 = Joel 3:13   Mt 13:32 and Mk 4:32 and Lk 13:19 = Daniel 4:12,21 and Ezekiel 17:23; 31:6
Mt 13:33 and Lk 13:21 = Genesis 18:6   Mt 13:35 = Psalm 78:2
NC references: Mt 13:31-32 and Mk 4:30-32 and Lk 13:18-19 = GT 20   Mt 13:33 and Lk 13:20-21 = GT 96

MATT 13

L^L the harvest is [1]the close of the age, and the reapers are angels. Just as the 40 weeds are gathered and burned with fire, so will it be at [1]the close of the age. The Son of man will send his 41 angels, and they will gather out of his kingdom all causes of sin and all evildoers, and throw them into the 42 furnace of fire; there men will weep and gnash their teeth. Then the right- 43 eous will shine like the sun in the kingdom of their Father.

M^M He who has ears, let him hear.

N "The kingdom of heaven is like 44 treasure hidden in a field, which a man found and covered up; then [2]in his joy he goes and sells all that he has and buys that field.

O "Again, the kingdom of heaven is 45 like a merchant in search of fine pearls, who, on finding one pearl of 46 great value, went and sold all that he had and bought it.

P "Again, the kingdom of heaven is 47 like a [3]net which was thrown into the sea and gathered fish of every kind; when it was full, men drew it ashore 48 and sat down and sorted the good into vessels but threw away the bad.

Q^Q So it will be at [1]the close of the 49 age. The angels will come out and separate the evil from the righteous, and throw them into the furnace of 50 fire; there men will weep and gnash their teeth.

---

1 Or *the consummation*   2 Or *for joy thereof*   3 Greek *drag-net*

HS references; Mt 13:43 = Daniel 12:3
NC references: Mt 13:44 = GT 109   Mt 13:45-46 = GT 76   Mt 13:47-48 = GT 8

L I tell you, many will come from east and west and sit at table with Abraham, Isaac, and Jacob in the kingdom of heaven, while the sons of the kingdom will be thrown into the outer darkness; there men will weep and gnash their teeth. (§ 39 D = Mt 8:11-12)

L There you will weep and gnash your teeth, when you see Abraham and Isaac and Jacob and all the prophets in the kingdom of God and you yourselves thrust out. And men will come from east and west, and from north and south, and sit at table in the kingdom of God. (§ 100 G = Lk 13:28-29)

L And throw them into the furnace of fire; there men will weep and gnash their teeth. (§ 48 Q = Mt 13:50)

L And cast him into the outer darkness; there men will weep and gnash their teeth. (§ 129 P = Mt 22:13)

L And will punish him, and put him with the hypocrites; there men will weep and gnash their teeth. (§ 136 D = Mt 24:51)

L And will punish him, and put him with the unfaithful. (§ 94 E = Lk 12:46)

L And cast the worthless servant into the outer darkness; there men will weep and gnash their teeth. (§ 136 Q = Mt 25:30)

M Compare § 47 F and attached references

Q Compare portion L above and attached references

MATT 13

R "Have you understood all this?" 51 They said to him, "Yes." And he said 52 to them, "Therefore every scribe who has been trained for the kingdom of heaven is like a householder who brings out of his treasure what is new and what is old."

S And when Jesus had finished these 53 parables, he went away from there, (+§ 54)

§ 49 Basis of Real Relationship to Jesus[*]

MATT 12:46-50	MARK 3:31-35	LUKE 8:19-21
A *While he was still speaking to the* 46 *people, behold, his mother and his brothers stood outside, asking to speak to him.*	**A** *And his mother and his brothers* 31 *came; and standing outside they sent to him and called him. And a crowd* 32 *was sitting about him;*	**A** Then his mother and his brothers 19 came to him, but they could not reach him for the crowd.
B *See note 1 below*	**B** *and they said to him, "Your mother and your brothers[2] are outside, asking for you."*	**B** And he was told, "Your mother 20 and your brothers are standing outside, desiring to see you."
C *But he replied to the man who told* 48 *him,*	**C** *And he replied,* 33	**C** But he said to them, 21
D *"Who is my mother, and who are my brothers?" And stretching out his* 49 *hand toward his disciples, he said, "Here are my mother and my brothers!*	**D** *"Who are my mother and my brothers?" And looking around on* 34 *those who sat about him, he said, "Here are my mother and my brothers!*	
E *For whoever does the will of my* 50 *Father in heaven is my brother, and sister, and mother." (§ 46 A-E)*	**E** *Whoever does the will of God is my* 35 *brother, and sister, and mother." (§ 46 A-E)*	**E** "My mother and my brothers are those who hear the word of God and do it."

---

1 Some ancient authorities add verse 47: *Some one told him, "Your mother and your brothers are standing outside, asking to speak to you."*
2 Some ancient authorities add *and your sisters*

---

* With these accounts compare the record in § 87

Chapter IX

THE PLACE OF FAITH IN THE WORK OF JESUS

§ 50 "Have you no faith?"

(§ 25 +) MATT 8:18-27	MARK 4:35-41	LUKE 8:22-25
A Now when Jesus saw great crowds 18 around him, he gave orders to go over to the other side.	**A** On that day, when evening had 35 come, he said to them, "Let us go across to the other side."	**A** One day he got into a boat with his 22 disciples, and he said to them, "Let us go across to the other side of the lake."
B And ¹a scribe came up and said to 19 him, "Teacher, I will follow you wherever you go." And Jesus said to 20 him, "Foxes have holes, and birds of the air have ²nests; but the Son of man has nowhere to lay his head." Another of the disciples said to him, 21 "Lord, let me first go and bury my father." But Jesus said to him, 22 "Follow me, and leave the dead to bury their own dead."		**B** *As they were going along the road,* 9: *a man said to him, "I will follow you* 57 *wherever you go." And Jesus said to* 58 *him, "Foxes have holes, and birds of the air have ²nests; but the Son of man has nowhere to lay his head." To* 59 *another he said, "Follow me." But he said, "Lord, let me first go and bury my father." But he said to him,* 60 *"Leave the dead to bury their own dead; but as for you, go and proclaim the kingdom of God." Another said, "I* 61 *will follow you, Lord, but let me first say farewell to those at my home." Jesus said to him, "No one who puts* 62 *his hand to the plow and looks back is fit for the kingdom of God."* (§ 81 AB)
C And when he got into the boat, his 23 disciples followed him.	**C** And leaving the crowd, they took 36 him with them in the boat, just as he was. And other boats were with him.	**C** So they set out,
D And behold, there arose a great 24 storm on the sea, so that the boat was being swamped by the waves; but he was asleep. And they went and woke 25 him, saying, "Save, Lord; we are perishing."	**D** And a great storm of wind arose, 37 and the waves beat into the boat, so that the boat was already filling. But 38 he was in the stern, asleep on the cushion; and they woke him and said to him, "Teacher, do you not care if we perish?"	**D** and as they sailed he fell asleep. 23 And a storm of wind came down on the lake, and they were filling with water, and were in danger. And they 24 went and woke him, saying, "Master, Master, we are perishing!"
E And he said to them, "Why are you 26 afraid, O men of little faith?"	**E** *Compare portion G below*	**E** *Compare portion G below*
F Then he rose and rebuked the winds and the sea; and there was a great calm.	**F** And he awoke and rebuked the 39 wind, and said to the sea, "Peace! Be still!" And the wind ceased, and there was a great calm.	**F** And he awoke and rebuked the wind and the raging waves; and they ceased, and there was a calm.
G *Compare portion E above* 27	**G** He said to them, "Why are you 40 afraid? ³Have you no faith?"	**G** He said to them, "Where is your 25 faith?"
H And the men marveled, saying, "What sort of man is this,	**H** And they were filled with awe, and 41 said to one another,	**H** And they were afraid, and they marveled, saying to one another,

---

1 Greek *one scribe* 2 Greek *lodging-places* 3 Some ancient authorities add *Why*

HS references: Mt 8:26 and Mk 4:39 and Lk 8:24 = Psalm 89:9 and Psalm 107:23-32
NC references: Mt 8:20 and Lk 9:58 = GT 86

MATT 8	MARK 4	LUKE 8
that even winds and sea obey him?"	"Who then is this, that even wind and sea obey him?"	"Who then is this, that he commands even wind and water, and they obey him?"

§ 51 Attitude of the Gerasenes

MATT 8:28-34	MARK 5:1-20	LUKE 8:26-39
A And when he came to the other side, to the country of the Gadarenes, 28	A They came to the other side of the sea, to the country of the Ger'asenes. 1	A Then they arrived at the country of the [1]Ger'asenes, which is opposite Galilee. 26
B two demoniacs met him, coming out of the tombs,	B And when he had come out of the boat, there met him out of the tombs a man with an unclean spirit, who lived among the tombs; 2 3	B And as he stepped out on land, there met him a man from the city who had demons; for a long time he had worn no clothes, and he lived not in a house but among the tombs. 27
C so fierce that no one could pass that way.	C and no one could bind him any more, even with a chain; for he had often been bound with fetters and chains, but the chains he wrenched apart, and the fetters he broke in pieces; and no one had the strength to subdue him. Night and day among the tombs and on the mountains he was always crying out, and bruising himself with stones. 4 5	C *Compare portion F below*
D And behold, they cried out, "What have you to do with us, O Son of God? Have you come here to torment us before the time?" 29	D And when he saw Jesus from afar, he ran and worshiped him; and crying out with a loud voice, he said, "What have you to do with me, Jesus, Son of the Most High God? I adjure you by God, do not torment me." 6 7	D When he saw Jesus, he cried out and fell down before him, and said with a loud voice, "What have you to do with me, Jesus, Son of the Most High God? I beseech you, do not torment me." 28
	E For he had said to him, "Come out of the man, you unclean spirit!" 8	E For he had commanded the unclean spirit to come out of the man. 29
F *Compare portion C above*	F *Compare portion C above*	F (For [2]many a time it had seized him; he was kept under guard, and bound with chains and fetters, but he broke the bonds and was driven by the demon into the desert.)
	G And [3]Jesus asked him, "What is your name?" He replied, "My name is Legion; for we are many." And he begged him eagerly not to send them out of the country. 9 10	G Jesus then asked him, "What is your name?" And he said, "Legion"; for many demons had entered him. And they begged him not to command them to depart into the abyss. 30 31
H Now a herd of many swine was feeding at some distance from them. And the demons begged him, "If you cast us out, send us away into the herd of swine." And he said to them, "Go." 30 31 32	H Now a great herd of swine was feeding there on the hillside; and they begged him, "Send us to the swine, let us enter them." So he gave them leave. 11 12 13	H Now a large herd of swine was feeding there on the hillside; and they begged him to let them enter these. So he gave them leave. 32

1 Many ancient authorities read *Gergesenes*; others, *Gadarenes*: and so in verse 37   2 Or *of a long time*   3 Greek *he*

HS references: Mt 8:29 = Judges 11:12 and II Samuel 16:10

MATT 8	MARK 5	LUKE 8
I So they came out and went into the swine; and behold, the whole herd rushed down the steep bank into the sea, and perished in the waters.	I And the unclean spirits came out, and entered the swine; and the herd, numbering about two thousand, rushed down the steep bank into the sea, and were drowned in the sea.	I Then the demons came out of the 33 man and entered the swine, and the herd rushed down the steep bank into the lake and were drowned.
J The herdsmen fled, and going into 33 the city they told everything, and what had happened to the demoniacs. And behold, all the city came out to 34 meet Jesus;	J The herdsmen fled, and told it in 14 the city and in the country. And people came to see what it was that had happened.	J When the herdsmen saw what had 34 happened, they fled, and told it in the city and in the country. Then people 35 went out to see what had happened,
	K And they came to Jesus, and saw 15 the demoniac sitting there, clothed and in his right mind, the man who had had the legion; and they were afraid. And those who had seen it told 16 what had happened to the demoniac and to the swine.	K and they came to Jesus, and found the man from whom the demons had gone, sitting at the feet of Jesus, clothed and in his right mind; and they were afraid. And those who had 36 seen it told them how he who had been possessed with demons was ¹healed.
L and when they saw him, they begged him to leave their neighborhood.	L And they began to beg ²Jesus to 17 depart from their neighborhood.	L Then all the people of the 37 surrounding country of the Ger'asenes asked him to depart from them; for they were seized with great fear;
	M And as he was getting into the 18 boat, the man who had been possessed with demons begged him that he might be with him. But he refused, 19 and said to him, "Go home to your friends, and tell them how much the Lord has done for you, and how he has had mercy on you." And he went 20 away and began to proclaim in the Decap'olis how much Jesus had done for him; and all men marveled.	M so he got into the boat and 38 returned. The man from whom the demons had gone begged that he might be with him; but he sent him away, saying, "Return to your home, 39 and declare how much God has done for you." And he went away, proclaiming throughout the whole city how much Jesus had done for him.

§ 52 "Fear not, Only Believe"

MATT 9:1,(§ 31+)18-26	MARK 5:21-43	LUKE 8:40-56
A And getting into a boat he crossed 1 over and came to his own city. (+ § 29)	A And when Jesus had crossed again 21 in the boat to the other side, a great crowd gathered about him; and he was beside the sea.	A Now when Jesus returned, the 40 crowd welcomed him, for they were all waiting for him.
B While he was thus speaking to 18 them, behold, ³a ruler came in and knelt before him, saying, "My daughter has just died; but come and lay your hand on her, and she will live."	B Then came one of the rulers of the 22 synagogue, Ja'irus by name; and seeing him, he fell at his feet, and 23 besought him, saying, "My little daughter is at the point of death. Come and lay your hands on her, so that she may be made well, and live."	B And there came a man named 41 Ja'irus, who was a ruler of the synagogue; and falling at Jesus' feet he besought him to come to his house, for he had an only daughter, 42 about twelve years of age, and she was dying.

1 Or *saved*   2 Greek *him*   3 Greek *one ruler*

MATT 9	MARK 5	LUKE 8
C And Jesus rose and followed him, 19 with his disciples.	C And he went with him. And a great 24 crowd followed him and thronged about him.	C As he went, the people pressed round him.
D And behold, a woman who had 20 suffered from a hemorrhage for twelve years came up behind him and touched the fringe of his garment; for 21 she said to herself, "If I only touch his garment, I shall be [1]made well."	D And there was a woman who had 25 had a flow of blood for twelve years, and who had suffered much under 26 many physicians, and had spent all that she had, and was no better but rather grew worse. She had heard the 27 reports about Jesus, and came up behind him in the crowd and touched his garment. For she said, "If I touch 28 even his garments, I shall be [1]made well."	D And a woman who had had a flow 43 of blood for twelve years and[2] could not be healed by any one, came up 44 behind him, and touched the fringe of his garment;
E *Compare portion K below*	E And immediately the hemorrhage 29 ceased; and she felt in her body that she was healed of her [3]disease.	E and immediately her flow of blood ceased.
	F And Jesus, perceiving in himself 30 that power had gone forth from him, immediately turned about in the crowd, and said, "Who touched my garments?"	F And Jesus said, "Who was it that 45 touched me?" *Compare portion H below*
	G And his disciples said to him, "You 31 see the crowd pressing around you, and yet you say, 'Who touched me?'"	G When all denied it, Peter[4] said, "Master, the multitudes surround you and press upon you!"
	H *Compare portion F above*	H But Jesus said, "Some one touched 46 me; for I perceive that power has gone forth from me."
	I And he looked around to see who 32 had done it. But the woman, knowing 33 what had been done to her, came in fear and trembling and fell down before him, and told him the whole truth.	I And when the woman saw that she 47 was not hidden, she came trembling, and falling down before him declared in the presence of all the people why she had touched him, and how she had been immediately healed.
J Jesus turned, and seeing her he 22 said, "Take heart, daughter; your faith has [5]made you well."	J And he said to her, "Daughter, your 34 faith has [5]made you well; go in peace, and be healed of your [3]disease."	J And he said to her, "Daughter, your 48 faith has [5]made you well; go in peace."
K And instantly the woman was made well.	K *Compare portion E above*	K *Compare portion E above*
	L While he was still speaking, there 35 came from the ruler's house some who said, "Your daughter is dead; why trouble the Teacher any further?"	L While he was still speaking, a man 49 from the ruler's house came and said, "Your daughter is dead; do not trouble the Teacher any more."

---

1 Or *saved*   2 Some ancient authorities add *had spent all her living upon physicians, and*   3 Greek *scourge*
4 Some ancient authorities add *and they that were with him*   5 Or *saved you*

HS references: Mt 9:20 = Numbers 15:38 and Deuteronomy 22:12   Mk 5:25 and Lk 8:43 = Leviticus 15:25-30

MATT 9	MARK 5	LUKE 8
	M But ¹ignoring what they said, Jesus 36 said to the ruler of the synagogue, "Do not fear, only believe."	M But Jesus on hearing this answered 50 him, "Do not fear; only believe, and she shall be ²well."
	N And he allowed no one to follow 37 him except Peter and James and John the brother of James.	N And when he came to the house, he 51 permitted no one to enter with him, except Peter and John and James,
	O *Compare portion Q below*	O and the father and mother of the child.
P And when Jesus came to the ruler's 23 house, and saw the flute players, and the crowd making a tumult, he said, 24 "Depart; for the girl is not dead but sleeping." And they laughed at him.	P When they came to the house of the 38 ruler of the synagogue, he saw a tumult, and people weeping and wailing loudly. And when he had 39 entered, he said to them, "Why do you make a tumult and weep? The child is not dead but sleeping." And 40 they laughed at him.	P And all were weeping and 52 bewailing her; but he said, "Do not weep; for she is not dead but sleeping." And they laughed at him, 53 knowing that she was dead.
Q But when the crowd had been put 25 outside, he went in and took her by the hand, and the girl arose.	Q But he put them all outside, and took the child's father and mother and those who were with him, and went in where the child was. Taking her by 41 the hand he said to her, "Tal'itha cu'mi"; which means, "Little girl, I say to you, arise." And immediately 42 the girl got up and walked	Q But taking her by the hand he 54 called, saying, "Child, arise." And 55 her spirit returned, and she got up at once; *Compare portion O above*
	R (she was twelve years of age),	R *Compare portion B above*
	S *Compare portion U below*	S and he directed that something should be given her to eat.
T And ³the report of this went 26 through all that district.	T and they were immediately overcome with amazement. And he 43 strictly charged them that no one should know this,	T And her parents were amazed; but 56 he charged them to tell no one what had happened.
	U and told them to give her something to eat.	U *Compare portion S above*

§ 53 "Do You Believe That I Am Able?"

MATT 9:27-34

A And as Jesus passed on from there, two blind men 27 followed him, crying aloud, "Have mercy on us, Son of David." When he entered the house, the blind men came to 28 him; and Jesus said to them, "Do you believe that I am able to do this?" They said to him, "Yes, Lord." Then he 29 touched their eyes, saying, "According to your faith be it done to you." And their eyes were opened. And Jesus 30 sternly charged them, "See that no one knows it." But they 31 went away and spread his fame through all that district.

A *For an account in Matt-Mark-Luke of similar general content, compare § 121*

---

1 Or *overhearing*   2 Or *saved*   3 Greek *this fame*

MATT 9   LUKE

B As they were going away, behold, a dumb demoniac was 32 brought to him. And when the demon had been cast out, 33 the dumb man spoke; and the crowds marveled, saying, "Never was anything like this seen in Israel." But the 34 Pharisees said, "He casts out demons ¹by the prince of demons." (+ § 55)

B *For an account in Matt-Mark-Luke of similar general content, compare § 45 ABC*

§ 54 "Because of Their Unbelief"

(§ 48 +) MATT 13:54-58   MARK 6:1-6a   LUKE 4:16-30

A and coming to his own country he 54 taught them in their synagogue,

A He went away from there and came 1 to his own country; and his disciples followed him. And on the sabbath he 2 began to teach in the synagogue;

A *And he come to Nazareth, where he 16 had been brought up; and he went to the synagogue, as his custom was, on the sabbath day. And he stood up to read;*

B *and there was given to him ²the 17 book of the prophet Isaiah. He opened the ³book and found the place where it was written,*
> *"The Spirit of the Lord is upon   18*
>   *me,*
> *⁴because he has anointed me to*
>   *preach good news to the poor.*
> *He has sent me to proclaim*
>   *release to the captives*
> *and recovering of sight to the*
>   *blind,*
> *to set at liberty those who are*
>   *oppressed,*
> *to proclaim the acceptable year   19*
>   *of the Lord."*

And he closed the ³book, and gave it 20 back to the attendant, and sat down; and the eyes of all in the synagogue were fixed on him. And he began to 21 say to them, "Today this scripture has been fulfilled in your hearing."

C so that they were astonished, and said, "Where did this man get this wisdom and these ⁶mighty works?
  Compare portion E below

C and ⁵many who heard him were astonished, saying, "Where did this man get all this? What is the wisdom given to him? What ⁶mighty works are wrought by his hands!

C *And all spoke well of him, and 22 wondered at the gracious words which proceeded out of his mouth;*

---

1 Or *in*   2 Or *a roll*   3 Or *roll*   4 Or *wherefore*   5 Some ancient authorities insert *the*   6 Greek *powers*

HS references: Lk 4:18-19 = Isaiah 61:1-2

MATT 13	MARK 6	LUKE 4
D Is not this the carpenter's son? Is 55 not his mother called Mary? And are not his brothers James and Joseph and Simon and Judas? And are not all his 56 sisters with us?	**D** Is not this the carpenter, the son of 3 Mary and brother of James and Joses and Judas and Simon, and are not his sisters here with us?"	**D** *and they said, "Is not this Joseph's son?"*
E Where then did this man get all this?"	**E** *Compare portion C above*	
F And they ¹took offense at him. 57	**F** And they ¹took offense at him.	**F** *Compare portion K below*
		G *And he said to them, "Doubtless 23 you will quote to me this proverb, 'Physician, heal yourself; what we have heard you did at Caper'na-um, do here also in your own country.'"*
H But Jesus said to them, "A prophet is not without honor except in his own country and in his own house."	**H** And Jesus said to them, "A prophet 4 is not without honor, except in his own country, and among his own kin, and in his own house."	**H** *And he said, "Truly, I say to you, 24 no prophet is acceptable in his own country.*
		I *But in truth, I tell you, there were 25 many widows in Israel in the days of Eli'jah, when the heaven was shut up three years and six months, when there came a great famine over all the land; and Eli'jah was sent to none of 26 them but only to ²Zar'ephath, in the land of Sidon, to a woman who was a widow. And there were many lepers in 27 Israel in the time of the prophet Eli'sha; and none of them was cleansed, but only Na'aman the Syrian."*
J And he did not do many ³mighty 58 works there, because of their unbelief. (+ § 58)	**J** And he could do no ⁴mighty work 5 there, except that he laid his hands upon a few sick people and healed them. And he marveled because of 6 their unbelief.	
K *Compare portion F above*	**K** *Compare portion F above*	**K** *When they heard this, all in the 28 synagogue were filled with wrath. And 29 they rose up and put him out of the city, and led him to the brow of the hill on which their city was built, that they might throw him down headlong. But passing through the midst of them 30 he went away.* (§ 22 A-K)

---

1 Greek *were caused to stumble*   2 Greek *Sarepta*   3 Greek *powers*   4 Greek *power*

HS references: Lk 4:25 = I Kings 17:1 and 18:1-2   Lk 4:26 = I Kings 17:8-9   Lk 4:27 = II Kings 5:1,14
NC references: Mt 13:57 and Mk 6:4 and Lk 4:23-24 = GT 31

Chapter X

TOUR OF THE DISCIPLES AND RESULTANT EVENTS

§ 55 Jesus Tours in Galilee

(§ 53+) MATT 9:35

A And Jesus went about all the cities 35 and villages, teaching in their synagogues

B^B and preaching the gospel of the kingdom, and healing every disease and every infirmity.

MARK 6:6b

A And he went about among the 6b villages teaching.

§ 56 Discourse on the Mission of the Disciples

MATT 9:36-11:1

A When he saw the crowds, he had 36 compassion for them, because they were harassed and helpless, like sheep without a shepherd.

B Then he said to his disciples, "The 37 harvest is plentiful, but the laborers are few; pray therefore the Lord of 38 the harvest to send out laborers into his harvest."

C^C And he called to him his twelve 10: disciples and gave them authority over 1 unclean spirits, to cast them out, and to heal every disease and every infirmity.

D The names of the twelve apostles 2 are these: first, Simon, who is called Peter, and Andrew his brother; James the son of Zeb'edee, and John his brother; Philip and Bartholomew; 3 Thomas and Matthew the tax collector; James the son of Alphaeus, and Thaddaeus; Simon the 4 [1]Cananaean, and Judas Iscariot, who [3]betrayed him.

MARK 6:7-13

A *As he went ashore he saw a great* 6: *throng, and he had compassion on* 34 *them, because they were like sheep without a shepherd; (§ 60 B)*

C^C And he called to him the twelve, 7 and began to send them out two by two, and gave them authority over the unclean spirits.

D *Simon whom he surnamed Peter;* 3: *James the son of Zeb'edee and John* 16 *the brother of James, whom he* 17 *surnamed Boaner'ges, that is, sons of thunder; Andrew, and Philip, and* 18 *Bartholomew, and Matthew, and Thomas, and James the son of Alphaeus, and Thaddaeus, and Simon the* [1]*Cananaean, and Judas Iscariot,* 19 *who betrayed him. (§ 35 C)*

LUKE 9:1-6

B *And he said to them, "The harvest* 10: *is plentiful, but the laborers are few;* 2 *pray therefore the Lord of the harvest to send out laborers into his harvest. (§ 82 B)*

C^C And he called the twelve together 1 and gave them power and authority over all demons and to cure diseases,

D *He called his disciples, and chose* 6: *from them twelve, whom he named* 13b *apostles; Simon, whom he named* 14 *Peter, and Andrew his brother, and James and John, and Philip, and Bartholomew, and Matthew, and* 15 *Thomas, and James the son of Alphaeus, and Simon who was called the Zealot, and Judas the* [2]*son of* 16 *James, and Judas Iscariot, who became a traitor. (§ 35 BC)*

---

1 Or *Zealot*: see Lk 6:15 and Acts 1:13   2 Or, brother: see Jude I   3 Or *delivered him up*: and so always

HS references: Mt 9:36 and Mk 6:34 = Numbers 27:17 and I Kings 22:17 and Ezekiel 34:5 and Zechariah 10:2
NC references: Mt 9:37-38 and Lk 10:2 = GT 73

B Compare the latter half of the Matthew record in § 26 D
C After this the Lord appointed seventy others, and sent them on ahead of him, two by two, into every town and place where he himself was about to come. (§ 82 A = Lk 10:1)

MATT 10	MARK 6	LUKE 9
E[E] These twelve Jesus sent out, 5 charging them, "Go nowhere among the Gentiles, and enter no town of the Samaritans, but go rather to the lost 6 sheep of the house of Israel.		
F[F] And preach as you go, saying, 7 'The kingdom of heaven is at hand.' Heal the sick, raise the dead, cleanse 8 lepers, cast out demons. You received without paying, give without pay.		**F**[F] and he sent them out to preach the 2 kingdom of God and to heal.[1]
G[G] Take no gold, nor silver, nor 9 copper in your belts, no bag for your 10 journey, nor two tunics, nor sandals, nor a staff;	**G**[G] He charged them to take nothing 8 for their journey except a staff; no bread, no bag, no [2]money in their belts; but to wear sandals and not put 9 on two tunics.	**G**[G] And he said to them, "Take 3 nothing for your journey, no staff, nor bag, nor bread, nor money; and do not have two tunics.
H for the laborer deserves his food.		**H** *for the laborer deserves his wages.* 10: (§ 82 H) 7
I[I] And whatever town or village you 11 enter, find out who is worthy in it, and stay with him until you depart.	**I**[I] And he said to them, "Where you 10 enter a house, stay there until you leave the place.	**I**[I] And whatever house you enter, stay 4 there, and from there depart.
J As you enter the house, salute it. 12 And if the house is worthy, let your 13 peace come upon it; but if it is not worthy, let your peace return to you.		**J** *Whatever house you [3]enter, first say,* 10: *'Peace be to this house!' And if a son* 5 *of peace is there, your peace shall* 6 *rest upon [4]him; but if not, it shall return to you.* (§ 82 G)
K[K] And if any one will not receive 14 you or listen to your words, shake off the dust from your feet as you leave that house or town.	**K**[K] And if any place will not receive 11 you and they refuse to hear you, when you leave, shake off the dust that is on your feet for a testimony against them."	**K**[K] And wherever they do not receive 5 you, when you leave that town shake off the dust from your feet as a testimony against them."
L Truly, I say to you, it shall be 15 more tolerable on the day of judgment for the land of Sodom and Gomor'rah than for that town.		**L** *I tell you, it shall be more tolerable* 10: *on that day for Sodom than for that* 12 *town.* (§ 82 L)
But I tell you that it shall be more 11: *tolerable on the day of judgment for* 24 *the land of Sodom than for you."* (§ 41 O)		

---

1 Some ancient authorities add *the sick*   2 Greek *brass*   3 Or *enter first, say*   4 Or *it*

E With the Matthew report here, compare the Matthew form of the record in § 64 D
F Heal the sick in it and say to them, The kingdom of God has come near to you. (§ 82 I = Lk 10:9)
F Nevertheless know this, that the kingdom of God has come near. (§ 82 K = Lk 10:11)
G Carry no purse, no bag, no sandals; and salute no one on the road. (§ 82 E = Lk 10:4)
I And remain in the same house, eating and drinking what they provide . . . do not go from house to house. Whenever you enter a town and they receive you, eat what is set before you. (§ 82 H = Lk 10:7-8)
K But whenever you enter a town and they do not receive you, go into its streets and say, 'Even the dust of your town that clings to our feet, we wipe off against you.' (§ 82 J = Lk 10:10-11)

MATT 10   LUKE

M "Behold, I send you out as sheep 16
in the midst of wolves; so be wise as
serpents and ¹innocent as doves.

M *Go your way; behold, I send you* 10:
out as lambs in the midst of wolves. 3
(§ 82 D)

§ 57 Discourse on the Mission of the Disciples (concluded)

MATT 10   MARK   LUKE

A Beware of men; for they will 17
deliver you up to councils, and flog
you in their synagogues, and you will 18
be dragged before governors and
kings for my sake, to bear testimony
before them and the Gentiles.
"Then they shall deliver you up to 24:
tribulation, (§ 134 G)   9a

A *"But take heed to yourselves; for* 13:
they will deliver you up to councils; 9
and you will be beaten in synagogues;
and you will stand before governors
and kings for my sake, to bear
testimony before them.

A *But before all this they will lay* 21:
their hands on you and persecute you, 12
delivering you up to the synagogues
and prisons, and you ²will be brought
before kings and governors for my
name's sake. This will be a time for 13
you to bear testimony.

B   *Compare portion F below*
   Compare § 134 portion N

B *And the gospel must first be* 10
preached to all nations.

Cᶜ When they deliver you up, do not 19
be anxious how you are to speak or
what you are to say; for what you are
to say will be given to you in that
hour; for it is not you who speak, but 20
the Spirit of your Father speaking
through you.

Cᶜ *And when they bring you to trial* 11
and deliver you up, do not be anxious
beforehand what you are to say; but
say whatever is given you in that
hour, for it is not you who speak, but
the Holy Spirit.

Cᶜ *Settle it therefore in your minds,* 14
not to meditate beforehand how to
answer; for I will give you a mouth 15
and wisdom, which none of your
adversaries will be able to withstand
or contradict.

D Brother will deliver up brother to 21
death, and the father his child, and
children will rise against parents and
³have them put to death;
   and put you to death;   24:
   (§ 134 J)   9b

D *And brother will deliver up brother* 12
to death, and the father his child, and
children will rise against parents and
³have them put to death;

D *You will be delivered up even by* 16
parents and brothers and kinsmen and
friends, and some of you they will put
to death;

E and you will be hated by all for my 22
name's sake. But he who endures to
the end will be saved.
and you will be hated by all nations 24:
for my name's sake." . . . But he who 9c
endures to the end will be saved. 13
(§ 134 K-M)

E *and you will be hated by all for my* 13
name's sake. But he who endures to
the end will be saved. (§ 134 G-M)

E *you will be hated by all for my* 17
name's sake. But not a hair of your 18
head will perish. By your endurance 19
you will gain your lives. (§ 134 G-M)

F When they persecute you in one 23
town, flee to the next; for truly, I say
to you, you will not have gone
through all the towns of Israel, before
the Son of man comes.

F   *Compare portion B above*

---

1 Or *simple*   2 Greek *being brought*   3 Or *put them to death*

HS references: Mt 10:16 = Genesis 3:1   Lk 21:18 = I Samuel 14:45
NC references: Mt 10:16b = GT 39

C And when they bring you before the synagogues and the rulers and the authorities, do not be anxious how or what you are to answer or what you are to
say; for the Holy Spirit will teach you in that very hour what you ought to say. (§ 91 I = Lk 12:11-12)

MATT 10   LUKE

G "A disciple is not above his 24 teacher, nor a ¹servant above his ²master; it is enough for the disciple 25 to be like his teacher, and the ¹servant like his ²master. If they have called the master of the house Be-el'zebul, how much more will they malign those of his household.

G *A disciple is not above his teacher,* 6: *but every one when he is fully taught* 40 *will be like his teacher.* (§ 38 H)

Hᴴ "So have no fear of them; for 26 nothing is covered that will not be revealed, or hidden that will not be known. What I tell you in the dark, 27 utter in the light; and what you hear whispered, proclaim upon the housetops.

Hᴴ *Nothing is covered up that will not* 12: *be revealed, or hidden that will not be* 2 *known. Therefore whatever you have* 3 *said in the dark shall be heard in the light, and what you have whispered in private rooms shall be proclaimed upon the housetops.*

I And do not fear those who kill the 28 body but cannot kill the soul; rather fear him who can destroy both soul and body in ⁴hell.

I *"I tell you, my friends, do not fear* 4 *those who kill the body, and after that have no more that they can do. But I* 5 *will warn you whom to fear; fear him who, after he has killed, has ³power to cast into ⁴hell; yes, I tell you, fear him!*

Jᴶ Are not two sparrows sold for a 29 penny? And not one of them will fall to the ground without your Father's will. But even the hairs of your head 30 are all numbered. Fear not, therefore; 31 you are of more value than many sparrows.

Jᴶ *Are not five sparrows sold for two* 6 *pennies? And not one of them is forgotten before God. Why, even the* 7 *hairs of your head are all numbered. Fear not; you are of more value than many sparrows.*

Kᴷ So every one who acknowledges 32 ⁵me before men, I also will acknowledge before my Father who is 33 in heaven; but whoever denies me before men, I also will deny before my Father who is in heaven.

Kᴷ *"And I tell you, every one who* 8 *acknowledges ⁵me before men, the Son of man also will acknowledge before the angels of God; but he who denies* 9 *me before men will be denied before the angels of God.* (§ 91 C-G)

L "Do not think that I have come to 34 ⁶bring peace on earth; I have not

L *Do you think that I have come to* 12: *give peace on earth? No, I tell you,* 51

---

1 Or *slave* 2 Greek *teacher* 3 Or *authority* 4 Greek *Gehenna* 5 Greek *in me* 6 Greek *cast*

HS references: Mt 10:25 = II Kings 1:2
NC references: Mt 10:26 and Lk 12:1-2 = GT 5,6   Mt 10:27 and Lk 12:3 = GT 33   Mt 10:34-36 and Lk 12:51-53 = GT 16

H For there is nothing hid, except to be made manifest; nor is anything secret, except to come to light. (§ 47 R = Mk 4:22)

H For nothing is hid that shall not be made manifest, nor anything secret that shall not be known and come to light. (§ 47 R = Lk 8:17)

J But not a hair of your head will perish. (§ 134 M = Lk 21:18)
K For the son of man is to come with his angels in the glory of his Father, and then he will repay every man for what he has done. (§ 73 C = Mt 16:27)

K For whoever is ashamed of me and of my words in this adulterous and sinful generation, of him will the Son of man also be ashamed, when he comes in the glory of his Father with the holy angels. (§ 73 C = Mk 8:38)

K For whoever is ashamed of me and of my words, of him will the Son of man be ashamed when he comes in his glory and the glory of the Father and of the holy angels. (§ 73 C = Lk 9:26)

MATT 10	MARK 6	LUKE 9
come to ¹bring peace, but a sword. For I have come to set a man against 35 his father, and a daughter against her mother, and a daughter-in-law against her mother-in-law; and a man's foes 36 will be those of his own household.		*but rather division; for henceforth in 52 one house there will be five divided, three against two and two against three; they will be divided, father 53 against son and son against father, mother against daughter and daughter against her mother, mother-in-law against her daughter-in-law and daughter-in-law against her mother-in-law." (§ 95 B)*
M He who loves father or mother 37 more than me is not worthy of me; and he who loves son or daughter more than me is not worthy of me;		**M** *"If any one comes to me and does 14: not hate his own father and mother 26 and wife and children and brothers and sisters, yes, and even his own life, he cannot be my disciple.*
Nᴺ and he who does not take his cross 38 and follow me is not worthy of me.		**Nᴺ** *Whoever does not bear his own 27 cross and come after me, cannot be my disciple." (§ 104 BC)*
Oᴼ He who ²finds his ³life will ⁴lose 39 it, and he who ⁵loses his ³life for my sake will find it.⁷		**Oᴼ** *Whoever seeks to gain his ³life will 17: ⁴lose it, but whoever ⁵loses his ³life 33 will ⁶preserve it. (§ 112 J)*
P "He who receives you receives me, 40 and he who receives me receives him who sent me. He who receives a 41 prophet because he is a prophet shall receive a prophet's reward, and he who receives a righteous man because he is a righteous man shall receive a righteous man's reward.	**P** *and whoever receives me, receives 9: not me but him who sent me." 37b (§ 78 G)*	**P** *"Whoever receives this child in my 9: name receives me, and whoever 48 receives me receives him who sent me; (§ 78 G)*
		"He who hears you hears me, and he 10: who rejects you rejects me, and he 16 who rejects me rejects him who sent me." (§ 82 Q)
Q And whoever gives to one of these 42 little ones even a cup of cold water because he is a disciple, truly, I say to you, he shall not lose his reward."	**Q** *For truly, I say to you, whoever 9: gives you a cup of water to drink 41 because ⁸you bear the name of Christ, will by no means lose his reward. (§ 78 J)*	
R And when Jesus had finished 11: instructing his twelve disciples, he 1 went on from there to teach and preach in their cities. (+ § 41)	**R** So they went out and preached that 12 men should repent. And they cast out 13 many demons, and anointed with oil many that were sick and healed them.	**R** And they departed and went 6 through the villages, preaching the gospel and healing everywhere.

---

1 Greek *cast*   2 Or *found*   3 Or *soul*   4 Greek *destroy*   5 Or *lost (destroys,* or *destroyed)*   6 Greek *save it alive*
7 See also the notes on the Greek at § 73 B   8 Greek *in name you are*

HS references: Mt 10:35-36 and Lk 12:52-53 = Micah 7:6
NC references: Mt 10:37-38 and Lk 14:26-27 = GT 55, 101

N If any man would come after me, let him deny himself and take up his cross and follow me.
O For whoever would save his life will lose it, and whoever loses his life for my sake will find it. (§ 73 AB = Mt 16:24-25)

N If any man would come after me, let him deny himself and take up his cross and follow me.
O For whoever would save his life will lose it; and whoever loses his life for my sake and the gospel's will save it.
(§ 73 AB = Mk 8:34-35)

N If any man would come after me, let him deny himself and take up his cross daily and follow me.
O For whoever would save his life will lose it; and whoever loses his life for my sake, he will save it. (§ 73 AB = Lk 9:23-24)

§ 58 Fate of John the Baptist

(§ 54+) MATT 14:1-12	MARK 6:14-29	LUKE 9:7-9
A At that time Herod the tetrarch 1 heard about the fame of Jesus; and he 2 said to his servants, "This is John the Baptist, he has been raised from the dead; that is why these powers are at work in him."	**A** King Herod heard of it; for [1]Jesus' 14 name had become known. [2]Some said, "John the baptizer has been raised from the dead; that is why these powers are at work in him."	**A** Now Herod the tetrarch heard of 7 all that was done, and he was perplexed, because it was said by some that John had been raised from the dead,
	B[B] But others said, "It is Eli'jah." 15 And others said, "It is a prophet, like one of the prophets of old."	**B**[B] by some that Eli'jah had appeared, 8 and by others that one of the old prophets had risen.
	C[C] But when Herod heard of it he 16 said, "John, whom I beheaded, has been raised."	**C**[C] Herod said, "John I beheaded; but 9 who is this about whom I hear such things?" And he sought to see him.
D For Herod had seized John and 3 bound him and put him in prison, for the sake of Hero'di-as, his brother Philip's wife; because John said to 4 him, "It is not lawful for you to have her."	**D** For Herod had sent and seized 17 John, and bound him in prison for the sake of Hero'di-as, his brother Philip's wife; because he had married her. For John said to Herod, "It is 18 not lawful for you to have your brother's wife."	**D** *So, with many other exhortations,* 3: *he preached good news to the people.* 18 *But Herod the tetrarch, who had been* 19 *reproved by him for Hero'di-as, his brother's wife, and for all the evil things that Herod had done, added* 20 *this to them all, that he shut up John in prison. (§ 17 R)*
E And though he wanted to put him 5 to death, he feared the people, because they held him to be a prophet.	**E** And Hero'di-as had a grudge 19 against him, and wanted to kill him. But she could not, for Herod feared 20 John, knowing that he was a righteous and holy man, and kept him safe. When he heard him, he [3]was much perplexed; and yet he heard him gladly.	
F But when Herod's birthday came, 6 the daughter of Hero'di-as danced before the company, and pleased Herod, so that he promised with an 7 oath to give her whatever she might ask.	**F** But an opportunity came when 21 Herod on his birthday gave a banquet for his [4]courtiers and officers and the leading men of Galilee. For when 22 [5]Hero'di-as' daughter came in and danced, [6]she pleased Herod and his guests; and the king said to the girl, "Ask me for whatever you wish, and I will grant it." And he vowed to her, 23 "Whatever you ask me, I will give you, even half of my kingdom."	
G Prompted by her mother, she said, 8 "Give me the head of John the Baptist here on a platter."	**G** And she went out, and said to her 24 mother, "What shall I ask?" And she said, "The head of John the baptizer."	

---

1 Greek *his*   2 Many ancient authorities read *he*   3 Many ancient authorities read *did many things*   4 Or *military tribunes* Greek *chiliarchs*
5 Some ancient authorities read *his daughter Herodias*   6 Or *it*

HS references: Mt 14:4 and Mk 6:18 and Lk 3:19 = Leviticus 18:16 and 20:21   Mk 6:23 = Esther 5:3,6

BC For another record of these estimates of Jesus, compare § 71 C

MATT 14   MARK 6

And she came in immediately with 25
haste to the king, and asked, saying,
"I want you to give me at once the
head of John the Baptist on a platter."

H And the king was sorry; but 9   **H** And the king was exceedingly 26
because of his oaths and his guests he   sorry; but because of his oaths and his
commanded it to be given; he sent 10   guests he did not want to break his
and had John beheaded in the prison,   word to her. And immediately the 27
and his head was brought on a platter 11   king sent a soldier of the guard and
and given to the girl, and she brought   gave orders to bring his head. He
it to her mother.   went and beheaded him in the prison,
                                           and brought his head on a platter, and 28
                                           gave it to the girl; and the girl gave it
                                           to her mother.

I And his disciples came and took the 12   **I** When his disciples heard of it, they 29
body and buried it; and they went and   came and took his body, and laid it in
told Jesus.   a tomb.

§ 59 Report of Associates on their Tour*

              MARK 6:30-31   LUKE 9:10a

The apostles returned to Jesus, and 30   On their return the apostles told him 10a
told him all that they had done and   what they had done.
taught. And he said to them, "Come 31
away by yourselves to a lonely place,
and rest a while." For many were
coming and going, and they had no
leisure even to eat.

§ 60 Teaching and Feeding the Multitude

      MATT 14:13-23a   MARK 6:32-46   LUKE 9:10b-17

A Now when Jesus heard this, he 13   **A** And they went away in the boat to 32   **A** And he took them and withdrew 10b
withdrew from there in a boat to a   a lonely place by themselves. Now 33   apart to a city called Beth-sa'ida.
lonely place apart. But when the   many saw them going, and knew   When the crowds learned it, they 11
crowds heard it, they followed him   them, and they ran there [1]on foot   followed him;
[1]on foot from the towns.   from all the towns, and got there
                                       ahead of them.

B[B] As he went ashore he saw a great 14   **B**[B] As he went ashore he saw a great 34   **B**[B] and he welcomed them and spoke
throng; and he had compassion on   throng, and he had compassion on   to them of the kingdom of God, and
them, and healed their sick.   them, because they were like sheep   cured those who had need of healing.
                                       without a shepherd; and he began to
                                       teach them many things.

---

1 Or *by land*

HS references: Mk 6:34 (Mt 9:36) = Numbers 27:17 and I Kings 22:17 and Ezekiel 34:5 and Zechariah 10:2

B When he saw the crowds, he had compassion for them, because they were harassed and helpless, like sheep without a shepherd. (§ 56 A = Mt 9:36)

* For another record of a report on a Tour, compare § 82 R

MATT 14	MARK 6	LUKE 9
C When it was evening, the disciples 15 came to him and said, "This is a lonely place, and the day is now over; send the crowds away to go into the villages and buy food for themselves."	C And when it grew late, his 35 disciples came to him and said, "This is a lonely place, and the hour is now 36 late; send them away, to go into the country and villages round about and buy themselves something to eat."	C Now the day began to wear away; 12 and the twelve came and said to him, "Send the crowd away, to go into the villages and country round about, to lodge and get provisions; for we are here in a lonely place."
D Jesus said, "They need not go 16 away; you give them something to eat." They said to him, "We have 17 only five loaves here and two fish." And he said, "Bring them here to 18 me."	D But he answered them, "You give 37 them something to eat." And they said to him, "Shall we go and buy two hundred ¹denarii worth of bread, and give it to them to eat?" And he said 38 to them, "How many loaves have you? Go and see." And when they had found out, they said, "Five, and two fish."	D But he said to them, "You give 13 them something to eat." They said, "We have no more than five loaves and two fish--unless we are to go and buy food for all these people."
E *Compare portion I below*	E *Compare portion I below*	E For there were about five thousand 14 men.
F Then he ordered the crowds to ²sit 19 down on the grass;	F Then he commanded them all to 39 ²sit down by companies upon the green grass. So they sat down in 40 groups, by hundreds and by fifties.	F And he said to his disciples, "Make them ²sit down in companies, about fifty each." And they did so, and 15 made them all sit down.
G and taking the five loaves and the two fish he looked up to heaven, and blessed, and broke and gave the loaves to the disciples, and the disciples gave them to the crowds.	G And taking the five loaves and the 41 two fish he looked up to heaven, and blessed, and broke the loaves, and gave them to the disciples to set before the people; and he divided the two fish among them all.	G And taking the five loaves and the 16 two fish he looked up to heaven, and blessed and broke them, and gave them to the disciples to set before the crowd.
H And they all ate and were satisfied. 20 And they took up twelve baskets full of the broken pieces left over.	H And they all ate and were satisfied. 42 And they took up twelve baskets full 43 of broken pieces and of the fish.	H And all ate and were satisfied. And 17 they took up what was left over, twelve baskets of broken pieces.
I And those who ate were about five 21 thousand men, besides women and children.	I And those who ate the loaves were 44 five thousand men.	I *Compare portion E above*
J Then he made the disciples get into 22 the boat and go before him to the other side, while he dismissed the crowds.	J Immediately he made his disciples 45 get into the boat and go before him to the other side, to Beth-sa'ida, while he dismissed the crowd.	
K And after he had dismissed the 23a crowds, he went up on the mountain by himself to pray.	K And after he had taken leave of 46 them, he went up on the mountain to pray.	K *Compare § 71 portion A*

§ 61 Across the Sea of Galilee

MATT 14:23b-33	MARK 6:47-52
A When evening came, he was there 23b alone, but the boat by this time was 24 many furlongs distant from the land,	A And when evening came, the boat 47 was out on the sea, and he was alone on the land. And he saw that they 48

---

1 The word in the Greek denotes a coin worth about forty cents. The denarius was a day's wage for a laborer.   2 Greek *recline*

HS references: Mt 14:16-17 and Mk 6:37 and Lk 9:13 = II Kings 4:42-44   Mk 6:48 = Job 9:8 and Psalm 77:19 and Isaiah 43:16

MATT 14

MARK 6

beaten by the waves; for the wind was against them. And in the fourth 25 watch of the night he came to them, walking on the sea.

B But when the disciples saw him 26 walking on the sea, they were terrified, saying, "It is a ghost!" And they cried out for fear. But 27 immediately he spoke to them, saying, "Take heart, it is I; have no fear."

C And Peter answered him, "Lord, if 28 it is you, bid me come to you on the water." He said, "Come." So Peter 29 got out of the boat and walked on the water and came to Jesus; but when he 30 saw the wind,[1] he was afraid, and beginning to sink he cried out, "Lord, save me." Jesus immediately reached 31 out his hand and caught him, saying to him, "O man of little faith, why did you doubt?"

D And when they got into the boat, 32 the wind ceased. And those in the 33 boat worshiped him, saying, "Truly you are the Son of God."

were making headway painfully, for the wind was against them. And about the fourth watch of the night he came to them, walking on the sea.

B He meant to pass by them, but 49 when they saw him walking on the sea they thought it was a ghost, and cried out; for they all saw him, and 50 were terrified. But immediately he spoke to them and said, "Take heart, it is I; have no fear."

D And he got into the boat with them 51 and the wind ceased. And they were utterly astounded, for they did not 52 understand about the loaves, but their hearts were hardened.

§ 62 Many Sick Brought to Jesus

MATT 14:34-36

MARK 6:53-56

A And when they had crossed over, 34 they came to land at Gen-nes'aret. And when the men of that place 35 recognized him, they sent round to all that region and brought to him all that were sick,

A And when they had crossed [2]over, 53 they came to land at Gen-nes'aret, and moored to the shore. And when 54 they got out of the boat, immediately the people recognized him, and ran 55 about the whole neighborhood and began to bring sick people on their pallets to any place where they heard he was.

B And wherever he came, in villages, 56 cities, or country, they laid the sick in the market places,

C and besought him that they might 36 only touch the fringe of his garment; and as many as touched it were made well.

C and besought him that they might touch even the fringe of his garment; and as many as touched it were made well.

---

1 Many ancient authorities add *strong*   2 Or *crossed over to the land, they came to Gennesaret*

HS references: Mt 14:36 and Mk 6:56 = Numbers 15:38

Chapter XI

DEMAND BY PHARISEES FOR CONFORMITY AND CREDENTIALS

§ 63 Concerning Traditions about Defilement

MATT 15:1-20	MARK 7:1-23	LUKE
A Then Pharisees and scribes came to Jesus from Jerusalem and said,	**A** Now when the Pharisees gathered together to him, with some of the scribes, who had come from Jerusalem, they saw that some of his disciples ate with ¹hands defiled, that is, unwashed.	**A** *Compare § 90 portion A*
	B (For the Pharisees, and all the Jews, do not eat unless they wash their hands², observing the tradition of the elders; and when they come from the market place, they do not eat unless they ³purify themselves; and there are many other traditions which they observe, the ⁴washing of cups and pots and vessels of bronze⁵.)	
C "Why do your disciples transgress the tradition of the elders? For they do not wash their hands when they eat."	**C** And the Pharisees and the scribes asked him, "Why do your disciples not live according to the tradition of the elders, but eat with ¹hands defiled?"	
D He answered them, "And why do you transgress the commandment of God for the sake of your tradition? For God commanded, 'Honor your father and your mother,' and, 'He who speaks evil of father or mother, let him surely die.'	**D** *Compare portion G below*	
E But you say, 'If any one tells his father or his mother, What you would have gained from me is given to God, he need not honor his father.⁶' So, for the sake of your tradition, you have made void the ⁷word of God.	**E** *Compare portion H below*	
F You hypocrites! Well did Isaiah prophesy of you, when he said: 'This people honors me with their lips, but their heart is far from me; in vain do they worship me, teaching as doctrines the precepts of men.'"	**F** And he said to them, "Well did Isaiah prophesy of you hypocrites, as it is written, 'This people honors me with their lips, but their heart is far from me; in vain do they worship me, teaching as doctrines the precepts of men.'	

---

1 Or *common hands*   2 That is, *up to the elbows:* Greek *with the fist*   3 Greek *sprinkle:* some ancient authorities read *baptize*   4 Greek *baptizing*   5 Many ancient authorities add *and couches*   6 Some ancient authorities add *or his mother*   7 Some ancient authorities read *law*

HS references: Mt 15:4 and Mk 7:10 = Exodus 20:12 and Deuteronomy 5:16 and Exodus 21:17 and Leviticus 20:9
Mt 15:8-9 and Mk 7:6-7 = Isaiah 29:13

MATT 15	MARK 7	LUKE

G *Compare portion D above*

G You leave the commandment of 8 God, and hold fast the tradition of men." And he said to them, "You 9 have a fine way of rejecting the commandment of God, in order to keep your tradition! For Moses said, 10 'Honor your father and your mother'; and, 'He who speaks evil of father or mother, let him surely die';

H *Compare portion E above*

H but you say, 'If a man tells his 11 father or his mother, What you would have gained from me is Corban' (that is, given to God)--then you no longer 12 permit him to do anything for his father or mother, thus making void 13 the word of God through your tradition which you hand on. And many such things you do."

I And he called the people to him and 10 said to them, "Hear and understand: not what goes into the mouth defiles a 11 man, but what comes out of the mouth, this defiles a man."

I And he called the people to him 14 again, and said to them, "Hear me, all of you, and understand: there is 15 nothing outside a man which by going into him can defile him; but the things which come out of a man are what defile him."[1]

J Then the disciples came and said to 12 him, "Do you know that the Pharisees were [2]offended when they heard this saying?" He answered, "Every [3]plant 13 which my heavenly Father has not planted will be rooted up. Let them 14 alone; they are blind guides. And if a blind man leads a blind man, both will fall into a pit."

J *He also told them a parable: "Can 6: a blind man lead a blind man? Will 39 they not both fall into a pit? (§ 38 G)*

K But Peter said to him, "Explain the 15 parable to us." And he said, "Are you 16 also still without understanding? Do 17 you not see that whatever goes into the mouth passes into the stomach, and so passes on?

K And when he had entered the 17 house, and left the people, his disciples asked him about the parable. And he said to them, "Then are you 18 also without understanding? Do you not see that whatever goes into a man from outside cannot defile him, since 19 it enters, not his heart but his stomach, and so passes on?" (Thus he declared all foods clean.)

---

1 Many ancient authorities insert verse 16: *If any man has ears to hear, let him hear*   2 Greek *caused to stumble*   3 Greek *planting*

HS references: Mk 7:10 = compare page 79   Mt 15:13 = Isaiah 60:21   Mk 7:11 = Leviticus 1:2
NC references: Mt 15:11 and Mk 7:15 = GT 14   Mt 15:13 = GT 40   Mt 15:14 and Lk 6:39 = GT 34

MATT 15   MARK 7

L But what comes out of the mouth 18 proceeds from the heart, and this defiles a man. For out of the heart 19 come evil thoughts, murder, adultery, fornication, theft, false witness, slander. These are what defile a man; 20 but to eat with unwashed hands does not defile a man."

L And he said, "What comes out of a 20 man is what defiles a man. For from 21 within, out of the heart of man, [1]come evil thoughts, fornication, theft, murder, adultery, coveting, 22 wickedness, deceit, licentiousness, [2]envy, [3]slander, pride, foolishness. All 23 these evil things come from within, and they defile a man."

§ 64 Withdrawal Toward Tyre and Sidon

MATT 15:21-28   MARK 7:24-30

A And Jesus went away from there 21 and withdrew to the district of Tyre and Sidon.

A And from there he arose and went 24 away to the region of Tyre[4] and Sidon. And he entered a house, and would not have any one know it; yet he could not be hid.

B And behold, a Canaanite woman 22 from that region came out and cried, "Have mercy on me, O Lord, Son of David; my daughter is severely possessed by a demon."

B But immediately a woman, whose 25 little daughter was possessed by an unclean spirit, heard of him, and came and fell down at his feet. Now 26 the woman was a Greek, a Syrophoeni'cian by birth. And she begged him to cast the demon out of her daughter.

C But he did not answer her a word. 23 And his disciples came and begged him, saying, "Send her away, for she is crying after us."

D[D] He answered, "I was sent only to 24 the lost sheep of the house of Israel."

D[D] And he said to her, "Let the 27 children first be fed,

E But she came and knelt before him, 25 saying, "Lord, help me." And he 26 answered, "It is not fair to take the children's [5]bread and throw it to the dogs." She said, "Yes, Lord, yet even 27 the dogs eat the crumbs that fall from their masters' table."

E for it is not right to take the children's [5]bread and throw it to the dogs." But she answered him, "Yes, 28 Lord; yet even the dogs under the table eat the children's crumbs."

F Then Jesus answered her, "O 28 woman, great is your faith! Be it done for you as you desire." And her daughter was healed instantly.

F And he said to her, "For this 29 saying you may go your way; the demon has left your daughter." And 30 she went home, and found the child lying in bed, and the demon gone.

---

1 Greek *thoughts that are evil come forth*   2 Greek *an evil eye*   3 Greek *blasphemy*   4 Some ancient authorities omit *and Sidon*
5 Or *loaf*

D With the Matthew form of the record here, compare the Matthew report in § 56 E

§ 65 Return Journey Through Decapolis

MATT 15:29a   MARK 7:31

And Jesus went on from there and 29a
passed along the Sea of Galilee.

Then he returned from the region of 31
Tyre, and went through Sidon to the
Sea of Galilee, through the region of
the Decap'olis.

§ 66 The Deaf and Dumb Man

MARK 7:32-37

A And they brought to him a man 32
who was deaf and had an impediment
in his speech; and they besought him
to lay his hand upon him. And taking 33
him aside from the multitude
privately, he put his fingers into his
ears, and he spat and touched his
tongue; and looking up to heaven, he 34
sighed, and said to him,
"Eph'phatha," that is, "Be opened."
And his ears were opened, his tongue 35
was released, and he spoke plainly.

B And he charged them to tell no 36
one; but the more he charged them,
the more zealously they proclaimed it.

C And they were astonished beyond 37
measure, saying, "He has done all
things well; he even makes the deaf
hear and the dumb speak."

§ 67 Healing and Feeding the Multitude

MATT 15:29b-39   MARK 8:1-10

A And he went up on the mountain, 29b
and sat down there. And great crowds 30
came to him, bringing with them the
lame, the maimed, the blind, the
dumb, and many others, and they put
them at his feet, and he healed them,

A In those days, when again a great 1
crowd had gathered, and they had
nothing to eat,

B so that the throng wondered, when 31
they saw the dumb speaking, the
maimed whole, the lame walking, and
the blind seeing; and they glorified
the God of Israel.

B   *Compare § 66 portion C*

C Then Jesus called his disciples to 32
him and said, "I have compassion on
the crowd, because they have been
with me now three days, and have
nothing to eat; and I am unwilling to
send them away hungry, lest they
faint on the way."

C he called his disciples to him, and
said to them, "I have compassion on 2
the crowd, because they have been
with me now three days, and have
nothing to eat; and if I send them 3
away hungry to their homes, they will
faint on the way; and some of them
have come a long way."

HS references: Mk 7:37 = Isaiah 35:5

MATT 15	MARK 8
D And the disciples said to him, 33 "Where are we to get bread enough in the desert to feed so great a crowd?" And Jesus said to them, "How many 34 loaves have you?" They said, "Seven, and a few small fish."	**D** And his disciples answered him, 4 "How can one feed these men with [1]bread here in the desert?" And he 5 asked them, "How many loaves have you?" They said, "Seven." *Compare portion G below*
E And commanding the crowd to sit 35 down on the ground,	**E** And he commanded the crowd to 6 sit down on the ground;
F he took the seven loaves and the 36 fish, and having given thanks he broke them and gave them to the disciples, and the disciples gave them to the crowds.	**F** and he took the seven loaves, and having given thanks he broke them and gave them to his disciples to set before the people; and they set them before the crowd.
G *Compare portion D above*	**G** And they had a few small fish; and 7 having blessed them, he commanded that these also should be set before them.
H And they all ate and were satisfied; 37 and they took up seven baskets full of the broken pieces left over.	**H** And they ate, and were satisfied; 8 and they took up the broken pieces left over, seven baskets full.
I Those who ate were four thousand 38 men, besides women and children.	**I** And there were about four thousand 9 people.
J And sending away the crowds, he 39 got into the boat and went to the region of Mag'adan.	**J** And he sent them away; and 10 immediately he got into the boat with his disciples, and went to the district of Dalmanu'tha.

§ 68 Pharisees Demand Signs from Jesus

MATT 16:1-4	MARK 8:11-13	LUKE
A[A] And the Pharisees and Sad'ducees 1 came, and to test him they asked him to show them a sign from heaven.	**A**[A] The Pharisees came and began to 11 argue with him, seeking from him a sign from heaven, to test him.	
B He answered them, [2]"When it is 2 evening, you say, 'It will be fair weather; for the sky is red.' And in 3 the morning, 'It will be stormy today, for the sky is red and threatening.' You know how to interpret the appearance of the sky, but you cannot interpret the signs of the times.		**B** *He also said to the multitudes,* 12: *"When you see a cloud rising in the* 54 *west, you say at once, 'A shower is coming'; and so it happens. And when* 55 *you see the south wind blowing, you say, 'There will be* [3]*scorching heat'; and it happens. You hypocrites! You* 56 *know how to*

---

1 Greek *loaves*   2 The following words, to the end of verse 3, are omitted by some of the most ancient and other important authorities
3 Or *hot wind*

NC references: Mt 16:1-3 and Lk 12:56 = GT 91

A Then some of the scribes and Pharisees said to him. "Teacher, we wish to see a sign from you." (§ 45 Q = Mt 12:38)   A Others, to test him, sought from him a sign from heaven. (§ 86 D = Lk 11:16)

MATT 16	MARK 8	LUKE
		[1]interpret the appearance of earth and sky; but why do you not know how to [1]interpret the present time? (§ 96 A)
C[C] An evil and adulterous generation 4 seeks for a sign, but no sign shall be given to it except the sign of Jonah."	C[C] And he sighed deeply in his spirit, 12 and said, "Why does this generation seek a sign? Truly, I say to you, no sign shall be given to this generation."	
D So he left them and departed.	D And he left them, and getting into 13 the boat again he departed to the other side.	

§ 69 The Leaven of the Pharisees

MATT 16:5-12	MARK 8:14-21	LUKE
A When the disciples reached the 5 other side, they had forgotten tn bring any [2]bread. Jesus said to them, "Take 6 heed and beware of the leaven of the Pharisees and Sad'ducees."	A Now they had forgotten to bring 14 bread; and they had only one loaf with them in the boat. And he 15 cautioned them, saying, "Take heed, beware of the leaven of the Pharisees and the leaven of Herod."	A *Compare portion D below*
B And they discussed it among 7 themselves, saying,[4] "We brought no [2]bread." But Jesus, aware of this, 8 said, "O men of little faith, why do you discuss among yourselves the fact that you have no [2]bread?	B And they discussed it with one 16 another,[3] saying,[5] "We have no bread." And being aware of it, Jesus 17 said to them, "Why do you discuss the fact that you have no bread?	
C Do you not yet perceive? Do you 9 not remember the five loaves of the five thousand, and how many [6]baskets you gathered? Or the seven loaves of 10 the four thousand, and how many [6]baskets you gathered? How is it that 11 you fail to perceive that I did not speak about [2]bread?	C Do you not yet perceive or understand? Are your hearts hardened? Having eyes do you not 18 see, and having ears do you not hear? And do you not remember? When I 19 broke the five loaves for the five thousand, how many [7]baskets full of broken pieces did you take up?" They said to him, "Twelve." "And the 20 seven for the four thousand, how many [7]baskets full of broken pieces did you take up?" And they said to him, "Seven." And he said to them, 21 "Do you not yet understand?"	
D Beware of the leaven of the Pharisees and Sad'ducees." Then they 12 understood that he did not tell them to beware of the leaven of [2]bread, but of the teaching of the Pharisees and Sad'ducees.	D *Compare portion A above*	D "Beware of the leaven of the 12: Pharisees, which is hypocrisy. 1 (§ 91 B)

1 Greek *prove*   2 Greek *loaves*   3 Some ancient authorities read *because they had no bread*   4 Or, It is *because we took no bread*   5 Or, It is *because we have no bread*   6 *Basket* in verses 9 and 10 represents different Greek words   7 *Basket* in verses 19 and 20 represents different Greek words.

HS references: Mt 16:4 = Jonah 3:1-4   Mk 8:18 = Jeremiah 5:21 and Ezekiel 12:2 and Isaiah 6:9-10

C But he answered them, "An evil and adulterous generation seeks for a sign; but no sign shall be given to it except the sign of the prophet Jonah." (§ 45 R = Mt 12:39)

C When the crowds were increasing, he began to say, "This generation is an evil generation; it seeks a sign, but no sign shall be given to it except the sign of Jonah." (§ 88 B = Lk 11:29)

§ 70 The Blind Man of Bethsaida

MARK 8:22-26

A And they came to Beth-sa'ida. And 22
some people brought to him a blind
man, and begged him to touch him.
And he took the blind man by the 23
hand, and led him out of the village;
and when he had spit on his eyes and
laid his hands upon him, he asked
him, "Do you see anything?" And he 24
looked up and said, "I see men; but
they look like trees, walking." Then 25
again he laid his hands upon his eyes;
and he looked intently and was
restored, and saw everything clearly.

B And he sent him away to his home, 26
saying, "Do not even enter the
village."

Chapter XII

FORECASTS OF CONFLICT WITH THE JERUSALEM AUTHORITIES

§ 71 Opinion of Disciples about Jesus

MATT 16:13-20	MARK 8:27-30	LUKE 9:18-21
A *Compare § 60 portion K*	**A** *Compare § 60 portion K*	**A** Now it happened that as he was 18 praying alone
B Now when Jesus came into the dis- 13 trict of Caesare'a Philip'pi, he asked his disciples, "Who do men say ¹that the Son of man is?"	**B** And Jesus went on with his 27 disciples, to the villages of Caesare'a Philip'pi; and on the way he asked his disciples, "Who do men say that I am?"	**B** the disciples ²were with him; and he asked them, "Who do the people say that I am?"
Cᶜ And they said, "Some say John 14 the Baptist, others say Eli'jah, and others Jeremiah or one of the prophets."	**C**ᶜ And they told him, "John the Bap- 28 tist; and others say, Eli'jah; and others one of the prophets."	**C**ᶜ And they answered, "John the 19 Baptist; but others say, Eli'jah; and others, that one of the old prophets has risen."
D He said to them, "But who do you 15 say that I am?" Simon Peter replied, 16 "You are the Christ, the Son of the living God."	**D** And he asked them, "But who do 29 you say that I am?" Peter answered him, "You are the Christ."	**D** And he said to them, "But who do 20 you say that I am?" And Peter answered, "The Christ of God."
E And Jesus answered him, "Blessed 17 are you, Simon Bar-Jona! For flesh and blood has not revealed this to you, but my Father who is in heaven. 18 And I tell you, you are ³Peter, and on this ⁴rock I will build my church, and the ⁵powers of death shall not prevail against it.		
Fᶠ I will give you the keys of the 19 kingdom of heaven, and whatever you bind on earth shall be bound in heaven, and whatever you loose on earth shall be loosed in heaven."		
G Then he strictly ⁶charged the dis- 20 ciples to tell no one that he was the Christ.	**G** And he ⁶charged them to tell no 30 one about him.	**G** But he ⁶charged and commanded 21 them to tell this to no one,

---

1 Many ancient authorities read *that I the Son of man am:* see Mark 8:27 and Luke 9:18   2 Codex Vaticanus reads *met him*   3 Greek *Petros*
4 Greek *petra*   5 Greek *gates of Hades*   6 Greek *rebuked*

HS references: Mt 16:19 = Isaiah 22:22

C For another record of these estimates of Jesus, compare § 58 BC
F Truly, I say to you, whatever you bind on earth shall be bound in heaven, and whatever you loose on earth shall be loosed in heaven.
(§ 78 T = Mt 18:18)

§ 72   Jesus Foretells Events at Jerusalem

MATT 16:21-23	MARK 8:31-33	LUKE 9:22
A^A From that time [1]Jesus began to 21 show his disciples that he must go to Jerusalem and suffer many things from the elders and chief priests and scribes, and be killed, and on the third day be raised.	A^A And he began to teach them that 31 the Son of man must suffer many things, and be rejected by the elders and the chief priests and the scribes, and be killed, and after three days rise again. And he said this plainly. 32	A^A saying, "The Son of man must 22 suffer many things, and be rejected by the elders and chief priests and scribes, and be killed, and on the third day be raised."
B And Peter took him and began to 22 rebuke him, saying, [2]"God forbid, Lord! This shall never happen to you." But he turned and said to Peter, 23 "Get behind me, Satan! You are a [3]hindrance to me; [4]for you are not on the side of God, but of men."	B And Peter took him, and began to rebuke him. But turning and seeing 33 his disciples, he rebuked Peter, and said, "Get behind me, Satan! [4]For you are not on the side of God, but of men."	

§ 73   Some Costs of Discipleship

MATT 16:24-28	MARK 8:34-9:1	LUKE 9:23-27
A^A Then Jesus told his disciples, "If 24 any man would come after me, let him deny himself and take up his cross and follow me.	A^A And he called to him the multi- 34 tude with his disciples, and said to them, "If any man would come after me, let him deny himself and take up his cross and follow me.	A^A And he said to all, "If any man 23 would come after me, let him deny himself and take up his cross daily and follow me.
B^B For whoever would save his [5]life 25 will [6]lose it, and whoever [6]loses his [5]life for my sake will find it.[8] For 26 what will it profit a man, if he gains the whole world and forfeits his [5]life? Or what shall a man give in return for his [5]life?	B^B For whoever would save his [5]life 35 will [6]lose it; and whoever [6]loses his [5]life [7]for my sake and the gospel's will save it.[8] For what does it profit a 36 man, to gain the whole world and forfeit his [5]life? For what can a man 37 give in return for his [5]life?	B^B For whoever would save his [5]life 24 will [6]lose it; and whoever [6]loses his [5]life for my sake, he will save it.[8] For 25 what does it profit a man if he gains the whole world and loses or forfeits himself?

---

1 Some very ancient authorities read *Jesus Christ*   2 Or, God *have mercy on you*   3 Greek *cause of stumbling*   4 Greek *for you do not heed the things of God but the human things*   5 Or *soul (psyche)*   6 Greek *destroy, destroys*   7 The third century Chester Beatty Papyri and some other ancient authorities read *for the gospel's sake*   8 See also the note on the Greek at § 57 N, O and § 112 J

HS references: Mt 16:26 and Mk 8:37 = Psalm 49:7-8
NC references: Mt 16:24 and Mk 8:34 and Lk 9:23 = GT 55, 101

A The Son of man is to be delivered into the hands of men, and they will kill him, and he will be raised on the third day. (§ 76 B = Mt 17:22-23)	A The Son of man will be delivered into the hands of men, and they will kill him; and when he is killed, after three days he will rise. (§ 76 B = Mk 9:31)	A Let these words sink into your ears; for the Son of man is to be delivered into the hands of men. (§ 76 B = Lk 9:44)
A But first he must suffer many things and be rejected by this generation. (§ 112 D = Lk 17:25)		
A Behold, we are going up to Jerusalem; and the Son of man will be delivered to the chief priests and scribes, and they will condemn him to death, and deliver him to the Gentiles to be mocked and scourged and crucified, and he will be raised on the third day. (§ 119 C-F = Mt 20:18-19)	A Behold, we are going up to Jerusalem; and the Son of man will be delivered to the chief priests and the scribes, and they will condemn him to death, and deliver him to the Gentiles; and they will mock him, and spit upon him, and scourge him, and kill him; and after three days he will rise. (§ 119 C-F = Mk 10:33-34)	A Behold, we are going up to Jerusalem, and everything that is written of the Son of man by the prophets will be accomplished. For he will be delivered to the Gentiles and will be mocked and shamefully treated and spit upon, and they will scourge him and kill him, and on the third day he will rise. (§ 119 C-F = Lk 18:31-33)

A For other references to these events, compare § 74 I-N & § 101.

A And he who does not take his cross and follow me is not worthy of me.	A Whoever does not bear his own cross and come after me, cannot be my disciple. (§ 104 C = Lk 14:27)
B He who finds his life will lose it, and he who loses his life for my sake will find it. (§ 57 NO = Mt 10:38-39)	B Whoever seeks to gain his life will lose it, but whoever loses his life will preserve it. (§ 112 J = Lk 17:33)

MATT 16	MARK 8	LUKE 9
C^C For the Son of man is to come 27 with his angels in the glory of his Father, and then he will repay every man for what he has done.	C^C For whoever is ashamed of me 38 and of my words in this adulterous and sinful generation, of him will the Son of man also be ashamed, when he comes in the glory of his Father with the holy angels."	C^C For whoever is ashamed of me 26 and of my words, of him will the Son of man be ashamed when he comes in his glory and the glory of the Father and of the holy angels.
D Truly, I say to you, there are some 28 standing here who will not taste death before they see the Son of man coming in his kingdom."	D And he said to them, "Truly, I say 9: to you, there are some standing here 1 who will not taste death before they see that the kingdom of God has come with power."	D But I tell you truly, there are some 27 standing here who will not taste death before they see the kingdom of God."

§ 74 The Transfiguration of Jesus

MATT 17:1-13	MARK 9:2-13	LUKE 9:28-36
A And after six days Jesus took with 1 him Peter and James and John his brother, and led them up a high mountain apart.	A And after six days Jesus took with 2 him Peter and James and John, and led them up a high mountain apart by themselves;	A Now about eight days after these 28 sayings he took with him Peter and John and James, and went up on the mountain to pray.
B And he was transfigured before 2 them, and his face shone like the sun, and his garments became white as light.	B and he was transfigured before them, and his garments became 3 glistening, intensely white, as no fuller on earth could bleach them.	B And as he was praying, the 29 appearance of his countenance was altered, and his raiment became dazzling white.
C And behold, there appeared to them 3 Moses and Eli'jah, talking with him.	C And there appeared to them Eli'jah 4 with Moses; and they were talking to Jesus.	C And behold, two men talked with 30 him, Moses and Eli'jah, who 31 appeared in glory and spoke of his departure, which he was to accomplish at Jerusalem. Now Peter 32 and those who were with him were heavy with sleep, and when they wakened they saw his glory and the two men who stood with him.
D And Peter said to Jesus, "Lord, it 4 is well that we are here; if you wish, I will make three booths here, one for you and one for Moses and one for Eli'jah."	D And Peter said to Jesus, [1]"Master, 5 it is well that we are here; let us make three booths, one for you and one for Moses and one for Eli'jah." For he did not know what to say, for 6 they were exceedingly afraid.	D And as the men were parting from 33 him, Peter said to Jesus, "Master, it is well that we are here; let us make three booths, one for you and one for Moses and one for Eli'jah"--not knowing what he said.
E^E He was still speaking, when lo, a 5 bright cloud overshadowed them, and a voice from the cloud said, "This is [2]my beloved Son, with whom I am well pleased; listen to him."	E^E And a cloud overshadowed them, 7 and a voice came out of the cloud, "This is [2]my beloved Son; listen to him."	E^E As he said this, a cloud came and 34 overshadowed them; and they were afraid as they entered the cloud. And 35 a voice came out of the cloud, saying, "This is [3]my Son, my Chosen; listen to him!"

---

1 Greek *Rabbi*   2 Or *my son, my (or the) Beloved*   3 Many ancient authorities read *my beloved son; Codex Bezae adds with whom I am well pleased*: see Matt 17:5 and Mark 9:7

HS references: Mt 16:27 = Psalm 62:12 and Proverbs 24:12   Mt 17:2 and Mk 9:3 and Lk 9:29 = Exodus 34:29-35
Mt 17:5 and Mk 9:7 and Lk 9:35 = Deuteronomy 18:15 and Isaiah 42:1 and Psalm 2:7

C But whoever denies me before men, I also will deny before my Father who is in heaven. (§ 57 K = Mt 10:33)
E Compare § 18 portion D

C But he who denies me before men will be denied before the angels of God. (§ 91 G = Lk 12:9)

MATT 17	MARK 9	LUKE 9
F When the disciples heard this, they 6 fell on their faces, and were filled with awe. But Jesus came and touched 7 them, saying, "Rise, and have no fear."		
G And when they lifted up their eyes, 8 they saw no one but Jesus only.	G And suddenly looking around they 8 no longer saw any one with them but Jesus only.	G And when the voice ¹had spoken, 36 Jesus was found alone.
	H *Compare portion J below*	H And they kept silence and told no one in those days anything of what they had seen.
I¹ And as they were coming down the 9 mountain, Jesus commanded them, "Tell no one the vision, until the Son of man is raised from the dead."	I¹ And as they were coming down the 9 mountain, he charged them to tell no one what they had seen, until the Son of man should have risen from the dead.	
	J So they kept the matter to them- 10 selves, questioning what the rising from the dead meant.	J *Compare portion H above*
K And the disciples asked him, "Then 10 why do the scribes say that first Eli'jah must come?" He replied, 11 "Eli'jah does come, and he is to restore all things;	K And they asked him, "Why do the 11 scribes say that first Eli'jah must come?" And he said to them, "Eli'jah 12 does come first to restore all things;	
L^L *Compare portion N below*	L^L and how is it written of the Son of man, that he should suffer many things and be treated with contempt?	
M^M but I tell you that Eli'jah has 12 already come, and they did not know him, but did to him whatever they pleased.	M^M But I tell you that Eli'jah has 13 come, and they did to him whatever they pleased, as it is written of him."	
N^N So also the Son of man will suffer at their hands."	N^N *Compare portion L above*	
O Then the disciples understood that 13 he was speaking to them of John the Baptist.		

§ 75 The Youth with the Dumb Spirit

MATT 17:14-20	MARK 9:14-29	LUKE 9:37-43a
A And when they came to the crowd, 14	A And when they came to the dis- 14 ciples, they saw a great crowd about them, and scribes arguing with them. And immediately all the crowd, when 15	A On the next day, when they had 37 come down from the mountain, a great crowd met him.

1 Or *was past*

HS references: Mt 17:10-11 and Mk 9:11-12 = Malachi 4:5-6   Mt 17:12 and Mk 9:13 = I Kings 19:2,10

I-N For accounts of the forecast of suffering and death, compare § 72 A and attached references
L Compare § 119 portion D
M For another record of the identification of John the Baptist with Elijah by Jesus, compare § 41 G

MATT 17	MARK 9	LUKE 9
	they saw him, were greatly amazed, and ran up to him and greeted him. And he asked them, "What are you 16 discussing with them?"	
B a man came up to him and kneeling before him said, "Lord, have mercy 15 on my son, for he is an epileptic and he suffers terribly; for often he falls into the fire, and often into the water. And I brought him to your disciples, 16 and they could not heal him."	**B** And one of the crowd answered 17 him, "Teacher, I brought my son to you, for he has a dumb spirit; and 18 wherever it seizes him, it dashes him down; and he foams and grinds his teeth and becomes rigid; and I asked your disciples to cast it out, and they were not able."	**B** And behold, a man from the crowd 38 cried, "Teacher, I beg you to look upon my son, for he is my only child; and behold, a spirit seizes him, and 39 he suddenly cries out; it convulses him till he foams, and shatters him, and will hardly leave him. And I 40 begged your disciples to cast it out, but they could not."
C And Jesus answered, "O faithless 17 and perverse generation, how long am I to be with you? How long am I to bear with you? Bring him here to me."	**C** And he answered them, "O 19 faithless generation, how long am I to be with you? How long am I to bear with you? Bring him to me."	**C** Jesus answered, "O faithless and 41 perverse generation, how long am I to be with you and bear with you? Bring your son here."
	D And they brought the boy to him; 20 and when the spirit saw him, immediately it convulsed the boy, and he fell on the ground and rolled about, foaming at the mouth. And ¹Jesus 21 asked his father, "How long has he had this?" And he said, "From childhood. And it has often cast him 22 into the fire and into the water, to destroy him; but if you can do anything, have pity on us and help us." And Jesus said to him, "If you 23 can! All things are possible to him who believes." Immediately the father 24 of the child cried out and said,² "I believe; help my unbelief!"	**D** While he was coming, the demon 42 tore him and convulsed him.
E And Jesus rebuked him, and the 18 demon came out of him, and the boy was cured instantly.	**E** And when Jesus saw that a crowd 25 came running together, he rebuked the unclean spirit, saying to it, "You dumb and deaf spirit, I command you, come out of him, and never enter him again." And after crying out and con- 26 vulsing him terribly, it came out, and the boy was like a corpse; so that most of them said, "He is dead." But 27 Jesus took him by the hand and lifted him up, and he arose.	**E** But Jesus rebuked the unclean spirit, and healed the boy, and gave him back to his father.
		F And all were astonished at the 43a majesty of God.
G Then the disciples came to Jesus 19 privately and said, "Why could we not cast it out?" He said to them, 20 "Because of your little faith.	**G** And when he had entered the 28 house, his disciples asked him privately, "Why could we not cast it out?" And he said to them, "This kind 29	

---

1 Greek *he*   2 Many ancient authorities add *with tears*

MATT 17	MARK	LUKE
	cannot be driven out by anything but prayer[1]."	
H[H] For truly, I say to you, if you have faith as a grain of mustard seed, you will say to this mountain, 'Move from here to there,' and it will move;		**H**[H] *And the Lord said, "If you had* 17: *faith as a grain of mustard seed, you* 6 *could say to this sycamine tree, 'Be rooted up, and be planted in the sea,' and it would obey you. (§ 109 F)*
I and nothing will be impossible to you."[2]		

§ 76 Jesus Repeats his Forecast of Events

MATT 17:22-23	MARK 9:30-32	LUKE 9:43b-45
A As they were [3]gathering in Galilee, 22 Jesus said to them,	**A** They went on from there and 30 passed through Galilee. And he would not have any one know it; for he was 31 teaching his disciples, saying to them,	**A** But while they were all marveling 43b at everything he did, he said to his disciples,
B[B] "The Son of man is to be delivered into the hands of men, and they 23 will kill him, and he will be raised on the third day."	**B**[B] "The Son of man will be delivered into the hands of men, and they will kill him; and when he is killed, after three days he will rise."	**B**[B] "Let these words sink into your 44 ears; for the Son of man is to be delivered into the hands of men."
C And they were greatly distressed.	**C** But they did not understand the 32 saying, and they were afraid to ask him.	**C** But they did not understand this 45 saying, and it was concealed from them, that they should not perceive it; and they were afraid to ask him about this saying.

§ 77 The Problem of Tribute Payment

MATT 17:24-27

A When they came to Caper'na-um, 24 the collectors of the [4]half-shekel tax went up to Peter and said, "Does not your teacher pay the tax?" He said, 25 "Yes." And when he came home, Jesus spoke to him first, saying, "What do you think, Simon? From whom do kings of the earth take toll or tribute? From their sons or from others?" And when he said, "From 26 others," Jesus said to him, "Then the sons are free.

---

1 Many ancient authorities add *and fasting*　2 Many authorities, some ancient, insert verse 21: *But this kind never comes out except by prayer and fasting*: see Mark 9:29　3 Some ancient authorities read *living*　4 Greek *didrachma*

HS references: Mt 17:24 = Exodus 30:11-15 and 38:26
NC references: Mt 17:21 and Lk 17:6 = GT 48, 106

H Truly, I say to you, if you have faith and never doubt, you will not only do what has been done to the fig tree, but even if you say to this mountain, 'Be taken up and cast into the sea,' it will be done.
(§ 127 C = Mt 21:21)

H Have faith in God. Truly, I say to you, whoever says to this mountain, 'Be taken up and cast into the sea,' and does not doubt in his heart, but believes that what he says will come to pass, it will be done for him.
(§ 127 C = Mk 11:22-23)

B For other records of these forecasts, compare § 72 A and attached references.

MATT 17

B However, not to give offense to 27 them, go to the sea and cast a hook, and take the first fish that comes up, and when you open its mouth you will find a [1]shekel; take that and give it to them for me and for yourself."

§ 78 Discourse on Standards of Greatness

MATT 18:1-35	MARK 9:33-50	LUKE 9:46-50
A At that time the disciples came to Jesus, saying, "Who is the [2]greatest in the kingdom of heaven?" (1)	**A** And they came to Caper'na-um; 33 and when he was in the house he asked them, "What were you discussing on the way?" But they 34 were silent; for on the way they had discussed with one another who was the [2]greatest.	**A** And an argument arose among 46 them as to which of them was the [2]greatest.
B[B] *Compare portion E below*	**B**[B] And he sat down and called the 35 twelve; and he said to them, "If any one would be first, he must be last of all and servant of all."	**B**[B] *Compare portion H below*
C And calling to him a child, he put 2 him in the midst of them, and said, 3	**C** And he took a child, and put him 36 in the midst of them; and taking him in his arms, he said to them,	**C** But when Jesus perceived the 47 thought of their hearts, he took a child and put him by his side, and 48 said to them,
D "Truly, I say to you, unless you turn and become like children, you will never enter the kingdom of heaven.	**D** *Truly, I say to you, whoever does* 10: *not receive the kingdom of God like a* 15 *child shall not enter it." (§ 116 C)*	**D** *Truly, I say to you, whoever does* 18: *not receive the kingdom of God like a* 17 *child shall not enter it." (§ 116 C)*
E Whoever humbles himself like this 4 child, he is the [2]greatest in the kingdom of heaven.	**E** *Compare portion B above*	**E** *Compare portion H below*
F "Whoever receives one such child 5 in my name receives me;	**F** "Whoever receives one such child 37 in my name receives me;	**F** "Whoever receives this child in my name receives me,
G[G] *"He who receives you receives me,* 10: *and he who receives me receives him* 40 *who sent me. (§ 57 P)*	**G**[G] and whoever receives me, receives not me but him who sent me."	**G**[G] and whoever receives me receives him who sent me;
H *Compare portion E above*	**H** *Compare portion B above*	**H** for he who is [3]least among you all is the one who is great."

---

1 Greek *stater*   2 Greek *greater*   3 Greek *lesser*

NC references: Mt 18:3 and Mk 10:15 and Lk 18:17 = GT 22

B It shall not be so among you; but whoever would be great among you must be your servant, and whoever would be first among you must be your slave. (§ 120 J = Mt 20:26-27)
B He who is greatest among you shall be your servant. (§ 132 G = Mt 23:11)

B But it shall not be so among you; but whoever would be great among you must be your servant, and whoever would be first among you must be slave of all. (§ 120 J = Mk 10:43-44)

B But not so with you; rather let the greatest among you become as the youngest, and the leader as one who serves. (§ 138 M = Lk 22:26)

G He who hears you hears me, and he who rejects you rejects me, and he who rejects me rejects him who sent me, (§ 82 Q = Lk 10:16)

MATT 18	MARK 9	LUKE 9
	I[1] John said to him, "Teacher, we saw 38 a man casting out demons in your name, and we forbade him, because he was not following us." But Jesus 39 said, "Do not forbid him; for no one who does a [1]mighty work in my name will be able soon after to speak evil of me. For he that is not against us is 40 for us.	I[1] John answered, "Master, we saw a 49 man casting out demons in your name, and we forbade him, because he does not follow with us." But 50 Jesus said to him, "Do not forbid him; for he that is not against you is for you."
J *"And whoever gives to one of these* 10: *little ones even a cup of cold water* 42 *because he is a disciple, truly, I say to you, he shall not lose his reward."* *(§ 57 Q)*	J For truly, I say to you, whoever 41 gives you a cup of water to drink because you bear the name of Christ, will by no means lose his reward.	
K but whoever causes one of these 6 little ones who believe in me to [3]sin, it would be better for him to have [4]a great millstone fastened round his neck and to be drowned in the depth of the sea.	K "Whoever causes one of these little 42 ones who believe[2] in me to [3]sin, it would be better for him if [4]a great millstone were hung round his neck and he were thrown into the sea.	K *It would be better for him if a* 17: *millstone were hung round his neck* 2 *and he were cast into the sea, than that he should cause one of these little ones to* [3]*sin. (§ 109 B)*
L "Woe to the world for temptations 7 to [3]sin! For it is necessary that temptations come, but woe to the man by whom the temptation comes!		L *"Temptations to* [3]*sin are sure to* 17: *come; but woe to him by whom they* 1 *come! (§ 109 A)*
M[M] And if your hand or your foot 8 causes you to [3]sin, cut it off and throw it away; it is better for you to enter life maimed or lame than with two hands or two feet to be thrown into the eternal fire. And if your eye 9 causes you to [3]sin, pluck it out and throw it away; it is better for you to enter life with one eye than with two eyes to be thrown into the [7]hell of fire.	M[M] And if your hand causes you to 43 [3]sin, cut it off; it is better for you to enter life maimed than with two hands to go to [5]hell, to the unquenchable fire.[6] And if your foot causes you to 45 [3]sin, cut it off; it is better for you to enter life lame than with two feet to be thrown into [5]hell.[6] And if your eye 47 causes you to [3]sin, pluck it out; it is better for you to enter the kingdom of God with one eye than with two eyes to be thrown into [5]hell, N where their worm does not die, and 48 the fire is not quenched. For every 49 one will be salted with fire.[8]	
O *"You are the salt of the earth; but* 5: *if salt has lost its taste, how shall* 13	O Salt is good; but if the salt has lost 50 its saltness, how will you season it?	O *"Salt is good; but if salt has lost its* 14: *taste, how shall its saltness be* 34

---

1 Greek *power*   2 Many ancient authorities omit *in me*   3 Greek *stumble*   4 Greek *a millstone turned by an ass*   5 Greek *Gehenna*
6 Verses 44 and 46 (which are identical with verse 48) are omitted by the best ancient authorities   7 Greek *Gehenna of fire*   8 Many ancient
authorities add *and every sacrifice shall be salted with salt*: see Leviticus 2:13

HS references: Mk 9:38-40 and Lk 9:49-50 = Numbers 11:27-29   Mk 9:48 = Isaiah 66:24   Mk 9:49 = Leviticus 2:13

I With the last verse of this portion, compare § 45 H and § 86 H
M If your right eye causes you to sin, pluck it out and throw it away; it is better that you lose one of your members than that your whole body be thrown into hell. And if your right hand causes you to sin, cut it off and throw it away; it is better that you lose one of your members than that your whole body go into hell. (§ 37 C = Mt 5:29-30)

MATT 18

its saltness be restored? It is no longer good for anything except to be thrown out and trodden under foot by men. (§ 36 KL)

P "See that you do not despise one of 10 these little ones; for I tell you that in heaven their angels always behold the face of my Father who is in heaven.[1]

Q What do you think? If a man has a 12 hundred sheep, and one of them has gone astray, does he not leave the ninety-nine on the mountains and go in search of the one that went astray? And if he finds it, truly, I say to you, 13 he rejoices over it more than over the ninety-nine that never went astray. So 14 it is not [2]the will of [3]my Father who is in heaven that one of these little ones should perish.

R "If your brother sins [4]against you, 15 go and tell him his fault, between you and him alone. If he listens to you, you have gained your brother.

S But if he does not listen, take one 16 or two others along with you, that every word may be confirmed by the evidence of two or three witnesses. If 17 he refuses to listen to them, tell it to the [5]church; and if he refuses to listen even to the [5]church, let him be to you as a Gentile and a tax collector.

T[T] Truly, I say to you, whatever you 18 bind on earth shall he bound in heaven, and whatever you loose on earth shall be loosed in heaven.

U Again I say to you, if two of you 19 agree on earth about anything they ask, it will be done for them by my Father in heaven. For where two or 20

MARK 9

Have salt in yourselves, and be at peace with one another."

LUKE

restored? It is fit neither for the land 35 nor for the dunghill; men throw it away. (§ 104 E)

Q *"What man of you, having a* 15: *hundred sheep, if he has lost one of* 4 *them, does not leave the ninety-nine in the wilderness and go after the one which is lost, until he finds it? And* 5 *when he has found it, he lays it on his shoulders, rejoicing. And when he* 6 *comes home, he calls together his friends and his neighbors, saying to them, 'Rejoice with me, for I have found my sheep which was lost.' Just* 7 *so, I tell you, there will be more joy in heaven over one sinner who repents than over ninety-nine righteous persons who need no repentance.* (§ 105 B)

R *Take heed to yourselves; if your* 17: *brother sins, rebuke him, and if he* 3 *repents, forgive him;*

---

1 Many authorities, some ancient, insert verse 11: *For the Son of man came to save that which was lost:* see Luke 19:10   2 Greek *a thing willed before your Father*   3 Many ancient authorities read *your*   4 Some ancient authorities omit *against you*   5 Or *congregation*

HS references: Mt 18:15-17 = Leviticus 19:17   Mt 18:16 = Deuteronomy 19:15
NC references: Mt 18:12-14 and Lk 15:3-7 = GT 107

T I will give you the keys of the kingdom of heaven, and whatever you bind on earth shall be bound in heaven, and whatever you loose on earth shall be loosed in heaven. (§ 71 F= Mt 16:19)

MATT **18**   LUKE

three are gathered in my name, there
am I in the midst of them."

V Then Peter came up and said to 21
him, "Lord, how often shall my
brother sin against me, and I forgive
him? As many as seven times?" Jesus 22
said to him, "I do not say to you
seven times, but ¹seventy times seven.

W "Therefore the kingdom of heaven 23
may be compared to a king who
wished to settle accounts with his
²servants. When he began the 24
reckoning, one was brought to him
who owed him ten thousand ³talents;
and as he could not pay, his lord 25
ordered him to be sold, with his wife
and children and all that he had, and
payment to be made. So the ⁴servant 26
fell on his knees, imploring him,
'Lord, have patience with me, and I
will pay you everything.' And out of 27
pity for him the lord of that ⁴servant
released him and forgave him the
⁵debt. But that same ⁴servant, as he 28
went out, came upon one of his
fellow servants who owed him a
hundred ⁶denarii; and seizing him by
the throat he said, 'Pay what you
owe.' So his fellow servant fell down 29
and besought him, 'Have patience
with me, and I will pay you.' He re- 30
fused and went and put him in prison
till he should pay the debt. When his 31
fellow servants saw what had taken
place, they were greatly distressed,
and they went and reported to their
lord all that had taken place. Then his 32
lord summoned him and said to him,
'You wicked ⁴servant! I forgave you
all that debt because you besought
me; and should not you have had 33
mercy on your fellow servant, as I
had mercy on you?' And in anger his 34
lord delivered him to the jailers, till
he should pay all his debt.

Xˣ So also my heavenly Father will 35
do to every one of you, if you do not
forgive your brother from your
heart."

V *and if he sins against you seven* 4
times in the day, and turns to you
seven times, and says, 'I repent,' you
must forgive him." (§ 109 CD)

---

1 Or *seventy times and seven*   2 Greek *slaves*   3 This talent was more than fifteen years' wages of a laborer.   4 Greek *slave*   5 Greek *loan*
6 The denarius was a day's wage for a laborer.

HS references: Mt 18:21-22 = Genesis 4:24

X But if you do not forgive men their trespasses, neither will your father forgive your trespasses. (§ 37 X = Mt 6:15)
X And whenever you stand praying, forgive, if you have anything against any one; so that your Father also who is in heaven may forgive you your
trespasses. (§ 127 E = Mk 11:25)

Chapter XIII

DEPARTURE FROM GALILEE FOR JERUSALEM

§ 79 General Statement of Journey

MATT 19:1-2   MARK 10:1   LUKE 9:51

Now when Jesus had finished these 1 sayings, he went away from Galilee and entered the region of Judea beyond the Jordan; and large crowds 2 followed him, and he healed them there.

And he left there and went to the 1 region of Judea and beyond the Jordan, and crowds gathered to him again; and again, as his custom was, he taught them.

When the days¹ drew near for him to 51 be received up, he set his face to go to Jerusalem.

§ 80 Attitude of Samaritans Toward Jesus

LUKE 9:52-56

And he sent messengers ahead of him, who went and 52 entered a village of the Samaritans, to make ready for him; but the people would not receive him, because his face was 53 set toward Jerusalem. And when his disciples James and 54 John saw it, they said, "Lord, do you want us to bid fire come down from heaven and consume them?"² But he 55 turned and rebuked them.³ And they went on to another 56 village.

§ 81 Some Tests of Discipleship

MATT 8:19-22   LUKE 9:57-62

A *And ⁴a scribe came up and said to him, "Teacher, I will 19 follow you wherever you go." And Jesus said to him, 20 "Foxes have holes, and birds of the air have ⁵nests; but the Son of man has nowhere to lay his head."*

B *Another of the disciples said to him, "Lord, let me first 21 go and bury my father." But Jesus said to him, "Follow me, 22 and leave the dead to bury their own dead." (§ 50 B)*

A As they were going along the road, a man said to him, 57 "I will follow you wherever you go." And Jesus said to 58 him, "Foxes have holes, and birds of the air have ⁵nests; but the Son of man has nowhere to lay his head."

B To another he said, "Follow me." But he said, "Lord, let 59 me first go and bury my father." But he said to him, 60 "Leave the dead to bury their own dead; but as for you, go and proclaim the kingdom of God."

C Another said, "I will follow you, Lord; but let me first 61 say farewell to those at my home." Jesus said to him, "No 62 one who puts his hand to the plow and looks back is fit for the kingdom of God."

---

1 Greek *were being fulfilled*   2 Many ancient authorities add *even as Elijah did*   3 Some ancient authorities add *and said, You know not what manner of spirit you are of*: some, but fewer, add also *For the Son of man came not to destroy people's lives but to save them*   4 Greek *one scribe*   5 Greek *lodging-places*

HS references: Lk 9:54 = II Kings 1:10-12   Lk 9:61 = I Kings 19:20

§ 82 The Mission of the Disciples

MATTHEW   LUKE 10:1-24

A   Compare § 56 portion C

A After this the Lord appointed seventy[1] others, and sent 1 them on ahead of him, two by two, into every town and place where he himself was about to come.

B Then he said to his disciples, "The harvest is plentiful, 9: but the laborers are few; pray therefore the Lord of the 37 harvest to send out laborers into his harvest." (§ 56 B)   38

B And he said to them, "The harvest is plentiful, but the 2 laborers are few; pray therefore the Lord of the harvest to send out laborers into his harvest.

C^C — rendered as **C**^C

C^C And preach as you go, saying, 'The kingdom of heaven 10: is at hand.' Heal the sick, raise the dead, cleanse lepers, 7 cast out demons. You received without paying, give without 8 pay.

C^C   Compare portion I below
Compare portion K below

D   Compare portion M below

D Go your way; behold, I send you out as lambs in the 3 midst of wolves.

E^E Take no gold, nor silver, nor copper in your belts, no 9 bag for your journey, nor two tunics, nor sandals, nor a 10 staff;

E^E Carry no purse, no bag, no sandals; and salute no one 4 on the road.

F^F for the laborer deserves his food. And whatever town or 11 village you enter, find out who is worthy in it, and stay with him until you depart.

F^F   Compare portion H below

G As you enter the house, salute it. And if the house is 12 worthy, let your peace come upon it; but if it is not worthy, 13 let your peace return to you.

G Whatever house you [2]enter, first say, 'Peace be to this 5 house!' And if a son of peace is there, your peace shall rest 6 upon [3]him; but if not, it shall return to you.

H   Compare portion F above

H And remain in the same house, eating and drinking what 7 they provide, for the laborer deserves his wages; do not go from house to house. Whenever you enter a town and they 8 receive you, eat what is set before you;

I   Compare portion C above

I heal the sick in it and say to them, 'The kingdom of God 9 has come near to you.'

J^J And if any one will not receive you or listen to your 14 words, shake off the dust from your feet as you leave that house or town.

J^J But whenever you enter a town and they do not receive 10 you, go into its streets and say, 'Even the dust of your 11 town that clings to our feet, we wipe off against you;

---

1 Many ancient authorities add *and two*: and so in verse 17   2 Or *enter first, say*   3 Or *it*

HS references: Lk 10:5 = I Samuel 25:6   Lk 10:7 = Deuteronomy 24:15

C *Matt parallel shown above under C*

E *Matt parallel shown above under E*

F *Matt parallel shown above under F*

J *Matt parallel shown above under J*

E He charged them to take nothing for their journey except a staff; no bread, no bag, no money in their belts; but to wear sandals and not put on two tunics.

F And he said to them, Where you enter a house, stay there until you leave the place.

J And if any place will not receive you and they refuse to hear you, when you leave, shake off the dust that is on your feet for a testimony against them.
(§ 56 G-K = Mk 6:8-11)

C And he sent them out to preach the kingdom of God and to heal.

E And he said to them, Take nothing for your journey, no staff, nor bag, nor bread, nor money; and do not have two tunics.

F And whatever house you enter, stay there, and from there depart.

J And wherever they do not receive you, when you leave that town shake off the dust from your feet as a testimony against them.
(§ 56 F-K = Lk 9:2-5)

MATTHEW

LUKE 10

K   *Compare portion C above*

K nevertheless know this, that the kingdom of God has come near.'

L[L] *Truly, I say to you, it shall be more tolerable on the day* 15 *of judgment for the land of Sodom and Gomor'rah than for that town.*
        Compare portion P below

L[L] I tell you, it shall be more tolerable on that day for 12 Sodom than for that town.

M *"Behold, I send you out as sheep in the midst of wolves;* 16 *so be wise as serpents and* [1]*innocent as doves. (§ 56 F-M)*

M   *Compare portion D above*

N *"Woe to you, Chora'zin! woe to you, Beth-sa'ida! for if* 11: *the* [2]*mighty works done in you had been done in Tyre and* 21 *Sidon, they would have repented long ago in sackcloth and ashes. But I tell you, it shall be more tolerable on the day* 22 *of judgment for Tyre and Sidon than for you. And you,* 23 *Caper'na-um, will you be exalted to heaven? You shall be brought down to Hades.*

N *"Woe to you, Chora'zin! woe to you, Beth-sa'ida! for if* 13 *the* [2]*mighty works done in you had been done in Tyre and Sidon, they would have repented long ago, sitting in sackcloth and ashes. But it shall be more tolerable in the* 14 *judgment for Tyre and Sidon than for you. And you,* 15 *Caper'na-um, will you be exalted to heaven? You shall be brought down to Hades.*

O *For if the mighty works done in you had been done in Sodom, it would have remained until this day.*

P[P] *But I tell you that it shall be more tolerable an the day* 24 *of judgment for the land of Sodom than for you."*
(§ 41 L-O)

P[P]   *Compare portion L above*

Q[Q] *"He who receives you receives me, and he who receives* 10: *me receives him who sent me. (§ 57 P)*   40

Q[Q] *"He who hears you hears me, and he who rejects you* 16 *rejects me, and he who rejects me rejects him who sent me."*

R[R] The seventy returned with joy, saying, "Lord, even the 17 demons are subject to us in your name!" And he said to 18 them, "I saw Satan fall like lightning from heaven. Behold, 19 I have given you authority to tread upon serpents and scorpions, and over all the power of the enemy; and nothing shall hurt you. Nevertheless do not rejoice in this, 20 that the spirits are subject to you; but rejoice that your names are written in heaven."

S *At that time Jesus declared, "I* [4]*thank thee, Father, Lord* 11: *of heaven and earth, that thou hast hidden these things from* 25 *the wise and understanding and revealed them to babes; yea, Father,* [5]*for such was thy gracious will.*   26

S In that same hour he rejoiced [3]*in the Holy Spirit and* 21 said, "I [4]*thank thee, Father, Lord of heaven and earth, that thou hast hidden these things from the wise and understanding and revealed them to babes; yea, Father,* [5]*for such was thy gracious will.*

---

1 Or *simple*   2 Greek *powers*   3 Or *by*   4 Or *praise*   5 Greek *for so it was well-pleasing before you*

HS references: Mt 10:15 and Lk 10:12 = Genesis 19:24-28   Mt 11:23a and Lk 10:15 = Isaiah 14:13-15   Mt 11:23b-24 and Lk 10:12 = Genesis 19:24 Lk 10:20 = Exodus 32:32 and Psalm 69:28 and Daniel 12:1

L Compare portion P below
P Compare portion L above
Q Whoever receives one such child in my name receives me. (§ 78 F = Mt 18:5)   Q Whoever receives one such child in my name receives me; and whoever receives me, receives not me but him who sent me. (§ 78 FG = Mk 9:37)   Q Whoever receives this child in my name receives me, and whoever receives me receives him who sent me. (§ 78 FG = Lk 9:48)
R For another record of a report on a Tour, compare § 59
R And these signs will accompany those who believe: in my name they will cast out demons; they will speak in new tongues; they will pick up serpents, and if they drink any deadly thing, it will not hurt them; they will lay their hands on the sick, and they will recover. (§ 150 footnote E)

MATTHEW

T^T *All things have been delivered to me by my Father; and* 27 *no one knows the Son except the Father, and no one knows the Father except the Son and any one to whom the Son chooses to reveal him. (§ 41 PQ)*

U *But blessed are your eyes, for they see, and your ears,* 13: *for they hear. Truly, I say to you, many prophets and* 16 *righteous men longed to see what you see, and did not see* 17 *it, and to hear what you hear, and did not hear it. (§ 47 K)*

LUKE 10

T^T All things have been delivered to me by my Father; and 22 no one knows who the Son is except the Father, or who the Father is except the Son and any one to whom the Son chooses to reveal him."

U Then turning to the disciples he said privately, "Blessed 23 are the eyes which see what you see! For I tell you that 24 many prophets and kings desired to see what you see, and did not see it, and to hear what you hear, and did not hear it."

§ 83 The Way of Eternal Life
LUKE 10:25-37

A *For an account in Matt-Mark of somewhat similar general content, compare § 130 L-N*

A And behold, a lawyer stood up to put him to the test, 25 saying, "Teacher, what shall I do to inherit eternal life?" He said to him, "What is written in the law? How do you 26 read?" And he answered, "You shall love the Lord your 27 God [1]with all your heart, and with all your soul, and with all your strength, and with all your mind; and your neighbor as yourself." And he said to him, "You have 28 answered right; do this, and you will live."

B But he, desiring to justify himself, said to Jesus, "And 29 who is my neighbor?" Jesus replied,   30

C "A man was going down from Jerusalem to Jericho, and he fell among robbers, who stripped him and beat him, and departed, leaving him half dead. Now by chance a priest 31 was going down that road; and when he saw him he passed by on the other side. So likewise a Levite, when he came 32 to the place and saw him, passed by on the other side. But 33 a Samaritan, as he journeyed, came to where he was; and when he saw him, he had compassion, and went to him and 34 bound up his wounds, pouring on oil and wine; then he set him on his own beast and brought him to an inn, and took care of him. And the next day he took out two [2]denarii and 35 gave them to the innkeeper, saying, 'Take care of him; and whatever more you spend, I will repay you when I come back.'

D Which of these three, do you think, proved neighbor to 36 the man who fell among the robbers?" He said, "The one 37 who showed mercy on him." And Jesus said to him, "Go and do likewise."

§ 84 Many Things *vs* One Thing
LUKE 10:38-42

Now as they went on their way, he entered a village; and a 38 woman named Martha received him into her house. And 39 she had a sister called Mary, who sat at the Lord's feet and listened to his teaching. But Martha was distracted with 40 much serving; and she went to him and said, "Lord, do you not care that my sister has left me to serve alone? Tell her then to help me." But the Lord answered her, 41 [3]"Martha, Martha, you are anxious and troubled about many things; [4]one thing is needful. Mary has chosen the   42

---

1 Greek *from*   2 The word in the Greek denotes a coin worth about forty cents. The denarius was a day's wage for a laborer.   3 A few ancient authorities read *Martha, Martha, you are troubled: Mary has chosen etc.*   4 Many very ancient authorities read *but few things are needful, or one*

HS references Lk 10:27 = Deuteronomy 6:5 and Leviticus 19:18   Lk 10:28 = Leviticus 18:5

T All authority in heaven and on earth has been given to me. (§ 151 B = Mt 28:18)

LUKE **10**
good portion, which shall not be taken away from her."

§ 85 Elements of Prevailing Prayer

MATTHEW

LUKE **11**:1-13

A He was praying in a certain place, and when he ceased, 1 one of his disciples said to him, "Lord, teach us to pray, as John taught his disciples."

B *Pray then like this:*
 Our Father who art in heaven,
 Hallowed be thy name.
 Thy kingdom come,
 Thy will be done,
  On earth as it is in heaven.
 Give us this day ³our daily bread;
 And forgive us our debts,
  As we also have forgiven our debtors;
 And lead us not into temptation,
  But deliver us from evil.⁴ (§ 37 W)

6:
9

10

11
12

13

B And he said to them, "When you pray, say: 2 ¹"Father, hallowed be thy name. Thy kingdom come². Give 3 us each day ³our daily bread; and forgive us our sins, for 4 we ourselves forgive every one who is indebted to us; and lead us not into temptation."

C And he said to them, "Which of you who has a friend 5 will go to him at midnight and say to him, 'Friend, lend me three loaves; for a friend of mine has arrived on a 6 journey, and I have nothing to set before him'; and he will 7 answer from within, 'Do not bother me; the door is now shut, and my children are with me in bed; I cannot get up and give you anything'? I tell you, though he will not get 8 up and give him anything because he is his friend, yet because of his importunity he will rise and give him whatever he needs.

D *"Ask, and it will be given you; seek, and you will find;* 7: *knock, and it will be opened to you. For every one who* 7 *asks receives, and he who seeks finds, and to him who* 8 *knocks it will be opened. Or what man of you, if his son* 9 *asks him for bread, will give him a stone? Or if he asks for* 10 *a fish, will give him a serpent? If you then, who are evil,* 11 *know how to give good gifts to your children, how much more will your Father who is in heaven give good things to those who ask him! (§ 38 K)*

D And I tell you, Ask, and it will be given you; seek, and 9 you will find; knock, and it will be opened to you. For 10 every one who asks receives, and he who seeks finds, and to him who knocks it will be opened. What father among 11 you, if his son asks for⁵ a fish, will instead of a fish give him a serpent; or if he asks for an egg, will give him a 12 scorpion? If you then, who are evil, know how to give 13 good gifts to your children, how much more will the heavenly Father give the Holy Spirit to those who ask him!"

§ 86 A Charge of Alliance with Satan

MATTHEW 12

LUKE **11**:14-26

Aᴬ *Then a blind and dumb demoniac was brought to him,* 22 *and he healed him, so that the dumb man spoke and saw.*

Aᴬ Now he was casting out a demon that was dumb; when 14 the demon had gone out, the dumb man spoke,

Bᴮ *And all the people were amazed, and said, "Can this be* 23 *the Son of David?"*

Bᴮ and the people marveled.

Cᶜ *But when the Pharisees heard it they said, "it is only* 24 *⁶by Beelzebul, the prince of demons, that*

Cᶜ But some of them said, "He casts out demons ⁶by 15 Be-el'zebul, the prince of demons";

---

1 Many ancient authorities read *Our Father, who art in heaven*: see Matt 6:9 2 Many ancient authorities add *Thy will be done, on earth as it is in heaven*: see Matt 6:10 3 Greek *our bread for the coming day* 4 Many authorities, some ancient, but with variations, add *For Thine is the kingdom, and the power, and the glory, for ever. Amen* 5 Some ancient authorities add *a loaf, will he give him a stone? or if he asks for* 6 Or in

---

ABC For another Matthew account covering portions ABC, compare § 53 B
C *Matt parallel shown above under C*

C And the scribes who came down from Jerusalem said, "He is possessed by Beelzebul, and by the prince of demons he casts out the demons." (§ 45 C = Mk 3:22)

MATT 12   LUKE 11

this man casts out demons."

D *Compare § 45 Q and attached references*

D while others, to test him, sought from him a sign from 16 heaven.

E[E] *Knowing their thoughts, he said to them, "Every* 25 *kingdom divided against itself is laid waste, and no city or house divided against itself will stand; and if Satan casts* 26 *out Satan, he is divided against himself; how then will his kingdom stand?*

E[E] But he, knowing their thoughts, said to them, "Every 17 kingdom divided against itself is laid waste, [1]and a divided household falls. And if Satan also is divided against 18 himself, how will his kingdom stand? For you say that I cast out demons by Be-el'zebul.

F *And if I cast out demons* [2]*by Be-el'zebul, by whom do* 27 *your sons cast them out? Therefore they shall be your judges. But if it is* [2]*by the Spirit of God that I cast out* 28 *demons, then the kingdom of God has come upon you.*

F And if I cast out demons [2]by Be-el'zebul, by whom do 19 your sons cast them out? Therefore they shall be your judges. But if it is by the finger of God that I cast out 20 demons, then the kingdom of God has come upon you.

G[G] *Or how can one enter a strong man's house and* 29 *plunder his goods, unless he first binds the strong man? Then indeed he may plunder his house.*

G[G] When a strong man, fully armed, guards his own 21 palace, his goods are in peace; but when one stronger than 22 he assails him and overcomes him, he takes away his armor in which he trusted, and divides his spoil.

H[H] *He who is not with me is against me, and he who does* 30 *not gather with me scatters. (§ 45 A-H)*

H[H] He who is not with me is against me, and he who does 23 not gather with me scatters.

I *"When the unclean spirit has gone out of a man,* [3]*he* 43 *passes through waterless places seeking rest, but* [3]*he finds none. Then* [3]*he says, 'I will return to my house from which* 44 *I came.' And when* [3]*he comes he finds it empty, swept, and put in order. Then* [3]*he goes and brings with* [4]*him seven* 45 *other spirits more evil than* [4]*himself, and they enter and dwell there; and the last state of that man becomes worse than the first. So shall it be also with this evil generation." (§ 45 W)*

I "When the unclean spirit has gone out of a man, [3]he 24 passes through waterless places seeking rest; and finding none he says, 'I will return to my house from which I came.' And when he comes he finds it swept and put in 25 order. Then [3]he goes and brings seven other spirits more 26 evil than [4]himself, and they enter and dwell there; and the last state of that man becomes worse than the first."

§ 87 Basis of Real Relationship to Jesus

LUKE 11:27-28

For an account in Matt-Mark-Luke of similar general content, compare § 46

As he said this, a woman in the crowd raised her voice and 27 said to him, "Blessed is the womb that bore you, and the breasts that you sucked!" But he said, "Blessed rather are 28 those who hear the word of God and keep it!"

---

1 Or *and house falls upon house*   2 Or *in*   3 Or *it*   4 Or *itself*

NC references: Lk 11:27-28 = GT 79

E *Matt parallel shown above under E*

E And he called them to him, and said to them in parables, How can Satan cast out Satan? If a kingdom is divided against itself, that kingdom cannot stand. And if a house is divided against itself, that house will not be able to stand. And if Satan has risen up against himself and is divided, he cannot stand, but is coming to an end.

G *Matt parallel shown above under G*

G But no one can enter a strong man's house and plunder his goods, unless he first binds the strong man; then indeed he may plunder his house. (§ 45 E-G = Mk 3:23-27)

H With the first half of this saying, compare the last verse of § 78 portion I

Chapter XIV

CONDEMNATION FOR OPPONENTS AND CONCERN FOR DISCIPLES

§ 88 Pharisees Demand Signs from Jesus

MATT 12:38-42	LUKE 11:29-32
A *Then some of the scribes and Pharisees said to him,* 38 *"Teacher, we wish to see a sign from you."*	**A** *Compare § 86 portion D*
B^B *But he answered them, "An evil and adulterous gener-* 39 *ation seeks for a sign; but no sign shall be given to it except the sign of the prophet Jonah.*	**B**^B When the crowds were increasing, he began to say, 29 "This generation is an evil generation; it seeks a sign, but no sign shall be given to it except the sign of Jonah.
C *For as Jonah was three days and three nights in the belly* 40 *of the ¹whale, so will the Son of man be three days and three nights in the heart of the earth.*	**C** For as Jonah became a sign to the men of Nin'eveh, so 30 will the Son of man be to this generation.
D *Compare portion F below*	**D** The queen of the South will arise at the judgment with 31 the men of this generation and condemn them; for she came from the ends of the earth to hear the wisdom of Solomon, and behold, ²something greater than Solomon is here.
E *The men of Nin'eveh will arise at the judgment with this* 41 *generation and condemn it; for they repented at the preaching of Jonah, and behold, ²something greater than Jonah is here.*	**E** The men of Nin'eveh will arise at the judgment with this 32 generation and condemn it; for they repented at the preaching of Jonah, and behold, ²something greater than Jonah is here.
F *The queen of the South will arise at the judgment with* 42 *this generation and condemn it; for she came from the ends of the earth to hear the wisdom of Solomon, and behold, ²something greater than Solomon is here.* (§ 45 Q-V)	**F** *Compare portion D above*

§ 89 The Use and Test of Truth

MATTHEW	LUKE 11:33-36
A *Nor do men light a lamp and put it under a bushel, but* 5: *on a stand, and it gives light to all in the house.* 15 (§ 36 N)	**A** "No one after lighting a lamp puts it in a cellar or 33 under a bushel, but on a stand, that those who enter may see the light.

---

1 Greek *sea-monster* 2 Greek *more than*

HS references: Mt 12:39 and Lk 11:29 = Jonah 3:1-4   Mt 12:40 = Jonah 1:17   Mt 12:42 and Lk 11:31 = I Kings 10:1-3 and II Chronicles 9:1-9
Mt 12:41 and Lk 11:32 = Jonah 3:5-10
NC references: Mt 5:15 and Lk 11:33 = GT 33

A And the Pharisees and Sadducees came, and to test him they asked him to show them a sign from heaven. B He answered them, . . . An evil and adulterous generation seeks for a sign, but no sign shall be given to it except the sign of Jonah. So he left them and departed. (§ 68 A-D = Mt 16:1-4)	A The Pharisees came and began to argue with him, seeking from him a sign from heaven, to test him. B And he sighed deeply in his spirit, and said, Why does this generation seek a sign? Truly, I say to you, no sign shall be given to this generation. And he left them, and getting into the boat again he departed to the other side. (§ 68 A-D = Mk 8:11-13)	

	A Is a lamp brought in to be put under a bushel, or under a bed, and not on a stand? (§ 47 Q = Mk 4:21)	A No one after lighting a lamp covers it with a vessel, or puts it under a bed, but puts it on a stand, that those who enter may see the light. (§ 47 Q = Lk 8:16)

MATTHEW	LUKE 11
B *"The eye is the lamp of the body. So, if your eye is* 6: *¹sound, your whole body will be full of light; but if your eye* 22 *is ²not sound, your whole body will be full of darkness.* 23	**B** Your eye is the lamp of your body; when your eye is 34 ¹sound, your whole body is full of light; but when it is ²not sound, your body is full of darkness.
C *If then the light in you is darkness, how great is the darkness! (§ 38 B)*	**C** Therefore be careful lest the light in you be darkness. 35
	D If then your whole body is full of light, having no part 36 dark, it will be wholly bright, as when a lamp with its rays gives you light."

§ 90   Discourse on the Scribes and Pharisees

MATTHEW 23	LUKE 11:37-54
A *Compare § 63 portions ABC*	**A** While he was speaking, a Pharisee asked him to ³dine 37 with him; so he went in and sat at table. The Pharisee was 38 astonished to see that he did not first wash before ³dinner. And the Lord said to him, 39
B *"Woe to you, scribes and Pharisees, hypocrites! for you* 25 *cleanse the outside of the cup and of the plate, but inside they are full of extortion and rapacity. You blind Pharisee!* 26 *first cleanse the inside of the cup and of the plate, that the outside also may be clean. (§ 132 M)*	**B** "Now you Pharisees cleanse the outside of the cup and of the dish, but inside you are full of extortion and wickedness. You fools! Did not he who made the outside 40 make the inside also? But give for alms those things which 41 ⁴are within; and behold, everything is clean for you.
C *"Woe to you, scribes and Pharisees, hypocrites! for you* 23 *tithe mint and dill and cummin, and have neglected the weightier matters of the law, justice and mercy and faith; these you ought to have done, without neglecting the others. You blind guides, straining out a gnat and swallowing a* 24 *camel! (§ 132 L)*	**C** "But woe to you Pharisees! for you tithe mint and rue 42 and every herb, and neglect justice and the love of God; these you ought to have done, without neglecting the others.
Dᴰ *They do all their deeds to be seen by men; for they* 5 *make their phylacteries broad and their fringes long, and* 6 *they love the place of honor at feasts and the best seats in the synagogues, and salutations in the market places, and* 7 *being called rabbi by men. (§ 132 D)*	**Dᴰ** Woe to you Pharisees! for you love the best seat in the 43 synagogues and salutations in the market places.
E *"Woe to you, scribes and Pharisees, hypocrites! for you* 27 *are like whitewashed tombs, which outwardly appear beautiful, but within they are full of dead men's bones and all uncleanness. So you also outwardly appear righteous to* 28 *men, but within you are full of hypocrisy and iniquity. (§ 132 N)*	**E** Woe to you! for you are like graves which are not seen, 44 and men walk over them without knowing it."
	F One of the lawyers answered him, "Teacher, in saying 45 this you reproach us also." And he said, 46
G *They bind heavy burdens, ⁵hard to bear, and lay them on* 4 *men's shoulders; but they themselves will not move them with their finger. (§ 132 C)*	**G** "Woe to you lawyers also! for you load men with burdens hard to bear, and you yourselves do not touch the burdens with one of your fingers.

---

1 Greek *single*   2 Greek *evil*   3 Or *breakfast*   4 Or *you can*   5 Many ancient authorities omit *hard to bear*

HS references: Mt 23:5 = Exodus 13:9 and Numbers 15:38-39 and Deuteronomy 6:8 and 11:18   Mt 23:23 and Lk 11:42 = Leviticus 27:30 and Micah 6:8
NC references: Mt 6:22-23 and Lk 11:34-36 = GT 24

D *Matt parallel shown above under D*	D Beware of the scribes, who like to go about in long robes, and to have salutations in the market places and the best seats in the synagogues and the places of honor at feasts. (§ 132 D = Mk 12:38-39)	D Beware of the scribes, who like to go about in long robes, and love salutations in the market places and the best seats in the synagogues and the places of honor at feasts. (§ 132 D = Lk 20:46)

MATT 23	LUKE 11
H *"Woe to you, scribes and Pharisees, hypocrites! for you* 29 *build the tombs of the prophets and adorn the monuments of* 30 *the righteous, saying, 'If we had lived in the days of our* 30 *fathers, we would not have taken part with them in shedding the blood of the prophets.' Thus you witness* 31 *against yourselves, that you are sons of those who murdered the prophets. (§ 132 O)*	**H** Woe to you! for you build the tombs of the prophets 47 whom your fathers killed. So you are witnesses and consent 48 to the deeds of your fathers; for they killed them, and you build their tombs.
I *Therefore I send you prophets and wise men and scribes,* 34 *some of whom you will kill and crucify, and some you will scourge in your synagogues and persecute from town to town, that upon you may come all the righteous blood shed* 35 *on earth, from the blood of innocent Abel to the blood of Zechari'ah the son of Barachi'ah, whom you murdered between the sanctuary and the altar. Truly, I say to you, all* 36 *this will come upon this generation. (§ 132 Q)*	**I** Therefore also the Wisdom of God said, 'I will send them 49 prophets and apostles, some of whom they will kill and persecute,' that the blood of all the prophets, shed from the 50 foundation of the world, may be required of this generation, from the blood of Abel to the blood of 51 Zechari'ah, who perished between the altar and the ¹sanctuary. Yes, I tell you, it shall be required of this generation.
J *"But woe to you, scribes and Pharisees, hypocrites!* 13 *because you shut the kingdom of heaven ²against men; for you neither enter yourselves, nor allow those who would enter to go in.³ (§ 132 I)*	**J** Woe to you lawyers! for you have taken away the key of 52 knowledge; you did not enter yourselves, and you hindered those who were entering."
	K As he went away from there, the scribes and the 53 Pharisees began to ⁴press him hard, and to provoke him to speak of ⁵many things, lying in wait for him, to catch at 54 something he might say.

§ 91 Injunctions for the Future of the Disciples

MATTHEW	LUKE 12:1-12
	A In the meantime, when ⁶so many thousands of the 1 multitude had gathered together that they trod upon one another, he began to ⁷say to his disciples first,
Bᴮ *Beware of the leaven of the Pharisees and Sadducees.* 16: *(§ 69 D)* 11	**B**ᴮ "Beware of the leaven of the Pharisees, which is hypocrisy.
Cᶜ *for nothing is covered that will not be revealed, or* 10: *hidden that will not be known.* 26	**C**ᶜ Nothing is covered up that will not be revealed, or 2 hidden that will not be known.
D *What I tell you in the dark, utter in the light; and what* 27 *you hear whispered, proclaim upon the housetops.*	**D** Therefore whatever you have said in the dark shall be 3 heard in the light, and what you have whispered in private rooms shall be proclaimed upon the housetops.
E *And do not fear those who kill the body but cannot kill* 28 *the soul; rather fear him who can destroy both soul and body in ⁹hell.*	**E** "I tell you, my friends, do not fear those who kill the 4 body, and after that have no more that they can do. But I 5 will warn you whom to fear: fear him who, after he has killed, has ⁸power to cast into ⁹hell; yes, I tell you, fear him!

---

1 Greek *house*   2 Greek *before*   3 Some authorities insert here, or after verse 12, verse 14: *Woe to you, scribes and Pharisees, hypocrites! for you devour widows' houses, and for a pretense you make long prayers; therefore you will receive the greater condemnation:* see Mark 12:40 and Luke 20:47
4 Or *set themselves vehemently against him*   5 Or *more*   6 Greek *the myriads of*   7 Or *say to his disciples, First of all beware you*
8 Or *authority*   9 Greek *Gehenna*

HS references: Mt 23:35 and Lk 11:50-51 = Genesis 4:8 and II Chronicles 24:20-21
NC references: Mt 10:26 and Lk 12:2 = GT 5,6

| B Take heed and beware of the leaven of the Pharisees and Sadducees. (§ 69 A = Mt 16:6) | B Take heed, beware of the leaven of the Pharisees and the leaven of Herod. (§ 69 A = Mk 8:15) | |
| | C For there is nothing hid, except to be made manifest; nor is anything secret, except to come to light. (§ 47 R = Mk 4:22) | C For nothing is hid that shall not be made manifest, nor anything secret that shall not be known and come to light. (§ 47 R = Lk 8:17) |

MATTHEW

F^F *Are not two sparrows sold for a penny? And not one of* 10: *them will fall to the ground without your Father's will. But* 29 *even the hairs of your head are all numbered. Fear not,* 30 *therefore; you are of more value than many sparrows.* 31

G^G *So every one who acknowledges* ¹*me before men,* ²*I also* 32 *will acknowledge before my Father who is in heaven; but* 33 *whoever denies me before men, I also will deny before my Father who is in heaven. (§ 57 H-K)*

H^H *And whoever says a word against the Son of man will* 12: *be forgiven; but whoever speaks against the Holy Spirit will* 32 *not be forgiven, either in this age or in the age to come.* *(§ 45 J)*

I^I *When they deliver you up, do not be anxious how you are* 10: *to speak or what you are to say; for what you are to say* 19 *will be given to you in that hour; for it is not you who* 20 *speak, but the Spirit of your Father speaking through you.* *(§ 57 C)*

LUKE 12

F^F Are not five sparrows sold for two pennies? And not 6 one of them is forgotten before God. Why, even the hairs 7 of your head are all numbered. Fear not; you are of more value than many sparrows.

G^G "And I tell you, every one who acknowledges ¹me 8 before men, ²the Son of man also will acknowledge before the angels of God; but he who denies me before men will 9 be denied before the angels of God.

H^H And every one who speaks a word against the Son of 10 man will be forgiven; but he who blasphemes against the Holy Spirit will not be forgiven.

I^I And when they bring you before the synagogues and the 11 rulers and the authorities, do not be anxious how or what you are to answer or what you are to say; for the Holy 12 Spirit will teach you in that very hour what you ought to say."

§ 92 Teachings Against Concern about Wealth

LUKE 12:13-21

A One of the multitude said to him, "Teacher, bid my 13 brother divide the inheritance with me." But he said to him, 14 "Man, who made me a judge or divider over you?" And he 15 said to them, "Take heed, and beware of all covetousness; ³for a man's life does not consist in the abundance of his possessions."

B And he told them a parable, saying, "The land of a rich 16 man brought forth plentifully; and he thought to himself, 17 'What shall I do, for I have nowhere to store my crops?' And he said, 'I will do this: I will pull down my barns, 18 and build larger ones; and there I will store all my grain and my goods. And I will say to my ⁴soul, 'Soul, you have 19 ample goods laid up for many years; take your ease, eat,

---

1 Greek *in me*   2 Greek *in him*   3 Greek *for not in a man's abundance consists his life, from the things which he possesses*   4 Or *life*

NC references: Lk 12:13-14 = GT 72

F But not a hair of your head will perish. (§ 134 M = Lk 21:18)

G For the Son of man is to come with his angels in the glory of his Father, and then he will repay every man for what he has done. (§ 73 C = Mt 16:27)

H Therefore I tell you, every sin and blasphemy will be forgiven men, but the blasphemy against the Spirit will not be forgiven . . . either in this age or in the age to come. (§ 45 I-K = Mt 12:31-32)

G For whoever is ashamed of me and of my words in this adulterous and sinful generation, of him will the Son of man also be ashamed, when he comes in the glory of his Father with the holy angels. (§ 73 C = Mk 8:38)

H Truly, I say to you, all sins will be forgiven the sons of men, and whatever blasphemies they utter; but whoever blasphemes against the Holy Spirit never has forgiveness, but is guilty of an eternal sin. (§ 45 I-K = Mk 3:28-30)

I And when they bring you to trial and deliver you up, do not be anxious beforehand what you are to say; but say whatever is given you in that hour, for it is not you who speak, but the Holy Spirit. (§ 134 I = Mk 13:11)

G For whoever is ashamed of me and of my words, of him will the Son of man be ashamed when he comes in his glory and the glory of the Father and of the holy angels. (§ 73 C = Lk 9:26)

I Settle it therefore in your minds, not to meditate beforehand how to answer; for I will give you a mouth and wisdom, which none of your adversaries will be able to withstand or contradict. (§ 134 I = Lk 21:14-15)

LUKE 12

drink, be merry.' But God said to him, 'Fool! This night 20 [1]your [2]soul is required of you; and the things you have prepared, whose will they be?'

C So is he who lays up treasure for himself, and is not rich 21 toward God."

§ 93 Teaching against Anxiety about Food and Clothing

MATTHEW 6   LUKE 12:22-34

A And he said to his disciples,   22

B *"Therefore I tell you, do not be anxious about your life,* 25 *what you shall eat or what you shall drink, nor about your body, what you shall put on. Is not life more than food, and the body more than clothing?*

B "Therefore I tell you, do not be anxious about your life, what you shall eat, nor about your body, what you shall put on. For [3]life is more than food, and the body more than 23 clothing.

C *Look at the birds of the air; they neither sow nor reap* 26 *nor gather into barns, and yet your heavenly Father feeds them. Are you not of more value than they?*

C Consider the ravens: they neither sow nor reap, they 24 have neither storehouse nor barn, and yet God feeds them. Of how much more value are you than the birds!

D *And which of you by being anxious can add one cubit to* 27 *his [4]span of life? And why are you anxious about clothing?* 28

D And which of you by being anxious can add a cubit to 25 his [4]span of life? If then you are not able to do as small a 26 thing as that, why are you anxious about the rest?

E *Consider the lilies of the field, how they grow; they* *neither toil nor spin; yet I tell you, even Solomon in all his* 29 *glory was not arrayed like one of these. But if God so* 30 *clothes the grass of the field, which today is alive and tomorrow is thrown into the oven, will he not much more clothe you, O men of little faith?*

E Consider the lilies, how they grow; they neither toil nor 27 spin; yet I tell you, even Solomon in all his glory was not arrayed like one of these. But if God so clothes the grass 28 which is alive in the field today and tomorrow is thrown into the oven, how much more will he clothe you, O men of little faith!

F[F] *Therefore do not be anxious, saying, 'What shall we* 31 *eat?' or 'What shall we drink?' or 'What shall we wear?' For the Gentiles seek all these things; and your heavenly* 32 *Father knows that you need them all.*

F[F] And do not seek what you are to eat and what you are 29 to drink, nor be of anxious mind. For all the nations of the 30 world seek these things; and your Father knows that you need them.

G *But seek first his kingdom and his righteousness, and all* 33 *these things shall be yours as well.*

G Instead, seek [5]his kingdom, and these things shall be 31 yours as well.

H *"Therefore do not be anxious about tomorrow, for* 34 *tomorrow will be anxious for itself. Let the day's own trouble be sufficient for the day. (§ 38 DE)*

H "Fear not, little flock, for it is your Father's good 32 pleasure to give you the kingdom.

I *"Do not lay up for yourselves treasures on earth, where* 19 *moth and rust consume and where thieves [6]break in and steal,*

I Sell your possessions, and give alms;   33

J *but lay up for yourselves treasures in heaven, where* 20 *neither moth nor rust consumes and where thieves do not* [6]*break in and steal.*

J provide yourselves with purses that do not grow old, with a treasure in the heavens that does not fail, where no thief approaches and no moth destroys.

K *For where your treasure is, there will your heart be also.* 21 *(§ 38 A)*

K For where your treasure is, there will your heart be also. 34

---

1 Greek *they require your soul*   2 Or *life*   3 Or *the soul*   4 Or *stature*   5 Many very ancient authorities read *the kingdom of God*
6 Greek *dig through*

HS references: Lk 12:20 = Jeremiah 17:11 and Job 27:8 and Psalm 90:10-12   Mt 6:29 and Lk 12:27 = I Kings 10:1-10
NC references: Lk 12:16-21 = GT 63   Mt 6:25 and Lk 12:22-23 = GT 36   Mt 6:19-20 and Lk 12:33 = GT 76

F Do not be like them, for your Father knows what you need before you ask him. (§ 37 V = Mt 6:8)

§ 94 Teachings about the Future

MATT 24:43-51   LUKE 12:35-48

A *Compare the parable recorded in § 136 portion E = Matt 25:1-10*

A "Let your loins be girded and your lamps burning, and 35 be like men who are waiting for their master to come home 36 from the marriage feast, so that they may open to him at once when he comes and knocks. Blessed are those 37 [1]servants whom the master finds awake when he comes; truly, I say to you, he will gird himself and have them sit at table, and he will come and serve them. If he comes in 38 the second watch, or in the third, and finds them so, blessed are those servants!

B [2]*But know this, that if the householder had known in what part of the night the thief was coming, he would have watched and would not have let his house be broken into.* 43

B [2]But know this, that if the householder had known at 39 what hour the thief was coming, he would [3]not have left his house to be [4]broken into.

C[C] *Therefore you also must be ready; for the Son of man is coming at an hour you do not expect.* 44

C[C] You also must be ready; for the Son of man is coming 40 at an unexpected hour."

D Peter said, "Lord, are you telling this parable for us or 41 for all?" And the Lord said, 42

E *"Who then is the faithful and wise [6]servant, whom his master has set over his household, to give them their food at the proper time? Blessed is that [6]servant whom his master when he comes will find so doing. Truly, I say to you, he will set him over all his possessions. But if that wicked [6]servant says to himself, 'My master is delayed,' and begins to beat his fellow servants, and eats and drinks with the drunken, the master of that [6]servant will come on a day when he does not expect him and at an hour he does not know, and will [7]punish him, and put him with the hypocrites;* 45 46 47 48 49 50 51

E "Who then is [5]the faithful and wise steward, whom his master will set over his household, to give them their portion of food at the proper time? Blessed is that [6]servant 43 whom his master when he comes will find so doing. Truly, 44 I say to you, he will set him over all his possessions. But if 45 that [6]servant says to himself, 'My master is delayed in coming,' and begins to beat the menservants and the maidservants, and to eat and drink and get drunk, the 46 master of that [6]servant will come on a day when he does not expect him and at an hour he does not know, and will [7]punish him, and put him with the unfaithful.

F[F] *there men will weep and gnash their teeth. (§ 136 A-D)*

G And that [6]servant who knew his master's will, but did 47 not make ready or act according to his will, shall receive a severe beating. But he who did not know, and did what 48 deserved a beating, shall receive a light beating.

H Every one to whom much is given, of him will much be required; and of him to whom men commit much they will demand the more.

---

1 Or *slaves*   2 Or *But this you know*   3 Some ancient authorities add *have watched, and*   4 Greek *digged through*
5 Or *the faithful steward the wise* man *whom etc.*   6 Or *slave*   7 Or *cut him in pieces*

HS references: Lk 12:47-48 = Deuteronomy 25:2-3 and Numbers 15:29-30

C Compare § 136 B and attached references
F Compare § 136 D and attached references

Chapter XV
DEEP FEELING AND DIRECT TEACHING

§ 95 Phases of the Mission of Jesus

MATT 10:34-36

LUKE 12:49-53

A^ "I came to cast fire upon the earth; and [1]would that it were already kindled! I have a baptism to be baptized with; and how I am [2]constrained until it is accomplished! 49 50

B *"Do not think that I have come to [3]bring peace on earth;* 34 *I have not come to [3]bring peace, but a sword. For I have* 35 *come to set a man against his father, and a daughter against her mother, and a daughter-in-law against her mother-in-law; and a man's foes will be those of his own* 36 *household. (§ 57 L)*

B Do you think that I have come to give peace on earth? 51 No, I tell you, but rather division; for henceforth in one 52 house there will be five divided, three against two and two against three; they will be divided, father against son and 53 son against father, mother against daughter and daughter against her mother, mother-in-law against her daughter-in-law and daughter-in-law against her mother-in-law."

§ 96 The Signs of the Times

MATTHEW

LUKE 12:54-59

A *He answered them,*[4] *"When it is evening, you say, 'It will* 16: *be fair weather; for the sky is red.' And in the morning, 'It* 2 *will be stormy today, for the sky is red and threatening.'* 3 *You know how to interpret the appearance of the sky, but you cannot interpret the signs of the times. (§ 68 B)*

A He also said to the multitudes, "When you see a cloud 54 rising in the west, you say at once, 'A shower is coming'; and so it happens. And when you see the south wind 55 blowing, you say, 'There will be [5]scorching heat'; and it happens. You hypocrites! You know how to [6]interpret the 56 appearance of earth and sky; but why do you not know how to [6]interpret the present time?

B "And why do you not judge for yourselves what is right? 57

C *Make friends quickly with your accuser, while you are* 5: *going with him to court, lest your accuser hand you over to* 25 *the judge, and the judge [7]to the guard, and you be put in prison; truly, I say to you, you will never get out till you* 26 *have paid the last penny. (§ 37 B)*

C As you go with your accuser before the magistrate, make 58 an effort to settle with him on the way, lest he drag you to the judge, and the judge hand you over to the [8]officer, and the [8]officer put you in prison. I tell you, you will never get 59 out till you have paid the very last copper."

§ 97 Warnings of Impending Fate

LUKE 13:1-9

A There were some present at that very time who told him 1 of the Galileans whose blood Pilate had mingled with their sacrifices. And he answered them, "Do you think that these 2 Galileans were worse sinners than all the other Galileans, because they suffered thus? I tell you, No; but unless you 3 repent you will all likewise perish.

B Or those eighteen upon whom the tower in Silo'am fell 4 and killed them, do you think that they were worse [9]offenders than all the others who dwelt in Jerusalem? I tell 5 you, No; but unless you repent you will all likewise perish."

---

1 Greek *what will I if it is already kindled?*   2 Greek *straitened*   3 Greek *cast*   4 The following words, to the end of verse 3, are omitted by some of the most ancient and other important authorities   5 Or *hot wind*   6 Greek *prove*   7 Some ancient authorities add *deliver you* 8 Greek *exactor* 9 Greek *debtors*

HS references: Mt 10:35-36 and Lk 12:52-53 = Micah 7:6

A Or to be baptized with the baptism with which I am baptized? (§ 120 D = Mk 10:38)
A And with the baptism with which I am baptized, you will be baptized. (§ 120 F = Mk 10:39)

LUKE 13

C And he told this parable: "A man had a fig tree planted 6 in his vineyard; and he came seeking fruit on it and found none. And he said to the vinedresser, 'Lo, these three years 7 I have come seeking fruit on this fig tree, and I find none. Cut it down; why should it use up the ground?' And he 8 answered him, 'Let it alone, sir, this year also, till I dig about it and put on manure. And if it bears fruit next year, 9 well and good; but if not, you can cut it down.'"

§ 98 Jesus Censured for Sabbath Healing

LUKE 13:10-17

A Now he was teaching in one of the synagogues on the 10 sabbath. And there was a woman who had had a spirit of 11 infirmity for eighteen years; she was bent over and could not fully straighten herself. And when Jesus saw her, he 12 called her and said to her, "Woman, you are freed from your infirmity." And he laid his hands upon her, and 13 immediately she was made straight, and she praised God.

B But the ruler of the synagogue, indignant because Jesus 14 had healed on the sabbath, said to the people, "There are six days on which work ought to be done; come on those days and be healed, and not on the sabbath day."

C Then the Lord answered him, "You hypocrites! Does not 15 each of you on the sabbath untie his ox or his ass from the manger, and lead it away to water it? And ought not this 16 woman, a daughter of Abraham whom Satan bound for eighteen years, be loosed from this bond on the sabbath day?"

D As he said this, all his adversaries were put to shame; 17 and all the people rejoiced at all the glorious things that were done by him.

§ 99 Parables of the Kingdom of God

MATT 13:31-33

A^ *Another parable he put before them, saying, "The 31 kingdom of heaven is like a grain of mustard seed which a man took and sowed in his field; it is the smallest of all 32 seeds, but when it has grown it is the greatest of shrubs and becomes a tree, so that the birds of the air come and make nests in its branches."*

LUKE 13:18-21

A^ He said therefore, "What is the kingdom of God like? 18 And to what shall I compare it? It is like a grain of 19 mustard seed which a man took and sowed in his garden; and it grew and became a tree, and the birds of the air made nests in its branches."

HS references: Mt 13:32 and Lk 13:19 = Daniel 4:10-12 and 20-22   Lk 13:14 = Exodus 20:8-11 and Deuteronomy 5:12-15

A Matt parallel shown above under A

A And he said, "With what can we compare the kingdom of God, or what parable shall we use for it? It is like a grain of mustard seed, which, when sown upon the ground, is the smallest of all the seeds on earth; yet when it is sown it grows up and becomes the greatest of all shrubs, and puts forth large branches, so that the birds of the air can make nests in its shade." (§ 48 E = Mk 4:30-32)

MATTHEW 13   LUKE 13

B *He told them another parable. "The kingdom of heaven is* 33 *like leaven which a woman took and hid in three* [1]*measures of flour, till it was all leavened." (§ 48 EF)*

B And again he said, "To what shall I compare the 20 kingdom of God? It is like leaven which a woman took and 21 hid in three [1]measures of flour, till it was all leavened."

§ 100 Limits of the Kingdom of God

MATTHEW   LUKE 13:22-30

A He went on his way through towns and villages, 22 teaching, and journeying toward Jerusalem.

B And some one said to him, "Lord, will those who are 23 saved be few?" And he said to them,

C *"Enter by the narrow gate; for*[2] *the gate is wide and the* 7: *way is easy, that leads to destruction, and those who enter* 13 *by it are many.* [3]*For the gate is narrow and the way is* 14 *hard, that leads to life, and those who find it are few.* (§ 38 M)

C "Strive to enter by the narrow door; for many, I tell 24 you, will seek to enter and will not be [4]able.

D *and the door was shut. Afterward the other maidens* 25: *came also, saying, 'Lord, lord, open to us.' But he replied,* 11 *'Truly, I say to you, I do not know you.' (§ 136 F)* 12

D When once the householder has risen up and shut the 25 door, you will begin to stand outside and to knock at the door, saying, 'Lord, open to us.' He will answer you, 'I do not know where you come from.'

E *On that day many will say to me, 'Lord, Lord, did we* 7: *not prophesy in your name, and cast out demons in your* 22 *name, and do many* [5]*mighty works in your name?'*

E Then you will begin to say, 'We ate and drank in your 26 presence, and you taught in our streets.'

F *And then will I declare to them, 'I never knew you;* 23 *depart from me, you evildoers.' (§ 38 V)*

F But he will say, 'I tell you, I do not know where you 27 come from; depart from me, all you workers of iniquity!'

G[G] *"I tell you, many will come from east and west and* [6]*sit* 8: *at table with Abraham, Isaac, and Jacob in the kingdom of* 11 *heaven, while the sons of the kingdom will be thrown into* 12 *the outer darkness; there men will weep and gnash their teeth." (§ 39 D)*

G[G] There you will weep and gnash your teeth, when you 28 see Abraham and Isaac and Jacob and all the prophets in the kingdom of God and you yourselves thrust out. And 29 men will come from east and west, and from north and south, and [6]sit at table in the kingdom of God.

H[H] *"So the last will be first, and the first last."* (§ 118 B)   20:

H[H] And behold, some are last who will be first, and some 30 16 are first who will be last."

---

1 The word in the Greek denotes the Hebrew *seah*, a measure containing nearly a peck and a half   2 Some ancient authorities read *For wide and broad is the way that leads to destruction. . . .*   3 Many ancient authorities read *How narrow is the gate, and straitened the way, etc.*   4 Or *able, when once*   5 Greek *powers*   6 Greek *recline*

HS references: Mt 7:23 and Lk 13:27 = Psalm 6:8   Mt 8:11 and Lk 13:29 = Psalm 107:3 and Isaiah 49:12
NC references: Mt 20:16 and Lk 13:30 = GT 4

G And throw them into the furnace of fire; there men will weep and gnash their teeth. (§ 48 L = Mt 13:42)
G And throw them into the furnace of fire; there men will weep and gnash their teeth. (§ 48 Q = Mt 13:50)
G And cast him into the outer darkness; there men will weep and gnash their teeth. (§ 129 P = Mt 22:13)
G And will punish him, and put him with the hypocrites; there men will weep and gnash their teeth. (§ 136 D = Mt 24:51)
G And cast the worthless servant into the outer darkness; there men will weep and gnash their teeth. (§ 136 Q = Mt 25:30)
G And will punish him, and put him with the unfaithful. (§ 94 E = Lk 12:46)
H But many that are first will be last, and the last first.(§ 117 N = Mt 19:30)
H But many that are first will be last, and the last first.(§ 117 N = Mk 10:31)

§ 101 Forecast of His Death by Jesus

MATT 23:37-39   LUKE 13:31-35

A *For other forecasts of forthcoming events at Jerusalem, compare § 72 A and attached references.*

A At that very hour some Pharisees came, and said to him, 31 "Get away from here, for Herod wants to kill you." And 32 he said to them, "Go and tell that fox, 'Behold, I cast out demons and perform cures today and tomorrow, and the third day I finish my course. Nevertheless I must go on my 33 way today and tomorrow and the day following; for it cannot be that a prophet should perish away from Jerusalem.'

B *"O Jerusalem, Jerusalem, killing the prophets and 37 stoning those who are sent to you! How often would I have gathered your children together as a hen gathers her brood under her wings, and you would not! Behold, your house is 38 forsaken[1] and desolate. For I tell you, you will not see me 39 again, until you say, 'Blessed is he who comes in the name of the Lord.'" (§ 132 R)*

B O Jerusalem, Jerusalem, killing the prophets and stoning 34 those who are sent to you! How often would I have gathered your children together as a hen gathers her brood under her wings, and you would not! Behold, your house is 35 forsaken. And I tell you, you will not see me until you say, 'Blessed is he who comes in the name of the Lord!'"

§ 102 Again Censured for Sabbath Healing

MATT 12:11-12   LUKE 14:1-6

A One sabbath when he went to dine at the house of a ruler 1 who belonged to the Pharisees, they were watching him. And behold, there was a man before him who had dropsy. 2

B[B] And Jesus spoke to the lawyers and Pharisees, saying, 3 "Is it lawful to heal on the sabbath, or not?" But they were 4 silent.

C Then he took him and healed him, and let him go.

D *He said to them, "What man of you, if he has one sheep 11 and it falls into a pit on the sabbath, will not lay hold of it and lift it out? Of how much more value is a man than a 12 sheep! (§ 33 D)*

D And he said to them, "Which of you, having a son or an 5 ox that has fallen into a well, will not immediately pull him out on a sabbath day?"

E And they could not reply to this.   6

§ 103 Teachings at the Table of a Pharisee

MATT 22:2-10   LUKE 14:7-24

A Now he told a parable to those who were invited, when 7 he marked how they chose the places of honor, saying to them, "When you are invited by any one to a marriage 8 feast, do not [2]sit down in a place of honor, lest a more eminent man than you be invited by him; and he who 9 invited you both will come and say to you, 'Give place to this man,' and then you will begin with shame to take the lowest place. But when you are invited, go and sit in the   10

---

1 Some ancient authorities omit *and desolate*   2 Greek *recline*

HS references: Mt 23:38 and Lk 13:35a = Jeremiah 12:7 and 22:5   Mt 23:39 and Lk 13:35b = Psalm 118:26   Lk 14:8 = Proverbs 25:6-7

B So it is lawful to do good on the sabbath. (§ 33 E = Mt 12:12)

B And he said to them, Is it lawful on the sabbath to do good or to do harm, to save life or to kill? But they were silent. (§ 33 E = Mk 3:4)

B And Jesus said to them, I ask you, is it lawful on the sabbath to do good or to do harm, to save life or to destroy it? (§ 33 E = Lk 6:9)

MATT 22

LUKE 14

lowest place, so that when your host comes he may say to you, 'Friend, go up higher'; then you will be honored in the presence of all who sit at table with you.

B[B] For every one who exalts himself will be humbled, and 11 he who humbles himself will be exalted."

C He said also to the man who had invited him, "When 12 you give a dinner or a banquet, do not invite your friends or your brothers or your kinsmen or rich neighbors, lest they also invite you in return, and you be repaid. But when 13 you give a feast, invite the poor, the maimed, the lame, the blind, and you will be blessed, because they cannot repay 14 you. You will be repaid at the resurrection of the just."

D When one of those who sat at table with him heard this, 15 he said to him, "Blessed is he who shall eat bread in the kingdom of God!"

E *"The kingdom of heaven may be compared to a king who* 2 *gave a marriage feast for his son, and sent his* [1]*servants to* 3 *call those who were invited to the marriage feast; but they would not come. Again he sent other* [1]*servants, saying, 'Tell* 4 *those who are invited, Behold, I have made ready my dinner, my oxen and my fat calves are killed, and everything is ready; come to the marriage feast.'*

E But he said to him, "A man once gave a great banquet, 16 and invited many; and at the time for the banquet he sent 17 his [2]servant to say to those who had been invited, 'Come; for all is now ready.'

F *But they made light of it and went off, one to his farm,* 5 *another to his business, while the rest seized his* [1]*servants,* 6 *treated them shamefully, and killed them.*

F But they all alike began to make excuses. The first said 18 to him, 'I have bought a field, and I must go out and see it; I pray you, have me excused.' And another said, 'I have 19 bought five yoke of oxen, and I go to examine them; I pray you, have me excused.' And another said, 'I have married 20 a wife, and therefore I cannot come.' So the [2]servant came 21 and reported this to his master.

G *The king was angry, and he sent his troops and* 7 *destroyed those murderers and burned their city.*

H *Then he said to his* [1]*servants, 'The wedding is ready, but* 8 *those invited were not worthy. Go therefore to the* 9 *thoroughfares, and invite to the marriage feast as many as you find.' And those* [1]*servants went out into the streets and* 10 *gathered all whom they found, both bad and good; so the wedding hall was filled with guests. (§ 129 L-O)*

H Then the householder in anger said to his [2]servant, 'Go out quickly to the streets and lanes of the city, and bring in the poor and maimed and blind and lame.' And the 22 [2]servant said, 'Sir, what you commanded has been done, and still there is room.' And the master said to the 23 [2]servant, 'Go out to the highways and hedges, and compel people to come in, that my house may be filled. For I tell 24 you, none of those men who were invited shall taste my banquet.'"

---

1 Or *slaves*   2 Or *slave*

HS references: Lk 14:20 = Deuteronomy 24:5
NC references: Mt 22:2-10 and Lk 14:15-24 = GT 64

B For every one who exalts himself will be humbled, but he who humbles himself will be exalted. (§ 114 B = Lk 18:14)
B Whoever exalts himself will be humbled, and whoever humbles himself will be exalted. (§ 132 H = Mt 23:12)

§ 104   The Costs of Discipleship

MATTHEW   LUKE 14:25-35

A Now great multitudes accompanied him; and he turned 25 and said to them,

B *He who loves father or mother more than me is not* 10: *worthy of me; and he who loves son or daughter more than* 37 *me is not worthy of me;*

B "If any one comes to me and does not hate his own 26 father and mother and wife and children and brothers and sisters, yes, and even his own life, he cannot be my disciple.

Cᶜ *and he who does not take his cross and follow me is not* 38 *worthy of me. (§ 57 MN)*

Cᶜ Whoever does not bear his own cross and come after 27 me, cannot be my disciple.

D For which of you, desiring to build a tower, does not 28 first sit down and count the cost, whether he has enough to complete it? Otherwise, when he has laid a foundation, and 29 is not able to finish, all who see it begin to mock him, saying, 'This man began to build, and was not able to 30 finish.' Or what king, going to encounter another king in 31 war, will not sit down first and take counsel whether he is able with ten thousand to meet him who comes against him with twenty thousand? And if not, while the other is yet a 32 great way off, he sends an embassy and asks terms of peace. So therefore, whoever of you does not renounce all 33 that he has cannot be my disciple.

Eᴱ *"You are the salt of the earth; but if salt has lost its* 5: *taste, how shall its saltness be restored? It is no longer* 13 *good for anything except to be thrown out and trodden underfoot by men. (§ 36 KL)*

Eᴱ "Salt is good; but if salt has lost its taste, how shall its 34 saltness be restored? It is fit neither for the land nor for the 35 dunghill; men throw it away.

Fᶠ *He who has ears ¹to hear, let him hear. (§ 41 H)*

11: 15

Fᶠ He who has ears to hear, let him hear."

---

1 Some ancient authorities omit *to hear*

C If any man would come after me, let him deny himself and take up his cross and follow me. (§ 73 A = Mt 16:24)

C If any man would come after me, let him deny himself and take up his cross and follow me. (§ 73 A = Mk 8:34)

C If any man would come after me, let him deny himself and take up his cross daily and follow me. (§ 73 A = Lk 9:23)

E Salt is good; but if the salt has lost its saltness, how will you season it? Have salt in yourselves, and be at peace with one another. (§ 78 O = Mk 9:50)

F He who has ears, let him hear. (§ 47 F = Mt 13:9)

F He who has ears to hear, let him hear. (§ 47 F = Mk 4:9)

F He who has ears to hear, let him hear. (§ 47 F = Lk 8:8)

F If any man has ears to hear, let him hear. (§ 47 S = Mk 4:23)

F He who has ears, let him hear. (§ 48 M = Mt 13:43)

Chapter XVI

MANY TRUTHS TAUGHT IN PARABLES

§ 105 Parables on the Worth of Sinners

MATT 18:12-14

LUKE 15:1-32

A Now the tax collectors and sinners were all drawing near 1 to hear him. And the Pharisees and the scribes murmured, 2 saying, "This man receives sinners and eats with them." So 3 he told them this parable:

B *What do you think? If a man has a hundred sheep, and 12 one of them has gone astray, does he not leave the ninety-nine on the mountains and go in search of the one that went astray? And if he finds it, truly, I say to you, he 13 rejoices over it more than over the ninety-nine that never went astray. So it is not ¹the will of ²my father who is in 14 heaven that one of these little ones should perish. (§ 78 Q)*

B "What man of you, having a hundred sheep, if he has 4 lost one of them, does not leave the ninety-nine in the wilderness, and go after the one which is lost, until he finds it? And when he has found it, he lays it on his 5 shoulders, rejoicing. And when he comes home, he calls 6 together his friends and his neighbors, saying to them, 'Rejoice with me, for I have found my sheep which was lost.' Just so, I tell you, there will be more joy in heaven 7 over one sinner who repents than over ninety-nine righteous persons who need no repentance.

C "Or what woman, having ten silver ³coins, if she loses 8 one coin, does not light a lamp and sweep the house and seek diligently until she finds it? And when she has found 9 it, she calls together her friends and neighbors, saying, 'Rejoice with me, for I have found the coin which I had lost.' Just so, I tell you, there is joy before the angels of 10 God over one sinner who repents."

D And he said, "There was a man who had two sons; and 11 the younger of them said to his father, 'Father, give me the 12 share of property that falls to me.' And he divided his living between them. Not many days later, the younger son 13 gathered all he had and took his journey into a far country, and there he squandered his property in loose living. And 14 when he had spent everything, a great famine arose in that country, and he began to be in want. So he went and joined 15 himself to one of the citizens of that country, who sent him into his fields to feed swine. And he would gladly have fed 16 on ⁴the pods that the swine ate; and no one gave him anything. But when he came ⁵to himself he said, 'How 17 many of my father's hired servants have bread enough and to spare, but I perish here with hunger! I will arise and go 18 to my father, and I will say to him, "Father, I have sinned against heaven and before you; I am no longer worthy to 19 be called your son; treat me as one of your hired servants."' And he arose and came to his father.   20

---

1 Greek *a thing willed before your Father*   2 Some ancient authorities read *your*   3 Greek *drachma*, a coin worth about thirty cents   4 Greek *the pods of the carob tree*   5 Greek *into*

HS references: Lk 15:12 = Deuteronomy 21:15-17

LUKE 15

But while he was yet at a distance, his father saw him and had compassion, and ran and embraced him and [1]kissed him. And the son said to him, 'Father, I have sinned 21 against heaven and before you; I am no longer worthy to be called your son.'[2] But the father said to his [3]servants, 22 'Bring quickly the best robe, and put it on him; and put a ring on his hand, and shoes on his feet; and bring the fatted 23 calf and kill it, and let us eat and make merry; for this my 24 son was dead, and is alive again; he was lost, and is found.' And they began to make merry.

"Now his elder son was in the field; and as he came and 25 drew near to the house, he heard music and dancing. And 26 he called one of the servants and asked what this meant. And he said to him, 'Your brother has come, and your 27 father has killed the fatted calf, because he has received him safe and sound.' But he was angry and refused to go 28 in. His father came out and entreated him, but he answered 29 his father, 'Lo, these many years I have served you, and I never disobeyed your command; yet you never gave me a kid, that I might make merry with my friends. But when 30 this son of yours came, who has devoured your living with harlots, you killed for him the fatted calf!' And he said to 31 him, "Son, you are always with me, and all that is mine is yours. It was fitting to make merry and be glad, for this 32 your brother was dead, and is alive; he was lost, and is found.'"

§ 106 Parable of the Steward

LUKE 16:1-12

He also said to the disciples, "There was a rich man who 1 had a steward, and charges were brought to him that this man was wasting his goods. And he called him and said to 2 him, 'What is this that I hear about you? Turn in the account of your stewardship, for you can no longer be steward.' And the steward said to himself, 'What shall I 3 do, since my master is taking the stewardship away from me? I am not strong enough to dig, and I am ashamed to beg. I have decided what to do, so that people may receive 4 me into their houses when I am put out of the stewardship.' So, summoning his master's debtors one by one, he said to 5 the first, 'How much do you owe my master?' He said, 'A 6 hundred [5]measures of oil.' And he said to him, 'Take your [6]bill, and sit down quickly and write fifty.' Then he said to 7 another, 'And how much do you owe?' He said, 'A hundred [7]measures of wheat.' He said to him, 'Take your [8]bill, and write eighty.' The master commended the 8 [8]dishonest steward for his shrewdness; for the sons of this [9]world are more shrewd in dealing with their own generation than the sons of light. And I tell you,   9

---

1 Greek *kissed him much*   2 Some ancient authorities add *make me as one of your hired servants*; see verse 19   3 Or *slave*   4 Greek *Child*   5 Greek *baths*, the bath being a Hebrew measure: see Ezekiel 45:10,11,14   6 Greek *writings*   7 Greek *cors*, the cor being a Hebrew measure: see Ezekiel 45:14   8 Greek *the steward of unrighteousness*   9 Greek *age*

HS references: Lk 15:22 = Genesis 41:42 and Zechariah 3:4

LUKE 16

make friends for yourselves ¹by means of unrighteous mammon, so that when it fails they may receive you into the eternal habitations. "He who is faithful in a very little is 10 faithful also in much; and he who is dishonest in a very little is dishonest also in much. If then you have not been 11 faithful in the unrighteous mammon, who will entrust to you the true riches? And if you have not been faithful in 12 that which is another's, who will give you that which is ²your own?

§ 107 Several Sayings of Jesus

MATTHEW

A *"No one can serve two masters; for either he will hate* 6: *the one and love the other, or he will be devoted to the one* 24 *and despise the other. You cannot serve God and mammon.* (§ 38 C)

C *From the days of John the Baptist until now the kingdom* 11: *of heaven has ⁴suffered violence, and men of violence take it* 12 *by force. For all the prophets and the law prophesied until* 13 *John;* (§ 41 F)

D *For truly, I say to you, till heaven and earth pass away,* 5: *not an iota, not a dot, will pass from the law until all is* 18 *accomplished.* (§ 36 Q)

Eᴱ *But I say to you that every one who divorces his wife,* 5: *except on the ground of unchastity, makes her an* 32 *adulteress; and whoever marries a divorced woman commits adultery.* (§ 37 E)

LUKE 16:13-18

A No ³servant can serve two masters; for either he will 13 hate the one and love the other, or he will be devoted to the one and despise the other. You cannot serve God and mammon."

B The Pharisees, who were lovers of money, heard all this, 14 and they scoffed at him. But he said to them, "You are 15 those who justify yourselves before men, but God knows your hearts; for what is exalted among men is an abomination in the sight of God.

C "The law and the prophets were until John; since then 16 the good news of the kingdom of God is preached, and every one enters it violently.

D But it is easier for heaven and earth to pass away, than 17 for one dot of the law to become void.

Eᴱ "Every one who divorces his wife and marries another 18 commits adultery, and he who marries a woman divorced from her husband commits adultery.

§ 108 Parable of the Rich Man and the Beggar

LUKE 16:19-31

"There was a rich man, who was clothed in purple and fine 19 linen and who ⁵feasted sumptuously every day. And at his 20 gate lay a poor man named Laz'arus, full of sores, who 21 desired to be fed with what fell from the rich man's table; moreover the dogs came and licked his sores. The poor 22 man died and was carried by the angels to Abraham's bosom. The rich man also died and was buried; and in 23 Hades, being in torment, he lifted up his

---

1 Greek *out of* 2 Some ancient authorities read *our own* 3 Greek *household servant* 4 Or *has been coming violently* 5 Or *lived in mirth and splendor every day*

HS references: Lk 16:15 = I Samuel 16:7 and Proverbs 21:2
NC references: Mt 5:18 and Lk 16:17 = GT 11 Mt 6:24 and Lk 16:13 = GT 47

E And I say to you: whoever divorces his wife, except for unchastity, and marries another, commits adultery. (§ 115 F = Mt 19:9)

E And he said to them, Whoever divorces his wife and marries another, commits adultery against her; and if she divorces her husband and marries another, she commits adultery. (§ 115 F = Mk 10:11-12)

LUKE 16

eyes, and saw Abraham far off and Laz'arus in his bosom. And he called out, 'Father Abraham, have mercy upon me, 24 and send Laz'arus to dip the end of his finger in water and cool my tongue; for I am in anguish in this flame.' But 25 Abraham said, "¹Son, remember that you in your lifetime received your good things, and Laz'arus in like manner evil things; but now he is comforted here, and you are in anguish. And ²besides all this, between us and you a great 26 chasm has been fixed, in order that those who would pass from here to you may not be able, and none may cross from there to us.' And he said, 'Then I beg you, father, to 27 send him to my father's house, for I have five brothers, so 28 that he may warn them, lest they also come into this place of torment.' But Abraham said, 'They have Moses and the 29 prophets; let them hear them.' And he said, 'No, father 30 Abraham; but if some one goes to them from the dead, they will repent.' He said to him, 'If they do not hear 31 Moses and the prophets, neither will they be convinced if some one should rise from the dead.'"

§ 109 Several Sayings of Jesus

MATTHEW 18	LUKE 17:1-6
A *"Woe to the world for temptations to sin! For it is 7 necessary that ³temptations come, but woe to the man by whom the temptation comes! (§ 78 L)*	**A** And he said to his disciples, "³Temptations to sin are 1 sure to come; but woe to him by whom they come!
Bᴮ *but whoever causes one of these little ones who believe 6 in me to ⁴sin, it would be better for him to have ⁵a great millstone fastened round his neck and to be drowned in the depth of the sea. (§ 78 K)*	**B**ᴮ It would be better for him if a millstone were hung 2 round his neck and he were cast into the sea, than that he should cause one of these little ones to ⁴sin.
C *"If your brother sins ⁶against you, go and tell him his 15 fault, between you and him alone. If he listens to you, you have gained your brother. (§ 78 R)*	**C** Take heed to yourselves; if your brother sins, rebuke 3 him, and if he repents, forgive him;
D *Then Peter came up and said to him, "Lord, how often 21 shall my brother sin against me, and I forgive him? As many as seven times?" Jesus said to him, "I do not say to 22 you seven times, but ⁷seventy times seven. (§ 78 V)*	**D** and if he sins against you seven times in the day, and 4 turns to you seven times, and says, 'I repent,' you must forgive him."
	E The apostles said to the Lord, "Increase our faith!" 5
Fᶠ *For truly, I say to you, if you have faith as a grain of 17: mustard seed, you will say to this mountain, 'Move from 20 here to there,' and it will move; and nothing will be impossible to you." (§ 75 H)*	**F**ᶠ And the Lord said, "If you had faith as a grain of 6 mustard seed, you could say to this sycamine tree, 'Be rooted up, and be planted in the sea,' and it would obey you.

---

1 Greek *Child*   2 Or *in all these things*   3 Greek *occasion of stumbling*   4 Greek *stumble*   5 Greek *a millstone turned by an ass*
6 Some ancient authorities omit *against you*   7 Or *seventy times and seven*

B *Matt parallel shown above under B*	B Whoever causes one of these little ones who believe in me to sin, it would be better for him if a great millstone were hung round his neck and he were thrown into the sea. (§ 78 K = Mk 9:42)
F Truly, I say to you, if you have faith and never doubt, you will not only do what has been done to the fig tree, but even if you say to this mountain, 'Be taken up and cast into the sea,' it will be done. (§ 127 C = Mt 21:21)	F Have faith in God. Truly, I say to you, whoever says to this mountain, 'Be taken up and cast into the sea,' and does not doubt in his heart, but believes that what he says will come to pass, it will be done for him. (§ 127 C = Mk 11:22-23)

§ 110 Parable on Duty

LUKE 17:7-10

"Will any one of you, who has a [1]servant plowing or 7 keeping sheep, say to him when he has come in from the field, 'Come at once and sit down at table'? Will he not 8 rather say to him, 'Prepare supper for me, and gird yourself and serve me, till I eat and drink; and afterward you shall eat and drink'? Does he thank the [1]servant because he 9 did what was commanded? So you also, when you have 10 done all that is commanded you, say, 'We are unworthy [2]servants; we have only done what was our duty.'"

§ 111 The Healing of the Lepers

LUKE 17:11-19

A On the way to Jerusalem he was passing along between 11 Samar'ia and Galilee.

B And as he entered a village, he was met by ten lepers, 12 who stood at a distance and lifted up their voices and said, 13 "Jesus, Master, have mercy on us." When he saw them he 14 said to them, "Go and show yourselves to the priests." And as they went they were cleansed. Then one of them, when 15 he saw that he was healed, turned back, praising God with a loud voice; and he fell on his face at Jesus' feet, giving 16 him thanks. Now he was a Samaritan. Then said Jesus, 17 "Were not ten cleansed? Where are the nine? [3]Was no one 18 found to return and give praise to God except this [4]foreigner?" And he said to him, "Rise and go your way; 19 your faith has [5]made you well."

§ 112 The Day of the Son of Man

MATTHEW 24   LUKE 17:20-37

A Being asked by the Pharisees when the kingdom of God 20 was coming, he answered them, "The kingdom of God is not coming with signs to be observed; nor will they say, 21 'Lo, here it is!' or 'There!' for behold, the kingdom of God is [6]in the midst of you."

B And he said to the disciples, "The days are coming when 22 you will desire to see one of the days of the Son of man, and you will not see it.

C[c] *So, if they say to you, 'Lo, he is in the wilderness,' do 26 not go out; if they say, 'Lo, he is in the inner rooms,' do not believe [7]it. For as the lightning comes from the east and 27 shines as far as the west, so will be the [8]coming of the Son of man. (§ 135 CD)*

C[c] And they will say to you, 'Lo, there!' or 'Lo, here!' Do 23 not go, do not follow them. For as the lightning flashes and 24 lights up the sky from one side to the other, so will the Son of man be [9]in his day.

---

1 Or *slave*   2 Or *slaves*   3 Or *There was no one found . . . except this foreigner*   4 Or *alien*   5 Or *saved you*   6 Or *within you*
7 Or, *them*   8 Greek *presence*   9 Some ancient authorities omit *in his day*

HS references: Lk 17:12 = Leviticus 13:45-46   Lk 17:14 = Leviticus 13:49 and 14:1-3
NC references: Lk 17:20-21 = GT 3, 113

C Compare § 134 portion D
C Then if any one says to you, 'Lo, here is the Christ!' or 'There he is!' do not believe it. (§ 135 A = Mt 24:23)

C And then if any one says to you, 'Look, here is the Christ!' or 'Look, there he is!' do not believe it. (§ 135 A = Mk 13:21)

MATT 24   LUKE 17

D^D   *Compare § 72 A and attached references*

D^D But first he must suffer many things and be rejected by 25 this generation.

E *As were the days of Noah, so will be the ¹coming of the* 37 *Son of man. For as in those days before the flood they were* 38 *eating and drinking, marrying and giving in marriage, until the day when Noah entered the ark, and they did not know* 39 *until the flood came and swept them all away,*

E As it was in the days of Noah, so will it be in the days 26 of the Son of man. They ate, they drank, they married, 27 they were given in marriage, until the day when Noah entered the ark, and the flood came and destroyed them all.

F Likewise as it was in the days of Lot--they ate, they 28 drank, they bought, they sold, they planted, they built, but 29 on the day when Lot went out from Sodom fire and sulphur rained from heaven and destroyed them all--

G *so will be the ¹coming of the Son of man. (§ 135 LM)*

G so will it be on the day when the Son of man is 30 revealed.

H^H   *Compare with portions P and Q of § 134*

H^H On that day, let him who is on the housetop, with his 31 goods in the house, not come down to take them away; and likewise let him who is in the field not turn back.

I Remember Lot's wife.   32

J^J *He who ²finds his ³life will ⁴lose it, and he who ⁵loses his* 10: *³life for my sake will find it. (§ 57 O)*   39

J^J Whoever seeks to gain his ³life will ⁴lose it, but whoever 33 ⁵loses his ³life will ⁶preserve it.⁷

K *Then two men will be in the field; one is taken and one* 24: *is left. Two women will be grinding at the mill; one is taken* 40 *and one is left. (§ 135 N)*   41

K I tell you, in that night there will be two in one bed; one 34 will be taken and the other left. There will be two women 35 grinding together; one will be taken and the other left."⁸

L And they said to him, "Where, Lord?"   37

M *Wherever the body is, there the ⁹eagles will be gathered* 28 *together. (§ 135 E)*

M He said to them, "Where the body is, there the ⁹eagles will be gathered together."

§ 113 Parable of the Widow and the Judge

LUKE 18:1-8

A And he told them a parable, to the effect that they ought 1 always to pray and not lose heart. He said, "In a certain 2 city there was a judge who neither feared God nor regarded man; and there was a widow in that city who kept coming 3 to him and saying, 'Vindicate me against my adversary.' For a while he refused; but afterward he said to himself, 4 'Though I neither fear God nor regard man, yet because 5 this widow bothers me, I will

---

1 Greek *presence*   2 Or *found*   3 Or *soul*   4 Greek *destroy*   5 Or *lost;* Greek *destroys,* or *destroyed*   6 Greek *save it alive*
7 See also the notes on the Greek at § 73 B   8 Some ancient authorities add verse 36: *"Two men will be in the field; one will be taken, and the other left."*   9 Or *vultures*

HS references: Mt 24:28 and Lk 17:37 = Job 39:30   Mt 24:37-39 and Lk 17:26-27 = Genesis 6:11-13 and 7:7, 21-23   Lk 17:28 = Genesis 18:20-22
Lk 17:29 = Genesis 19:24-25   Lk 17:32 = Genesis 19:26

D Compare § 72 A and attached references
H Compare with portions P and Q of § 134

J For whoever would save his life will lose it, and whoever loses his life for my sake will find it. (§ 73 B = Mt 16:25)	J For whoever would save his life will lose it; and whoever loses his life for my sake and the gospel's will save it, (§ 73 B = Mk 8:35)	J For whoever would save his life will lose it; and whoever loses his life for my sake, he will save it. (§ 73 B = Lk 9:24)

LUKE 18

vindicate her, or she will [1]wear me out by her continual coming.'"

B And the Lord said, "Hear what [2]the unrighteous judge 6 says. And will not God vindicate his elect, who cry to him 7 day and night? Will he delay long over them? I tell you, he 8 will vindicate them speedily. Nevertheless, when the Son of man comes, will he find [3]faith on earth?"

§ 114 Parable of the Publican and the Pharisee

LUKE 18:9-14

A He also told this parable to some who trusted in 9 themselves that they were righteous and despised others: "Two men went up into the temple to pray, one a Pharisee 10 and the other a tax collector. The Pharisee stood and 11 prayed thus with himself, 'God, I thank thee that I am not like other men, extortioners, unjust, adulterers, or even like this tax collector. I fast twice a week, I give tithes of all 12 that I get.' But the tax collector, standing far off, would 13 not even lift up his eyes to heaven, but beat his breast, saying, 'God, be [4]merciful to me [5]a sinner!' I tell you, this 14 man went down to his house justified rather than the other;

B[B] for every one who exalts himself will be humbled, but he who humbles himself will be exalted."

---

1 Greek *bruise*   2 Greek *the judge of unrighteousness*   3 Or *the faith*   4 Or *propitious*   5 Or *the sinner*

B For every one who exalts himself will be humbled, and he who humbles himself will be exalted. (§ 103 B = Lk 14:11)
B Whoever exalts himself will be humbled, and whoever humbles himself will be exalted. (§ 132 H = Mt 23:12)

Chapter XVII

TEACHING AND JOURNEYING ON TO JERUSALEM

§ 115 Teachings about Divorce

MATT 19:3-12	MARK 10:2-12
A And [1]Pharisees came up to him and 3 tested him by asking, "Is it lawful to divorce one's wife for any cause?"	**A** And Pharisees came up and in 2 order to test him asked, "Is it lawful for a man to divorce his wife?"
B He answered, 4	**B** He answered them, 3
C *Compare portion E below*	**C** "What did Moses command you?" They said, "Moses allowed a man to 4 write a certificate of divorce, and to put her away." But Jesus said to 5 them, "For your hardness of heart he wrote you this commandment.
D "Have you not read that he who [2]made them from the beginning made them male and female, and said, 'For 5 this reason a man shall leave his father and mother and be joined to his wife, and the two shall become one flesh'? So they are no longer two but 6 one flesh. What therefore God has joined together, let not man put asunder."	**D** But from the beginning of creation, 6 'God made them male and female.' 'For this reason a man shall leave his 7 father and mother [3]and be joined to his wife, and the two shall become 8 one flesh.' So they are no longer two but one flesh. What therefore God has 9 joined together, let not man put asunder."
E They said to him, "Why then did 7 Moses command one to give a certificate of divorce, and to put her away?" He said to them, "For your 8 hardness of heart Moses allowed you to divorce your wives, but from the beginning it was not so.	**E** *Compare portion C above*
F^F And I say to you: whoever 9 divorces his wife, [4]except for unchastity, and marries another, commits adultery."	**F**^F And in the house the disciples 10 asked him again about this matter. And he said to them, "Whoever 11 divorces his wife and marries another, commits adultery against her; and if 12 she divorces her husband and marries another, she commits adultery."

---

1 Many authorities, some ancient, insert *the*   2 Some ancient authorities read *created*   3 Some ancient authorities omit *and be joined to his wife*
4 Some ancient authorities read *except on the ground of unchastity, makes her an adulteress*: as in Matt 5:32

HS references: Mt 19:4 and Mk 10:6 = Genesis 1:27 and 5:2   Mt 19:5 and Mk 10:7-8 = Genesis 2:24
Mt 19:7 and Mk 10:4 = Deuteronomy 24:1-4

F But I say to you that every one who divorces his wife, except on the ground of unchastity, makes her an adulteress; and whoever marries a divorced woman commits adultery. (§ 37 E = Mt 5:32)

F Every one who divorces his wife and marries another commits adultery, and he who marries a woman divorced from her husband commits adultery. (§ 107 E = Lk 16:18)

MATT 19

G The disciples said to him, "If such 10 is the case of a man with his wife, it is not expedient to marry." But he 11 said to them, "Not all men can receive this saying, but only those to whom it is given. For there are 12 eunuchs who have been so from birth, and there are eunuchs who have been made eunuchs by men, and there are eunuchs who have made themselves eunuchs for the sake of the kingdom of heaven. He who is able to receive this, let him receive it."

§ 116 Attitude of Jesus toward Children

MATT 19:13-15	MARK 10:13-16	LUKE 18:15-17
A Then children were brought to him 13 that he might lay his hands on them and pray. The disciples rebuked the people;	**A** And they were bringing children to 13 him, that he might touch them; and the disciples rebuked them.	**A** Now they were bringing even 15 infants to him that he might touch them; and when the disciples saw it, they rebuked them.
B but Jesus said, "Let the children 14 come to me, and do not hinder them; for to such belongs the kingdom of heaven."	**B** But when Jesus saw it he was 14 indignant, and said to them, "Let the children come to me, do not hinder them; for to such belongs the kingdom of God.	**B** But Jesus called them to him, 16 saying, "Let the children come to me, and do not hinder them; for to such belongs the kingdom of God.
C *"Truly, I say to you, unless you* 18: *turn and become like children, you* 3 *will never enter the kingdom of heaven. (§ 78 D)*	**C** Truly, I say to you, whoever does 15 not receive the kingdom of God like a child shall not enter it."	**C** Truly, I say to you, whoever does 17 not receive the kingdom of God like a child shall not enter it."
D And he laid his hands on them and 15 went away.	**D** And he took them in his arms and 16 blessed them, laying his hands upon them.	

§ 117 Relation of Riches to Eternal Life

MATT 19:16-30	MARK 10:17-31	LUKE 18:18-30
A And behold, one came up to him, 16 saying, "[1]Teacher, what good deed must I do, to have eternal life?"	**A** And as he was setting out on his 17 journey, a man ran up and knelt before him, and asked him, "Good Teacher, what must I do to inherit eternal life?"	**A** And a ruler asked him, "Good 18 Teacher, what shall I do to inherit eternal life?"
B And he said to him, "[2]Why do you 17 ask me about what is good? One there is who is good.	**B** And Jesus said to him, "Why do 18 you call me good? No one is good but God alone.	**B** And Jesus said to him, "Why do 19 you call me good? No one is good but God alone.

---

1 Some ancient authorities read *Good Teacher*: see Mark 10:17 and Luke 18:18   2 Some ancient authorities read *Why do you call me good? No one is good save one*, even *God*: see Mark 10:18 and Luke 18:19

HS references: Mt 19:16 = Leviticus 18:5

MATT 19	MARK 10	LUKE 18
C If you would enter life, keep the commandments." He said to him, 18 "Which?" And Jesus said, "You shall not kill, You shall not commit adultery, You shall not steal, You shall not bear false witness, Honor 19 your father and mother, and, You shall love your neighbor as yourself."	**C** You know the commandments: 'Do 19 not kill, Do not commit adultery, Do not steal, Do not bear false witness, Do not defraud, Honor your father and mother.'"	**C** You know the commandments: 'Do 20 not commit adultery, Do not kill, Do not steal, Do not bear false witness, Honor your father and mother.'"
D The young man said to him, "All 20 these I have observed; what do I still lack?"	**D** And he said to him, "Teacher, all 20 these I have observed from my youth."	**D** And he said, "All these I have 21 observed from my youth."
E Jesus said to him, "If you would be 21 perfect, go, sell what you possess and give to the poor, and you will have treasure in heaven; and come, follow me."	**E** And Jesus looking upon him loved 21 him, and said to him, "You lack one thing; go, sell what you have, and give to the poor, and you will have treasure in heaven; and come, follow me."	**E** And when Jesus heard it, he said to 22 him, "One thing you still lack. Sell all that you have and distribute to the poor, and you will have treasure in heaven; and come, follow me."
F When the young man heard this he 22 went away sorrowful; for he had great possessions.	**F** At that saying his countenance fell, 22 and he went away sorrowful; for he had great possessions.	**F** But when he heard this he became 23 sad, for he was very rich.
G And Jesus said to his disciples, 23 "Truly, I say to you, it will be hard for a rich man to enter the kingdom of heaven.	**G** And Jesus looked around and said 23 to his disciples, "How hard it will be for those who have riches to enter the kingdom of God!"	**G** Jesus looking at him said, "How 24 hard it is for those who have riches to enter the kingdom of God!
	H And the disciples were amazed at 24 his words. But Jesus said to them again, "Children, how hard it is [1]to enter the kingdom of God!	
I Again I tell you, it is easier for a 24 camel to go through the eye of a needle than for a rich man to enter the kingdom of God."	**I** It is easier for a camel to go 25 through the eye of a needle than for a rich man to enter the kingdom of God."	**I** For it is easier for a camel to go 25 through the eye of a needle than for a rich man to enter the kingdom of God."
J When the disciples heard this they 25 were greatly astonished, saying, "Who then can be saved?" But Jesus looked 26 at them and said to them, "With men this is impossible, but with God all things are possible."	**J** And they were exceedingly 26 astonished, and said [2]to him, "Then who can be saved?" Jesus looked at 27 them and said, "With men it is impossible, but not with God; for all things are possible with God."	**J** Those who heard it said, "Then 26 who can be saved?" But he said, 27 "What is impossible with men is possible with God."
K Then Peter said in reply, "Lo, we 27 have left everything and followed you. What then shall we have?"	**K** Peter began to say to him, "Lo, we 28 have left everything and followed you."	**K** And Peter said, "Lo, we have left 28 our homes and followed you."
L Jesus said to them, "Truly, I say to 28 you, in the new world,		**L** *"You are those who have continued* 22: *with me in my trials;* 28

---

1 Some ancient authorities add *for those who trust in riches*   2 Many ancient authorities read *to one another*

HS references: Mt 19:18-19a and Mk 10:19 and Lk 18:20 = Exodus 20:12-16 and Deuteronomy 5:16-20   Mt 19:19b = Leviticus 19:18b
Mt 19:24 and Mk 10:25 and Lk 18:25 = Psalm 62:10   Mt 19:26 and Mk 10:27 and Lk 18:27 = Genesis 18:14 and Job 42:2 and Jeremiah 32:17

MATT 19	MARK 10	LUKE 18

and I assign to you, as my Father 22: *assigned to me, a kingdom, that you* 29 *may eat and drink at my table in my* 30 *kingdom, and sit on thrones judging the twelve tribes of Israel.*

when the Son of man shall sit on his glorious throne, you who have followed me will also sit on twelve thrones, judging the twelve tribes of Israel.

M And every one who has left houses 29 or brothers or sisters or father or mother[1] or children or lands, for my name's sake, will receive [2]a hundredfold, and inherit eternal life.

M Jesus said, "Truly, I say to you, 29 there is no one who has left house or brothers or sisters or mother or father or children or lands, for my sake and for the gospel, who will not receive a 30 hundredfold now in this time, houses and brothers and sisters and mothers and children and lands, with persecutions, and in the age to come eternal life.

M And he said to them, "Truly, I say 29 to you, there is no man who has left house or wife or brothers or parents or children, for the sake of the kingdom of God, who will not receive 30 manifold more in this time, and in the age to come eternal life."

N[N] But many that are first will be 30 last, and the last first.

N[N] But many that are first will be 31 last, and the last first."

§ 118 Parable of the Householder and the Laborers

MATT 20:1-16   LUKE

A "For the kingdom of heaven is like a householder who 1 went out early in the morning to hire laborers for his vineyard. After agreeing with the laborers for a [3]denarius a 2 day, he sent them into his vineyard. And going out about 3 the third hour he saw others standing idle in the market place; and to them he said, 'You go into the vineyard too, 4 and whatever is right I will give you.' So they went. Going 5 out again about the sixth hour and the ninth hour, he did the same. And about the eleventh hour he went out and 6 found others standing; and he said to them, 'Why do you stand here idle all day?' They said to him, 'Because no one 7 has hired us.' He said to them, 'You go into the vineyard too.' And when evening came, the owner of the vineyard 8 said to his steward, 'Call the laborers and pay them their wages, beginning with the last, up to the first.' And when 9 those hired about the eleventh hour came, each of them received a [3]denarius. Now when the first came, they 10 thought they would receive more; but each of them also received a [3]denarius. And on receiving it they grumbled at 11 the householder, saying, 'These last worked only one hour, 12 and you have made them equal to us who have borne the burden of the day and the [4]scorching heat.' But he replied 13 to one of them, 'Friend, I am doing you no wrong; did you not agree with me for a [3]denarius? Take what belongs to   14

---

1 Many ancient authorities add *or wife*: as in Luke 18:29   2 Some ancient authorities read *manifold*   3 The word in the Greek denotes a coin worth about forty cents. The denarius was a day's wage for a laborer.   4 Or *hot wind*

HS references: Mt 20:8 = Leviticus 19:13 and Deuteronomy 24:15   Mt 20:13 = Deuteronomy 15:9
NC references: Mt 19:30 and Mk 10:31 = GT 4

N So the last will be first, and the first last. (§ 118 B = Mt 20:16)   N And behold, some are last who will be first, and some are first who will be last. (§ 100 H = Lk 13:30)

MATT 20   LUKE 13

you, and go; I choose to give to this last as I give to you.
Am I not allowed to do what I choose with what belongs to 15
me? ¹Or do you begrudge my generosity?'

Bᴮ So the last will be first, and the first last."   16 **B**ᴮ *And behold, some are last who will be first, and some* 30
are first who will be last." (§ 100 H)

§ 119 Jesus Forecasts Events at Jerusalem

MATT 20:17-19	MARK 10:32-34	LUKE 18:31-34
A And as Jesus was going up to 17 Jerusalem,	**A** And they were on the road, going 32 up to Jerusalem, and Jesus was walking ahead of them; and they were amazed, ²and those who followed were afraid.	
B he took the twelve disciples aside, and on the way he said to them,	**B** And taking the twelve again, he began to tell them what was to happen to him, saying, 33	**B** And taking the twelve, he said to 31 them,
Cᶜ "Behold, we are going up to 18 Jerusalem;	**C**ᶜ "Behold, we are going up to Jerusalem;	**C**ᶜ "Behold, we are going up to Jerusalem,
		Dᴰ and everything that is written of the Son of man ³by the prophets will be accomplished.
Eᴱ and the Son of man will be delivered to the chief priests and scribes, and they will condemn him to death,	**E**ᴱ and the Son of man will be delivered to the chief priests and the scribes, and they will condemn him to death,	
Fᶠ and deliver him to the Gentiles to 19 be mocked and scourged and crucified, and he will be raised on the third day."	**F**ᶠ and deliver him to the Gentiles; and they will mock him, and spit 34 upon him, and scourge him, and kill him; and after three days he will rise."	**F**ᶠ For he will be delivered to the 32 Gentiles, and will be mocked and shamefully treated and spit upon; they 33 will scourge him and kill him, and on the third day he will rise."
		G But they understood none of these 34 things; this saying was hid from them, and they did not grasp what was said.

§ 120 Teaching on Standards of Greatness

MATT 20:20-28	MARK 10:35-45
A Then the mother of the sons of 20 Zeb'edee came up to him, with her sons, and kneeling before him she asked him for something.	**A** And James and John, the sons of 35 Zeb'edee, came forward to him, and said to him, "Teacher, we want you to do for us whatever we ask of you."

---

1 Greek *or is your eye evil because I am good?*   2 Or *but some as they followed were afraid*   3 Or *through*

NC references: Mt 20:16 and Lk 13:30 = GT 4

B But many that are first will be last, and the   B But many that are first will be last, and the
last first. (§ 117 N = Mt 19:30)   last first. (§ 117 N = Mk 10:31)
CEF For other records of these forecasts, compare § 72 A and attached references
D Compare § 74 portion L

MATT 20	MARK 10	LUKE 22:24-27
B And he said to her, "What do you 21 want?" She said to him, "Command that these two sons of mine may sit, one at your right hand and one at your left, in your kingdom."	**B** And he said to them, "What do you 36 want me to do for you?" And they 37 said to him, "Grant us to sit, one at your right hand and one at your left, in your glory."	**B** *A dispute also arose among them,* 24 *which of them was to be regarded as the* [1]*greatest.*
C But Jesus answered, "You do not 22 know what you are asking. Are you able to drink the cup that I am to drink?"	**C** But Jesus said to them, "You do 38 not know what you are asking. Are you able to drink the cup that I drink,	
	D[D] or to be baptized with the baptism with which I am baptized?"	
E They said to him, "We are able." He said to them, "You will drink my 23 cup,	**E** And they said to him, "We are 39 able." And Jesus said to them, "The cup that I drink you will drink;	
	F[F] and with the baptism with which I am baptized, you will be baptized;	
G but to sit at my right hand and at my left is not mine to grant, but it is for those for whom it has been prepared by my Father."	**G** but to sit at my right hand or at my 40 left is not mine to grant, but it is for those for whom it has been prepared."	
H And when the ten heard it, they 24 were indignant at the two brothers.	**H** And when the ten heard it, they 41 began to be indignant at James and John.	
I But Jesus called them to him and 25 said, "You know that the rulers of the Gentiles lord it over them, and their great men exercise authority over them.	**I** And Jesus called them to him and 42 said to them, "You know that those who are supposed to rule over the Gentiles lord it over them, and their great men exercise authority over them.	**I** *And he said to them, "The kings of* 25 *the Gentiles exercise lordship over them; and those in authority over them are called benefactors.*
J[J] It shall not be so among you; but 26 whoever would be great among you must be your servant, and whoever 27 would be first among you must be your slave;	**J**[J] But it shall not be so among you; 43 but whoever would be great among you must be your servant, and 44 whoever would be first among you must be slave of all.	**J**[J] *But not so with you; rather let the* 26 *greatest among you become as the youngest, and the leader as one who serves.*
K even as the Son of man came not 28 to be served but to serve, and to give his life as a ransom for many."	**K** For the Son of man also came not 45 to be served but to serve, and to give his life as a ransom for many."	**K** *For which is the greater, one who* 27 [2]*sits at table, or one who serves? Is it not the one who* [2]*sits at table? But I am among you as one who serves.* (§ 138 LM)

---

1 Greek *greater*   2 Greek *reclines*

D I came to cast fire upon the earth; and would that it were already kindled! I have a baptism to be baptized with; and how I am constrained until it is accomplished! (§ 95 A = Lk 12:49-50)
D Compare also portion F below
F Compare portion D above and attached references

J Whoever humbles himself like this child, he is the greatest in the kingdom of heaven. (§ 78 E = Mt 18:4)	**J** If any one would be first, he must be last of all and servant of all. (§ 78 B = Mk 9:35)	**J** For he who is least among you all is the one who is great. (§ 78 H = Lk 9:48)

J He who is greatest among you shall be your servant. (§ 132 G = Mt 23:11)

§ 121 The Blind Beggar of Jericho

MATT 20:29-34*	MARK 10:46-52	LUKE 18:35-43
A And as they went out of Jericho, a 29 great crowd followed him. And 30 behold, two blind men sitting by the roadside,	A And they came to Jericho; and as 46 he was leaving Jericho with his disciples and a great multitude, Bartimae'us, a blind beggar, the son of Timae'us, was sitting by the roadside.	A As he drew near to Jericho, a blind 35 man was sitting by the roadside begging;
B when they heard that Jesus was passing by, cried out, "¹Have mercy on us, Son of David!"	B And when he heard that it was 47 Jesus of Nazareth, he began to cry out and say, "Jesus, Son of David, have mercy on me!"	B and hearing a multitude going by, 36 he inquired what this meant. They 37 told him, "Jesus of Nazareth is passing by." And he cried, "Jesus, 38 Son of David, have mercy on me!"
C The crowd rebuked them, telling 31 them to be silent; but they cried out the more, "¹Lord, have mercy on us, Son of David!"	C And many rebuked him, telling him 48 to be silent; but he cried out all the more, "Son of David, have mercy on me!"	C And those who were in front 39 rebuked him, telling him to be silent; but he cried out all the more, "Son of David, have mercy on me!"
D And Jesus stopped and called them, 32 saying, "What do you want me to do for you?"	D And Jesus stopped and said, "Call 49 him." And they called the blind man, saying to him, "Take heart; rise, he is calling you." And throwing off his 50 mantle he sprang up and came to Jesus. And Jesus said to him, "What 51 do you want me to do for you?"	D And Jesus stopped, and commanded 40 him to be brought to him; and when he came near, he asked him, "What 41 do you want me to do for you?"
E They said to him, "Lord, let our 33 eyes be opened." And Jesus in pity 34 touched their eyes,	E And the blind man said to him, "²Master, let me receive my sight." And Jesus said to him, "Go your 52 way; your faith has ³made you well."	E He said, "Lord, let me receive my sight." And Jesus said to him, 42 "Receive your sight; your faith has made you well."
F and immediately they received their sight and followed him.	F And immediately he received his sight and followed him on the way.	F And immediately he received his 43 sight and followed him, glorifying God;
		G and all the people, when they saw it, gave praise to God.

§ 122 The Rich Publican of Jericho

LUKE 19:1-10

He entered Jericho and was passing through. And there was 1 a man named Zacchae'us; he was a chief tax collector, and 2 rich. And he sought to see who Jesus was, but could not, 3 on account of the crowd, because he was small of stature. So he ran on ahead and climbed up into a sycamore tree to 4 see him, for he was to pass that way. And when Jesus 5 came to the place, he looked up and said to him, "Zacchae'us, make haste and come down; for I must stay at your house today." So he made haste and came down, and 6 received him joyfully. And when they saw it they all 7 murmured, "He has gone in to be the guest of a man who

---

1 Important ancient authorities read *Lord, have mercy on us* or *Have mercy on us, Jesus*   2 Greek *Rabbi*: see John 20:16   3 Or *saved you*

HS references: Lk 19:8 = Exodus 22:1 and Numbers 5:6-7 and Leviticus 6:5

---

* For another Matthew account of similar general content, compare § 53 A

LUKE 19

is a sinner." And Zacchae'us stood and said to the Lord, 8 "Behold, Lord, the half of my goods I give to the poor; and if I have defrauded any one of anything, I restore it 9 fourfold." And Jesus said to him, "Today salvation has come to this house, since he also is a son of Abraham. For 10 the Son of man came to seek and to save the lost."

§ 123 Appearance of the Kingdom of God

MATT 25:14-30

LUKE 19:11-28

A As they heard these things, he proceeded to tell a 11 parable, because he was near to Jerusalem, and because they supposed that the kingdom of God was to appear immediately.

B *"For it will be as when a man going on a journey called* 14 *his ¹servants and entrusted to them his property; to one he* 15 *gave five ²talents, to another two, to another one, to each according to his ability. Then he went away.*

B He said therefore, "A nobleman went into a far country 12 to receive a kingdom and then return. Calling ten of his 13 ¹servants, he gave them ten ³pounds, and said to them, 'Trade with these till I come.'

C But his citizens hated him and sent an embassy after 14 him, saying, 'We do not want this man to reign over us.'

D *He who had received the five talents went at once and* 16 *traded with them; and he made five talents more. So also,* 17 *he who had the two talents made two talents more. But he* 18 *who had received the one talent went and dug in the ground and hid his master's money.*

E *Now after a long time the master of those ¹servants came* 19 *and settled accounts with them.*

E When he returned, having received the kingdom, he 15 commanded these ¹servants, to whom he had given the money, to be called to him, that he might know what they had gained by trading.

F *And he who had received the five talents came forward,* 20 *bringing five talents more, saying, 'Master, you delivered to me five talents; here I have made five talents more.' His* 21 *master said to him, 'Well done, good and faithful ⁴servant; you have been faithful over a little, I will set you over much; enter into the joy of your master.'*

F The first came before him, saying, 'Lord, your pound 16 has made ten pounds more.' And he said to him, 'Well 17 done, good ⁴servant! Because you have been faithful in a very little, you shall have authority over ten cities.'

G *And he also who had the two talents came forward,* 22 *saying, 'Master, you delivered to me two talents; here I have made two talents more.' His master said to him, 'Well* 23 *done, good and faithful ⁴servant; you have been faithful over a little, I will set you over much; enter into the joy of your master.'*

G And the second came, saying, 'Lord, your pound has 18 made five pounds.' And he said to him, 'And you are to be 19 over five cities.'

H *He also who had received the one talent came forward,* 24 *saying, 'Master, I knew you to be a hard man, reaping where you did not sow, and gathering where you did not winnow; so I was afraid, and I went and hid your talent in* 25 *the ground. Here you have what is yours.'*

H Then ⁵another came, saying, 'Lord, here is your pound, 20 which I kept laid away in a napkin; for I was afraid of you, 21 because you are a severe man; you take up what you did not lay down, and reap what you did not sow.'

---

1 Or *slaves*   2 This talent was more than 15 years' wages of a laborer. 3 *Mina*, here translated a pound, is equal to about twenty dollars. It was about 3 months' wages for a laborer.   4 Or *slave*   5 Greek *the other*

HS references: Lk 19:10 = Ezekiel 34:16

MATT 25   LUKE 19

I *But his master answered him, 'You wicked and slothful* 26 *servant! You knew that I reap where I have not sowed, and gather where I have not winnowed? Then you ought to have* 27 *invested my money with the bankers, and at my coming I should have received what was my own with interest. So* 28 *take the talent from him, and give it to him who has the ten talents.*

J¹ *For to every one who has will more be given, and he will* 29 *have abundance; but from him who has not, even what he has will be taken away.*

Kᵏ *And cast the worthless ¹servant into the outer darkness;* 30 *there men will weep and gnash their teeth.' (§ 136 H-Q)*

I He said to him, 'I will condemn you out of your own 22 mouth, you wicked ¹servant! You knew that I was a severe man, taking up what I did not lay down and reaping what I 23 did not sow? Why then did you not put my money into the bank, and at my coming I should have collected it with interest?' And he said to those who stood by, 'Take the 24 pound from him, and give it to him who has the ten pounds.' (And they said to him, 'Lord, he has ten 25 pounds!')

J¹ 'I tell you, that to every one who has will more be 26 given; but from him who has not, even what he has will be taken away.

L But as for these enemies of mine, who did not want me 27 to reign over them, bring them here and slay them before me.'"

M And when he had said this, he went on ahead, going up 28 to Jerusalem.

---

1 Or *slave*

NC references: Mt 25:29 and Lk 19:26 = GT 41

J For to him who has will more be given, and he will have abundance; but from him who has not, even what he has will be taken away. (§ 47 H = Mt 13:12)

J For to him who has will more be given; and from him who has not, even what he has will be taken away. (§ 47 V = Mk 4:25)

J For to him who has will more be given, and from him who has not, even what he thinks that he has will be taken away. (§ 47 V = Lk 8:18)

K I tell you, many will come from east and west and sit at table with Abraham, Isaac, and Jacob in the kingdom of heaven, while the sons of the kingdom will be thrown into the outer darkness; there men will weep and gnash their teeth. (§ 39 D = Mt 8:11-12)

K There you will weep and gnash your teeth, when you see Abraham and Isaac and Jacob and all the prophets in the kingdom of God and you yourselves thrust out. And men will come from east and west, and from north and south, and sit at table in the kingdom of God. (§ 100 G = Lk 13:28-29)

K And throw them into the furnace of fire; there men will weep and gnash their teeth. (§ 48 L = Mt 13:42)
K And throw them into the furnace of fire; there men will weep and gnash their teeth. (§ 48 Q = Mt 13:50)
K And cast him into the outer darkness; there men will weep and gnash their teeth. (§ 129 P = Mt 22:13)
K And will punish him, and put him with the hypocrites; there men will weep and gnash their teeth. (§ 136 D = Mt 24:51)

K And will punish him, and put him with the unfaithful. (§ 94 E = Lk 12:46)

Chapter XVIII

CHALLENGE OF THE JERUSALEM LEADERS BY JESUS

§ 124 Jesus Enters Jerusalem as a Popular Leader

MATT 21:1-11	MARK 11:1-11	LUKE 19:29-44
A And when they drew near to Jerusalem and came to Beth'phage, to the Mount of Olives, then Jesus sent two disciples, saying to them,	**A** And when they drew near to Jerusalem, to Beth'phage and Bethany, at the Mount of Olives, he sent two of his disciples, and said to them,	**A** When he drew near to Beth'phage and Bethany, at the mount that is called Olivet, he sent two of the disciples, saying,
B "Go into the village opposite you, and immediately you will find an ass tied, and a colt with her; untie them and bring them to me. If any one says anything to you, you shall say, 'The Lord has need of them,' and he will send them immediately."	**B** "Go into the village opposite you, and immediately as you enter it you will find a colt tied, on which no one has ever sat; untie it and bring it. If any one says to you, 'Why are you doing this?' say, 'The Lord has need of it and [1]will send it [2]back here immediately.'"	**B** "Go into the village opposite, where on entering you will find a colt tied, on which no one has ever yet sat; untie it and bring it here. If any one asks you, 'Why are you untying it?' you shall say this, 'The Lord has need of it.'"
C This took place to fulfill what was spoken [3]by the prophet, saying, "Tell the daughter of Zion, Behold, your king is coming to you, humble, and mounted on an ass, and on a colt, the foal of an ass."		
D The disciples went and did as Jesus had directed them;	**D** And they went away, and found a colt tied at the door out in the open street; and they untied it. And those who stood there said to them, "What are you doing, untying the colt?" And they told them what Jesus had said; and they let them go.	**D** So those who were sent went away and found it as he had told them. And as they were untying the colt, its owners said to them, "Why are you untying the colt?" And they said, "The Lord has need of it."
E they brought the ass and the colt, and put their garments on them, and he sat thereon.	**E** And they brought the colt to Jesus, and threw their garments on it; and he sat upon it.	**E** And they brought it to Jesus, and throwing their garments on the colt they set Jesus upon it.
F Most of the crowd spread their garments on the road, and others cut branches from the trees and spread them on the road.	**F** And many spread their garments on the road, and others spread [4]leafy branches which they had cut from the fields.	**F** And as he rode along, they spread their garments on the road.
G And the crowds that went before him and that followed him shouted, "Hosanna to the Son of David! Blessed is he who	**G** And those who went before and those who followed cried out, "Hosanna! Blessed is he who comes in the name of the	**G** As he was now drawing near, at the descent of the Mount of Olives, the whole multitude of the disciples began to rejoice and

Verse numbers: MATT — 1, 2, 3, 4, 5, 6, 7, 8, 9; MARK — 1, 2, 3, 4, 5, 6, 7, 8, 9; LUKE — 29, 30, 31, 32, 33, 34, 35, 36, 37

---

1 Greek *sends*   2 Or *again*   3 Or *through*   4 Greek *layers of leaves*

HS references: Mt 21:5 = Isaiah 62:11 and Zechariah 9:9   Mt 21:8 and Mk 11:8 and Lk 9:36 = II Kings 9:13

MATT 21	MARK 11	LUKE 19
comes in the name of the Lord! Hosanna in the highest!"	Lord! Blessed is the kingdom of our 10 father David that is coming! Hosanna in the highest!"	praise God with a loud voice for all the [1]mighty works that they had seen, saying, "Blessed is the King who 38 comes in the name of the Lord! Peace in heaven and glory in the highest!"
H Compare § 126 portions GH		H And some of the Pharisees in the 39 multitude said to him, "Teacher, rebuke your disciples." He answered, 40 "I tell you, if these were silent, the very stones would cry out."
		I And when he drew near and saw the 41 city he wept over it, saying, "[2]Would 42 that even today you knew the things that make for peace! But now they are hid from your eyes. For the days 43 shall come upon you, when your enemies will cast up a [3]bank about you and surround you, and hem you in on every side, and dash you to the 44 ground, you and your children within you, and they will not leave one stone upon another in you; because you did not know the time of your visitation."
J And when he entered Jerusalem, all 10 the city was stirred, saying, "Who is this?" And the crowds said, "This is 11 the prophet Jesus from Nazareth of Galilee."		
	K And he entered Jerusalem, and 11 went into the temple; and when he had looked round at everything, as it was already late, he went out to Bethany with the twelve.	

§ 125 Jesus Returns to Jerusalem

MATT 21:18-19	MARK 11:12-14
In the morning, as he was returning 18 to the city, he was hungry. And seeing 19 [4]a fig tree by the wayside he went to it, and found nothing on it but leaves only. And he said to it, "May no fruit ever come from you again!" (§ 127 A)	On the following day, when they 12 came from Bethany, he was hungry. And seeing in the distance a fig tree 13 in leaf, he went to see if he could find anything on it. When he came to it, he found nothing but leaves, for it was not the season for figs. And he 14 said to it, "May no one ever eat fruit from you again." And his disciples heard it.

1 Greek *powers*   2 Or *O that you had known*   3 Greek *barricade*   4 Or *a single*

HS references: Mt 21:9 and Mk 11:9-10 and Lk 19:38 = Psalm 118:25-26   Lk 19:40 = Habakkuk 2:11   Lk 19:43 = Isaiah 29:3 and Jeremiah 6:6 and Ezekiel 4:2   Lk 19:44 = Psalm 137:9

§ 126 Jesus Casts Commerce from the Temple

MATT 21:12-17	MARK 11:15-19	LUKE 19:45-48
A And Jesus entered the temple [1]of God and drove out all who sold and bought in the temple, and he overturned the tables of the moneychangers and the seats of those who sold pigeons. [12]	A And they came to Jerusalem. And he entered the temple and began to drive out those who sold and those who bought in the temple, and he overturned the tables of the moneychangers and the seats of those who sold pigeons; [15]	A And he entered the temple and began to drive out those who sold, [45]
	B and he would not allow any one to carry anything through the temple. [16]	
C He said to them, "It is written, 'My house shall be called a house of prayer'; but you make it a den of robbers." [13]	C And he taught, and said to them, "Is it not written, 'My house shall be called a house of prayer for all the nations'? But you have made it a den of robbers." [17]	C saying to them, "It is written, 'My house shall be a house of prayer'; but you have made it a den of robbers." [46]
		D And he was teaching daily in the temple. [47]
E _Compare § 130 portion I_	E And the chief priests and the scribes heard it and sought a way to destroy him; for they feared him, because all the multitude was astonished at his teaching. [18]	E The chief priests and the scribes and the principal men of the people sought to destroy him; but they did not find anything they could do, for all the people hung upon his words. [48]
F And the blind and the lame came to him in the temple, and he healed them. [14]		
G But when the chief priests and the scribes saw the wonderful things that he did, and the children crying out in the temple, "Hosanna to the Son of David!" they were indignant; and they said to him, "Do you hear what these are saying?" [15][16]		G _Compare § 124 portion H_
H And Jesus said to them, "Yes; have you never read, 'Out of the mouth of babes and sucklings thou hast brought perfect praise'?"		H _Compare § 124 portion H_
I And leaving them, he went out of the city to Bethany and lodged there. [17]	I And [2]when evening came [3]they went out of the city. [19]	I _And every day he was teaching in the temple, but at night he went out and lodged on the mount called Olivet. And early in the morning all the people came to him in the temple to hear him._ [21:37][38]

1 Many ancient authorities omit _of God_   2 Greek _whenever evening came_   3 Some ancient authorities read _he_

HS references: Mt 21:12 and Mk 11:15 and Lk 19:45 = Exodus 30:13 and Leviticus 1:14   Mt 21:13 and Mk 11:17 and Lk 19:46 = Isaiah 56:7 and Jeremiah 7:11   Mt 21:16 = Psalm 8:2

§ 127 Faith as a Power

MATT 21:18-22   MARK 11:20-25

A In the morning, as he was returning 18 to the city, he was hungry. And 19 seeing [1]a fig tree by the wayside he went to it, and found nothing on it but leaves only. And he said to it, "May no fruit ever come from you again!"

A *On the following day, when they* 11: *came from Bethany, he was hungry.* 12 *And seeing in the distance a fig tree* 13 *in leaf, he went to see if he could find anything on it. When he came to it, he found nothing but leaves, for it was not the season for figs. And he said to* 14 *it, "May no one ever eat fruit from you again." And his disciples heard it.* (§ 125)

B And the fig tree withered at once. When the disciples saw it they 20 marveled, saying, "How did the fig tree wither at once?"

B As they passed by in the morning, 20 they saw the fig tree withered away to its roots. And Peter remembered and 21 said to him, "[2]Master, look! The fig tree which you cursed has withered."

C[C] And Jesus answered them, "Truly, 21 I say to you, if you have faith and never doubt, you will not only do what has been done to the fig tree, but even if you say to this mountain, 'Be taken up and cast into the sea,' it will be done.

C[C] And Jesus answered them, "Have 22 faith in God. Truly, I say to you, 23 whoever says to this mountain, 'Be taken up and cast into the sea,' and does not doubt in his heart, but believes that what he says will come to pass, it will be done for him.

D And whatever you ask in prayer, 22 you will receive, if you have faith."

D Therefore I tell you, whatever you 24 ask in prayer, believe that you have received it, and it will be yours.

E[E] *For if you forgive men their* 6: *trespasses, your heavenly Father also* 14 *will forgive you; but if you do not* 15 *forgive men their trespasses, neither will your Father forgive your trespasses.* (§ 37 X)

E[E] And whenever you stand praying, 25 forgive, if you have anything against any one; so that your Father also who is in heaven may forgive you your trespasses."[3]

---

1 Or *a single*   2 Greek *Rabbi*   3 Many ancient authorities add verse 26: *But if you do not forgive, neither will your Father which is in heaven forgive your trespasses*

NC references: Mt 21:21 and Mk 11:22-23 = GT 48,106

C He said to them, Because of your little faith. For truly, I say to you, if you have faith as a grain of mustard seed, you will say to this mountain, 'Move from here to there,' and it will move. (§ 75 GH = Mt 17:20)

C And the Lord said, If you had faith as a grain of mustard seed, you could say to this sycamine tree, 'Be rooted up, and be planted in the sea,' and it would obey you. (§ 109 F = Lk 17:6)

E So also my heavenly Father will do to every one of you, if you do not forgive your brother from your heart. (§ 78 X = Mt 18:35)

Chapter XIX

FINAL CONTEST OF JESUS WITH THE JEWISH RULERS

§ 128 Jewish Rulers Challenge the Authority of Jesus

MATT 21:23-27	MARK 11:27-33	LUKE 20:1-8
A And when he entered the temple, 23 the chief priests and the elders of the people came up to him as he was teaching, and said, "By what authority are you doing these things, and who gave you this authority?"	A And they came again to Jerusalem. 27 And as he was walking in the temple, the chief priests and the scribes and the elders came to him, and they said 28 to him, "By what authority are you doing these things, or who gave you this authority to do them?"	A One day, as he was teaching the 1 people in the temple and preaching the gospel, the chief priests and the scribes with the elders came up and 2 said to him, "Tell us by what authority you do these things, or who it is that gave you this authority."
B Jesus answered them, "I also will 24 ask you a ¹question; and if you tell me the answer, then I also will tell you by what authority I do these things. The baptism of John, whence 25 was it? From heaven or from men?"	B Jesus said to them, "I will ask you 29 a ¹question; answer me, and I will tell you by what authority I do these things. Was the baptism of John from 30 heaven or from men? Answer me."	B He answered them, "I also will ask 3 you a ¹question; now tell me, Was the 4 baptism of John from heaven or from men?"
C And they argued with one another, "If we say, 'From heaven,' he will say to us, 'Why then did you not believe him?' But if we say, 'From 26 men,' we are afraid of the multitude; for all hold that John was a prophet."	C And they argued with one another, 31 "If we say, 'From heaven,' he will say, 'Why then did you not believe him?' But shall we say, 'From 32 men'?"--they were afraid of the people, ²for all held that John was a real prophet.	C And they discussed it with one 5 another, saying, "If we say, 'From heaven,' he will say, 'Why did you not believe him?' But if we say, 6 'From men,' all the people will stone us; for they are convinced that John was a prophet."
D So they answered Jesus, "We do 27 not know." And he said to them, "Neither will I tell you by what authority I do these things.	D So they answered Jesus, "We do 33 not know." And Jesus said to them, "Neither will I tell you by what authority I do these things."	D So they answered that they did not 7 know whence it was. And Jesus said 8 to them, "Neither will I tell you by what authority I do these things."

§ 129 Parables in Condemnation of Jewish Leaders

MATT 21:28-22:14	MARK 12:1-12	LUKE 20:9-19
A "What do you think? A man had 28 two sons; and he went to the first and said, '³Son, go and work in the vineyard today.' And he answered, 'I 29 will not'; but afterward he repented and went. And he went to the second 30 and said the same; and he answered, 'I go, sir,' but did not go. Which of 31 the two did the will of his father?" They said, "The first."		

---

1 Greek *word* 2 Or *for all indeed held John to be a prophet* 3 Greek *Child*

MATT 21	MARK 12	LUKE 20
B Jesus said to them, "Truly, I say to you, the tax collectors and the harlots go into the kingdom of God before you. For John came to you in the way 32 of righteousness, and you did not believe him, but the tax collectors and the harlots believed him; and even when you saw it, you did not afterward repent and believe him.		**B** *(When they heard this all the people* 7: *and the tax collectors justified God,* 29 *having been baptized with the baptism of John; but the Pharisees and the* 30 *lawyers rejected the purpose of God for themselves, not having been baptized by him.) (§ 41 I)*
C "Hear another parable. There was a 33 householder who planted a vineyard, and set a hedge around it, and dug a wine press in it, and built a tower, and let it out to tenants, and went into another country.	**C** And he began to speak to them in 1 parables. "A man planted a vineyard, and set a hedge around it, and dug a pit for the wine press, and built a tower, and let it out to tenants, and went into another country.	**C** And he began to tell the people this 9 parable: "A man planted a vineyard, and let it out to tenants, and went into another country for a long while.
D When the season of fruit drew 34 near, he sent his [1]servants to the tenants, to get [3]his fruit; and the 35 tenants took his [1]servants and beat one, killed another, and stoned another.	**D** When the time came, he sent a 2 [2]servant to the tenants, to get from them some of the fruit of the vineyard. And they took him and beat 3 him, and sent him away empty-handed.	**D** When the time came, he sent a 10 [2]servant to the tenants, that they should give him some of the fruit of the vineyard; but the tenants beat him, and sent him away empty-handed.
E Again he sent other [1]servants, more 36 than the first; and they did the same to them.	**E** Again he sent to them another 4 [2]servant, and they wounded him in the head, and treated him shamefully. And he sent another, and him they 5 killed; and so with many others, some they beat and some they killed.	**E** And he sent another [2]servant; him 11 also they beat and treated shamefully, and sent him away empty-handed. And he sent yet a third; this one they 12 wounded and cast out.
F Afterward he sent his son to them, 37 saying, 'They will respect my son.' But when the tenants saw the son, 38 they said to themselves, 'This is the heir; come, let us kill him and have his inheritance.' And they took him 39 and cast him out of the vineyard, and killed him.	**F** He had still one other, a beloved 6 son; finally he sent him to them, saying, 'They will respect my son.' But those tenants said to one another, 7 'This is the heir; come, let us kill him, and the inheritance will be ours.' And they took him and killed him, 8 and cast him out of the vineyard.	**F** Then the owner of the vineyard 13 said, 'What shall I do? I will send my beloved son; it may be they will respect him.' But when the tenants 14 saw him, they said to themselves, 'This is the heir; let us kill him, that the inheritance may be ours.' And 15 they cast him out of the vineyard and killed him.
G When therefore the owner of the 40 vineyard comes, what will he do to those tenants?" They said to him, "He 41 will put those wretches to a miserable death, and let out the vineyard to other tenants who will give him the fruits in their seasons."	**G** What will the owner of the 9 vineyard do? He will come and destroy the tenants, and give the vineyard to others.	**G** What then will the owner of the vineyard do to them? He will come 16 and destroy those tenants, and give the vineyard to others."

---

1 Or *slaves*   2 Or *slave*   3 Or *the fruits of it*

HS references: Mt 21:33 and Mk 12:1 and Lk 20:9 = Isaiah 5:1-2
NC references: Mt 21:33-46 and Mk 12:1-12 and Lk 20:9-19 = GT 65

MATT 21-22	MARK 12	LUKE 20

H Jesus said to them, "Have you 42 never read in the scriptures:
'The very stone which the
    builders rejected
has become the head of the
    corner;
this was the Lord's doing,
and it is marvelous in our eyes'?
	H Have you not read this scripture:
	'The very stone which the
	    builders rejected
	has become the head of the
	    corner;
	this was the Lord's doing,
	and it is marvelous in our
	    eyes'?"
		H When they heard this, they said, 10
		[1]"God forbid!" But he looked at them 17
		and said, "What then is this that is
		written:
		'The very stone which the
		    builders rejected 11
		has become the head of the
		    corner'?

I Therefore I tell you, the kingdom of 43 God will be taken away from you and given to a nation producing the fruits of it."		
J *See note 2 below*		**J** Every one who falls on that stone 18 will be broken to pieces; but when it falls on any one it will crush him."
K When the chief priests and the 45 Pharisees heard his parables, they perceived that he was speaking about them. But when they tried to arrest 46 him, they feared the multitudes, because they held him to be a prophet.	**K** And they tried to arrest him, but 12 feared the multitude, for they perceived that he had told the parable against them; so they left him and went away.	**K** The scribes and the chief priests 19 tried to lay hands on him at that very hour, but they feared the people; for they perceived that he had told this parable against them.
L And again Jesus spoke to them in 22: parables, saying, "The kingdom of 1 heaven may be compared to a king 2 who gave a marriage feast for his son, and sent his [3]servants to call 3 those who were invited to the marriage feast; but they would not come. Again he sent other [3]servants, 4 saying, 'Tell those who are invited, Behold, I have made ready my dinner, my oxen and my fat calves are killed, and everything is ready; come to the marriage feast.'		**L** *But he said to him, "A man once 14: gave a great banquet, and invited 16 many; and at the time for the banquet 17 he sent his [4]servant to say to those who had been invited, 'Come, for all is now ready.'*
M But they made light of it and went 5 off, one to his farm, another to his business, while the rest seized his 6 [3]servants, treated them shamefully, and killed them.		**M** *But they all alike began to make 18 excuses. The first said to him, 'I have bought a field, and I must go out and see it. I pray you, have me excused.' And another said, 'I have bought five 19 yoke of oxen, and I go to examine them; I pray you, have me excused.' And another said, 'I have married a 20 wife, and therefore I cannot come.' So 21 the [4]servant came and reported this to his master.*

---

1 Greek *May it not be*   2 Many ancient authorities add verse 44: *"And he who falls on this stone will be broken to pieces; but when it falls on any one, it will crush him."*   3 Or *slaves*   4 Or *slave*

HS references: Mt 21:42 and Mk 12:10-11 and Lk 20:17 = Psalm 118:22-23   Mt 21:44 and Lk 20:18 = Isaiah 8:14-15
NC references: Mt 21:42 and Mk 12:10 and Lk 20:17 = GT 66

MATT 22   LUKE

N The king was angry, and he sent 7 his troops and destroyed those murderers and burned their city.

O Then he said to his ¹servants, 'The 8 wedding is ready, but those invited were not worthy. Go therefore to the 9 thoroughfares, and invite to the marriage feast as many as you find.' And those ¹servants went out into the 10 streets and gathered all whom they found, both bad and good; so the wedding hall was filled with guests.

O *Then the householder in anger said to his servant, 'Go out quickly to the streets and lanes of the city; and bring in the poor and maimed and blind and lame.' And the servant said, 'Sir, 22 what you commanded has been done, and still there is room.' And the 23 master said to the servant, 'Go out to the highways and hedges, and compel people to come in, that my house may be filled. For I tell you, none of those 24 men who were invited shall taste my banquet.'"* (§ 103 E-H)

Pᵖ "But when the king came in to 11 look at the guests, he saw there a man who had no wedding garment; and he 12 said to him, 'Friend, how did you get in here without a wedding garment?' And he was speechless. Then the king 13 said to the ²attendants, 'Bind him hand and foot, and cast him into the outer darkness; there men will weep and gnash their teeth.' For many are 14 called, but few are chosen."

§ 130 Efforts to Accumulate Evidence Against Jesus

MATT 22:15-40   MARK 12:13-34   LUKE 20:20-40

A Then the Pharisees went and took 15 counsel how to entangle him in his talk. And they sent their disciples to 16 him, along with the Hero'di-ans,

A And they sent to him some of the 13 Pharisees and some of the Hero'di-ans, to entrap him in his talk.

A So they watched him, and sent 20 spies, who pretended to be sincere, that they might take hold of what he said, so as to deliver him up to the authority and jurisdiction of the governor.

---

1 Or *slaves*   2 Or *ministers*

NC references: Mt 22:2-10 and Lk 14:16-24 = GT 64

P I tell you, many will come from east and west and sit at table with Abraham, Isaac, and Jacob in the kingdom of heaven, while the sons of the kingdom will be thrown into the outer darkness; there men will weep and gnash their teeth. (§ 39 D = Mt 8:11-12)

P And throw them into the furnace of fire; there men will weep and gnash their teeth. (§ 48 L = Mt 13:42)
P And throw them into the furnace of fire; there men will weep and gnash their teeth. (§ 48 Q = Mt 13:50)
P And will punish him, and put him with the hypocrites; there men will weep and gnash their teeth. (§ 136 D = Mt 24:51)
P And cast the worthless servant into the outer darkness; there men will weep and gnash their teeth. (§ 136 Q = Mt 25:30)

P There you will weep and gnash your teeth, when you see Abraham and Isaac and Jacob and all the prophets in the kingdom of God and you yourselves thrust out. And men will come from east and west, and from north and south, and sit at table in the kingdom of God. (§ 100 G = Lk 13:28-29)

P And will punish him, and put him with the unfaithful. (§ 94 E = Lk 12:46)

MATT 22 | MARK 12 | LUKE 20

B saying, "Teacher, we know that you are true, and teach the way of God truthfully, and care for no man; for you do not regard the position of men. Tell us, then, what you think. Is 17 it lawful to pay taxes to Caesar, or not?"

C But Jesus, aware of their malice, 18 said, "Why put me to the test, you hypocrites? Show me the money for 19 the tax." And they brought him a ¹coin. And Jesus said to them, 20 "Whose likeness and inscription is this?" They said, "Caesar's." Then he 21 said to them, "Render therefore to Caesar the things that are Caesar's, and to God the things that are God's."

D When they heard it, they marveled; 22 and they left him and went away.

E The same day Sad'ducees came to 23 him, ²who say that there is no resurrection; and they asked him a question, saying, 24

F "Teacher, Moses said, 'If a man dies, having no children, his brother ³must marry the widow, and raise up children for his brother.' Now there 25 were seven brothers among us; the first married, and died, and having no children left his wife to his brother. So too the second and third, down to 26 the ⁵seventh. After them all, the 27 woman died. In the resurrection, 28 therefore, to which of the seven will she be wife? For they all had her."

G But Jesus answered them, "You are 29 wrong, because you know neither the scriptures nor the power of God. For 30 in the resurrection they neither marry nor are given in marriage, but are like angels⁶ in heaven.

B And they came and said to him, 14 "Teacher, we know that you are true, and care for no man; for you do not regard the position of men, but truly teach the way of God. Is it lawful to pay taxes to Caesar, or not? Should 15 we pay them, or should we not?"

C But knowing their hypocrisy, he said to them, "Why put me to the test? Bring me a ¹coin, and let me look at it." And they brought one. 16 And he said to them, "Whose likeness and inscription is this?" They said to him, "Caesar's." Jesus said to them, 17 "Render to Caesar the things that are Caesar's, and to God the things that are God's."

D And they were amazed at him.

E And Sad'ducees came to him, who 18 say that there is no resurrection; and they asked him a question, saying,

F "Teacher, Moses wrote for us that 19 if a man's brother dies and leaves a wife, but leaves no child, ⁴the man must take the wife, and raise up children for his brother. There were 20 seven brothers; the first took a wife, and when he died left no children; and the second took her, and died, 21 leaving no children; and the third likewise; and the seven left no 22 children. Last of all the woman also died. In the resurrection whose wife 23 will she be? For the seven had her as wife."

G Jesus said to them, "Is not this why 24 you are wrong, that you know neither the scriptures nor the power of God? For when they rise from the dead, 25 they neither marry nor are given in marriage, but are like angels in heaven.

B They asked him, "Teacher, we 21 know that you speak and teach rightly, and show no partiality, but truly teach the way of God. Is it 22 lawful for us to give tribute to Caesar, or not?"

C But he perceived their craftiness, 23 and said to them, "Show me a ¹coin. 24 Whose likeness and inscription has it?" They said, "Caesar's." He said to 25 them, "Then render to Caesar the things that are Caesar's, and to God the things that are God's."

D And they were not able in the 26 presence of the people to catch him by what he said; but marveling at his answer they were silent.

E There came to him some 27 Sad'ducees, those who say that there is no resurrection, and they asked him 28 a question, saying,

F "Teacher, Moses wrote for us that if a man's brother dies, having a wife but no children, the man must take the wife and raise up children for his brother. Now there were seven 29 brothers; the first took a wife, and died without children; and the second 30 and the third took her, and likewise 31 all seven left no children and died. Afterward the woman also died. In 32 the resurrection, therefore, whose 33 wife will the woman be? For the seven had her as wife."

G And Jesus said to them, "The sons 34 of this age marry and are given in marriage; but those who are 35 accounted worthy to attain to that age and to the resurrection from the dead neither marry nor are given in marriage, for they cannot die any 36 more,

---

1 Greek *denarius*, a coin worth about forty cents. The denarius was a day's wage for a laborer.   2 Greek *saying*   3 Greek *shall perform the duty of a husband's brother to his wife*: compare Deuteronomy 25:5   4 Greek *his brother*   5 Greek *seven*   6 Many ancient authorities add *of God*

HS references: Mt 22:24 and Mk 12:19 and Lk 20:28 = Deuteronomy 25:5-6 (compare Genesis 38:8)
NC references: Mt 22:15-22 and Mk 12:13-17 and Lk 20:22-25 = GT 100

MATT **22**   MARK **12**   LUKE **20**

because they are equal to angels and are sons of God, being sons of the resurrection.

H And as for the resurrection of the 31 dead, have you not read what was said to you by God, 'I am the God of 32 Abraham, and the God of Isaac, and the God of Jacob'? He is not God of the dead, but of the living."

H And as for the dead being raised, 26 have you not read in the book of Moses, in the passage about the bush, how God said to him, 'I am the God of Abraham, and the God of Isaac, and the God of Jacob'? He is not God 27 of the dead, but of the living; you are quite wrong."

H But that the dead are raised, even 37 Moses showed, in the passage about the bush, where he calls the Lord the God of Abraham and the God of Isaac and the God of Jacob. Now he is not 38 God of the dead, but of the living; for all live to him."

I And when the crowd heard it, they 33 were astonished at his teaching.

I   *Compare § 126 portion E*

I   *Compare § 126 portion E*

J   *Compare portion O below*

J And some of the scribes answered, 39 "Teacher, you have spoken well."

K   *Compare § 131 portion D*

K   *Compare portion Q below*

K For they no longer dared to ask 40 him any question.

L But when the Pharisees heard that 34 he had silenced the Sad'ducees, they came together. And one of them, a 35 lawyer, asked him a question, to test him. "Teacher, which is the great 36 commandment in the law?"

L And one of the scribes came up and 28 heard them disputing with one another, and seeing that he answered them well, asked him, "Which commandment is the first of all?"

L *And behold, a lawyer stood up to* 10: *put him to the test, saying, "Teacher,* 25 *what shall I do to inherit eternal life?" He said to him, "What is* 26 *written in the law? How do you read?"*

M And he said to him, "You shall 37 love the Lord your God with all your heart, and with all your soul, and with all your mind. This is the great 38 and first commandment. And a second 39 is like it, You shall love your neighbor as yourself.

M Jesus answered, "The first is, 29 'Hear, O Israel: The Lord our God, the Lord is one; and you shall love 30 the Lord your God [1]with all your heart, and [1]with all your soul, and [1]with all your mind, and [1]with all your strength.' The second is this, 31 'You shall love your neighbor as yourself.'

M *And he answered, "You shall love* 27 *the Lord your God* [1]*with all your heart, and with all your soul, and with all your strength, and with all your mind; and your neighbor as yourself."*

N[N] On these two commandments 40 depend all the law and the prophets."

N[N] There is no other commandment greater than these."

N[N] *And he said to him, "You have* 28 *answered right; do this, and you will live." (§ 83 A)*

O And the scribe said to him, "You 32 are right, Teacher; you have truly said that he is one, and there is no other but he; and to love him with all 33 the heart, and with all the understanding, and with all the strength, and to love one's neighbor as oneself, is much more than all whole burnt offerings and sacrifices."

O   *Compare portion J above*

---

1 Greek *from*

HS references: Mt 22:32 and Mk 12:26 and Lk 20:37 = Exodus 3:6   Mk 12:29 = Deuteronomy 6:4   Mt 22:37 and Mk 12:30 and Lk 10:27 = Deuteronomy 6:5   Mt 22:39 and Mk 12:31 and Lk 10:27 = Leviticus 19:18   Lk 10:28 = Leviticus 18:5   Mk 12:32 = Deuteronomy 6:4 and 4:35 Mk 12:33 = Deuteronomy 6:5 and Leviticus 19:18 and I Samuel 15:22 and Hosea 6:6 and Micah 6:6-8

N For this is the law and the prophets. (§ 38 L = Mt 7:12)

MATT 22	MARK 12	LUKE 20
	P And when Jesus saw that he 34 answered wisely, he said to him, "You are not far from the kingdom of God."	
Q *Compare § 131 portion D*	**Q** And after that no one dared to ask him any question.	**Q** *Compare portion K above*

§ 131 The Problem of the Christ

MATT 22:41-46	MARK 12:35-37	LUKE 20:41-44
A Now while the Pharisees were 41 gathered together, Jesus asked them a question, saying, "What do you think 42 of the Christ? Whose son is he?" They said to him, "The son of David."	**A** And as Jesus taught in the temple, 35 he said, "How can the scribes say that the Christ is the son of David?	**A** But he said to them, "How can 41 they say that the Christ is David's son?
B He said to them, "How is it then 43 that David, [1]inspired by the Spirit, calls him Lord, saying, 'The Lord said to my Lord, 44 Sit at my right hand, till I put thy enemies under thy feet'? If David thus calls him Lord, how is 45 he his son?"	**B** David himself, [1]inspired by the 36 Holy Spirit, declared, 'The Lord said to my Lord, Sit at my right hand, till I [2]put thy enemies under thy feet.' David himself calls him Lord; so how 37 is he his son?"	**B** For David himself says in the Book 42 of Psalms, 'The Lord said to my Lord, Sit at my right hand, till I make thy enemies a stool 43 for thy feet.' David thus calls him Lord; so how is 44 he his son?"
	C And the [3]great throng heard him gladly.	
D And no one was able to answer 46 him a word, nor from that day did any one dare to ask him any more questions.	**D** *Compare § 130 portion Q*	**D** *Compare § 130 portion K*

---

1 Greek *in*   2 Some ancient authorities read *make thy enemies the footstool of thy feet*   3 Or *the common people*

HS references: Mt 22:44 and Mk 12:36 and Lk 20:42-43 = Psalm 110:1

Chapter XX

DISCOURSE IN CONDEMNATION OF SCRIBES AND PHARISEES

§ 132 Discourse in Condemnation of Scribes and Pharisees

MATT 23:1-39	MARK 12:38-40	LUKE 20:45-47
A Then said Jesus to the crowds and 1 to his disciples,	**A** And in his teaching he said,	38 **A** And in the hearing of all the people 45 he said to his disciples,
B "The scribes and the Pharisees sit 2 on Moses' seat; so practice and 3 observe whatever they tell you, but not what they do; for they preach, but do not practice.		
C They bind heavy burdens, ¹hard to 4 bear, and lay them on men's shoulders; but they themselves will not move them with their finger.		**C** *"Woe to you lawyers also! for you* 11: *load men with burdens hard to bear,* 46 *and you yourselves do not touch the burdens with one of your fingers.* (§ 90 G)
D They do all their deeds to be seen 5 by men; for they make their phylacteries broad and their fringes long, and they love the place of honor 6 at feasts and the best seats in the synagogues, and salutations in the 7 market places, and being called rabbi by men.	**D** "Beware of the scribes, who like to go about in long robes, and to have salutations in the market places and 39 the best seats in the synagogues and the places of honor at feasts,	**D** "Beware of the scribes, who like to 46 go about in long robes, and love salutations in the market places and the best seats in the synagogues and the places of honor at feasts, *Woe to you Pharisees! for you love* 11: *the best seat in the synagogues and* 43 *salutations in the market places.* (§ 90 D)
	E who devour widows' houses and 40 for a pretense make long prayers. They will receive the greater condemnation."	**E** who devour widows' houses and 47 for a pretense make long prayers. They will receive the greater condemnation."
F But you are not to be called rabbi, 8 for you have one teacher, and you are all brethren. And call no man your 9 father on earth, for you have one Father, ²who is in heaven. Neither be 10 called masters, for you have one master, the Christ.		
Gᴳ He who is ³greatest among you 11 shall be your ⁴servant;		

---

1 Many ancient authorities omit *hard to bear*   2 Greek *the heavenly*   3 Greek *greater*   4 Or *minister*

HS references: Mt 23:5 = Exodus 13:9 and Numbers 15:38-39 and Deuteronomy 6:8 and 11:18

G Whoever humbles himself like this child, he is the greatest in the kingdom of heaven. (§ 78 E = Mt 18:4) G It shall be not so among you; but whoever would be great among you must be your servant, and whoever would be first among you must be your slave. (§ 120 J = Mt 20:26-27)	G If any one would be first, he must be last of all and servant of all. (§ 78 B = Mk 9:35) G But it shall not be so among you; but whoever would be great among you must be your servant, and whoever would be first among you must be slave of all. (§ 120 J = Mk 10:43-44)	G For he who is least among you all is the one who is great. (§ 78 H = Lk 9:48) G But not so with you; rather let the greatest among you become as the youngest, and the leader as one who serves. (§ 138 M = Lk 22:26)

MATT 23

H^H whoever exalts himself will be 12 humbled, and whoever humbles himself will be exalted.

I "But woe to you, scribes and 13 Pharisees, hypocrites! because you shut the kingdom of heaven ¹against men; for you neither enter yourselves, nor allow those who would enter to go in.²

J Woe to you, scribes and Pharisees, 15 hypocrites! for you traverse sea and land to make a single proselyte, and when he becomes a proselyte, you make him twice as much a child of ³hell as yourselves.

K "Woe to you, blind guides, who 16 say, 'If any one swears by the ⁴temple, it is nothing; but if any one swears by the gold of the ⁴temple, he is bound by his oath.' You blind 17 fools! For which is greater, the gold or the ⁴temple that has made the gold sacred? And you say, 'If any one 18 swears by the altar, it is nothing; but if any one swears by the gift that is on the altar, he is bound by his oath.' You blind men! For which is greater, 19 the gift or the altar that makes the gift sacred? So he who swears by the 20 altar, swears by it and by everything on it; and he who swears by the 21 ⁴temple, swears by it and by him who dwells in it; and he who swears by 22 heaven, swears by the throne of God and by him who sits upon it.

L "Woe to you, scribes and 23 Pharisees, hypocrites! for you tithe mint and dill and cummin, and have neglected the weightier matters of the law, justice and mercy and faith; these you ought to have done, without neglecting the others. You blind 24 guides, straining out a gnat and swallowing a camel!

LUKE 11

I *Woe to you lawyers! for you have* 52 *taken away the key of knowledge; you did not enter yourselves, and you hindered those who were entering."* (§ 90 J)

L *"But woe to you Pharisees! for you* 42 *tithe mint and rue and every herb, and neglect justice and the love of God; these you ought to have done, without neglecting the others.* (§ 90 C)

---

1 Greek *before*   2 Some authorities insert here, or after verse 12, verse 14: *Woe to you, scribes and Pharisees, hypocrites! for you devour widows' houses, and for a pretense you make long prayers; therefore you will receive the greater condemnation:* see Mark 12:40 and Luke 20:47
3 Greek *Gehenna*   4 Or *sanctuary*: as in verse 35

HS references: Mt 23:17 = Exodus 30:29   Mt 23:21 = I Kings 8:13 and Psalm 26:8   Mt 23:23 and Lk 11:42 = Leviticus 27:30 and Micah 6:8
NC references: Mt 23:13 and Lk 11:52 = GT 39, 102

H For every one who exalts himself will be humbled, and he who humbles himself will be exalted. (§ 103 P = Lk 14:11)
H For every one who exalts himself will be humbled, but he who humbles himself will be exalted. (§ 114 B = Lk 18:14)

MATT 23

M "Woe to you, scribes and 25 Pharisees, hypocrites! for you cleanse the outside of the cup and of the plate, but inside they are full of extortion and rapacity. You blind 26 Pharisee! first cleanse the inside of the cup and of the plate, that the outside also may be clean.

N "Woe to you, scribes and 27 Pharisees, hypocrites! for you are like whitewashed tombs, which outwardly appear beautiful, but within they are full of dead men's bones and all uncleanness. So you also outwardly 28 appear righteous to men, but within you are full of hypocrisy and iniquity.

O "Woe to you, scribes and 29 Pharisees, hypocrites! for you build the tombs of the prophets and adorn the monuments of the righteous, saying, 'If we had lived in the days of 30 our fathers, we would not have taken part with them in shedding the blood of the prophets.' Thus you witness 31 against yourselves, that you are sons of those who murdered the prophets.

P[P] Fill up, then, the measure of your 32 fathers. You serpents, you brood of 33 vipers, how are you to escape being sentenced to [2]hell?

Q Therefore I send you prophets and 34 wise men and scribes, some of whom you will kill and crucify, and some you will scourge in your synagogues and persecute from town to town, that 35 upon you may come all the righteous blood shed on earth, from the blood of innocent Abel to the blood of Zechari'ah the son of Barachi'ah, whom you murdered between the sanctuary and the altar. Truly, I say 36 to you, all this will come upon this generation.

LUKE 11

M *"Now you Pharisees cleanse the 39 outside of the cup and of the dish, but inside you are full of extortion and wickedness. You fools! Did not he 40 who made the outside make the inside also? But give for alms those things 41 which [1]are within; and behold, everything is clean for you.* (§ 90 B)

N *"Woe to you! for you are like 44 graves which are not seen, and men walk over them without knowing it."* (§ 90 E)

O *Woe to you! for you build the 47 tombs of the prophets whom your fathers killed. So you are witnesses 48 and consent to the deeds of your fathers; for they killed them, and you build their tombs.* (§ 90 H)

Q *Therefore also the Wisdom of God 49 said, 'I will send them prophets and apostles, some of whom they will kill and persecute,' that the blood of all 50 the prophets, shed from the foundation of the world, may be required of this generation, from the blood of Abel to 51 the blood of Zechari'ah, who perished between the altar and the [3]sanctuary. Yes, I tell you, it shall be required of this generation.* (§ 90 I)

---

1 Or *you can*   2 Greek *Gehenna*   3 Greek *house*

HS references: Mt 23:25-28 = Psalm 5:9   Mt 23:35 and Lk 11:51 = Genesis 4:8 and Zechariah 1:1 and II Chronicles 24:20-21
NC references: Mt 23:25-26 and Lk 11:39-41 = GT 89

P For the record of a saying by John the Baptist somewhat similar to verse 33, compare § 17 M. The saying is recorded of Jesus in § 45 N

MATT 23

R "O Jerusalem, Jerusalem, killing 37 the prophets and stoning those who are sent to you! How often would I have gathered your children together as a hen gathers her brood under her wings, and you would not! Behold, 38 your house is forsaken ¹and desolate. For I tell you, you will not see me 39 again, until you say, 'Blessed is he who comes in the name of the Lord.'"

LUKE

R *O Jerusalem, Jerusalem, killing the* 13: *prophets and stoning those who are* 34 *sent to you! How often would I have gathered your children together as a hen gathers her brood under her wings, and you would not! Behold,* 35 *your house is forsaken. And I tell you, you will not see me until you say, 'Blessed is he who comes in the name of the Lord.'"* (§ 101 B)

§ 133   The True Test of Giving

MARK 12:41-44

A And he sat down opposite the 41 treasury, and watched the multitude putting ³money into the treasury. Many rich people put in large sums. And ⁴a poor widow came, and put in 42 two copper coins, which make a penny.

B And he called his disciples to him, 43 and said to them, "Truly, I say to you, this poor widow has put in more than all those who are contributing to the treasury. For they all contributed 44 out of their abundance; but she out of her poverty has put in everything she had, her whole living."

LUKE 21:1-4

A He looked up ²and saw the rich 1 putting their gifts into the treasury; and he saw a poor widow put in two 2 copper coins.

B And he said, "Truly I tell you, this 3 poor widow has put in more than all of them; for they all contributed out 4 of their abundance, but she out of her poverty put in all the living that she had."

---

1 Some ancient authorities omit *and desolate*   2 Or *and saw them that were casting their gifts into the treasury, and they were rich*   3 Greek *brass*
4 Greek *one*

HS references: Mt 23:38 and Lk 13:35a = Jeremiah 12:7 and 22:5 and I Kings 9:7   Mt 23:39 and Lk 13:35b = Psalm 118:26

Chapter XXI

DISCOURSE ON EVENTS OF THE FUTURE

§ 134 Discourse on Events of the Future

MATT 24:1-25:46	MARK 13:1-37	LUKE 21:5-38
A Jesus left the temple and was going 1 away, when his disciples came to point out to him the buildings of the temple.	**A** And as he came out of the temple, 1 one of his disciples said to him, "Look, Teacher, what wonderful stones and what wonderful buildings!"	**A** And as some spoke of the temple, 5 how it was adorned with noble stones and offerings,
B But he answered them, "You see all 2 these, do you not? Truly, I say to you, there will not be left here one stone upon another, that will not be thrown down."	**B** And Jesus said to him, "Do you see 2 these great buildings? There will not be left here one stone upon another, that will not be thrown down."	**B** he said, "As for these things which 6 you see, the days will come when there shall not be left here one stone upon another that will not be thrown down."
C As he sat on the Mount of Olives, 3 the disciples came to him privately, saying, "Tell us, when will this be, and what will be the sign of your ¹coming and of the close of the age?"	**C** And as he sat on the Mount of 3 Olives opposite the temple, Peter and James and John and Andrew asked him privately, "Tell us, when will this 4 be, and what will be the sign when these things are all to be accomplished?"	**C** And they asked him, "Teacher, 7 when will this be, and what will be the sign when this is about to take place?"
Dᴰ And Jesus answered them, "Take 4 heed that no one leads you astray. For 5 many will come in my name, saying, 'I am the Christ,' and they will lead many astray.	**D**ᴰ And Jesus began to say to them, 5 "Take heed that no one leads you astray. Many will come in my name, 6 saying, 'I am he!' and they will lead many astray.	**D**ᴰ And he said, "Take heed that you 8 are not led astray; for many will come in my name, saying, 'I am he!' and, 'The time is at hand!' Do not go after them.
E And you will hear of wars and 6 rumors of wars; see that you are not alarmed; for this must take place, but the end is not yet.	**E** And when you hear of wars and 7 rumors of wars, do not be alarmed; this must take place, but the end is not yet.	**E** And when you hear of wars and 9 tumults, do not be terrified; for this must first take place, but the end will not be at once."
F For nation will rise against nation, 7 and kingdom against kingdom, and there will be famines and earthquakes in various places: all this is but the 8 beginning of the birth-pangs.	**F** For nation will rise against nation, 8 and kingdom against kingdom; there will be earthquakes in various places, there will be famines; this is but the beginning of the birth-pangs.	**F** Then he said to them, "Nation will 10 rise against nation, and kingdom against kingdom; there will be great 11 earthquakes, and in various places famines and pestilences; and there will be terrors and great signs from heaven.
G *Beware of men; for they will* 10: *deliver you up to councils, and flog* 17 *you in their synagogues, and you will* 18 *be dragged before governors and kings for my sake, to bear testimony before them and the Gentiles.* "Then they will deliver you up to 9a tribulation,	**G** "But take heed to yourselves; for 9 they will deliver you up to councils; and you will be beaten in synagogues; and you will stand before governors and kings for my sake, to bear testimony before them.	**G** But before all this they will lay 12 their hands on you and persecute you, delivering you up to the synagogues and prisons, and you ²will be brought before kings and governors for my name's sake. This will be a time for 13 you to bear testimony.

---

1 Greek *presence* 2 Greek *being brought*

HS references: Mt 24:7 and Mk 13:8 and Lk 21:10 = Isaiah 19:2 and II Chronicles 15:6

D Compare § 135 portions ABC

MATT 24	MARK 13	LUKE 21
H *Compare portion N below Compare § 57 portion F*	**H** And the gospel must first be 10 preached to all nations.	
I[I] *When they deliver you up, do not be* 19 *anxious how you are to speak or what you are to say; for what you are to say will be given to you in that hour;* 20 *for it is not you who speak, but the Spirit of your Father speaking through you.*	**I**[I] And when they bring you to trial 11 and deliver you up, do not be anxious beforehand what you are to say; but say whatever is given you in that hour, for it is not you who speak, but the Holy Spirit.	**I**[I] Settle it therefore in your minds, 14 not to meditate beforehand how to answer; for I will give you a mouth 15 and wisdom, which none of your adversaries will be able to withstand or contradict.
J *Brother will deliver up brother to* 21 *death, and the father his child, and children will rise against parents and* [1]*have them put to death;* and put you to death; 9b	**J** And brother will deliver up brother 12 to death, and the father his child, and children will rise against parents and [1]have them put to death;	**J** You will be delivered up even by 16 parents and brothers and kinsmen and friends, and some of you they will put to death;
K *and you will be hated by all for my* 22a *name's sake.* and you will be hated by all nations 9c for my name's sake.	**K** and you will be hated by all for my 13 name's sake.	**K** you will be hated by all for my 17 name's sake.
L And then many will [2]fall away, and 10 betray one another, and hate one another. And many false prophets will 11 arise and lead many astray. And 12 because wickedness is multiplied, most men's love will grow cold.		
M *But he who endures to the end will* 22b *be saved. (§ 57 A-E)* But he who endures to the end will be 13 saved.	**M** But he who endures to the end will be saved.	**M**[M] But not a hair of your head will 18 perish. By your endurance you will 19 gain your lives.
N And [3]this gospel of the kingdom 14 will be preached throughout the whole [4]world, as a testimony to all nations; and then the end will come.	**N** *Compare portion H above*	
O "So when you see the desolating 15 sacrilege spoken of [5]by the prophet Daniel, standing in [6]the holy place (let the reader understand), then let those 16 who are in Judea flee to the mountains;	**O** "But when you see the desolating 14 sacrilege set up where it ought not to be (let the reader understand), then let those who are in Judea flee to the mountains;	**O** "But when you see Jerusalem 20 surrounded by armies, then know that its desolation has come near. Then let 21 those who are in Judea flee to the mountains,

---

1 Or *put them to death*　2 Greek *stumble*　3 Or *these good tidings*　4 Greek *inhabited earth*　5 Or *through*　6 Or *a holy place*

HS references: Mt 10:21 and Mk 13:12 and Lk 21:16 = Micah 7:6　　　Mt 24:15 and Mk 13:14 and Lk 21:20 = Daniel 9:27, 11:31, and 12:11
Lk 21:19 = I Samuel 14:45

I And when they bring you before the synagogues and the rulers and the authorities, do not be anxious how or what you are to answer or what you are to say; for the Holy Spirit will teach you in that very hour what you ought to say. (§ 91 I = Lk 12:11-12)
M (Lk) But even the hairs of your head are all numbered.　　　　　　M (Lk) Why, even the hairs of your head are all numbered.
(§ 57 J = Mt 10:30)　　　　　　　　　　　　　　　　　　　　　　(§ 91 F = Lk 12:7)

MATT 24	MARK 13	LUKE 21
P *Compare portion Q below*	**P** *Compare portion Q below*	**P** and let those who are inside the city depart, and let not those who are out in the country enter it; for these are 22 days of vengeance, to fulfil all that is written.
Q let him who is on the housetop not 17 go down to take what is in his house; and let him who is in the field not 18 turn back to take his mantle.	**Q** let him who is on the housetop not 15 go down, nor enter his house, to take anything away; and let him who is in 16 the field not turn back to take his mantle.	**Q** *On that day, let him who is on the 17: housetop, with his goods in the house, 31 not come down to take them away; and likewise let him who is in the field not turn back. (§ 112 H)* *Compare portion P above*
R And alas for those who are with 19 child and for those who give suck in those days! Pray that your flight may 20 not be in winter or on a sabbath. For 21 then there will be great tribulation, such as has not been from the beginning of the world until now, no, and never will be.	**R** And alas for those who are with 17 child and for those who give suck in those days! Pray that it may not 18 happen in winter. For in those days 19 there will be such tribulation as has not been from the beginning of the creation which God created until now, and never will be.	**R** Alas for those who are with child 23 and for those who give suck in those days! For great distress shall be upon the earth and wrath upon this people; they will fall by the edge of the 24 sword, and be led captive among all nations; and Jerusalem will be trodden down by the Gentiles, until the times of the Gentiles are fulfilled.
S And if those days had not been 22 shortened, no human being would be saved; but for the sake of the elect those days will be shortened.	**S** And if the Lord had not shortened 20 the days, no human being would be saved; but for the sake of the elect, whom he chose, he shortened the days.	

§ 135 Discourse on Events of the Future (*continued*)

MATT 24	MARK 13	LUKE 21
A Then if any one says to you, 'Lo, 23 here is the Christ!' or 'There he is!' do not believe [1]it.	**A** And then if any one says to you, 21 'Look, here is the Christ!' or 'Look, there he is!' do not believe [1]it.	**A** *And they will say to you, 'Lo, 17: there!' or 'Lo, here!' Do not go, do 23 not follow them.*
B[B] For false Christs and false 24 prophets will arise and show great signs and wonders, so as to lead astray, if possible, even the elect. Lo, 25 I have told you beforehand.	**B**[B] False Christs and false prophets 22 will arise and show signs and wonders, to lead astray, if possible, the elect. But take heed; I have told 23 you all things beforehand.	
C So, if they say to you, 'Lo, he is in 26 the wilderness,' do not go out; if they say, 'Lo, he is in the inner rooms,' do not believe [2]it.		**C** *Compare portion A above*
D For as the lightning comes from the 27 east and shines as far as the west, so will be the [3]coming of the Son of man.		**D** *For as the lightning flashes and 24 lights up the sky from one side to the other, so will the Son of man be [4]in his day. (§ 112 C)*

---

1 Or, *him*   2 Or, *them*   3 Greek *presence*   4 Some ancient authorities omit *in his day*

HS references: Mt 24:21 and Mk 13:19 = Daniel 12:1 and Joel 2:2   Lk 21:24 = Isaiah 63:18 and Daniel 8:13
Mt 24:24 and Mk 13:22 = Deuteronomy 13:1-3
NC references: Mt 24:23 and Mk 13:21 and Lk 17:23 = GT 79

B Compare § 134 portion D

MATT 24	MARK 13	LUKE 21
E Wherever the body is, there the 28 ¹eagles will be gathered together.		E "Where the body is, there the 17: ¹eagles will be gathered together." 37 (§ 112 M)
F "Immediately after the tribulation of 29 those days the sun will be darkened, and the moon will not give its light, and the stars will fall from heaven, and the powers of the heavens will be shaken;	F "But in those days, after that 24 tribulation, the sun will be darkened, and the moon will not give its light, and the stars will be falling from 25 heaven, and the powers in the heavens will be shaken.	F "And there will be signs in sun and 25 moon and stars, and upon the earth distress of nations in perplexity at the roaring of the sea and the waves, men 26 ²fainting with fear and with foreboding of what is coming on ³the world; for the powers of the heavens will be shaken.
G then will appear the sign of the Son 30 of man in heaven, and then all the tribes of the earth will mourn,		
H and they will see the Son of man coming on the clouds of heaven with power and great glory; and he will 31 send out his angels ⁴with ⁵a loud trumpet call, and they will gather his elect from the four winds, from one end of heaven to the other.	H And then they will see the Son of 26 man coming in clouds with great power and glory. And then he will 27 send out the angels, and gather his elect from the four winds, from the ends of the earth to the ends of heaven.	H And then they will see the Son of 27 man coming in a cloud with power and great glory. Now when these 28 things begin to take place, look up and raise your heads, because your redemption is drawing near."
I "From the fig tree learn its lesson: 32 as soon as its branch becomes tender and puts forth its leaves, you know that summer is near. So also, when 33 you see all these things, you know that ⁶he is near, at the very gates.	I "From the fig tree learn its lesson: 28 as soon as its branch becomes tender and puts forth its leaves, you know that summer is near. So also, when 29 you see these things taking place, you know that ⁶he is near, at the very gates.	I And he told them a parable: "Look 29 at the fig tree, and all the trees; as 30 soon as they come out in leaf, you see for yourselves and know that the summer is already near. So also, 31 when you see these things taking place, you know that the kingdom of God is near.
J Truly, I say to you, this generation 34 will not pass away till all these things take place. Heaven and earth will pass 35 away, but my words will not pass away.	J Truly, I say to you, this generation 30 will not pass away before all these things take place. Heaven and earth 31 will pass away, but my words will not pass away.	J Truly, I say to you, this generation 32 will not pass away till all has taken place. Heaven and earth will pass 33 away, but my words will not pass away.
K "But of that day and hour no one 36 knows, not even the angels of heaven, ⁷nor the Son, but the Father only.	K "But of that day or that hour no 32 one knows, not even the angels in heaven, nor the Son, but only the Father.	
L As were the days of Noah, so will 37 be the ⁸coming of the Son of man. For as in those days before the flood 38 they were eating and drinking, marrying and giving in		L As it was in the days of Noah, so 17: will it be in the days of the Son of 26 man. They ate, they drank, they 27 married, they were given in marriage, until the day

---

1 Or *vultures*   2 Or *expiring*   3 Greek *the inhabited earth*   4 Many ancient authorities read *with a great trumpet, and they shall gather, etc.*
5 Or *a trumpet of great sound*   6 Or *it*   7 Many authorities, some ancient, omit *nor the son*   8 Greek *presence*

HS references: Mt 24:28 and Lk 17:37 = Job 39:30   Mt 24:29 and Mk 13:24-25 and Lk 21:25-26 = Isaiah 13:9-10 and 34:4 and Ezekiel 32:7-8 and Joel 2:1-2, 10-11, 30-31 and Amos 8:9 and Zephaniah 1:14-16   Mt 24:30a = Zechariah 12:12   Mt 24:30b and Mk 13:26 and Lk 21:27 = Daniel 7:13-14 (LXX)   Mt 24:31 and Mk 13:27 and Lk 21:28 = Deuteronomy 30:4 (LXX) and Isaiah 27:12-13 and Zechariah 2:6 (LXX)
Mt 24:37-39 and Lk 17:26-27 = Genesis 6:5-8, 11-14, and 7:7, 21-23

MATT 24	MARK 13	LUKE 21
marriage, until the day when Noah entered the ark, and they did not 39 know until the flood came and swept them all away,		when Noah entered the Ark, and the flood came and destroyed them all. (§ 112 E)
M so will be the ¹coming of the Son of man.		**M** *so will it be on the day when the* 17: *Son of man is revealed.* (§ 112 G) 30
N Then two men will be in the field; 40 one is taken and one is left. Two 41 women will be grinding at the mill; one is taken and one is left.		**N** *I tell you, in that night there will* 17: *be two in one bed; one will be taken* 34 *and the other left. There will be two* 35 *women grinding together; one will be taken and the other left.* "² (§ 112 K)
O° Watch therefore, for you do not 42 know on what day your Lord is coming.	**O**° Take heed, watch; ³for you do not 33 know when the time will come.	**O**° "But take heed to yourselves 34
P *Compare the parable recorded in* § 136 *portions H-R*	**P** It is like a man going on a journey, 34 when he leaves home and puts his ⁴servants in charge, each with his work, and commands the doorkeeper to be on the watch.	**P** lest your hearts be weighed down with dissipation and drunkenness and cares of this life, and that day come upon you suddenly like a snare; for it 35 will come upon all who dwell upon the face of the whole earth.
Q^Q *Compare the parable recorded in* § 136 *portions E-G*	**Q**^Q Watch therefore--for you do not 35 know when the master of the house will come, in the evening, or at midnight, or at cockcrow, or in the morning--lest he come suddenly and 36 find you asleep. And what I say to 37 you I say to all: Watch."	**Q**^Q But watch at all times, praying 36 that you may have strength to escape all these things that will take place, and to stand before the Son of man."
R *And leaving them, he went out of* 21: *the city to Bethany and lodged there.* 17 (§ 126 I)	**R** *And* ⁵*when evening came they went* 11: *out of the city.* (§ 126 I) 19	**R** And every day he was teaching in 37 the temple, but at night he went out and lodged on the mount called Olivet. And early in the morning all 38 the people came to him in the temple to hear him.

§ 136 Discourse on Events of the Future (*concluded*)

MATT 24		LUKE 21
A ⁶But know this, that if the 43 householder had known in what part of the night the thief was coming, he would have watched and would not have let his house be ⁸broken into.		**A** "⁶*But know this, that if the* 12: *householder had known at what hour* 39 *the thief was coming, he would* ⁷*not have left his house to be* ⁸*broken into.*

---

1 Greek *presence*   2 Some ancient authorities add verse 36: *Two men will be in the field; one will be taken, and the other left.*
3 Some ancient authorities add *and pray*   4 Or *slaves*   5 Greek *whenever evening came*   6 Or *But this you know*   7 Some ancient authorities add *have watched, and*   8 Greek *digged through*

NC references: Mt 24:37-51 and Lk 17:26-35 = GT 21   Mt 24:43 and Lk 12:39-40 = GT 103

O Compare portion Q below and also § 136 B and § 136 G
Q Compare portion O above and also § 136 B and § 136 G

MATT 24-25	MARK	LUKE
B^B Therefore you also must be ready; 44 for the Son of man is coming at an hour you do not expect.	B^B *Compare § 135 portion O* *Compare § 135 portion Q*	B^B *You also must be ready; for the 40 Son of man is coming at an unexpected hour." (§ 94 BC)*
C "Who then is the faithful and wise 45 ¹servant, whom his master has set over his household, to give them their food at the proper time? Blessed is 46 that ¹servant whom his master when he comes will find so doing. Truly, I 47 say to you, he will set him over all his possessions. But if that wicked 48 ¹servant says to himself, 'My master is delayed,' and begins to beat his 49 fellow servants, and eats and drinks with the drunken, the master of that 50 ¹servant will come on a day when he does not expect him and at an hour he does not know, and will punish him, 51 and put him with the hypocrites;		C *"Who then is ²the faithful and wise 12: steward, whom his master will set 42 over his household, to give them their portion of food at the proper time? Blessed is that ¹servant whom his 43 master when he comes will find so doing. Truly, I say to you, he will set 44 him over all his possessions. But if 45 that ¹servant says to himself, 'My master is delayed in coming,' and begins to beat the menservants and the maidservants, and to eat and drink and get drunk, the master of that 46 ¹servant will come on a day when he does not expect him and at an hour he does not know, and will ³punish him, and put him with the unfaithful. (§ 94 E)*
D^D there men will weep and gnash their teeth.		
E "Then the kingdom of heaven shall 25: be compared to ten maidens who took 1 their ⁴lamps and went to meet the bridegroom⁵. Five of them were 2 foolish, and five were wise. For when 3 the foolish took their ⁴lamps, they took no oil with them; but the wise 4 took flasks of oil with their ⁴lamps. As the bridegroom was delayed, they 5 all slumbered and slept. But at 6 midnight there was a cry, 'Behold, the bridegroom! Come out to meet him.' Then all those maidens rose and 7 trimmed their ⁴lamps. And the foolish 8 said to the wise, 'Give us some of your oil, for our ⁴lamps are going out.' But the wise replied, 'Perhaps 9 there will not be enough for us and for you; go rather to the dealers and buy for yourselves.' And while they 10	E *Compare the parable recorded in § 135 portion Q*	E *"Let your loins be girded and your 12: lamps burning, and be like men who 35 are waiting for their master to come 36 home from the marriage feast, so that they may open to him at once when he comes and knocks. Blessed are those 37 ⁶servants whom the master finds awake when he comes; truly, I say to you, he will gird himself and have them sit at table, and he will come and serve them. If he comes in the 38 second watch, or in the third, and finds them so, blessed are those ⁶servants! (§ 94 A)*

---

1 Or *slave*   2 Or *the faithful steward, the wise whom, etc.*   3 Or *cut him in pieces*   4 Or *torches*   5 Some ancient authorities add *and the bride*   6 Or *slaves*

B Compare portion G below and also § 135 O and § 135 Q

D I tell you, many will come from east and west and sit at table with Abraham, Isaac, and Jacob in the kingdom of heaven, while the sons of the kingdom will be thrown into the outer darkness; there men will weep and gnash their teeth. (§ 39 D = Mt 8:11-12)

D And throw them into the furnace of fire; there men will weep and gnash their teeth. (§ 48 L = Mt 13:42)

D And throw them into the furnace of fire; there men will weep and gnash their teeth. (§ 48 Q = Mt 13:50)

D And cast him into the outer darkness; there men will weep and gnash their teeth. (§ 129 P = Mt 22:13)

D And will punish him, and put him with the hypocrites; there men will weep and gnash their teeth. (§ 136 D = Mt 24:51)

D There you will weep and gnash your teeth, when you see Abraham and Isaac and Jacob and all the prophets in the kingdom of God and you yourselves thrust out. And men will come from east and west, and from north and south, and sit at table in the kingdom of God. (§ 100 G = Lk 13:28-29)

D And will punish him, and put him with the unfaithful. (§ 94 E = Lk 12:46)

D And cast the worthless servant into the outer darkness; there men will weep and gnash their teeth. (§ 136 Q = Mt 25:30)

MATT 25	MARK	LUKE
went to buy, the bridegroom came, and those who were ready went in with him to the marriage feast;		
F and the door was shut. Afterward 11 the other maidens came also, saying, 'Lord, lord, open to us.' But he 12 replied, 'Truly, I say to you, I do not know you.'		**F** *When once the householder has* 13: *risen up and shut the door, you will* 25 *begin to stand outside and to knock at the door, saying, 'Lord, open to us.' He will answer you, 'I do not know where you come from.' (§ 100 D)*
Gᴳ Watch therefore, for you know 13 neither the day nor the hour.	**G**ᴳ *Compare § 135 portion O* *Compare § 135 portion Q*	
H "For it will be as when a man 14 going on a journey called his ¹servants and entrusted to them his property; to 15 one he gave five ²talents, to another two, to another one, to each according to his ability. Then he went away.	**H** *Compare the parable recorded in § 135 portion P*	**H** *"A nobleman went into a far* 19: *country to receive a kingdom and then* 12 *return. Calling ten of his ¹servants, he* 13 *gave them ten ³pounds, and said to them, 'Trade with these till I come.'*
		I *But his citizens hated him and sent* 14 *an embassy after him, saying, 'We do not want this man to reign over us.'*
J He who had received the five 16 talents went at once and traded with them; and he made five talents more. So also, he who had the two talents 17 made two talents more. But he who 18 had received the one talent went and dug in the ground and hid his master's money.		
K Now after a long time the master 19 of those ¹servants came and settled accounts with them.		**K** *When he returned, having received* 15 *the kingdom, he commanded these ¹servants, to whom he had given the money, to be called to him, that he might know what they had gained by trading.*
L And he who had received the five 20 talents came forward, bringing five talents more, saying, 'Master, you delivered to me five talents; here I have made five talents more.' His 21 master said to him, 'Well done, good and faithful ⁴servant; you have been faithful over a little, I will set you over much; enter into the joy of your master.'		**L** *The first came before him, saying,* 16 *'Lord, your pound has made ten pounds more.' And he said to him,* 17 *'Well done, good ⁴servant! Because you have been faithful in a very little, you shall have authority over ten cities.'*
M And he also who had the two 22 talents came forward, saying,		**M** *And the second came, saying,* 18 *'Lord, your pound has*

---

1 Or *slaves*   2 This talent was more than fifteen years' wages of a laborer.   3 *Mina*, here translated a pound, is equal to about twenty dollars. It was about 3 months' wages for a laborer.   4 Or *slave*

G Compare portion B above and also § 135 O and § 135 Q

MATT **25**

'Master, you delivered to me two
[2]talents; here I have made two talents
more.' His master said to him, 'Well 23
done, good and faithful [3]servant; you
have been faithful over a little, I will
set you over much; enter into the joy
of your master.'

N He also who had received the one 24
talent came forward, saying, 'Master,
I knew you to be a hard man, reaping
where you did not sow, and gathering
where you did not winnow; so I was 25
afraid, and I went and hid your talent
in the ground. Here you have what is
yours.'

O But his master answered him, 'You 26
wicked and slothful [3]servant! You
knew that I reap where I have not
sowed, and gather where I have not
winnowed? Then you ought to have 27
invested my money with the bankers,
and at my coming I should have
received what was my own with
interest. So take the talent from him, 28
and give it to him who has the ten
talents.

P[P] For to every one who has will 29
more be given, and he will have
abundance; but from him who has
not, even what he has will be taken
away.

Q[Q] And cast the worthless [3]servant 30
into the outer darkness; there men
will weep and gnash their teeth.'

LUKE

made five [1]pounds.' And he said to 19
him, 'And you are to be over five
cities.'

N *Then [4]another came, saying, 'Lord,* 20
here is your pound, which I kept laid
away in a napkin; for I was afraid of 21
you, because you are a severe man;
you take up what you did not lay
down, and reap what you did not
sow.'

O *He said to him, 'I will condemn* 22
you out of your own mouth, you
wicked [3]servant! You knew that I was
a severe man, taking up what I did
not lay down and reaping what I did
not sow? Why then did you not put my 23
money into the bank, and at my
coming I should have collected it with
interest?' And he said to those who 24
stood by, 'Take the pound from him,
and give it to him who has the ten
pounds.' (And they said to him, 25
'Lord, he has ten pounds!')

P[P] *'I tell you, that to every one who* 26
has will more be given; but from him
who has not, even what he has will be
taken away.

R *But as for these enemies of mine,* 27
who did not want me to reign over
them, bring them here and slay them
before me.'" (§ 123 B-L)

---

1 *Mina*, here translated a pound, is equal to about twenty dollars. It was about 3 months' wages for a laborer. 2 This talent was more than fifteen years' wages of a laborer. 3 Or *slave* 4 Greek *the other*

NC references: Mt 25:29 and Lk 19:26 = GT 41

P For to him who has will more be given, and he will have abundance; but from him who has not, even what he has will be taken away. (§ 47 H = Mt 13:12)

Q Compare Portion D above and attached references

P For to him who has will more be given; and from him who has not, even what he has will be taken away. (§ 47 V = Mk 4:25)

P For to him who has will more be given, and from him who has not, even what he thinks that he has will be taken away. (§ 47 V = Lk 8:18)

MATT **25**   LUKE

S "When the Son of man comes in his 31 glory, and all the angels with him, then he will sit on his glorious throne. Before him will be gathered all the 32 nations, and he will separate them one from another as a shepherd separates the sheep from the ¹goats, and he will 33 place the sheep at his right hand, but the ¹goats at the left. Then the King 34 will say to those at his right hand, 'Come, O blessed of my Father, inherit the kingdom prepared for you from the foundation of the world; for 35 I was hungry and you gave me food, I was thirsty and you gave me drink, I was a stranger and you welcomed me, I was naked and you clothed me, 36 I was sick and you visited me, I was in prison and you came to me.' Then 37 the righteous will answer him, 'Lord, when did we see thee hungry and feed thee, or thirsty and give thee drink? And when did we see thee a stranger 38 and welcome thee, or naked and clothe thee? And when did we see 39 thee sick or in prison and visit thee?' And the King will answer them, 40 'Truly, I say to you, as you did it to one of the least of these my brethren, you did it to me.' Then he will say to 41 those at his left hand, ²'Depart from me, you cursed, into the eternal fire prepared for the devil and his angels; for I was hungry and you gave me no 42 food, I was thirsty and you gave me no drink, I was a stranger and you 43 did not welcome me, naked and you did not clothe me, sick and in prison and you did not visit me.' Then they 44 also will answer, 'Lord, when did we see thee hungry or thirsty or a stranger or naked or sick or in prison, and did not minister to thee?' Then he 45 will answer them, 'Truly, I say to you, as you did it not to one of the least of these, you did it not to me.' And they will go away into eternal 46 punishment, but the righteous into eternal life."

---

1 Or *kids*   2 Or *Depart from me under a curse*

HS references: Mt 25:31 = Zechariah 14:5b   Mt 25:32 = Ezekiel 34:17   Mt 25:35-36 = Isaiah 58:7   Mt 25:40 = Proverbs 19:17
Mt 25:46 = Daniel 12:2

§ 137 Conspiracy for the Arrest of Jesus

MATT 26:1-16	MARK 14:1-11	LUKE 22:1-6

A When Jesus had finished all these 1 sayings, he said to his disciples, "You 2 know that after two days the Passover is coming, and the Son of man will be delivered up to be crucified." Then 3 the chief priests and the elders of the people gathered in the palace of the high priest, who was called Ca'iaphas, and took counsel together 4 in order to arrest Jesus by stealth and kill him. But they said, "Not during 5 the feast, lest there be a tumult among the people."

A It was now two days before the 1 Passover and the feast of Unleavened Bread. And the chief priests and the scribes were seeking how to arrest him by stealth, and kill him; for they 2 said, "Not during the feast, lest there be a tumult of the people."

A Now the feast of Unleavened Bread 1 drew near, which is called the Passover. And the chief priests and 2 the scribes were seeking how to put him to death; for they feared the people.

B Now when Jesus was at Bethany in 6 the house of Simon the leper, a 7 woman came up to him with an alabaster flask of very expensive ointment, and she poured it on his head, as he sat at table.

B And while he was at Bethany in the 3 house of Simon the leper, as he sat at table, a woman came with an alabaster flask of ointment of [1]pure nard, very costly, and she broke the flask and poured it over his head.

B *Compare § 42 portion A*

C But when the disciples saw it, they 8 were indignant, saying, "Why this waste? For this ointment might have 9 been sold for a large sum, and given to the poor."

C But there were some who said to 4 themselves indignantly, "Why was the ointment thus wasted? For this 5 ointment might have been sold for more than three hundred [2]denarii, and given to the poor." And they reproached her.

D But Jesus, aware of this, said to 10 them, "Why do you trouble the woman? For she has done a beautiful thing to me. For you always have the 11 poor with you, but you will not always have me. In [3]pouring this 12 ointment on my body she has done it to prepare me for burial.

D But Jesus said, "Let her alone; why 6 do you trouble her? She has done a beautiful thing to me. For you always 7 have the poor with you, and whenever you will, you can do good to them; but you will not always have me. She 8 has done what she could; she has anointed my body beforehand for burying.

E Truly, I say to you, wherever [4]this 13 gospel is preached in the whole world, what she has done will be told in memory of her."

E And truly, I say to you, wherever 9 [4]the gospel is preached in the whole world, what she has done will be told in memory of her."

F Then one of the twelve, who was 14 called Judas Iscariot, went to the chief priests and said, "What will you give 15 me if I deliver him to you?" And they paid him thirty pieces of silver. And 16 from that moment he sought an opportunity to betray him.

F Then Judas Iscariot, [5]who was one 10 of the twelve, went to the chief priests in order to betray him to them. And when they heard it they were 11 glad, and promised to give him money. And he sought an opportunity to betray him.

F Then Satan entered into Judas 3 called Iscariot, who was of the number of the twelve; he went away 4 and conferred with the chief priests and officers how he might betray him to them. And they were glad, and 5 engaged to give him money. So he 6 agreed, and sought an opportunity to betray him to them [6]in the absence of the multitude.

---

1 Greek *pistic nard*, pistic being perhaps a local name: others take it to mean *genuine*; others, *liquid*   2 The word in the Greek denotes a coin worth about forty cents. The denarius was a day's wage for a laborer.   3 Greek *casting*   4 Or *these good tidings*   5 Greek *the one of the twelve* 6 Or *without tumult*

HS references: Mt 26:11 and Mk 14:7 = Deuteronomy 15:11   Mt 26:15 = Zechariah 11:12 and Exodus 21:32

Chapter XXII

FINAL HOURS OF JESUS WITH HIS DISCIPLES

§ 138 The Passover with the Disciples

MATT 26:17-29	MARK 14:12-25	LUKE 22:7-30

A Now on the first day of Unleavened 17 Bread the disciples came to Jesus, saying, "Where will you have us prepare for you to eat the passover?"

B He said, "Go into the city to a 18 certain one, and say to him, 'The Teacher says, My time is at hand; I will keep the passover at your house with my disciples.'"

C And the disciples did as Jesus had 19 directed them, and they prepared the passover.

D When it was evening, he sat at 20 table with the twelve [2]disciples; and as 21 they were eating, he said,

E "Truly, I say to you, one of you will betray me." And they were very 22 sorrowful, and began to say to him one after another, "Is it I, Lord?" He 23 answered, "He who has dipped his hand in the dish with me, will betray me. The Son of man goes as it is 24 written of him, but woe to that man by whom the Son of man is betrayed! It would have been better for [4]that man if he had not been born."

A And on the first day of Unleavened 12 Bread, when they sacrificed the passover lamb, his disciples said to him, "Where will you have us go and prepare for you to eat the passover?"

B And he sent two of his disciples, 13 and said to them, "Go into the city, and a man carrying a jar of water will meet you; follow him, and wherever 14 he enters, say to the householder, 'The Teacher says, Where is my guest room, where I am to eat the passover with my disciples?' And he will show 15 you a large upper room furnished and ready; there prepare for us."

C And the disciples set out and went 16 to the city, and found it as he had told them; and they prepared the passover.

D And when it was evening he came 17 with the twelve. And as they [3]were at 18 table eating, Jesus said,

E "Truly, I say to you, one of you will betray me, one who is eating with me." They began to be 19 sorrowful, and to say to him one after another, "Is it I?" He said to them, 20 "It is one of the twelve, one who is dipping bread into the dish with me. For the Son of man goes as it is 21 written of him, but woe to that man by whom the Son of man is betrayed! It would have been better for [4]that man if he had not been born."

A Then came the day of Unleavened 7 Bread, on which the passover lamb had to be sacrificed. So [1]Jesus sent 8 Peter and John, saying, "Go and prepare the passover for us, that we may eat it. "They said to him, 9 "Where will you have us prepare it?"

B He said to them, "Behold, when 10 you have entered the city, a man carrying a jar of water will meet you; follow him into the house which he enters, and tell the householder, 'The 11 Teacher says to you, Where is the guest room, where I am to eat the passover with my disciples?' And he 12 will show you a large upper room furnished; there make ready."

C And they went, and found it as he 13 had told them; and they prepared the passover.

D And when the hour came, he sat at 14 table, and the apostles with him. And 15 he said to them,

E *Compare portion K below*

---

1 Greek *he*   2 Many authorities, some ancient, omit *disciples*   3 Greek *reclined*   4 Greek *for him if that man, etc.*

HS references: Mt 26:17 and Mk 14:12 and Lk 22:7 = Exodus 12:17-20   Mt 26:19 and Mk 14:16 and Lk 22:13 = Deuteronomy 16:5-8
Mt 26:21 and Mk 14:18 = Psalm 41:9

MATT 26	MARK 14	LUKE 22

F Judas, who betrayed him, said, "Is 25 it I, ¹Master?" He said to him, "You have said so."

| | | **G** "I have earnestly desired to eat this passover with you before I suffer; for 16 I tell you I shall ²not eat it until it is fulfilled in the kingdom of God." |

H   *Compare portion J below* | **H**   *Compare portion J below* | **H** And he took a cup, and when he 17 had given thanks he said, "Take this, and divide it among yourselves; for I 18 tell you that from now on I shall not drink of the fruit of the vine until the kingdom of God comes."

I Now as they were eating, Jesus took 26 ³bread, and blessed, and broke it, and gave it to the disciples and said, "Take, eat; this is my body."

I And as they were eating, he took 22 ³bread, and blessed, and broke it, and gave it to them, and said, "Take; this is my body."

Iᴵ And he took ³bread, and when he 19 had given thanks he broke it and gave it to them, saying, "This is my body ⁴which is given for you. Do this in remembrance of me."

J And he took ⁵a cup, and when he 27 had given thanks he gave it to them, saying, "Drink of it, all of you; for 28 this is my blood of ⁶the ⁷covenant, which is poured out for many for the forgiveness of sins. I tell you I shall 29 not drink again of this fruit of the vine until that day when I drink it new with you in my Father's kingdom."

J And he took a cup, and when he 23 had given thanks he gave it to them, and they all drank of it. And he said 24 to them, "This is my blood of ⁶the ⁸covenant, which is poured out for many. Truly, I say to you, I shall not 25 drink again of the fruit of the vine until that day when I drink it new in the kingdom of God."

Jᴶ And likewise the cup after supper, 20 saying, "This cup which is poured out for you is the new ⁹covenant in my blood.
Compare portion H above

K   *Compare portion E above* | **K**   *Compare portion E above* | **K** But behold the hand of him who 21 betrays me is with me on the table. For the Son of man goes as it has 22 been determined; but woe to that man by whom he is betrayed!" And they 23 began to question one another, which of them it was that would do this.

| | | **Lᴸ** A dispute also arose among them, 24 which of them was to be regarded as the ¹⁰greatest. |

---

1 Greek *Rabbi*   2 Some ancient authorities read *never eat it again*   3 Or *a loaf*   4 Some ancient authorities omit verses 19b and 20 *which is given for you . . . in my blood*   5 Some ancient authorities read *the cup*   6 Or *the testament*   7 Many ancient authorities insert *new*
8 Some ancient authorities insert *new*   9 Or *testament*   10 Greek *greater*

HS references: Mt 26:28 and Mk 14:24 and Lk 22:20 = Exodus 24:8 and Zechariah 9:11 and Jeremiah 31:31 and Leviticus 4:18-20
Lk 22:21-23 = Psalm 41:9

IJ (Lk) The Lord Jesus on the night when he was betrayed took bread, and when he had given thanks, he broke it, and said, "This is my body which is for you. Do this in remembrance of me." In the same way also the cup, after supper, saying, "This cup is the new covenant in my blood. Do this, as often as you drink it, in remembrance of me." (I Corinthians 11:23-25)

L At that time the disciples came to Jesus, saying, Who is the greatest in the kingdom of heaven? (§ 78 A = Mt 18:1)

L And they came to Capernaum; and when he was in the house he asked them, What were you discussing on the way? But they were silent; for on the way they had discussed with one another who on was the greatest. (§ 78 A = Mk 9:33-34)

L And an argument arose among them as to which of them was the greatest. (§ 78 A = Lk 9:46)

MATT	MARK	LUKE 22
M^M *"You know that the rulers of the* 20: *Gentiles lord it over them, and their* 25 *great men exercise authority over them. It shall not be so among you;* 26 *but whoever would be great among you must be your servant, and* 27 *whoever would be first among you must be your slave; even as the Son* 28 *of man came not to be served but to serve, and to give his life as a ransom for many." (§ 120 I-K)*	M^M *"You know that those who are* 10: *supposed to rule over the Gentiles* 42 *lord it over them, and their great men exercise authority over them. But it* 43 *shall not be so among you; but whoever would be great among you must be your servant, and whoever* 44 *would be first among you must be slave of all. For the Son of man also* 45 *came not to be served but to serve, and to give his life as a ransom for many." (§ 120 I-K)*	M^M And he said to them, "The kings 25 of the Gentiles exercise lordship over them; and those in authority over them are called benefactors. But not 26 so with you; rather let the greatest among you become as the youngest, and the leader as one who serves. For which is the greater, one who ¹sits at 27 table, or one who serves? Is it not the one who sits at table? But I am among you as one who serves.
N *Jesus said to them, "Truly, I say to* 19: *you, in the new world, when the Son* 28 *of man shall sit on his glorious throne, you who have followed me will also sit on twelve thrones, judging the twelve tribes of Israel. (§ 117 L)*		N "You are those who have continued 28 with me in my trials; and I assign to 29 you, as my Father assigned to me, a kingdom, that you may eat and drink 30 at my table in my kingdom, and sit on thrones judging the twelve tribes of Israel.

§ 139 Withdrawal to the Mount of Olives

MATT 26:30-35	MARK 14:26-31	LUKE 22:31-38
A And when they had sung a hymn, 30 they went out to the Mount of Olives.	A And when they had sung a hymn, 26 they went out to the Mount of Olives.	A *And he came out, and went, as was* 22: *his custom, to the Mount of Olives;* 39 *and the disciples followed him. (§ 140 A)*
B Then Jesus said to them, "You will 31 all ²fall away because of me this night; for it is written, 'I will strike the shepherd, and the sheep of the flock will be scattered.'	B And Jesus said to them, "You will 27 all ²fall away; for it is written, 'I will strike the shepherd, and the sheep will be scattered.'	B "Simon, Simon, behold, Satan 31 demanded to have ³you, that he might sift ³you like wheat, but I have prayed 32 for you that your faith may not fail; and when you have turned again, strengthen your brethren."
C But after I am raised up, I will go 32 before you to Galilee."	C But after I am raised up, I will go 28 before you to Galilee."	
D Peter declared to him, "Though 33 they all fall away because of you, I will never fall away." Jesus said to 34 him, "Truly, I say to you, this very night, before the cock crows, you will deny me three times." Peter said to 35 him, "Even if I must die with you, I will not deny you." And so said all the disciples.	D Peter said to him, "Even though 29 they all fall away, I will not." And 30 Jesus said to him, "Truly, I say to you, this very night, before the cock crows ⁴twice, you will deny me three times." But he said vehemently, "If I 31 must die with you, I will not deny you." And they all said the same.	D And he said to him, "Lord, I am 33 ready to go with you to prison and to death." He said, "I tell you, Peter, 34 the cock will not crow this day, until you three times deny that you know me."

1 Greek *reclines*   2 Greek *be caused to stumble*   3 Greek *you* (plural)   4 Some ancient authorities omit *twice*

HS references: Mt 26:31 and Mk 14:27 = Zechariah 13:7   Lk 22:31 = Job 1:6-12 and Amos 9:9

M Whoever humbles himself like this child, he is the greatest in the kingdom of heaven. (§ 78 E = Mt 18:4)	M And he sat down and called the twelve; and he said to them, If any one would be first, he must be last of all and servant of all. (§ 78 B = Mk 9:35)	M For he who is least among you all is the one who is great. (§ 78 H = Lk 9:48)
M He who is greatest among you shall be your servant. (§ 132 G = Mt 23:11)		

LUKE **22**

E And he said to them, "When I sent 35 you out with no purse or bag or sandals, did you lack anything?" They said, "Nothing." He said to them, 36 "But now, let him who has a purse take it, and likewise a bag. And let him who has no sword sell his mantle and buy one. For I tell you that this 37 scripture must be fulfilled in me, 'And he was reckoned with transgressors'; for what is written about me has its [1]fulfilment." And they said, 38 "Look, Lord, here are two swords." And he said to them, "It is enough."

§ 140 At the Place Named Gethsemane

| MATT 26:36-46 | MARK 14:32-42 | LUKE 22:39-46 |

A *And when they had sung a hymn,* 26: *they went out to the Mount of Olives.* 30 (§ 139 A)

A *And when they had sung a hymn,* 14: *they went out to the Mount of Olives.* 26 (§ 139 A)

A And he came out, and went, as was 39 his custom, to the Mount of Olives; and the disciples followed him.

B Then Jesus went with them to [2]a 36 place called Gethsem'ane, and he said to his disciples, "Sit here, while I go yonder and pray." And taking with 37 him Peter and the two sons of Zeb'edee, he began to be sorrowful and troubled. Then he said to them, 38 "My soul is very sorrowful, even to death; remain here, and [3]watch with me."

B And they went to [2]a place which 32 was called Gethsem'ane; and he said to his disciples, "Sit here, while I pray." And he took with him Peter 33 and James and John, and began to be greatly distressed and troubled. And 34 he said to them, "My soul is very sorrowful, even to death; remain here, and [3]watch."

B And when he came to the place he 40 said to them, "Pray that you may not enter into temptation."

C And going a little farther he fell on 39 his face and prayed, "My Father, if it be possible, let this cup pass from me; nevertheless, not as I will, but as thou wilt."

C And going a little farther, he fell 35 on the ground and prayed that, if it were possible, the hour might pass from him. And he said, "Abba, 36 Father, all things are possible to thee; remove this cup from me; yet not what I will, but what thou wilt."

C And he withdrew from them about 41 a stone's throw, and knelt down and prayed, "Father, if thou art willing, 42 remove this cup from me; nevertheless not my will, but thine, be done."

D [4]And there appeared to him an 43 angel from heaven, strengthening him. And being in an agony he prayed 44 more earnestly; and his sweat became like great drops of blood falling down upon the ground.

---

1 Greek *end*   2 Greek *an enclosed piece of ground*   3 Or *keep awake*   4 Many ancient authorities omit verses 43 and 44

HS references: Lk 22:37 = Isaiah 53:12   Mt 26:38 and Mk 14:34 = Psalm 42:6

MATT 26	MARK 14	LUKE 22
E And he came to the disciples and 40 found them sleeping; and he said to Peter, "So, could you not ¹watch with me one hour? ¹Watch and pray that 41 you may not enter into temptation; the spirit indeed is willing, but the flesh is weak."	**E** And he came and found them 37 sleeping, and he said to Peter, "Simon, are you asleep? Could you not ¹watch one hour? ¹Watch and pray 38 that you may not enter into temptation; the spirit indeed is willing, but the flesh is weak."	**E** And when he rose from prayer, he 45 came to the disciples and found them sleeping for sorrow, and he said to 46 them, "Why do you sleep? Rise and pray that you may not enter into temptation."
F Again, for the second time, he went 42 away and prayed, "My Father, if this cannot pass unless I drink it, thy will be done." And again he came and 43 found them sleeping, for their eyes were heavy.	**F** And again he went away and 39 prayed, saying the same words. And 40 again he came and found them sleeping, for their eyes were very heavy; and they did not know what to answer him.	
G So, leaving them again, he went 44 away and prayed for the third time, saying the same words. Then he came 45 to the disciples and said to them, "Are you still sleeping and taking your rest? Behold, the hour is at hand, and the Son of man is betrayed into the hands of sinners. Rise, let us 46 be going; see, my betrayer is at hand."	**G** And he came the third time, and 41 said to them, "Are you still sleeping and taking your rest? It is enough; the hour has come; the Son of man is betrayed into the hands of sinners. Rise, let us be going; see, my 42 betrayer is at hand."	

§ 141 The Betrayal and Arrest of Jesus

MATT 26:47-56	MARK 14:43-52	LUKE 22:47-53
A While he was still speaking, Judas 47 came, one of the twelve, and with him a great crowd with swords and clubs, from the chief priests and the elders of the people.	**A** And immediately, while he was still 43 speaking, Judas came, one of the twelve, and with him a crowd with swords and clubs, from the chief priests and the scribes and the elders.	**A** While he was still speaking, there 47 came a crowd, and the man called Judas, one of the twelve, was leading them.
B Now the betrayer had given them a 48 sign, saying, "The one I shall kiss is the man; seize him." And he came up 49 to Jesus at once and said, "Hail, ²Master!" And he ³kissed him. Jesus 50 said to him, "Friend, ⁴why are you here?" Then they came up and laid hands on Jesus and seized him.	**B** Now the betrayer had given them a 44 sign, saying, "The one I shall kiss is the man; seize him and lead him away under guard." And when he came, he 45 went up to him at once, and said, ²"Master!" And he ³kissed him. And 46 they laid hands on him and seized him.	**B** He drew near to Jesus to kiss him; but Jesus said to him, "Judas, would 48 you betray the Son of man with a kiss?"
		C And when those who were about 49 him saw what would follow, they said, "Lord, shall we strike with the sword?"
D And behold, one of those who were 51 with Jesus stretched out his hand and drew his sword, and struck the slave of the high priest, and cut off his ear.	**D** But one of those who stood by 47 drew his sword, and struck the slave of the high priest and cut off his ear.	**D** And one of them struck the slave 50 of the high priest and cut off his right ear.

---

1 Or *keep awake*   2 Greek *Rabbi*   3 Greek *kissed him much*   4 Or *do that for which you have come*

MATT 26	MARK 14	LUKE 22
		E But Jesus said, "No more of this!" 51 And he touched his ear and healed him.
F Then Jesus said to him, "Put your 52 sword back into its place; for all who take the sword will perish by the sword. Do you think that I cannot 53 appeal to my Father, and he will at once send me more than twelve legions of angels? But how then 54 should the scriptures be fulfilled, that it must be so?"		
G At that hour Jesus said to the 55 crowds, "Have you come out as against a robber, with swords and clubs to capture me? Day after day I sat in the temple teaching, and you did not seize me.	G And Jesus said to them, "Have you 48 come out as against a robber, with swords and clubs to capture me? Day 49 after day I was with you in the temple teaching, and you did not seize me.	G Then Jesus said to the chief priests 52 and officers of the temple and elders, who had come out against him, "Have you come out as against a robber, with swords and clubs? When I was 53 with you day after day in the temple, you did not lay hands on me.
H But all this has taken place, that 56 the scriptures of the prophets might be fulfilled."	H But let the scriptures be fulfilled."	H But this is your hour, and the power of darkness."
I Then all the disciples forsook him and fled.	I And they all forsook him, and fled. 50	
	J And a young man followed him, 51 with nothing but a linen cloth about his body; and they seized him, but he 52 left the linen cloth and ran away naked.	

HS references: Mt 26:52 = Genesis 9:6

Chapter XXIII

JUDICIAL TRIALS AND CRUCIFIXION OF JESUS

§ 142 The Trial before the Jewish Authorities

MATT 26:57-75	MARK 14:53-72	LUKE 22:54-71
A Then those who had seized Jesus 57 led him to Ca'iaphas the high priest, where the scribes and the elders had gathered.	A And they led Jesus to the high 53 priest; and all the chief priests and the elders and the scribes were assembled.	A Then they seized him and led him 54 away, bringing him into the high priest's house.
B But Peter followed him at a 58 distance, as far as the courtyard of the high priest, and going inside he sat with the guards to see the end.	B And Peter had followed him at a 54 distance, right into the courtyard of the high priest; and he was sitting with the guards, and warming himself at the fire.	B Peter followed at a distance; and 55 when they had kindled a fire in the middle of the courtyard and sat down together, Peter sat among them.
C Now the chief priests and the 59 whole council sought false testimony against Jesus that they might put him to death, but they found none, though 60 many false witnesses came forward. At last two came forward and said, 61 "This fellow said, 'I am able to destroy the ¹temple of God, and to build it in three days.'"	C Now the chief priests and the 55 whole council sought testimony against Jesus to put him to death; but they found none. For many bore false 56 witness against him, and their witness did not agree. And some stood up and 57 bore false witness against him, saying, "We heard him say, 'I will 58 destroy this ²temple that is made with hands, and in three days I will build another, not made with hands.'" Yet 59 not even so did their testimony agree.	C *Compare portion M below*
D And the high priest stood up and 62 said, "Have you no answer to make? What is it that these men testify against you?" But Jesus was silent. 63	D And the high priest stood up in the 60 midst, and asked Jesus, "Have you no answer to make? What is it that these men testify against you?" But he was 61 silent and made no answer.	
E And the high priest said to him, "I adjure you by the living God, tell us if you are the Christ, the Son of God." Jesus said to him, "You have 64 said so. But I tell you, hereafter you will see the Son of man seated at the right hand of Power, and coming on the clouds of heaven."	E Again the high priest asked him, "Are you the Christ, the Son of the Blessed?" And Jesus said, ³"I am; and 62 you will see the Son of man seated at the right hand of Power, and coming with the clouds of heaven."	E *Compare portion N below*
F Then the high priest tore his robes, 65 and said, "He has uttered blasphemy. Why do we still need witnesses? You have now heard his blasphemy. What 66 is your judgment?" They answered, "He deserves death."	F And the high priest tore his 63 garments, and said, "Why do we still need witnesses? You have heard his 64 blasphemy. What is your decision?" And they all condemned him as ⁴deserving death.	F *Compare portion O below*

---

1 Or *sanctuary:* as in Matt 23:35 and 27:5   2 Or *sanctuary*   3 The Caesarean text family reads *You have said so.*   4 Greek *liable to*

HS references: Mt 26:63 and Mk 14:61 = Isaiah 53:7   Mt 26:64 and Mk 14:62 and Lk 22:69 = Psalm 110:1 and Daniel 7:13
NC references: Mt 26:61 and Mk 14:58 = GT 71

MATT 26	MARK 14	LUKE 22
G Then they spat in his face, and 67 struck him; and some slapped him, saying, "Prophesy to us, you Christ! 68 Who is it that struck you?"	**G** And some began to spit on him, 65 and to cover his face, and to strike him, saying to him, "Prophesy!" And the guards received him with blows.	**G** *Compare portion L below*
H Now Peter was sitting outside in 69 the courtyard. And a maid came up to him, and said, "You also were with Jesus the Galilean." But he denied it 70 before them all, saying, "I do not know what you mean."	**H** And as Peter was below in the 66 courtyard, one of the maids of the high priest came; and seeing Peter 67 warming himself, she looked at him, and said, "You also were with the Nazarene, Jesus." But he denied it, 68 saying, "I neither know nor understand what you mean."	**H** Then a maid, seeing him as he sat 56 in the light and gazing at him, said, "This man also was with him." But he 57 denied it, saying, "Woman, I do not know him."
I And when he went out to the porch, 71 another maid saw him, and she said to the bystanders, "This man was with Jesus of Nazareth." And again he 72 denied it with an oath, "I do not know the man."	**I** And he went out into the ¹gateway.² And the maid saw him, 69 and began again to say to the bystanders, "This man is one of them." But again he denied it. 70	**I** And a little later some one else saw 58 him and said, "You also are one of them." But Peter said, "Man, I am not."
J After a little while the bystanders 73 came up and said to Peter, "Certainly you are also one of them, for your accent betrays you." Then he began to 74 invoke a curse on himself and to swear, "I do not know the man."	**J** And after a little while again the bystanders said to Peter, "Certainly you are one of them; for you are a Galilean." But he began to invoke a 71 curse on himself and to swear, "I do not know this man of whom you speak."	**J** And after an interval of about an 59 hour still another insisted, saying, "Certainly this man also was with him; for he is a Galilean." But Peter 60 said, "Man, I do not know what you are saying."
K And immediately the cock crowed. And Peter remembered the saying of 75 Jesus, "Before the cock crows, you will deny me three times." And he went out and wept bitterly.	**K** And immediately the cock crowed 72 a second time. And Peter remembered how Jesus had said to him, "Before the cock crows twice, you will deny me three times." And he broke down and wept.	**K** And immediately, while he was still speaking, the cock crowed. And 61 the Lord turned and looked at Peter. And Peter remembered the word of the Lord, how he had said to him, "Before the cock crows today, you will deny me three times." And he 62 went out and wept bitterly.
L *Compare portion G above*	**L** *Compare portion G above*	**L** Now the men who were holding 63 ³Jesus mocked him and beat him; they 64 also blindfolded him and asked him, "Prophesy! Who is it that struck you?" And they spoke many other 65 words against him, reviling him.
M *Compare portion C above* *Compare § 143 portion A*	**M** *Compare portion C above* *Compare § 143 portion A*	**M** When day came, the assembly of 66 the elders of the people gathered together, both chief priests and scribes; and they led him away to their council,

---

1 Greek *forecourt*   2 Many ancient authorities add *and the cock crowed*   3 Greek *him*

HS references: Mt 26:65-66 and Mk 14:63-64 = Leviticus 24:16 and Numbers 14:6

MATT 26	MARK 14	LUKE 22
N *Compare portion E above*	**N** *Compare portion E above*	**N** and they said, "If you are the 67 Christ, tell us." But he said to them, "If I tell you, you will not believe; and if I ask you, you will not answer. 68 But from now on the Son of man 69 shall be seated at the right hand of the power of God."
O *Compare portion F above*	**O** *Compare portion F above*	**O** And they all said, "Are you the 70 Son of God, then?" And he said to them, ¹"You say that I am." And they 71 said, "What further testimony do we need? We have heard it ourselves from his own lips."

§ 143 The Trial before the Roman Authorities

MATT 27:1-31	MARK 15:1-20	LUKE 23:1-25
A When morning came, all the chief 1 priests and the elders of the people took counsel against Jesus to put him to death; and they bound him and led 2 him away and delivered him to Pilate the governor.	**A** And as soon as it was morning the 1 chief priests, with the elders and scribes, and the whole council held a consultation; and they bound Jesus and led him away and delivered him to Pilate.	**A** *Compare § 142 portion M* Then the whole company of them 1 arose, and brought him before Pilate.
B When Judas, his betrayer, saw that 3 he was condemned, he repented and brought back the thirty pieces of silver to the chief priests and the elders, saying, "I have sinned in 4 betraying ²innocent blood." They said, "What is that to us? See to it yourself." And throwing down the 5 pieces of silver in the temple, he departed; and he went and hanged himself. But the chief priests, taking 6 the pieces of silver, said, "It is not lawful to put them into the ³treasury, since they are blood money." So they 7 took counsel, and bought with them the potter's field, to bury strangers in. Therefore that field has been called 8 the Field of Blood to this day. Then 9 was fulfilled what had been spoken ⁴by the prophet Jeremiah, saying, "And ⁵they took the thirty pieces of silver, the price of him ⁶on whom a price had been set by some of the sons of Israel, and ⁷they gave them 10 for the potter's field, as the Lord directed me."		

---

1 Or *You say* it *because I am*   2 Many ancient authorities read *righteous*   3 Greek *corbanas*, that is, *sacred treasury*: compare Mark 7:11
4 Or *through*   5 Or *I took*   6 Or *whom they priced on the part of the Sons of Israel*   7 Some ancient authorities read *I gave*

HS references: Lk 22:69 = Psalm 110:1 and Daniel 7:13   Mt 27:3 = Exodus 21:32   Mt 27:6 = Deuteronomy 23:18
Mt 27:9-10 = Zechariah 11:12-13 and Jeremiah 32:6-15 and 18:1-4

MATT 27	MARK 15	LUKE 23
		C And they began to accuse him, 2 saying, "We found this man perverting our nation, and forbidding us to give tribute to Caesar, and saying that he himself is ¹Christ a king."
D Now Jesus stood before the 11 governor; and the governor asked him, "Are you the King of the Jews?" Jesus said, "You have said so."	**D** And Pilate asked him, "Are you the 2 King of the Jews?" And he answered him, "You have said so."	**D** And Pilate asked him, "Are you the 3 King of the Jews?" And he answered him, "You have said so."
E But when he was accused by the 12 chief priests and elders, he made no answer. Then Pilate said to him, "Do 13 you not hear how many things they testify against you?" But he gave him 14 no answer, not even to a single charge; so that the governor wondered greatly.	**E** And the chief priests accused him 3 of many things. And Pilate again 4 asked him, "Have you no answer to make? See how many charges they bring against you." But Jesus made no 5 further answer, so that Pilate wondered.	
		F And Pilate said to the chief priests 4 and the multitudes, "I find no crime in this man." But they were urgent, 5 saying, "He stirs up the people, teaching throughout all Judea, from Galilee even to this place." When 6 Pilate heard this, he asked whether the man was a Galilean. And when he 7 learned that he belonged to Herod's jurisdiction, he sent him over to Herod, who was himself in Jerusalem at that time.
		G When Herod saw Jesus, he was 8 very glad, for he had long desired to see him, because he had heard about him, and he was hoping to see some sign done by him. So he questioned 9 him at some length; but he made no answer. The chief priests and the 10 scribes stood by, vehemently accusing him. And Herod with his soldiers 11 treated him with contempt and mocked him; then, arraying him in gorgeous apparel, he sent him back to Pilate. And Herod and Pilate became 12 friends with each other that very day, for before this they had been at enmity with each other.
		H Pilate then called together the chief 13 priests and the rulers and

1 Or *an anointed king*

HS references: Mt 27:14 and Mk 15:5 = Isaiah 53:7

| MATT 27 | MARK 15 | LUKE 23 |

I Now at ¹the feast the governor was 15 accustomed to release for the crowd any one prisoner whom they wanted. And they had then a notorious 16 prisoner, called Barab'bas. So when 17 they had gathered, Pilate said to them, "Whom do you want me to release for you, Barab'bas or Jesus who is called Christ?" For he knew that it 18 was out of envy that they had delivered him up.

J Besides, while he was sitting on the 19 judgment seat, his wife sent word to him, "Have nothing to do with that righteous man, for I have suffered much over him today in a dream."

K Now the chief priests and the 20 elders persuaded the people to ask for Barab'bas and destroy Jesus. The 21 governor again said to them, "Which of the two do you want me to release for you?" And they said, "Barab'bas." Pilate said to them, "Then what shall 22 I do with Jesus who is called Christ?" They all said, "Let him be crucified." And he said, "Why, what evil has he 23 done?" But they shouted all the more, "Let him be crucified."

L So when Pilate saw that he was 24 gaining nothing, but rather that a riot was beginning, he took water and washed his hands before the crowd,

---

I Now at ¹the feast he used to release 6 for them one prisoner for whom they asked. And among the rebels in 7 prison, who had committed murder in the insurrection, there was a man called Barab'bas. And the crowd 8 came up and began to ask Pilate to do as he was wont to do for them. And 9 he answered them, "Do you want me to release for you the king of the Jews?" For he perceived that it was 10 out of envy that the chief priests had delivered him up.

K But the chief priests stirred up the 11 crowd to have him release for them Barab'bas instead. And Pilate again 12 said to them, "Then what shall I do with the man whom you call the King of the Jews?" And they cried out 13 again, "Crucify him." And Pilate said 14 to them, "Why, what evil has he done?" But they shouted all the more, "Crucify him."

---

the people, and said to them, "You 14 brought me this man as one who was perverting the people; and after examining him before you, behold, I did not find this man guilty of any of your charges against him; neither did 15 Herod, for he sent him back to us. Behold, nothing deserving death has been done by him;

I I will therefore chastise him and 16 release him."² But they all cried out 18 together, "Away with this man, and release to us Barab'bas"--a man who 19 had been thrown into prison for an insurrection started in the city, and for murder.

K Pilate addressed them once more, 20 desiring to release Jesus; but they 21 shouted out, "Crucify, crucify him!" A third time he said to them, "Why, 22 what evil has he done? I have found in him no crime deserving death; I will therefore chastise him and release him." But they were urgent, 23 demanding with loud cries that he should be crucified.

---

1 Or *a feast*   2 Many ancient authorities insert verse 17: *Now he was obliged to release one man to them at the festival*: others add the same words after verse 19

HS references: Mt 27:24 = Deuteronomy 21:6-9

MATT 27	MARK 15	LUKE 23

saying, "I am innocent of this [1]man's blood; see to it yourselves." And all 25 the people answered, "His blood be on us and on our children!"

M   Then he released for them 26 Barab'bas, and having scourged Jesus, delivered him to be crucified.

M So Pilate, wishing to satisfy the 15 crowd, released for them Barab'bas; and having scourged Jesus, he delivered him to be crucified.

M And their voices prevailed. So 24 Pilate gave sentence that their demand should be granted. He released the 25 man who had been thrown into prison for insurrection and murder, whom they asked for; but Jesus he delivered up to their will.

N Then the soldiers of the governor 27 took Jesus into the praetorium, and they gathered the whole [2]battalion before him. And they [3]stripped him 28 and put a scarlet robe upon him, and 29 plaiting a crown of thorns they put it on his head, and put a reed in his right hand. And kneeling before him they mocked him, saying, "Hail, King of the Jews!" And they spat upon 30 him, and took the reed and struck him on the head. And when they had 31 mocked him, they stripped him of the robe, and put his own clothes on him, and led him away to crucify him.

N And the soldiers led him away 16 inside the palace (that is, the praetorium); and they called together the whole [2]battalion. And they clothed 17 him in a purple cloak, and plaiting a crown of thorns they put it on him. And they began to salute him, "Hail, 18 King of the Jews!" And they struck 19 his head with a reed, and spat upon him, and they knelt down in homage to him. And when they had mocked 20 him, they stripped him of the purple cloak, and put his own clothes on him. And they led him out to crucify him.

N   *Compare verse 11 of portion G above*

§ 144   The Crucifixion of Jesus

MATT 27:32-56	MARK 15:21-41	LUKE 23:26-49

A As they went out, they came upon 32 a man of Cyre'ne, Simon by name; this man they [4]compelled to carry his cross.

A And they [4]compelled a passer-by, 21 Simon of Cyre'ne, who was coming in from the country, the father of Alexander and Rufus, to carry his cross.

A And as they led him away, they 26 seized one Simon of Cyre'ne, who was coming in from the country, and laid on him the cross, to carry it behind Jesus.

B And there followed him a great 27 multitude of the people, and of women who bewailed and lamented him. But Jesus turning to them said, 28 "Daughters of Jerusalem, do not weep for me, but weep for yourselves and for your children. For behold, the 29 days are coming when they will say, 'Blessed are the barren, and the wombs that never bore, and the breasts that never gave suck!' Then 30 they will begin to say to the mountains,

---

1 Many ancient authorities read *this righteous (innocent) man's blood*   2 Or *cohort*   3 Some ancient authorities read *clothed*   4 Greek *impressed*

HS references: Mt 27:25 = Joshua 2:19   Lk 23:30 = Hosea 10:8
NC references: Lk 23:29 = GT 79

MATT 27 | MARK 15 | LUKE 23

LUKE 23

'Fall on us'; and to the hills, 'Cover 31 us.' For if they do this when the wood is green, what will happen when it is dry?"

C And when they came to a place 33 called Gol'gotha (which means the place of a skull), they offered him 34 wine to drink, mingled with gall; but when he tasted it, he would not drink it. And when they had crucified him, 35 they divided his garments among them by casting lots; then they sat down 36 and kept watch over him there. And 37 over his head they put the charge against him, which read, "This is Jesus the King of the Jews." Then 38 two robbers were crucified with him, one on the right and one on the left.

C And they brought him to the place 22 called Gol'gotha (which means the place of a skull). And they offered 23 him wine mingled with myrrh; but he did not take it. And they crucified 24 him, and divided his garments among them, casting lots for them, to decide what each should take. And it was the 25 third hour, when they crucified him. And the inscription of the charge 26 against him read, "The King of the Jews." And with him they crucified 27 two robbers, one on his right and one on his left.[3]

C Two others also, who were 32 criminals, were led away to be put to death with him. And when they came 33 to the place which is called [1]The Skull, there they crucified him, and the criminals, one on the right and one on the left. [2]And Jesus said, 34 "Father, forgive them; for they know not what they do." And they cast lots to divide his garments.
Compare verse 38 of portion D below

D And those who passed by derided 39 him, wagging their heads and saying, 40 "You who would destroy the [4]temple and build it in three days, save yourself! If you are the Son of God, come down from the cross." So also 41 the chief priests, with the scribes and elders, mocked him, saying, "He 42 saved others; [5]he cannot save himself. He is the King of Israel; let him come down now from the cross, and we will believe in him. He trusts in God; 43 let God deliver him now, if he desires him; for he said, 'I am the Son of God.'"

D And those who passed by derided 29 him, wagging their heads, and saying, "Aha! You who would destroy the [4]temple and build it in three days, save yourself, and come down from 30 the cross!" So also the chief priests 31 mocked him to one another with the scribes, saying, "He saved others; [5]he cannot save himself. Let the Christ, 32 the King of Israel, come down now from the cross, that we may see and believe."

D And the people stood by, watching; 35 but the rulers scoffed at him, saying, "He saved others; let him save himself, if he is the Christ of God, his Chosen One!" The soldiers also 36 mocked him, coming up and offering him vinegar, and saying, "If you are 37 the King of the Jews, save yourself!" There was also an inscription over 38 him,[6] "This is the King of the Jews."

E And the robbers who were crucified 44 with him also reviled him in the same way.

E Those who were crucified with him also reviled him.

E One of the criminals who were 39 hanged railed at him, saying, "Are you not the Christ? Save yourself and us!" But the other rebuked him, 40 saying, "Do you not fear God, since you are under the same sentence of condemnation? And we indeed justly; 41 for we are receiving the due reward of our deeds; but this man has done nothing wrong." And he said, "Jesus, 42 remember me when you come into your kingdom." And he said to him, 43 "Truly, I say to you, today you will be with me in Paradise."

---

1 According to the Latin, *Calvary*, which has the same meaning   2 Some ancient authorities omit *And Jesus said, "Father, forgive them; for they know not what they do."*   3 Many ancient authorities insert verse 28: *And the scripture was fulfilled, which says, He was reckoned with transgressors*: see Luke 22:37   4 Or *sanctuary*   5 Or *can he not save himself?*   6 Many ancient authorities add *in letters of Greek and Latin and Hebrew*

HS references: Mt 27:34 and Mk 15:23 and Lk 23:36 = Psalm 69:21   Mt 27:35 and Mk 15:24 and Lk 23:34 = Psalm 22:18   Mt 27:39 and Mk 15:29 and Lk 23:35 = Psalm 22:7   Mt 27:43 = Psalm 22:8
NC references: Mt 27:40 and Mk 15:29-30 = GT 71

MATT 27	MARK 15	LUKE 23
F Now from the sixth hour there was 45 darkness over all the ¹land until the ninth hour.	**F** And when the sixth hour had come, 33 there was darkness over the whole ¹land until the ninth hour.	**F** It was now about the sixth hour, 44 and there was darkness over the whole ¹land until the ninth hour, while 45 ²the sun's light failed;
G And about the ninth hour Jesus 46 cried with a loud voice, "Eli, Eli, la'ma sabach-tha'ni?" that is, "My God, my God, ³why hast thou forsaken me?" And some of the 47 bystanders hearing it said, "This man is calling Eli'jah." And one of them 48 at once ran and took a sponge, filled it with vinegar, and put it on a reed, and gave it to him to drink. But the 49 others said, "Wait, let us see whether Eli'jah will come to save him."⁴	**G** And at the ninth hour Jesus cried 34 with a loud voice, "E'lo-i, E'lo-i, la'ma sabach-tha'ni?" which means, "My God, my God, ³why hast thou forsaken me?" And some of the 35 bystanders hearing it said, "Behold, he is calling Eli'jah." And one ran 36 and, filling a sponge full of vinegar, put it on a reed and gave it to him to drink, saying, "Wait, let us see whether Eli'jah will come to take him down."	**G** *Compare verse 36 of portion D above*
H And Jesus cried again with a loud 50 voice and yielded up his spirit. And 51 behold, the curtain of the ⁵temple was torn in two, from top to bottom;	**H** And Jesus uttered a loud cry, and 37 breathed his last. And the curtain of 38 the ⁵temple was torn in two, from top to bottom.	**H** and the curtain of the ⁵temple was torn in two. Then Jesus, crying with a 46 loud voice, said, "Father, into thy hands I commit my spirit!" And having said this he breathed his last.
I and the earth shook, and the rocks were split; the tombs also were 52 opened, and many bodies of the saints who had fallen asleep were raised, and coming out of the tombs after his 53 resurrection they went into the holy city and appeared to many.		
J When the centurion and those who 54 were with him, keeping watch over Jesus, saw the earthquake and what took place, they were filled with awe, and said, "Truly this was ⁷the son of God!"	**J** And when the centurion, who stood 39 facing him, saw that he thus⁶ breathed his last, he said, "Truly this man was ⁷the Son of God!"	**J** Now when the centurion saw what 47 had taken place, he praised God, and said, "Certainly this man was innocent!"
		K And all the multitudes who 48 assembled to see the sight, when they saw what had taken place, returned home beating their breasts.
L There were also many women 55 there, looking on from afar, who had followed Jesus from Galilee, ministering to him; among whom 56 were Mary Mag'dalene, and Mary the mother of James and Joseph, and the mother of the sons of Zeb'edee.	**L** There were also women looking on 40 from afar, among whom were Mary Mag'dalene, and Mary the mother of James the ⁸younger and of Joses, and Salo'me, who, when he was in 41 Galilee, followed him, and ministered to him; and also many other women who came up with him to Jerusalem.	**L** And all his acquaintances and the 49 women who had followed him from Galilee stood at a distance and saw these things.

---

1 Or *earth*   2 Greek *the sun failing*   3 Or *why didst thou forsake me?*   4 Many ancient authorities add *And another took a spear and pierced his side, and out came water and blood*: see John 19:34   5 Or *sanctuary*   6 Many ancient authorities add *cried out, and*   7 Or *a son of God* 8 Greek *little*

HS references: Mt 27:46 and Mk 15:34 = Psalm 22:1   Mt 27:48 and Mk 15:36 and Lk 23:36 = Psalm 69:21   Mt 27:51 and Mk 15:38 and Lk 23:45 = Exodus 26:31-51   Lk 23:46 = Psalm 31:5

§ 145 The Burial of Jesus

MATT 27:57-61	MARK 15:42-47	LUKE 23:50-55
A When it was evening, 57	A And when evening had come, since 42 it was the day of Preparation, that is, the day before the sabbath,	A *Compare portion E below*
B there came a rich man from Arimathe'a, named Joseph, who also was a disciple of Jesus. He went to 58 Pilate and asked for the body of Jesus.	B Joseph of Arimathe'a, a respected 43 member of the council, who was also himself looking for the kingdom of God, took courage and went to Pilate, and asked for the body of Jesus.	B Now there was a man named 50 Joseph from the Jewish town of Arimathe'a. He was a member of the council, a good and righteous man, who had not consented to their 51 purpose and deed, and he was looking for the kingdom of God. This man 52 went to Pilate and asked for the body of Jesus.
C Then Pilate ordered it to be given to him.	C And Pilate wondered if he were 44 already dead; and summoning the centurion, he asked him whether he ¹was already dead. And when he 45 learned from the centurion that he was dead, he granted the body to Joseph.	
D And Joseph took the body, and 59 wrapped it in a clean linen shroud, and laid it in his own new tomb, 60 which he had hewn in the rock; and he rolled a great stone to the door of the tomb, and departed.	D And he bought a linen shroud, and 46 taking him down, wrapped him in the linen shroud, and laid him in a tomb which had been hewn out of the rock; and he rolled a stone against the door of the tomb.	D Then he took it down and wrapped 53 it in a linen shroud, and laid him in a rock-hewn tomb, where no one had ever yet been laid.
E *Compare portion A above*	E *Compare portion A above*	E It was the day of Preparation, and 54 the sabbath ²was beginning.
F Mary Mag'dalene and the other 61 Mary were there, sitting opposite the sepulchre.	F Mary Mag'dalene and Mary the 47 mother of Joses saw where he was laid.	F The women who had come with 55 him from Galilee followed, and saw the tomb, and how his body was laid;

---

1 Many ancient authorities read *had been some time dead*   2 Greek *began to dawn*

HS references: Mt 27:57-60 and Mk 15:42-46 and Lk 23:50-54 = Deuteronomy 21:22-23

Chapter XXIV

EVENTS SUBSEQUENT TO THE DEATH OF JESUS

§ 146 The Guard for the Sepulchre

MATT 27:62-66

Next day, that is, after the day of 62 Preparation, the chief priests and the Pharisees gathered before Pilate and 63 said, "Sir, we remember how that impostor said, while he was still alive, 'After three days I will rise again.' Therefore order the sepulchre 64 to be made secure until the third day, lest his disciples go and steal him away, and tell the people, 'He has risen from the dead,' and the last fraud will be worse than the first." Pilate said to them, "¹You have a 65 guard of soldiers; go, make it as secure as you ²can." So they went and 66 made the sepulchre secure by sealing the stone and setting a guard.

§ 147 The Visit to the Sepulchre

MATT 28:1-10	MARK 16:1-8	LUKE 23:56-24:12
	A And when the sabbath was past, 1 Mary Mag'dalene, and Mary the mother of James, and Salo'me, bought spices, so that they might go and anoint him.	A then they returned, and prepared 56 spices and ointments. On the sabbath they rested according to the commandment.
B Now after the sabbath, toward the 1 dawn of the first day of the week, Mary Mag'dalene and the other Mary went to see the sepulchre.	B And very early on the first day of 2 the week they went to the tomb when the sun had risen.	B But on the first day of the week, at 24: early dawn, they went to the tomb, 1 taking the spices which they had prepared.
C And behold, there was a great 2 earthquake; for an angel of the Lord descended from heaven and came and rolled back the stone, and sat upon it.	C And they were saying to one 3 another, "Who will roll away the stone for us from the door of the tomb?" And looking up, they saw that 4 the stone was rolled back--it was very large.	C And they found the stone rolled 2 away from the tomb, but when they 3 went in they did not find the body.³
D His appearance was like lightning, 3 and his raiment white as snow. And 4 for fear of him the guards trembled and became like dead men. But the 5 angel said to the women, "Do not be afraid; for I know that you seek Jesus who was crucified. He is not here; for 6 he has risen, as he said.	D And entering the tomb, they saw a 5 young man sitting on the right side, dressed in a white robe; and they were amazed. And he said to them, 6 "Do not be amazed; you seek Jesus of Nazareth, who was crucified. He has risen, he is not here; see the place where they laid him.	D While they were perplexed about 4 this, behold, two men stood by them in dazzling apparel; and as they were 5 frightened and bowed their faces to the ground, the men said to them, "Why do you seek ⁴the living among the dead?⁵

---

1 Or *Take a guard*   2 Greek *know*   3 Some ancient authorities add *of the Lord Jesus*   4 Greek *him that lives*   5 Some ancient authorities add
He is not here, but has risen

HS references: Lk 23:56 = Exodus 12:16, 20:8-11 and Deuteronomy 5:12-15

MATT 28	MARK 16	LUKE 24

Come, see the place where ¹he lay.

| | | E Remember how he told you, while 6 he was still in Galilee, that the Son of 7 man must be delivered into the hands of sinful men, and be crucified, and on the third day rise." |

| F Then go quickly and tell his 7 disciples that he has risen from the dead, and behold, he is going before you to Galilee; there you will see him. Lo, I have told you." | F But go, tell his disciples and Peter 7 that he is going before you to Galilee; there you will see him, as he told you." | |

| G So they departed quickly from the 8 tomb with fear and great joy, and ran to tell his disciples. | G And they went out and fled from 8 the tomb; for trembling and astonishment had come upon them; and they said nothing to any one, for they were afraid.* | G And they remembered his words, 8 and returning ²from the tomb they told 9 all this to the eleven and to all the rest. |

| Hᴴ And behold, Jesus met them and 9 said, "Hail!" And they came up and took hold of his feet and worshiped him. Then Jesus said to them, "Do 10 not be afraid; go and tell my brethren to go to Galilee, and there they will see me." | | |

| | | Iᴵ Now it was Mary Mag'dalene and 10 Jo-an'na and Mary the mother of James and the other women with them who told this to the apostles; but these 11 words seemed to them an idle tale, and they did not believe them.³ |

§ 148   The Guard and the Authorities

MATT 28:11-15

While they were going, behold, some of the guard went 11
into the city and told the chief priests all that had taken
place. And when they had assembled with the elders and 12
taken counsel, they gave a sum of money to the soldiers
and said, "Tell people, 'His disciples came by night and   13

---

1 Some ancient authorities read *the Lord*   2 Some ancient authorities omit *from the tomb*   3 Some ancient authorities add verse 12: *But Peter rose and ran to the tomb; stooping and looking in, he saw the linen cloths by themselves, and he went home wondering at what had happened.*

---

* About the ending of the record of Mark, both ERV and ARV have the marginal statement: *The two oldest Greek manuscripts, and some other authorities, omit from verse 9 to the end. Some other authorities have a different ending to the Gospel.* From 16:9 to the end is therefore not placed in full parallelism, but is set forth in footnote form:
H 9 Now when he rose early on the first day of the week, he appeared first to Mary Mag'dalene, from whom he had cast out seven demons.
I 10 She went out and told those who had been with him, as they mourned and wept. 11 But when they heard that he was alive and had been seen by her, they would not believe it. (Mark 16:9-11)

MATT **28**

stole him away while we were asleep.' And if this ¹comes 14
to the governor's ears, we will satisfy him and keep you
out of trouble." So they took the money and did as they 15
were directed; and this story has been spread among the
Jews to this day.

§ 149 With the Disciples in the Country

LUKE **24**:13-32

Aᴬ That very day two of them were going to a village 13
named Emma'us, about seven miles from Jerusalem, and 14
talking with each other about all these things that had
happened. While they were talking and discussing together, 15
Jesus himself drew near and went with them. But their eyes 16
were kept from recognizing him.

B And he said to them, "What is this conversation which 17
you are holding with each other as you walk?" And they
stood still, looking sad. Then one of them, named 18
Cle'opas, answered him, "Are you the only visitor to
Jerusalem who does not know the things that have
happened there in these days?" And he said to them, "What 19
things?" And they said to him, "Concerning Jesus of
Nazareth, who was a prophet mighty in deed and word
before God and all the people, and how our chief priests 20
and rulers delivered him up to be condemned to death, and
crucified him. But we had hoped that he was the one to 21
redeem Israel.

C Yes, and besides all this, it is now the third day since
this happened. Moreover, some women of our company 22
amazed us. They were at the tomb early in the morning and 23
did not find his body; and they came back saying that they
had even seen a vision of angels, who said that he was
alive.

D Some of those who were with us went to the tomb, and 24
found it just as the women had said; but him they did not
see."

E And he said to them, "O foolish men, and slow of heart 25
to believe all that the prophets have spoken! Was it not 26
necessary that the Christ should suffer these things and
enter into his glory?" And beginning with Moses and all 27
the prophets, he interpreted to them in all the scriptures the
things concerning himself.

---

1 Or *comes to a hearing before the governor*

A 12 After this he appeared in another form to two of them, as they were walking into the country. (Mark 16:12)

LUKE **24**

F So they drew near to the village to which they were 28 going. He appeared to be going further, but they 29 constrained him, saying, "Stay with us, for it is toward evening and the day is now far spent." So he went in to stay with them. When he was at table with them, he took 30 the ¹bread and blessed, and broke it, and gave it to them. And their eyes were opened and they recognized him; and 31 he vanished out of their sight. They said to each other, 32 "Did not our hearts burn within us while he talked to us on the road, while he opened to us the scriptures?"

§ 150   With the Disciples in Jerusalem

MATT **28**:19-20   LUKE **24**:33-53

Aᴬ And they rose that same hour and returned to 33 Jerusalem; and they found the eleven gathered together and those who were with them, who said, "The Lord has risen 34 indeed, and has appeared to Simon!" Then they told what 35 had happened on the road, and how he was known to them in the breaking of the bread.

Bᴮ As they were saying this, Jesus himself stood among 36 them.² But they were startled and frightened, and supposed 37 that they saw a spirit. And he said to them, "Why are you 38 troubled, and why do questionings rise in your hearts? See 39 my hands and my feet, that it is I myself; handle me, and see; for a spirit has not flesh and bones as you see that I have."³

C And while they still disbelieved for joy, and wondered, 41 he said to them, "Have you anything here to eat?" They 42 gave him a piece of broiled fish,⁴ and he took it and ate 43 before them.

D Then he said to them, "These are my words which I 44 spoke to you, while I was still with you, that everything written about me in the law of Moses and the prophets and the psalms must be fulfilled." Then he opened their minds 45 to understand the scriptures, and said to them, "Thus it is 46 written, that the Christ should suffer and on the third day rise from the dead,

Eᴱ *Go therefore and make disciples of all nations, baptizing* 19 *them in the name of the Father and of the Son and of the Holy Spirit, teaching them to observe all that I have* 20 *commanded you; and lo, I am with you ⁷always, to the ⁸close of the age." (§ 151 C)*   **E**ᴱ and that repentance ⁵and forgiveness of sins should be 47 preached in his name to all ⁶nations, beginning from Jerusalem. You are witnesses of these things. And behold, I 48 send the promise of my Father upon you; but stay in the 49 city, until you are clothed with power from on high."

---

1 Or *loaf*   2 Some ancient authorities add *and said to them, "Peace to you!"*   3 Some ancient authorities add verse 40: *and when he had said this he showed them his hands and his feet*   4 Some ancient authorities add *and a honeycomb*   5 Some ancient authorities read *unto*   6 Or *nations. Beginning from Jerusalem, you are witnesses. . .*   7 Greek *all the days*   8 Or *consummation*   9 Some ancient authorities omit *new*

HS references: Lk 24:46 = Hosea 6:2

A 13 And they went back and told the rest, but they did not believe them.
B 14 Afterward he appeared to the eleven themselves as they sat at table; and he upbraided them for their unbelief and hardness of heart, because they had not believed those who saw him after he had risen.
E 15 And he said to them, "Go into all the world and preach the gospel to the whole creation. 16 He who believes and is baptized will be saved; but he who does not believe will be condemned. 17 And these signs will accompany those who believe: in my name they will cast out demons; they will speak in ⁹new tongues; 18 they will pick up serpents, and if they drink any deadly thing, it will not hurt them; they will lay their hands on the sick, and they will recover." (Mark 16:13-18)

LUKE **24**

F[F] Then he led them out as far as Bethany, and lifting up 50 his hands he blessed them. While he blessed them, he 51 parted from them, [1]and was carried up into heaven. And 52 they[2] returned to Jerusalem with great joy, and were 53 continually in the temple blessing God.

§ 151 With the Disciples in Galilee

MATT 28:16-20   LUKE 24:47-49

A Now the eleven disciples went to Galilee, to the 16 mountain to which Jesus had directed them. And when they 17 saw him they worshiped him; but some doubted.

B[B] And Jesus came and said to them, "All authority in 18 heaven and on earth has been given to me.

C[C] Go therefore and make disciples of all nations, baptizing 19 them in the name of the Father and of the Son and of the Holy Spirit, teaching them to observe all that I have 20 commanded you; and lo, I am with you [5]always, to the [6]close of the age."

C[C] *and that repentance [3]and forgiveness of sins should be 47 preached in his name to all [4]nations, beginning from Jerusalem. You are witnesses of these things. And behold, I 48 send the promise of my Father upon you; but stay in the 49 city, until you are clothed with power from on high."*
(§ 150 E)

---

1 Some ancient authorities omit *and was carried up into heaven*   2 Some ancient authorities add *worshiped him, and*   3 Some ancient authorities read *unto*   4 Or *nations. Beginning from Jerusalem, you are witnesses. . .*   5 Greek *all the days*   6 Or *consummation*

HS references: Mk 16:19 = Psalm 110:1

F 19 So then the Lord Jesus, after he had spoken to them, was taken up into heaven, and sat down at the right hand of God. 20 And they went forth and preached everywhere, while the Lord worked with them and confirmed the message by the signs that attended it. Amen. (Mark 16:19-20)

B All things have been delivered to me by my Father.
(§ 41 Q = Mt 11:27)
C Compare the reference attached to § 150 portion E

B All things have been delivered to me by my Father.
(§ 82 T = Lk 10:22)

BOOK II

THE RECORD OF JOHN

RECORDS OF THE LIFE OF JESUS

BOOK II

THE RECORD OF JOHN

Chapter I

PROLOGUE TO THE RECORD OF JOHN

§ 152 Prologue to the Record of John

JOHN 1:1-18   MT-MK-LK

A In the beginning was the Word, and the Word was with God, and the 1 Word was God. He was in the beginning with God; all things were made 2 through him, and without him ¹was not anything made that was made. In 3 him was life, and the life was the light of men. The light shines in the 4 darkness, and the darkness has not overcome it. 5

B There was a man sent from God, whose name was John. He came for 6 testimony, to bear witness to the light, that all might believe through him. 7 He was not the light, but came to bear witness to the light. The true light 8 that enlightens every man was coming into the world. 9

B *The Mt-Mk-Lk account of the activity of John is recorded in § 17*

C He was in the world, and the world was made through him, yet the world 10 knew him not. He came to ²his own home, and his own people received him 11 not. But to all who received him, who believed in his name, he gave power 12 to become children of God; who were ³born, not of ⁴blood nor of the will of 13 the flesh nor of the will of man, but of God.

D And the Word became flesh and ⁵dwelt among us, full of grace and truth; 14 we have beheld his glory, glory as ⁶of the only Son from the Father.

D *For the Mt-Mk-Lk reference to a beholding of the glory of Jesus, compare § 74 C (Lk)*

Eᴱ (John bore witness to him, and cried, "This was he of whom I said, 'He 15 who comes after me ranks before me, for he was before me.'")

E *Compare § 17 portion P*

F And from his fulness have we all received, grace upon grace. For the law 16 was given through Moses; grace and truth came through Jesus Christ. No 17 one has ever seen God; the only ⁷Son, who is in the bosom of the Father, he 18 has made him known.

---

1 Or *was not anything made. That which has been made was life in him.*   2 Greek *his own things*   3 Or *begotten*   4 Greek *bloods*
5 Greek *tabernacled*   6 Or *an only begotten from a father*   7 Other ancient authorities read *God*

HS references: John 1:1 = Genesis 1:3 and Psalms 33:6; 107:19-20 and Amos 3:7-8   John 1:3 = Proverbs 8:27-30   John 1:18 = Exodus 33:20

E Compare § 154 portion A

Chapter II

IN BETHANY BEYOND JORDAN

§ 153 Purpose of the Preaching of John

JOHN 1:19-28

MT-MK-LK

A And this is the testimony of John, when the Jews sent priests and Levites 19 from Jerusalem to ask him, "Who are you?" He confessed, he did not deny, 20 but confessed, "I am not the Christ."

A *Compare § 17 portion O*

B And they asked him, "What then? Are you Eli'jah?" He said, "I am not." 21 "Are you the prophet?" And he answered, "No." They said to him then, 22 "Who are you? Let us have an answer for those who sent us. What do you say about yourself?"

B *For records of the identification of John as Elijah or the prophet, compare § 41 G and § 74 M. For records of the identification of Jesus as Elijah or the prophet, compare § 58 BC and § 71 C*

C He said, "I am the voice of one crying in the wilderness, 'Make straight 23 the way of the Lord,' as the prophet Isaiah said."

C *Compare § 17 portions D-F Compare § 41 portion E*

D Now they had been sent from the Pharisees. They asked him, "Then why 24 are you baptizing, if you are neither the Christ, nor Eli'jah, nor the 25 prophet?"

E John answered them, "I baptize ¹with water; but among you stands one 26 whom you do not know, even he who comes after me, the thong of whose 27 sandal I am not worthy to untie."

E *Compare § 17 portion P*

F This took place in ²Bethany beyond the Jordan, where John was baptizing. 28

§ 154 Purpose of the Baptism by John

JOHN 1:29-34

A^A The next day he saw Jesus coming toward him, and said, "Behold, the 29 Lamb of God, who ³takes away the sin of the world! This is he of whom I 30 said, 'After me comes a man who ranks before me, for he was ⁴before me.'

A *Compare § 17 portion P*

B I myself did not know him; but for this I came baptizing ¹with water, that 31 he might be revealed to Israel."

B *Compare § 18 portion B*

C And John bore witness, "I saw the Spirit descend as a dove from heaven, 32 and it remained on him.

C *Compare § 18 portion C*

D I myself did not know him; but he who sent me to baptize ¹with water 33 said to me, 'He on whom you see the Spirit descend and remain, this is he who baptizes ¹with the Holy Spirit.' And I have seen and have borne witness 34 that this is the Son of God."

D *Compare § 18 portion B Compare § 18 portion C*

---

1 Or *in*   2 Many ancient authorities read *Bethabarah* some *Betharabah*   3 Or *bears the sin*   4 Greek *first in regard of me*

HS references: John 1:21 = II Kings 2:11 and Malachi 4:5 and Deuteronomy 18:15-18   John 1:23 = Isaiah 40:3
John 1:29 = Exodus 12:1-6 and Isaiah 53:7

A Compare § 152 portion E

§ 155   Transition of Disciples from John to Jesus

MT-MK-LK   JOHN 1:35-42

A *For the Mt-Mk-Lk record of the relation of Andrew and Simon Peter to Jesus, compare § 23 and § 27*

A The next day again John was standing with two of his disciples; and he 35 looked at Jesus as he walked, and said, "Behold, the Lamb of God!" The 36 two disciples heard him say this, and they followed Jesus. Jesus turned, and 37 saw them following, and said to them, "What do you seek?" And they said 38 to him, "Rabbi" (which means Teacher), "where are you staying?" He said 39 to them, "Come and see." They came and saw where he was staying; and they stayed with him that day, for it was about the tenth hour. One of the 40 two who heard John speak, and followed him, was Andrew, Simon Peter's brother. He first found his brother Simon, and said to him, "We have found 41 the Messiah" (which means [1]Christ). He brought him to Jesus.   42

B *In connection with the double name of Simon Peter, compare § 35 C, § 56 D, and § 71 E*

B Jesus looked at him, and said, "So you are Simon the son of [2]John? You shall be called Cephas" (which means [3]Peter).

§ 156   Jesus Wins Early Followers

JOHN 1:43-51

A *For the complete list of the close associates of Jesus, compare § 35 C and § 56 D*

A The next day Jesus decided to go to Galilee. And he found Philip and said 43 to him, "Follow me." Now Philip was from Beth-sa'ida, the city of Andrew 44 and Peter. Philip found Nathan'a-el, and said to him, "We have found him 45 of whom Moses in the law and also the prophets wrote, Jesus of Nazareth, the son of Joseph." Nathan'a-el said to him, "Can anything good come out 46 of Nazareth?" Philip said to him, "Come and see." Jesus saw Nathan'a-el 47 coming to him, and said of him, "Behold, an Israelite indeed, in whom is no guile!" Nathan'a-el said to him, "How do you know me?" Jesus answered 48 him, "Before Philip called you, when you were under the fig tree, I saw you." Nathan'a-el answered him, "Rabbi, you are the Son of God! You are 49 the King of Israel!" Jesus answered him, "Because I said to you, I saw you 50 under the fig tree, do you believe? You shall see greater things than these."

B *On the ministry of angels to Jesus, compare § 20 G and § 140 D*

B And he said to him, "Truly, truly, I say to you, you will see heaven 51 opened, and the angels of God ascending and descending upon the Son of man."

---

1 That is *Anointed*   2 Greek *Joanes:* called in Matthew 16:17, *Jonah*   3 That is *Rock* or *Stone* from the word for *rock* in both Aramaic and Greek, respectively.

HS references: John 1:47 = Genesis 27:35 and 32:28   John 1:51 = Genesis 28:12

Chapter III

IN THE PROVINCE OF GALILEE

§ 157 In Cana of Galilee

JOHN 2:1-11   MT-MK-LK

A On the third day there was a marriage at Cana in Galilee, and the mother 1
of Jesus was there; Jesus also was invited to the marriage, with his 2
disciples. When the wine gave out, the mother of Jesus said to him, "They 3
have no wine." And Jesus said to her, "O woman, what have you to do with 4
me? My hour has not yet come." His mother said to the servants, "Do 5
whatever he tells you."

B Now six stone jars were standing there, for the Jewish rites of 6
purification, each holding twenty or thirty gallons. Jesus said to them, "Fill 7
the jars with water." And they filled them up to the brim. He said to them, 8
"Now draw some out, and take it to the steward of the feast." So they took
it. When the steward of the feast tasted the water now become wine, and did 9
not know where it came from (though the servants who had drawn the water
knew), the steward of the feast called the bridegroom and said to him, 10
"Every man serves the good wine first; and when men have drunk freely,
then the poor wine; but you have kept the good wine until now."

C^c This, the first of his signs, Jesus did at Cana in Galilee, and manifested 11
his glory; and his disciples believed in him.

§ 158 At Capernaum in Galilee

JOHN 2:12

After this he went down to Caper'na-um, with his mother and his brothers 12   *Compare § 21 portion B*
and his disciples; and there they stayed for a few days.   *Compare § 24 portion A*

C Compare § 173 portion C

Chapter IV

IN JERUSALEM AT THE PASSOVER

§ 159 Jesus Casts Commerce from the Temple

JOHN 2:13-22   MT-MK-LK

A The Passover of the Jews was at hand, and Jesus went up to Jerusalem. 13

A *Compare § 137 portion A*

B In the temple he found those who were selling oxen and sheep and 14 pigeons, and the money-changers at their business. And making a whip of 15 cords, he drove them all, with the sheep and oxen, out of the temple; and he poured out the coins of the money-changers and overturned their tables.

B *Compare § 126 portion A*

C And he told those who sold the pigeons, "Take these things away; you 16 shall not make my Father's house a house of trade."

C *Compare § 126 portion C*

D His disciples remembered that it was written, "Zeal for thy house will 17 consume me."

E The Jews then said to him, "What sign have you to show us for doing 18 this?"

E *Compare § 128 portion A*

F Jesus answered them, "Destroy this ¹temple, and in three days I will raise 19 it up."

F *Compare § 142 portion C*
   Compare § 144 portion D

G The Jews then said, "It has taken forty-six years to build this ¹temple, and 20 will you raise it up in three days?" But he spoke of the ¹temple of his body. 21 When therefore he was raised from the dead, his disciples remembered that 22 he had said this; and they believed the scripture and the word which Jesus had spoken.

§ 160 Attitude in Jerusalem toward Jesus

JOHN 2:23-25

Now when he was in Jerusalem at the Passover feast, many believed in his 23 name when they saw the signs which he did; but Jesus did not trust himself 24 to them, because he knew all men and needed no one to bear witness of 25 ²man; for he himself knew what was in man.

§ 161 Discourse with a Jewish Teacher

JOHN 3:1-12

A^A Now there was a man of the Pharisees, named Nicode'mus, a ruler of 1 the Jews. This man came to Jesus by night and said to him,   2

B "Rabbi, we know that you are a teacher come from God; for no one can do these signs that you do, unless God is with him."

B *Compare § 130 portion B*

C Jesus answered him, "Truly, truly, I say to you, unless one is born 3 ³anew, he cannot see the kingdom of God."

C *Compare § 78 portion D*
   Compare § 116 portion C

---

1 Or *sanctuary*   2 Or *a man; for . . . the man*   3 Or *from above*

HS references: John 2:13 = Deuteronomy 16:1-6   John 2:17 = Psalm 69:9

A For other references to Nicodemus, compare § 189 H and § 218 E

MT-MK-LK   JOHN 3

D Nicode'mus said to him, "How can a man be born when he is old? Can 4 he enter a second time into his mother's womb and be born?" Jesus 5 answered, "Truly, truly, I say to you, unless one is born of water and the Spirit, he cannot enter the kingdom of God.

E That which is born of the flesh is flesh, and that which is born of the 6 Spirit is spirit. Do not marvel that I said to you, 'You must be born ¹anew.' 7 ²The wind blows where it wills, and you hear the sound of it, but you do 8 not know whence it comes or whither it goes; so it is with every one who is born of the Spirit."

F Nicode'mus said to him, "How can this be?" Jesus answered him, "Are 9 you a teacher of Israel, and yet you do not understand this?   10

G^G Truly, truly, I say to you, we speak of what we know, and bear witness 11 to what we have seen; but you do not receive our testimony. If I have told 12 you earthly things and you do not believe, how can you believe if I tell you heavenly things?

§ 162   Mission of the Son of Man and Son of God

JOHN 3:13-21

A No one has ascended into heaven but he who descended from heaven, the 13 Son of man.³ And as Moses lifted up the serpent in the wilderness, so must 14 the Son of man be lifted up, that whoever believes in him may have eternal 15 life."⁴

B^B For God so loved the world that he gave his only Son, that whoever 16 believes in him should not perish but have eternal life. For God sent the Son 17 into the world, not to condemn the world, but that the world might be saved through him. He who believes in him is not condemned; he who does not 18 believe is condemned already, because he has not believed in the name of the only Son of God.

C And this is the judgment, that the light has come into the world, and men 19 loved darkness rather than light, because their deeds were evil. For every 20 one who ⁵does evil hates the light, and does not come to the light, lest his deeds should be ⁶exposed. But he who does what is true comes to the light, 21 that it may be clearly seen ⁷that his deeds have been wrought in God.

---

1 Or *from above*   2 Or *The spirit*. The same Greek word means both *wind* and *spirit*.   3 Some ancient authorities add *who is in heaven*
4 Some interpreters hold that the quotation continues through verse 21   5 Or *practices*   6 Or *convicted*   7 Or *because*

HS references: John 3:5 = Ezekiel 36:25-27   John 3:8 = Ezekiel 37:9   John 3:13-15 = Numbers 21:9

G Compare § 166 portion A

B Compare § 166 portion C

Chapter V

IN THE LAND OF JUDEA

---

§ 163 Baptism of the Disciples of Jesus

JOHN 3:22   MT-MK-LK

After this Jesus and his disciples went into the land of Judea; there he 22
remained with them and baptized.*

§ 164 Baptism of Disciples by John

JOHN 3:23-24

John also was baptizing at Ae'non near Salim, because there ¹was much 23   *For the Mt-Mk-Lk account of the*
water there; and people came and were baptized. For John had not yet been 24   *imprisonment of John, compare*
put in prison.   *§ 17 R, § 41 A, and § 58 D.*

§ 165 Relation of John to Jesus

JOHN 3:25-30

A Now a discussion arose between John's disciples and a Jew over 25
purifying. And they came to John, and said to him, "Rabbi, he who was 26
with you beyond the Jordan, to whom you bore witness, here he is,
baptizing, and all are going to him." John answered, "No one can receive 27
anything except what is given him from heaven.

B^B You yourselves bear me witness, that I said, I am not the Christ, but I 28
have been sent before him.

C He who has the bride is the bridegroom; the friend of the bridegroom, 29
who stands and hears him, rejoices greatly at the bridegroom's voice;
therefore this joy of mine is now full. He must increase, but I must 30
decrease."²

§ 166 Relation of Truth to Source

JOHN 3:31-36

A^A He who comes from above is above all; he who is of the earth belongs 31
to the earth, and of the earth he speaks; ³he who comes from heaven is
above all. He bears witness to what he has seen and heard, yet no one 32
receives his testimony; he who receives his testimony sets his seal to this, 33
that God is true. For he whom God has sent utters the words of God, for it 34
is not by measure that he gives the Spirit;

B the Father loves the Son, and has given all things into his hand.   35   B *Compare § 41 Q and § 82 T*
                                                                                    Compare § 151 portion B

C^C He who believes in the Son has eternal life; he who does not ⁴obey the 36
Son shall not see life, but the wrath of God rests upon him.

---

1 Greek *were many waters*   2 Some interpreters hold that the quotation continues through verse 36   3 Some ancient authorities read *he that comes from heaven bears witness of what he has seen and heard*   4 Or *believe*

---

* Compare § 167

B Compare § 153

A Compare § 161 portion G
C Compare § 162 portion B

§ 167 Departure from Judea for Galilee

MT-MK-LK   JOHN 4:1-3

Compare § 21 portion A

Now when the Lord knew that the Pharisees had heard that Jesus was 1
making and baptizing more disciples than John (although Jesus himself did 2
not baptize, but only his disciples), he left Judea and departed again to 3
Galilee.

Chapter VI

IN THE PROVINCE OF SAMARIA

§ 168 Jesus Journeys to Sychar of Samaria

JOHN 4:4-6   MT-MK-LK

He had to pass through Samar'ia. So he came to a city of Samar'ia, called 4
Sy'char, near the field that Jacob gave to his son Joseph. Jacob's ¹well was 5
there, and so Jesus, wearied as he was with his journey, sat down beside the 6
¹well. It was about the sixth hour.

§ 169 Discourse with a Woman of Samaria

JOHN 4:7-26

A There came a woman of Samar'ia to draw water. Jesus said to her, "Give 7
me a drink." For his disciples had gone away into the city to buy food. The 8
Samaritan woman said to him, "How is it that you, a Jew, ask a drink of 9
me, a woman of Samar'ia?" ²For Jews have no dealings with Samaritans.

B Jesus answered her, "If you knew the gift of God, and who it is that is 10
saying to you, 'Give me a drink,' you would have asked him, and he would
have given you living water." The woman said to him, "Sir, you have 11
nothing to draw with, and the well is deep; where do you get that living
water? Are you greater than our father Jacob, who gave us the well, and 12
drank from it himself, and his sons, and his cattle?"

C Jesus said to her, "Every one who drinks of this water will thirst again, 13
but whoever drinks of the water that I shall give him will never thirst; the 14
water that I shall give him will become in him a spring of water welling up
to eternal life." The woman said to him, "³Sir, give me this water, that I 15
may not thirst, nor come here to draw."

D Jesus said to her, "Go, call your husband, and come here." The woman 16
answered him, "I have no husband." Jesus said to her, "You are right in 17
saying, 'I have no husband'; for you have had five husbands, and he whom 18
you now have is not your husband; this you said truly."

E The woman said to him, "³Sir, I perceive that you are a prophet. Our 19
fathers worshiped on this mountain; and you say that in Jerusalem is the 20
place where men ought to worship." Jesus said to her, "Woman, believe me, 21
the hour is coming when neither on this mountain nor in Jerusalem will you
worship the Father. You worship what you do not know; we worship what 22
we know, for salvation is from the Jews. But the hour is coming, and now 23
is, when the true worshipers will worship the Father in spirit and truth, for
such the Father seeks to worship him. God is spirit, and those who worship 24
him must worship in spirit and truth."

F The woman said to him, "I know that Messiah is coming (he who is 25
called Christ); when he comes, he will show us all things." Jesus said to 26
her, "I who speak to you am he."

---

1 Greek *spring*: and so in verse 14; but not in verses 11 and 12   2 Some ancient authorities omit *For Jews have no dealings with Samaritans*.
3 Or *Lord*

HS references: John 4:5 = Genesis 33:19; 48:22 and Joshua 24:32   John 4:9 = II Kings 17:24-34 and Ezra 4:3-6
John 4:10 = Jeremiah 2:13 and 17:13   John 4:20 = Deuteronomy 11:29 and Joshua 8:33   John 4:22 = II Kings 17:28-41

§ 170 Discourse with the Disciples

MT-MK-LK   JOHN 4:27-38

A Just then his disciples came. They marveled that he was talking with a 27 woman, but none said, "What do you wish?" or, "Why are you talking with her?"

B So the woman left her water jar, and went away into the city, and said to 28 the people, "Come, see a man who told me all that I ever did. Can this be 29 the Christ?" They went out of the city and were coming to him.   30

C Meanwhile the disciples besought him, saying, "Rabbi, eat." But he said 31 to them, "I have food to eat of which you do not know." So the disciples 32 said to one another, "Has any one brought him food?" Jesus said to them, 33 "My food is to do the will of him who sent me, and to accomplish his 34 work.

D *Compare § 56 portion B*
    Compare § 82 portion B

D Do you not say, 'There are yet four months, then comes the harvest'? I 35 tell you, lift up your eyes, and see how the fields are already white for harvest.

E He who reaps receives wages, and gathers fruit for eternal life, so that 36 sower and reaper may rejoice together. For here the saying holds true, 'One 37 sows and another reaps.' I sent you to reap that for which you did not labor; 38 others have labored, and you have entered into their labor."

§ 171 Stay of Jesus in Samaria

JOHN 4:39-42

Many Samaritans from that city believed in him because of the woman's 39 testimony, "He told me all that I ever did." So when the Samaritans came to 40 him, they asked him to stay with them; and he stayed there two days. And 41 many more believed because of his word. They said to the woman, "It is no 42 longer because of your words that we believe, for we have heard for ourselves, and we know that this is indeed the Savior of the world."

Chapter VII

IN THE PROVINCE OF GALILEE

§ 172 Attitude of Galileans toward Jesus

JOHN 4:43-45   MT-MK-LK

A After the two days he departed to Galilee. **43**

A Compare § 21 portion A

B For Jesus himself testified that a prophet has no honor in his own **44** country.

B Compare § 22 portion H
Compare § 54 portion H

C So when he came to Galilee, the Galileans welcomed him, having seen all **45** that he had done in Jerusalem at the feast, for they too had gone to the feast.

§ 173 In Cana of Galilee

JOHN 4:46-54

A^A So he came again to Cana in Galilee, where he had made the water **46** wine.

B And at Caper'na-um there was an official whose son was ill. When he **47** heard that Jesus had come from Judea to Galilee, he went and begged him to come down and heal his son, for he was at the point of death. Jesus **48** therefore said to him, "Unless you see signs and wonders you will not believe." The official said to him, "[1]Sir, come down before my child dies." **49** Jesus said to him, "Go; your son will live." The man believed the word that **50** Jesus spoke to him and went his way. As he was going down, his [2]servants **51** met him and told him that his son was living. So he asked them the hour **52** when he began to mend, and they said to him, "Yesterday at the seventh hour the fever left him." The father knew that was the hour when Jesus had **53** said to him, "Your son will live"; and he himself believed, and all his household.

B For an account in Mt-Lk of somewhat similar general content, compare § 39

C^C This was now the second sign that Jesus did when he had come from **54** Judea to Galilee.

---

1 Or *Lord* 2 Or *slaves*

NC references: John 4:44 = GT 31

A Compare § 157 portions AB
C Compare § 157 portion C

Chapter VIII

IN JERUSALEM AT A FEAST

§ 174   At the Pool of Bethesda

JOHN 5:1-9a   MT-MK-LK

A After this there was ¹a feast of the Jews, and Jesus went up to Jerusalem. 1

B Now there is in Jerusalem by the Sheep Gate a pool, in Hebrew called 2
²Beth-za'tha, which has five porticoes. In these lay a multitude of invalids, 3
blind, lame, paralyzed.³ One man was there, who had been ill for 5
thirty-eight years. When Jesus saw him and knew that he had been lying 6
there a long time, he said to him, "Do you want to be healed?" The sick 7
man answered him, "⁴Sir, I have no man to put me into the pool when the
water is troubled, and while I am going another steps down before me."

C Jesus said to him, "Rise, take up your pallet, and walk." And at once the 8   C *Compare § 29 portions GH*
man was healed, and he took up his pallet and walked.   9a

§ 175   Criticism for Activity on the Sabbath

JOHN 5:9b-18

A Now that day was the sabbath. So the Jews said to the man who was 9b   A *Compare § 32 portion B*
cured, "It is the sabbath, it is not lawful for you to carry your pallet."   10

B But he answered them, "The man who healed me said to me, 'Take up 11
your pallet, and walk.'" They asked him, "Who is the man who said to you, 12
'Take up your pallet, and walk'?" Now the man who had been healed did 13
not know who it was, for Jesus had withdrawn, as there was a crowd in the
place. Afterward, Jesus found him in the temple, and said to him, "See, you 14
are well! Sin no more, that nothing worse befall you." The man went away 15
and told the Jews that it was Jesus who had healed him.

Cᶜ And this was why the Jews persecuted Jesus, because he did this on the 16   C *Compare § 33 portion G*
sabbath. But Jesus answered them, "My Father is working still, and I am 17
working." This was why the Jews sought all the more to kill him, because 18
he not only broke the sabbath but also called God his own Father, making
himself equal with God.

§ 176   Discourse on Judgment and Life

JOHN 5:19-29

A Jesus said to them, "Truly, truly, I say to you, the Son can do nothing of 19
his own accord, but only what he sees the Father doing; for whatever he
does, that the Son does likewise. For the Father loves the Son, and shows 20
him all that he himself is doing;

---

1 Many ancient authorities read *the feast*   2 Some ancient authorities read *Bethsaida* others *Bethesda*   3 Many ancient authorities insert, wholly or
in part, *waiting for the moving of the water; 4 for an angel of the Lord went down at certain seasons into the pool, and troubled the water: whoever
stepped in first after the troubling of the water was healed of whatever disease he had.*   4 Or *Lord*

HS references: John 5:2 = Nehemiah 3:1; 12:39   John 5:10 = Exodus 20:10 and Deuteronomy 5:14 and Nehemiah 13:19 and Jeremiah 17:21

C Compare § 188 portion B and § 195 portion B

MT-MK-LK   JOHN 5

B *With verse 23b compare § 57 P and § 78 G and § 82 Q*

B and greater works than these will he show him, that you may marvel. For 21 as the Father raises the dead and gives them life, so also the Son gives life to whom he will. The Father judges no one, but has given all judgment to 22 the Son, that all may honor the Son, even as they honor the Father. He who 23 does not honor the Son does not honor the Father who sent him. Truly, 24 truly, I say to you, he who hears my word and believes him who sent me, has eternal life; he does not come into judgment, but has passed from death to life.

C "Truly, truly, I say to you, the hour is coming, and now is, when the 25 dead will hear the voice of the Son of God, and those who hear will live. For as the Father has life in himself, so he has granted the Son also to have 26 life in himself, and has given him authority to execute judgment, because he 27 is [1]the Son of man.

D *Compare verse 46 of § 136 portion S*

D Do not marvel at this; for the hour is coming when all who are in the 28 tombs will hear his voice and come forth, those who have done good, to the 29 resurrection of life, and those who have [2]done evil, to the resurrection of judgment.

§ 177   Witnesses to the Truth of Jesus

JOHN 5:30-47

A "I can do nothing on my own authority; as I hear, I judge; and my judg- 30 ment is just, because I seek not my own will but the will of him who sent me. If I bear witness to myself, my testimony is not true; there is another 31 who bears witness to me, and I know that the testimony which he bears to 32 me is true.

B You sent to John, and he has borne witness to the truth. Not that the 33 testimony which I receive is from man; but I say this that you may be 34 saved. He was a burning and shining lamp, and you were willing to rejoice 35 for a while in his light.

C But the testimony which I have is greater than that of John; for the works 36 which the Father has granted me to accomplish, these very works which I am doing, bear me witness that the Father has sent me.

D And the Father who sent me has himself borne witness to me. His voice 37 you have never heard, his form you have never seen; and you do not have 38 his word abiding in you, for you do not believe him whom he has sent.

E You search the scriptures, because you think that in them you have 39 eternal life; and it is they that bear witness to me; yet you refuse to come to 40 me that you may have life.

F I do not receive glory from men. But I know that you have not the love 41 of God within you. I have come in my Father's name, and you do not 42 receive me; if another comes in his own name, him you will receive. How 43 can you believe, who receive glory from one another and do not seek the 44 glory that comes from the only God?

G *Compare § 149 portion E*
Compare § 150 portion D

G Do not think that I shall accuse you to the Father; it is Moses who 45 accuses you, on whom you set your hope. If you believed Moses, you 46 would believe me, for he wrote of me. But if you do not believe his 47 writings, how will you believe my words?"

---

1 Or *a son of man*   2 Or *practiced*

HS references: John 5:29 = Daniel 12:2

Chapter IX

ABOUT THE SEA OF GALILEE

---

§ 178 Teaching and Feeding the Multitude

JOHN 6:1-13   MT-MK-LK

A After this Jesus went to the other side of the Sea of Galilee, which is the 1
Sea of Tibe'ri-as. And a multitude followed him, because they saw the signs 2
which he did on those who were diseased.

A *Compare § 60 portion A*
Compare § 65

B Jesus went up on the mountain, and there sat down with his disciples. 3
Now the Passover, the feast of the Jews, was at hand. Lifting up his eyes, 4
then, and seeing that a multitude was coming to him, 5

B *Compare § 60 portion B*
Compare § 67 portion A

C Jesus said to Philip, "How are we to buy ¹bread, so that these people may
eat?" This he said to test him, for he himself knew what he would do. 6

C *Compare § 60 portion C*
Compare § 67 portion C

D Philip answered him, "Two hundred ²denarii would not buy enough 7
¹bread for each of them to get a little." One of his disciples, Andrew, Simon 8
Peter's brother, said to him, "There is a lad here who has five barley loaves 9
and two fish; but what are they among so many?"

D *Compare § 60 portion D*
Compare § 67 portion D

E Jesus said, "Make the people sit down." Now there was much grass in the 10
place;

E *Compare § 60 portion F*
Compare § 67 portion E

F so the men sat down, in number about five thousand.

F *Compare § 60 portion I*
Compare § 67 portion I

G Jesus then took the loaves, and when he had given thanks, he distributed 11
them to those who were seated; so also the fish, as much as they wanted.

G *Compare § 60 portion G*
Compare § 67 portion F

H And when they had eaten their fill, he told his disciples, "Gather up the 12
fragments left over, that nothing may be lost." So they gathered them up 13
and filled twelve baskets with fragments from the five barley loaves, left by
those who had eaten.

H *Compare § 60 portion H*
Compare § 67 portion H

§ 179 Popular Attitude toward Jesus

JOHN 6:14-15

A When the people saw the ³sign which he had done, they said, "This is 14
indeed the prophet who is to come into the world!"

B Perceiving then that they were about to come and take him by force to 15
make him king, Jesus withdrew again to the mountain by himself.

B *Compare § 60 portion K*
Compare § 71 portion A

§ 180 Across the Sea of Galilee

JOHN 6:16-21

A When evening came, his disciples went down to the sea, got into a boat, 16
and started across the sea to Caper'na-um. 17

A *Compare § 60 portion J*
Compare § 67 portion J

B It was now dark, and Jesus had not yet come to them. The sea rose 18

B *Compare § 61 portion A*

---

1 Greek *loaves*   2 The word in Greek denotes a coin worth about forty cents. The denarius was a day's wage for a laborer.   3 Some ancient
authorities read *signs*

HS references: John 6:5-13 = II Kings 4:42-44   John 6:14 = Deuteronomy 18:15-18

MT-MK-LK   **JOHN 6**

because a strong wind was blowing. When they had rowed about [1]three or 19 four miles, they saw Jesus walking on the sea and drawing near to the boat.

C   *Compare § 61 portion B*   **C** They were frightened, but he said to them, "It is I; do not be afraid."   20

D   *Compare § 61 portion D*   **D** Then they were glad to take him into the boat, and immediately the boat 21
     Compare § 62 portion A   was at the land to which they were going.

§ 181   The Multitude in Capernaum

JOHN 6:22-26

On the next day the people who remained on the other side of the sea saw 22 that there had been only one [2]boat there, and that Jesus had not entered the boat with his disciples, but that his disciples had gone away alone. However, 23 boats from Tibe'ri-as came near the place where they ate the bread after the Lord had given thanks. So when the people saw that Jesus was not there, 24 nor his disciples, they themselves got into the [3]boats and went to Caper'na-um, seeking Jesus.

When they found him on the other side of the sea, they said to him, "Rabbi, 25 when did you come here?" Jesus answered them, "Truly, truly, I say to 26 you, you seek me, not because you saw signs, but because you ate your fill of the loaves.

§ 182   Discourse on the Bread of Life

JOHN 6:27-59

A Do not labor for the food which perishes, but for the food which endures 27 to eternal life, which the Son of man will give to you; for on him has God the Father set his seal." Then they said to him, "What must we do, to be 28 doing the works of God?" Jesus answered them, "This is the work of God, 29 that you believe in him whom [4]he has sent."

B   *Compare § 45 portion Q*   **B** So they said to him, "Then what sign do you do, that we may see, and 30
     Compare § 68 portion A   believe you? What work do you perform? Our fathers ate the manna in the 31
     Compare § 86 portion D   wilderness; as it is written, 'He gave them bread from heaven to eat.'"

C Jesus then said to them, "Truly, truly, I say to you, it was not Moses 32 who gave you the bread from heaven; my Father gives you the true bread from heaven. For the bread of God is that which comes down from heaven, 33 and gives life to the world." They said to him, "Lord, give us this bread 34 always."

Jesus said to them, "I am the bread of life; he who comes to me shall not 35 hunger, and he who believes in me shall never thirst.

D But I said to you that you have seen me and yet do not believe.   36

E All that the Father gives me will come to me; and him who comes to me 37 I will not cast out. For I have come down from heaven, not to do my own 38 will, but the will of him who sent me; and this is the will of him who sent 39 me, that I should lose nothing of all that he has given me, but raise it up at the last day. For this is the will of my Father, that every   40

---

1 Greek *twenty-five or thirty stadia*   2 Greek *little boat*   3 Greek *little boats*   4 Or *he sent*

HS references: John 6:19-21 = Psalm 107:29-30   John 6:31 = Exodus 16:4,15 and Numbers 11:8 and Psalms 78:24; 105:40 and Nehemiah 9:15

JOHN 6   MT-MK-LK

one who sees the Son and believes in him should have eternal life; and [1]I
will raise him up at the last day."

F The Jews then murmured at him, because he said, "I am the bread which 41   F *Compare § 22 portion D*
came down from heaven." They said, "Is not this Jesus, the son of Joseph, 42   *Compare § 54 portion D*
whose father and mother we know? How does he now say, 'I have come
down from heaven'?"

G Jesus answered them, "Do not murmur among yourselves. No one can 43
come to me unless the Father who sent me draws him; and I will raise him 44
up at the last day. It is written in the prophets, 'And they shall all be taught 45
by God.' Every one who has heard and learned from the Father comes to
me.

H Not that any one has seen the Father except him who is from God; he has 46   H *Compare § 41 portion Q*
seen the Father.   *Compare § 82 portion T*

I Truly, truly, I say to you, he who believes has eternal life. I am the bread 47
of life. Your fathers ate the manna in the wilderness, and they died. This is 48
the bread which comes down from heaven, that a man may eat of it and not 49
die. I am the living bread which came down from heaven; if any one eats of 50
this bread, he will live for ever; and the bread which I shall give for the life 51
of the world is my flesh."

J The Jews then disputed among themselves, saying, "How can this man 52
give us his flesh to eat?" So Jesus said to them, "Truly, truly, I say to you, 53
unless you eat the flesh of the Son of man and drink his blood, you have no
life in you; he who eats my flesh and drinks my blood has eternal life, and I 54
will raise him up at the last day. For my flesh is [2]food indeed, and my 55
blood is [3]drink indeed. He who eats my flesh and drinks my blood abides in 56
me, and I in him. As the living Father sent me, and I live because of the 57
Father, so he who eats me will live because of me. This is the bread which 58
came down from heaven, not such as the fathers ate and died; he who eats
this bread will live for ever."

K This he said in [4]the synagogue, as he taught at Caper'na-um.   59

§ 183 Effect of the Discourse on Disciples

JOHN 6:60-71

A Many of his disciples, when they heard it, said, "This is a hard saying; 60   A *In connection with the question*
who can listen to [5]it?" But Jesus, knowing in himself that his disciples 61   *recorded in verse 62, compare § 150*
murmured at it, said to them, "Do you take offense at this? Then what if 62   *portion F.*
you were to see the Son of man ascending where he was before? It is the 63
spirit that gives life, the flesh is of no avail; the words that I have spoken to
you are spirit and life.

B But there are some of you that do not believe." For Jesus knew from the 64   B *Compare § 138 portion E*
first who those were that did not believe, and who it was that would betray
him. And he said, "This is why I told you that no one can come to me 65
unless it is granted him by the Father."

---

1 Or *that I should raise him up*   2 Greek *true food*   3 Greek *true drink*   4 Or *a synagogue*   5 Or *him*

HS references: John 6:44-45 = Hosea 11:3-4   John 6:45 = Isaiah 54:13 and Jeremiah 31:33-34 and Joel 2:28-29

MT-MK-LK	JOHN 6

C *Compare § 71 portion D*

C After this many of his disciples drew back and no longer went about with 66 him. Jesus said to the twelve, "Do you also wish to go away?" Simon Peter 67 answered him, "Lord, to whom shall we go? You ¹have the words of eternal 68 life; and we have believed, and have come to know, that you are the Holy 69 One of God."

D *Compare § 35 portion B*
    Compare § 137 portion F
    Compare § 138 portion F

Dᴰ Jesus answered them, "Did I not choose you, the twelve, and one of you 70 is a devil?" He spoke of Judas the son of Simon Iscariot, for he, one of the 71 twelve, was to betray him.

§ 184   Jesus in Galilee

JOHN 7:1

Compare § 76 portion A

After this Jesus went about in Galilee; he would not go about in Judea, 1 because the ²Jews sought to kill him.

---

1 Or *have words*   2 Or *Judeans*

D Compare § 209 portions C (verse 11) and F and H

Chapter X

AT THE FEAST OF TABERNACLES

§ 185 Opinions of the Brothers of Jesus

JOHN 7:2-9   MT-MK-LK

A Now the Jews' feast of Tabernacles was at hand. So his brothers said to 2
him, "Leave here and go to Judea, that your disciples may see the works 3
you are doing. For no man works in secret if he seeks to be known openly. 4
If you do these things, show yourself to the world."

B For even his brothers did not believe in him.   5

B Compare § 44
Compare § 54 portion J

C Jesus said to them, "My time has not yet come, but your time is always 6
here. The world cannot hate you, but it hates me because I testify of it that 7
its works are evil. Go to the feast yourselves; I am not[1] going up to this 8
feast, for my time has not yet fully come." So saying, he remained in 9
Galilee.

§ 186 Popular Opinions about Jesus

JOHN 7:10-13

But after his brothers had gone up to the feast, then he also went up, not 10
publicly but in private. The Jews were looking for him at the feast, and 11
saying, "Where is he?" And there was much muttering about him among the 12
people. While some said, "He is a good man," others said, "No, he is lead-
ing the people astray." Yet for fear of the Jews no one spoke openly of him. 13

§ 187 Source of the Teaching of Jesus

JOHN 7:14-18

A About the middle of the feast Jesus went up into the temple and taught. 14
The Jews marveled at it, saying, "How is it that this man [2]has learning, 15
when he has never studied?"

A Compare § 22 portion C
Compare § 54 portion C

B So Jesus answered them, "My teaching is not mine, but his who sent me; 16
if any man's will is to do his will, he shall know whether the teaching is 17
from God or whether I am speaking on my own authority. He who speaks 18
on his own authority seeks his own glory; but he who seeks the glory of
him who sent him is true, and in him there is no falsehood.

§ 188 Concerning Healing on the Sabbath

JOHN 7:19-24

A Did not Moses give you the law? Yet none of you keeps the law. Why do 19
you seek to kill me?" The people answered, "You have a demon! Who is 20
seeking to kill you?"

*A On the possession of Jesus by a
devil, compare § 45 C and § 53 B
and § 86 C*

B[B] Jesus answered them, "I did one deed, and you all marvel at it. Moses 21
gave you circumcision (not that it is from Moses, but from the fathers), and 22
you circumcise a man upon the sabbath. If on the sabbath a man receives 23
circumcision, so that the law of Moses may not be broken, are you angry
with me because on the sabbath I made a man's whole body well? Do not 24
judge by appearances, but judge with right judgment."

---

1 Many ancient authorities add *yet*   2 Or *knows his letters*

HS references: John 7:2 = Leviticus 23:39-43 and Deuteronomy 16:13-15   John 7:22-23 = Genesis 17:9-14 and Leviticus 12:1-3

B Compare § 175 portion C and § 195 portion B

§ 189   Conflicting Judgments about Jesus

MT-MK-LK   JOHN 7:25-52

A Some of the people of Jerusalem therefore said, "Is not this the man 25 whom they seek to kill? And here he is, speaking openly, and they say 26 nothing to him! Can it be that the authorities really know that this is the Christ? Yet we know where this man comes from; and when the Christ 27 appears, no one will know where he comes from."

B *With verse 29a compare § 41 Q and § 82 T*

B So Jesus proclaimed, as he taught in the temple, "You know me, and you 28 know where I come from? But I have not come of my own accord; he who sent me is true, and him you do not know. I know him, for I come from 29 him, and he sent me."

C So they sought to arrest him; but no one laid hands on him, because his 30 hour had not yet come. Yet many of the people believed in him; they said, 31 "When the Christ appears, will he do more signs than this man has done?" The Pharisees heard the crowd thus muttering about him, and the chief 32 priests and Pharisees sent officers to arrest him.

D[D] Jesus then said, "I shall be with you a little longer, and then I go to him 33 who sent me; you will seek me and you will not find me; where I am you 34 cannot come." The Jews said to one another, "Where does this man intend 35 to go that we shall not find him? Does he intend to go to the Dispersion [1]among the Greeks and teach the Greeks? What does he mean by saying, 36 'You will seek me and you will not find me,' and, 'Where I am you cannot come'?"

E *On the promise of the Spirit after the death of Jesus, compare § 150 portion E*

E On the last day of the feast, the great day, Jesus stood up and proclaimed, 37 "If any one thirst, let him come to me and drink. He who believes in me[2], 38 as the scripture has said, 'Out of his heart shall flow rivers of living water.'" Now this he said about the Spirit, which those who believed in him 39 were to receive; for as yet the [3]Spirit had not been given, because Jesus was not yet glorified.

F *On Bethlehem as the source of the Christ, compare § 11 portion C*

F When they heard these words, some of the people said, "This is really the 40 prophet." Others said, "This is the Christ." But some said, "Is the Christ to 41 come from Galilee? Has not the scripture said that the Christ is descended 42 from David, and comes from Bethlehem, the village where David was?" So 43 there was a division among the people over him. Some of them wanted to 44 arrest him, but no one laid hands on him.

G *Compare § 24 portion B*
Compare § 24 portion E
Compare § 38 portion X

G The officers then went back to the chief priests and Pharisees, who said 45 to them, "Why did you not bring him?" The officers answered, "No man 46 ever spoke like this man!" The Pharisees answered them, "Are you led 47 astray, you also? Have any of the authorities or of the Pharisees believed in 48 him? But this crowd, who do not know the law, are accursed." 49

H[H] Nicode'mus, who had gone to him before, and who was one of them, 50 said to them, "Does our law judge a man without first giving him a hearing 51

---

1 Greek *of*   2 Or *let him come to me, and let him who believes in me drink*   3 Some ancient authorities read *the Holy Spirit*

HS references: John 7:37-39 = Numbers 20:2-13 and Isaiah 44:3 and 55:1 and 58:11   John 7:42 = II Samuel 7:12-17 and Psalm 89:19-37 and Psalm 132:11-12 and Micah 5:2   John 7:51 = Deuteronomy 1:16 and 17:4-6

D Compare § 209 portion M
H For other references to Nicodemus, compare § 161 A and § 218 E

and learning what he does?" They replied, "Are you from Galilee too? 52 Search and you will [1]see that no prophet is to rise from Galilee."

§ 190 The Adulterous Woman and her Accusers

JOHN 7:53-8:11

[2]They went each to his own house, but Jesus went to the Mount of Olives. 53 Early in the morning he came again to the temple; all the people came to 8:1 him, and he sat down and taught them. The scribes and the Pharisees 2 brought a woman who had been caught in adultery, and placing her in the 3 midst they said to him, "Teacher, this woman has been caught in the act of 4 adultery. Now in the law Moses commanded us to stone such. What do you 5 say about her?" This they said to test him, that they might have some charge 6 to bring against him. Jesus bent down and wrote with his finger on the ground. And as they continued to ask him, he stood up and said to them, 7 "Let him who is without sin among you be the first to throw a stone at her." And once more he bent down and wrote with his finger on the ground. But 8 when they heard it, they went away, one by one, beginning with the eldest, 9 and Jesus was left alone with the woman standing before him. Jesus looked 10 up and said to her, "Woman, where are they? Has no one condemned you?" She said, "No one, Lord." And Jesus said, "Neither do I condemn you; go, 11 and do not sin again."

§ 191 Discourse on the Light of Life

JOHN 8:12-20

A Again Jesus spoke to them, saying, "I am the light of the world; he who 12 follows me will not walk in darkness, but will have the light of life."

B The Pharisees then said to him, "You are bearing witness to yourself; 13 your testimony is not true." Jesus answered, "Even if I do bear witness to 14 myself, my testimony is true, for I know whence I have come and whither I am going, but you do not know whence I come or whither I am going.

C You judge according to the flesh, I judge no one. Yet even if I do judge, 15 my judgment is true, for it is not I alone that judge, but I and [3]he who sent 16 me.

D In your law it is written that the testimony of two men is true; I bear 17 witness to myself, and the Father who sent me bears witness to me." They 18 said to him therefore, "Where is your Father?" Jesus answered, "You know 19 neither me nor my Father; if you knew me, you would know my Father also."

E These words he spoke in the treasury, as he taught in the temple; but no 20 one arrested him, because his hour had not yet come.

§ 192 The Identity of Jesus

JOHN 8:21-30

A Again he said to them, "I go away, and you will seek me and die in your 21 sin; where I am going, you cannot come."

---

1 Or *see: for out of Galilee no prophet is to rise*   2 Most of the ancient authorities omit John 7:53-8:11: those which contain it vary much from each other   3 Other ancient authorities read *the Father*

HS references: John 8:5 = Leviticus 20:10 and Deuteronomy 22:22-24   John 8:8 = Jeremiah 17:13   John 8:17 = Deuteronomy 17:6 and 19:15

MT-MK-LK   JOHN 8

Then said the Jews, "Will he kill himself, since he says, 'Where I am 22
going, you cannot come'?" He said to them, "You are from below, I am 23
from above; you are of this world, I am not of this world. I told you that 24
you would die in your sins, for you will die in your sins unless you believe
that ¹I am he." They said to him, "Who are you?" Jesus said to them, 25
²"Even what I have told you from the beginning.

B I have much to say about you and much to judge; but he who sent me is 26
true, and I declare ³to the world what I have heard from him." They did not 27
understand that he spoke to them of the Father.

C So Jesus said, "When you have lifted up the Son of man, then you will 28
know that ⁴I am he, and that I do nothing on my own authority but speak
thus as the Father taught me. And he who sent me is with me; he has not 29
left me alone, for I always do what is pleasing to him." As he spoke thus, 30
many believed in him.

§ 193 Discourse on Freedom through Truth

JOHN 8:31-59

A Jesus then said to the Jews who had believed in him, "If you continue in 31
my word, you are truly my disciples, and you will know the truth, and the 32
truth will make you free." They answered him, "We are descendants of 33
Abraham, and have never been in bondage to any one. How is it that you
say, 'You will be made free'?" Jesus answered them, "Truly, truly, I say to 34
you, every one who commits sin is a slave to sin. The slave does not 35
continue in the house for ever; the son continues for ever. So if the Son 36
makes you free, you will be free indeed.

B I know that you are descendants of Abraham; yet you seek to kill me, 37
because my word finds no place in you. I speak of what I have seen with 38
⁵my Father, and you do what you have heard from ⁵your father." They 39
answered him, "Abraham is our father." Jesus said to them, "If you were
Abraham's children, you would do what Abraham did, but now you seek to 40
kill me, a man who has told you the truth which I heard from God; this is
not what Abraham did. You do what your father did."   41

C They said to him, "We were not born of fornication; we have one Father,
even God." Jesus said to them, "If God were your Father, you would love 42
me, for I proceeded and came forth from God; I came not of my own
accord, but he sent me. Why do you not understand what I say? It is 43
because you cannot bear to hear my word. You are of your father the devil, 44
and your will is to do your father's desires. He was a murderer from the
beginning, and has nothing to do with the truth, because there is no truth in
him. When he lies, he speaks according to his own nature, for he is a liar
and the father of lies. But, because I tell the truth, you do not believe me. 45
Which of you convicts me of sin? If I tell the truth, why do you not believe 46
me? He who is of God hears the words of God; the reason why you do not 47
hear them is that you are not of God."

---

1 Or *I am*   2 Or *Why do I talk to you at all?*   3 Greek *into*   4 Or *I am* or *I am* he: *and I do*   5 Or *the Father*

HS references: John 8:35 = Genesis 21:10   John 8:41 = Isaiah 63:16

JOHN **8**

D The Jews answered him, "Are we not right in saying that you are a 48 Samaritan and have a demon?" Jesus answered, "I have not a demon; but I 49 honor my Father, and you dishonor me. Yet I do not seek my own glory; 50 there is One who seeks it and he will be the judge.

E Truly, truly, I say to you, if any one keeps my word, he will never see 51 death." The Jews said to him, "Now we know that you have a demon. 52 Abraham died, as did the prophets; and you say, 'If any one keeps my word, he will never taste death.' Are you greater than our father Abraham, 53 who died? And the prophets died! Who do you claim to be?" Jesus 54 answered, "If I glorify myself, my glory is nothing; it is my Father who glorifies me, of whom you say that he is your God. But you have not known 55 him; I know him. If I said, I do not know him, I should be a liar like you; but I do know him and I keep his word. Your father Abraham rejoiced that 56 he was to see my day; he saw it and was glad." The Jews then said to him, 57 "You are not yet fifty years old, and have you seen Abraham?"[1] Jesus said 58 to them, "Truly, truly, I say to you, before Abraham [2]was, I am." So they 59 took up stones to throw at him; but Jesus [3]hid himself, and went out of the temple.[4]

D *On the possession of Jesus by a devil, compare § 45 C and § 53 B and § 86 C*

E *On verse 52a compare the references under portion D above*

---

1 Other ancient authorities read *has Abraham seen you?*   2 Greek *was born*   3 Or *was hidden, and went* etc.   4 Many ancient authorities add *and going through the midst of them went his way, and so passed by*

HS references: John 8:58 = Exodus 3:14

Chapter XI

AT THE FEAST OF THE DEDICATION

§ 194 The Blind Beggar of Jerusalem

JOHN 9:1-12   MT-MK-LK

A As he passed by, he saw a man blind from his birth. And his disciples 1 asked him, "Rabbi, who sinned, this man or his parents, that he was born 2 blind?" Jesus answered, "It was not that this man sinned, or his parents, but 3 that the works of God might be made manifest in him.

B We must work the works of him who sent me, while it is day; night 4 comes, when no one can work. As long as I am in the world, I am the light 5 of the world."

C As he said this, he spat on the ground and made clay of the spittle and 6 anointed the man's eyes with the clay, saying to him, "Go, wash in the pool 7 of Silo'am" (which means Sent). So he went and washed and came back seeing.

C For the Mt-Mk-Lk cases of the use of material means in healing, compare § 66 A and § 70 A

D The neighbors and those who had seen him before as a beggar, said, "Is 8 not this the man who used to sit and beg?" Some said, "It is he"; others 9 said, "No, but he is like him." He said, "I am the man." They said to him, 10 "Then how were your eyes opened?" He answered, "The man called Jesus 11 made clay and anointed my eyes and said to me, 'Go to Silo'am and wash'; so I went and washed and received my sight." They said to him, "Where is 12 he?" He said, "I do not know."

§ 195 Controversy about the Beggar and Jesus

JOHN 9:13-34

A They brought to the Pharisees the man who had formerly been blind. 13 Now it was a sabbath day when Jesus made the clay and opened his eyes. 14 The Pharisees again asked him how he had received his sight. And he said 15 to them, "He put clay on my eyes, and I washed, and I see."

B[B] Some of the Pharisees said, "This man is not from God, for he does not 16 keep the sabbath." But others said, "How can a man who is a sinner do such signs?" There was a division among them. So they again said to the blind 17 man, "What do you say about him, since he has opened your eyes?" He said, "He is a prophet."

B On the opposition to Jesus because of his attitude toward sabbath observance, compare § 32, § 33, § 98 and § 102

C The Jews did not believe that he had been blind and had received his 18 sight, until they called the parents of the man who had received his sight, and asked them, "Is this your son, who you say was born blind? How then 19 does he now see?" His parents answered, "We know that this is our son, 20 and that he was born blind; but how he now sees we do not know, nor do 21 we know who opened his eyes. Ask him; he is of age, he will speak for himself." His parents said this because they feared the Jews, for the Jews 22 had already agreed that if any one should confess him to be Christ, he was to be put out of the synagogue. Therefore his parents said, "He is of age, 23 ask him."

HS references: John 9:2 = Ezekiel 18:20   John 9:7 = II Kings 5:10

B Compare § 175 and § 188

D So for the second time they called the man who had been blind, and said 24 to him, "Give God the praise; we know that this man is a sinner." He 25 answered, "Whether he is a sinner, I do not know; one thing I know, that though I was blind, now I see." They said to him, "What did he do to you? 26 How did he open your eyes?" He answered them, "I have told you already, 27 and you would not listen. Why do you want to hear it again? Do you too want to become his disciples?" And they reviled him, saying, "You are his 28 disciple, but we are disciples of Moses. We know that God has spoken to 29 Moses, but as for this man, we do not know where he comes from." The 30 man answered, "Why, this is a marvel! You do not know where he comes from, and yet he opened my eyes. We know that God does not listen to 31 sinners, but if any one is a worshiper of God and does his will, God listens to him. Never since the world began has it been heard that any one opened 32 the eyes of a man born blind. If this man were not from God, he could do 33 nothing." They answered him, "You were born in utter sin, and would you 34 teach us?" And they cast him out.

§ 196 True Sight and False Sight

JOHN 9:35-41

A Jesus heard that they had cast him out, and having found him he said, 35 "Do you believe in [1]the Son of man?" He answered, "And who is he, sir, 36 that I may believe in him?" Jesus said to him, "You have seen him, and it is 37 he who speaks to you." He said, "Lord, I believe"; and he worshiped him. 38

B Jesus said, "For judgment I came into this world, that those who do not 39 see may see, and that those who see may become blind." Some of the 40 Pharisees near him heard this, and they said to him, "Are we also blind?" Jesus said to them, "If you were blind, you would have no guilt; but now 41 that you say, 'We see,' your guilt remains.

§ 197 Discourse on the Sheep and the Shepherd

JOHN 10:1-21

A "Truly, truly, I say to you, he who does not enter the sheepfold by the 1 door but climbs in by another way, that man is a thief and a robber; but he 2 who enters by the door is [2]the shepherd of the sheep. To him the gatekeeper 3 opens; the sheep hear his voice, and he calls his own sheep by name and leads them out. When he has brought out all his own, he goes before them, 4 and the sheep follow him, for they know his voice. A stranger they will not 5 follow, but they will flee from him, for they do not know the voice of strangers." This figure Jesus used with them, but they did not understand 6 what he was saying to them.

B So Jesus again said to them, "Truly, truly, I say to you, I am the door of 7 the sheep. All who came before me are thieves and robbers; but the sheep 8 did not heed them. I am the door; if any one enters by me, he will be 9 saved, and will go in and out and find pasture. The thief comes only to steal 10 and kill and destroy; I came that they may have life, and [3]have it abundantly.

---

1 Other ancient authorities read *the Son of God*　2 Or *a shepherd*　3 Or *have abundance*

HS references: John 9:24 = Joshua 7:19　　John 9:31 = Psalm 66:18-19 and Proverbs 15:29
John 9:39-41 = Isaiah 6:9-10 and Jeremiah 5:21 and Ezekiel 12:2　　John 10:8 = Jeremiah 23:1 and Ezekiel 34:2

JOHN 10   MT-MK-LK

C I am the good shepherd. The good shepherd lays down his life for the 11 sheep. He who is a hireling and not a shepherd, whose own the sheep are 12 not, sees the wolf coming and leaves the sheep and flees; and the wolf snatches them and scatters them. He flees because he is a hireling and cares 13 nothing for the sheep.

D I am the good shepherd; I know my own and my own know me, as the 14 Father knows me and I know the Father; and I lay down my life for the 15 sheep.

D *With verse 15a compare § 41 Q and § 82 T*

E And I have other sheep, that are not of this fold; I must ¹bring them also, 16 and they will heed my voice. So there shall be one flock, one shepherd.

F For this reason the Father loves me, because I lay down my life, that I 17 may take it again. No one ²takes it from me, but I lay it down of my own 18 accord. I have ³power to lay it down, and I have ³power to take it again; this charge I have received from my Father."

G There was again a division among the Jews because of these words. 19 Many of them said, "He has a demon, and he is mad; why listen to him?" 20 Others said, "These are not the sayings of one who has a demon. Can a 21 demon open the eyes of the blind?"

G *On the possession of Jesus by a devil, compare § 45 C and § 53 B and § 86 C*

§ 198 Bases of a Charge of Blasphemy

JOHN 10:22-39

A ⁴It was the feast of the Dedication at Jerusalem; it was winter, and Jesus 22 was walking in the temple, in the portico of Solomon. So the Jews gathered 23 round him and said to him, "How long will you keep us in suspense? If you 24 are the Christ, tell us plainly." Jesus answered them, "I told you, and you 25 do not believe. The works that I do in my Father's name, they bear witness to me;

B but you do not believe, because you do not belong to my sheep. My 26 sheep hear my voice, and I know them, and they follow me; and I give 27 them eternal life, and they shall never perish, and no one shall snatch them 28 out of my hand. ⁵My Father, who has given them to me, is greater than all, 29 and no one is able to snatch them out of the Father's hand.

C I and the Father are one." The Jews took up stones again to stone him. 30 Jesus answered them, "I have shown you many good works from the Father; 31 for which of these do you stone me?" The Jews answered him, "It is not for 32 a good work that we stone you but for blasphemy; because you, being a 33 man, make yourself God."

D Jesus answered them, "Is it not written in your law, 'I said, you are 34 gods'? If he called them gods to whom the word of God came (and scripture 35 cannot be broken), do you say of him whom the Father consecrated and sent 36 into the world, 'You are blaspheming,' because I said, 'I am the Son of God'?

---

1 Or *lead*   2 Some ancient authorities read *took it away*   3 Or *authority*   4 Some ancient authorities read *At that time was the feast*
5 Some ancient authorities read *What my Father has given to me*

HS references: John 10:11 = Isaiah 40:11 and Jeremiah 23:1-4 and Ezekiel 34:11   John 10:16 = Isaiah 56:8 and Ezekiel 34:23 and 37:24
John 10:33 = Leviticus 24:16   John 10:34 = Psalm 82:6

E If I am not doing the works of my Father, then do not believe me; but if 37 I do them, even though you do not believe me, believe the works, that you 38 may know and understand that the Father is in me and I am in the Father." Again they tried to arrest him, but he escaped from their hands. 39

Chapter XII

IN THE REGION OF JERUSALEM

---

§ 199 Withdrawal to Bethany beyond Jordan

JOHN 10:40-42   MT-MK-LK

He went away again across the Jordan to the place where John at first 40
baptized, and there he remained. And many came to him; and they said, 41
"John did no sign, but everything that John said about this man was true."
And many believed in him there.   42

§ 200 Return to Bethany Near Jerusalem

JOHN 11:1-16

A^ Now a certain man was ill, Laz'arus of Bethany, the village of Mary and 1   A *For the Mt-Mk-Lk reference to*
her sister Martha. It was Mary who anointed the Lord with ointment and 2   *Mary and Martha, compare § 84*
wiped his feet with her hair, whose brother Laz'arus was ill. So the sisters 3
sent to him, saying, "Lord, he whom you love is ill." But when Jesus heard 4
it he said, "This illness is not unto death; it is for the glory of God, so that
the Son of God may be glorified by means of it." Now Jesus loved Martha 5
and her sister and Laz'arus.

B So when he heard that he was ill, he stayed two days longer in the place 6
where he was. Then after this he said to the disciples, "Let us go into Judea 7
again." The disciples said to him, "Rabbi, the Jews were but now seeking to 8
stone you, and are you going there again?" Jesus answered, "Are there not 9
twelve hours in the day? If any one walks in the day, he does not stumble,
because he sees the light of this world. But if any one walks in the night, he 10
stumbles, because the light is not in him."

C Thus he spoke, and then he said to them, "Our friend Laz'arus has fallen 11
asleep, but I go to awake him out of sleep." The disciples said to him, 12
"Lord, if he has fallen asleep, he will ¹recover." Now Jesus had spoken of 13
his death, but they thought that he meant taking rest in sleep. Then Jesus 14
told them plainly, "Laz'arus is dead; and for your sake I am glad that I was 15
not there, so that you may believe. But let us go to him."

D Thomas, called the Twin, said to his fellow disciples, "Let us also go, 16
that we may die with him."

§ 201 Concerning Lazarus of Bethany

JOHN 11:17-44

A Now when Jesus came, he found that ²Laz'arus had already been in the 17
tomb four days. Bethany was near Jerusalem, about ³two miles off, and 18
many of the Jews had come to Martha and Mary to console them concerning 19
their brother.

B When Martha heard that Jesus was coming, she went and met him, while 20
Mary sat in the house. Martha said to Jesus, "Lord, if you had been here, 21
my brother would not have died. And even now I know that whatever you 22
ask from God, God will give you." Jesus said to her, "Your brother will 23
rise again." Martha said to him, "I know that he will rise again in the 24
resurrection at the last day."

---

1 Greek *be saved*   2 Greek *he*   3 Greek *fifteen stadia*

HS references: John 11:19 = Job 2:11   John 11:24 = Daniel 12:2

A On the anointing of Jesus by Mary, compare § 204 portion B

MT-MK-LK   **JOHN 11**

Jesus said to her, "I am the resurrection [1]and the life; he who believes in 25 me, though he die, yet shall he live, and whoever lives and believes in me 26 shall never die. Do you believe this?" She said to him, "Yes, Lord; I 27 believe that you are the Christ, the Son of God, he who is coming into the world."

C When she had said this, she went and called her sister Mary, saying 28 quietly, "The Teacher is here and is calling for you." And when she heard 29 it, she rose quickly and went to him. Now Jesus had not yet come to the 30 village, but was still in the place where Martha had met him. When the 31 Jews who were with her in the house, consoling her, saw Mary rise quickly and go out, they followed her, supposing that she was going to the tomb to [2]weep there. Then Mary, when she came where Jesus was and saw him, fell 32 at his feet, saying to him, "Lord, if you had been here, my brother would not have died."

D When Jesus saw her [3]weeping, and the Jews who came with her also 33 [3]weeping, he [4]was deeply moved in spirit and [5]troubled; and he said, "Where 34 have you laid him?" They said to him, "Lord, come and see." Jesus wept. 35 So the Jews said, "See how he loved him!" But some of them said, "Could 36 not he who opened the eyes of the blind man have kept this man from 37 dying?"

E Then Jesus, [6]deeply moved again, came to the tomb; it was a cave, and a 38 stone lay upon it. Jesus said, "Take away the stone." Martha, the sister of 39 the dead man, said to him, "Lord, by this time there will be an odor, for he has been dead four days." Jesus said to her, "Did I not tell you that if you 40 would believe you would see the glory of God?" So they took away the 41 stone.

F And Jesus lifted up his eyes and said, "Father, I thank thee that thou hast heard me. I knew that thou hearest me always, but I have said this on 42 account of the people standing by, that they may believe that thou didst send me." When he had said this, he cried with a loud voice, "Laz'arus, come 43 out." The dead man came out, his hands and feet bound with bandages, and 44 his face wrapped with a cloth. Jesus said to them, "Unbind him, and let him go."

§ 202   Plots for the Death of Jesus

JOHN 11:45-53

A Many of the Jews therefore, who had come with Mary and had seen 45 [7]what he did, believed in him; but some of them went to the Pharisees and 46 told them what Jesus had done.

B On the determination by the religious leaders to put Jesus to death, compare § 137 portion A

B So the chief priests and the Pharisees gathered the council, and said, 47 "What are we to do? For this man performs many signs. If we let him go 48 on thus, every one will believe in him, and the Romans will come and destroy both our [8]holy place and our nation."

C[c] But one of them, Ca'iaphas, who was high priest that year, said to them, 49 "You know nothing at all; you do not understand that it is expedient for you 50 that one man should die for the people, and that the whole nation should not perish."

---

1 Other ancient authorities omit *and the life*   2 Greek *wail*   3 Greek *wailing*   4 Or *was moved with indignation in the spirit*
5 Greek *troubled himself*   6 Or *being moved with indignation in himself*   7 Many ancient authorities read *the things which he did*   8 Greek *our place*

C Compare § 215 portion A

JOHN 11   MT-MK-LK

D He did not say this of his own accord, but being high priest that year he 51
prophesied that Jesus should die for the nation, and not for the nation only, 52
but to gather into one the children of God who are scattered abroad.

E So from that day on they took counsel how to put him to death.   53   **E** *Compare the reference under portion B above*

§ 203 Withdrawal of Jesus to Ephraim

JOHN 11:54-57

A Jesus therefore no longer went about openly among the Jews, but went 54
from there to the country near the wilderness, to a town called E'phraim;
and there he stayed with the disciples.

B Now the Passover of the Jews was at hand, and many went up from the 55
country to Jerusalem before the Passover, to purify themselves. They were 56
looking for Jesus and saying to one another as they stood in the temple,
"What do you think? That he will not come to the feast?"

C Now the chief priests and the Pharisees had given orders that if any one 57
knew where he was, he should let them know, so that they might arrest him.

§ 204 The Supper to Jesus at Bethany

JOHN 12:1-11

A Six days before the Passover, Jesus came to Bethany, where Laz'arus 1   **A** *On the statement about Martha, compare § 84*
was, whom Jesus had raised from the dead. There they made him a supper; 2
Martha served, and Laz'arus was one of those at table with him.

B Mary took a pound of costly ointment of ¹pure nard and anointed the feet 3   **B** *Compare § 42 portion A*
of Jesus and wiped his feet with her hair; and the house was filled with the   *Compare § 137 portion B*
fragrance of the ointment.

C But Judas Iscariot, one of his disciples (he who was to betray him), said, 4 **C** *Compare § 137 portion C*
"Why was this ointment not sold for three hundred ²denarii and given to the 5
poor?"

Dᴰ This he said, not that he cared for the poor but because he was a thief, 6
and as he had the money box he used to take what was put into it.

E Jesus said, "Let her alone, let her keep it for the day of my burial. The 7   **E** *Compare § 137 portion D*
poor you always have with you, but you do not always have me."   8

F When the great crowd of the Jews learned that he was there, they came, 9
not only on account of Jesus but also to see Laz'arus, whom he had raised
from the dead. So the chief priests planned to put Laz'arus also to death, 10
because on account of him many of the Jews were going away and believing 11
in Jesus.

---

1 Greek *pistic nard*, pistic being perhaps a local name: others take it to mean *genuine*; others *liquid*   2 The word in the Greek denotes a coin worth
about forty cents. The denarius was a day's wage for a laborer.

HS references: John 12:8 = Deuteronomy 15:11

D Compare § 209 portion K

Chapter XIII

CHALLENGE TO THE JERUSALEM LEADERS

§ 205 Jesus Enters Jerusalem as a Popular Leader

JOHN 12:12-19   MT-MK-LK

A The next day [1]a great crowd who had come to the feast heard that Jesus 12 was coming to Jerusalem. So they took branches of palm trees and went out 13 to meet him,

A *Compare § 124 portion F*

B crying, "Hosanna! Blessed is he who comes in the name of the Lord, even the King of Israel!"

B *Compare § 124 portion G*

C And Jesus found a young ass and sat upon it;   14

C *Compare § 124 portion E*

D as it is written,
    "Fear not, daughter of Zion;   15
    behold, your king is coming,
    sitting on an ass's colt!"
His disciples did not understand this at first; but when Jesus was glorified, 16 then they remembered that this had been written of him and had been done to him.

D *Compare § 124 portion C*

E The crowd that had been with him when he called Laz'arus out of the 17 tomb and raised him from the dead bore witness. The reason why the crowd 18 went to meet him was that they heard he had done this sign.

F The Pharisees then said to one another, "You see that you can do nothing; 19 look, the world has gone after him."

§ 206 Intimations of the Impending Death of Jesus

JOHN 12:20-36a

A Now among those who went up to worship at the feast were some 20 Greeks. So these came to Philip, who was from Beth-sa'ida in Galilee, and 21 said to him, "Sir, we wish to see Jesus." Philip went and told Andrew; 22 Andrew went with Philip and they told Jesus.

B And Jesus answered them, "The hour has come for the Son of man to be 23 glorified. Truly, truly, I say to you, unless a grain of wheat falls into the 24 earth and dies, it remains alone; but if it dies, it bears much fruit.

C He who loves his [2]life loses it, and he who hates his [2]life in this world 25 will keep it for eternal life. If any one serves me, he must follow me; and 26 where I am, there shall my servant be also; if any one serves me, the Father will honor him.

C *Compare § 57 portions NO*
Compare § 73 portions AB
Compare § 104 portion C
Compare § 112 portion J

D "Now is my soul troubled. And what shall I say? 'Father, save me from 27 this hour'? No, for this purpose I have come to this hour. Father, glorify 28 thy name." Then a voice came from heaven, "I have glorified it, and I will glorify it again." The crowd standing by heard it and said that it had 29 thundered. Others said, "An angel has spoken to him." Jesus answered, 30 "This voice has come for your sake, not for mine.

D *Compare § 95 portion A*
Compare § 140 portions BC
In reference to an angel, compare § 140 portion D

---

1 Some ancient authorities read *the common people*   2 or *soul*

HS references: John 12:13 = Psalm 118:25-26   John 12:15 = Isaiah 62:11 and Zechariah 9:9   John 12:27 = Psalm 42:6

MT-MK-LK   JOHN 12

E *With verse 31b compare verse 18 of § 82 portion R*

E Now is [1]the judgment of this world, now shall the ruler of this world be 31 cast out; and I, when I am lifted up [2]from the earth, will draw all men to 32 myself." He said this to show by what death he was to die. The crowd 33 answered him, "We have heard from the law that the Christ remains for 34 ever. How can you say that the Son of man must be lifted up? Who is this Son of man?"

F Jesus said to them, "The light is [3]with you for a little longer. Walk while 35 you have the light, lest the darkness overtake you; he who walks in the darkness does not know where he goes. While you have the light, believe in 36a the light, that you may become sons of light."

§ 207 Unbelief and Belief in Jesus

JOHN 12:36b-43

A When Jesus had said this, he departed and [4]hid himself from them. 36b Though he had done so many signs before them, yet they did not believe in 37 him; it was that the word spoken by the prophet Isaiah might be fulfilled: 38
"Lord, who has believed our report,
　　and to whom has the arm of the Lord been revealed?"

B *Compare § 47 portion J*

B Therefore they could not believe. For Isaiah again said,   39
"He has blinded their eyes and hardened their heart,   40
　　lest they should see with their eyes and perceive with their heart,
　　and turn for me to heal them."
Isaiah said this because he saw his glory and spoke of him.   41

C Nevertheless many even of the authorities believed in him, but for fear of 42 the Pharisees they did not confess it, lest they should be put out of the synagogue: for they loved the praise of men more than the praise of God.   43

§ 208 The Source of the Truth in Jesus

JOHN 12:44-50

A *Compare § 57 portion P*
Compare § 78 portion G
Compare § 82 portion Q

A And Jesus cried out and said, "He who believes in me, believes not in me 44 but in him who sent me. And he who sees me sees him who sent me.   45

B I have come as light into the world, that whoever believes in me may not 46 remain in darkness.

C If any one hears my sayings and does not keep them, I do not judge him; 47 for I did not come to judge the world but to save the world. He who rejects 48 me and does not receive my sayings has a judge; the word that I have spoken will be his judge on the last day.

D For I have not spoken on my own authority; the Father who sent me has 49 himself given me commandment what to say and what to speak. And I know 50 that his commandment is eternal life. What I say, therefore, I say as the Father has bidden me."

---

1 Or *a judgment*   2 Or *out of*   3 Or *in*   4 Or *was hidden from them*

HS references: John 12:34 = Isaiah 9:7 and Daniel 7:14   John 12:38 = Isaiah 53:1   John 12:40 = Isaiah 6:10 and Jeremiah 5:21 and Ezekiel 12:2
John 12:41 = Isaiah 6:1

Chapter XIV

FINAL HOURS WITH DISCIPLES

---

§ 209 The Passover with the Disciples

JOHN 13:1-38   MT-MK-LK

A Now before the feast of the Passover, when Jesus knew that his hour had 1
come to depart out of this world to the Father, having loved his own who
were in the world, he loved them ¹to the end.

B And during supper, when the devil had already put it into the heart of 2
Judas Iscariot, Simon's son, to betray him, Jesus, knowing that the Father 3
had given all things into his hands, and that he had come from God and was
going to God, rose from supper, laid aside his garments, and girded himself 4
with a towel. Then he poured water into a basin, and began to wash the 5
disciples' feet, and to wipe them with the towel with which he was girded.

B With verse 2 compare Luke 22:3 in § 137 portion F
With verse 3a compare § 41 Q and § 82 T and § 151 B
With verses 4-5 compare verse 37 in § 94 A

C He came to Simon Peter; and Peter said to him, "Lord, do you wash my 6
feet?" Jesus answered him, "What I am doing you do not know now, but 7
afterward you will understand." Peter said to him, "You shall never wash 8
my feet." Jesus answered him, "If I do not wash you, you have no part in
me." Simon Peter said to him, "Lord, not my feet only but also my hands 9
and my head!" Jesus said to him, "He who has bathed does not need to 10
wash, ²except for his feet, but he is clean all over; and ³you are clean, but
not every one of you." For he knew who was to betray him; that was why 11
he said, "You are not all clean."

C With verse 11 compare § 138 portion E

D When he had washed their feet, and taken his garments, and ⁴resumed his 12
place, he said to them, "Do you know what I have done to you? You call 13
me Teacher and Lord; and you are right, for so I am. If I then, your Lord 14
and Teacher, have washed your feet, you also ought to wash one another's
feet. For I have given you an example, that you also should do as I have 15
done to you.

D Compare § 78 portions BEH
Compare § 120 portion J
Compare § 138 portion M
Compare § 132 portion G

Eᴱ Truly, truly, I say to you, a ⁵servant is not greater than his master; nor is 16
⁶he who is sent greater than he who sent him. If you know these things, 17
blessed are you if you do them.

E Compare § 38 portion H
Compare § 57 portion G

F I am not speaking of you all; I know whom I have chosen; it is that the 18
scripture may be fulfilled, 'He who ate ⁷my bread has lifted his heel against
me.' I tell you this now, before it takes place, that when it does take place 19
you may believe that ⁸I am he.

F Compare § 138 portion E

G Truly, truly, I say to you, he who receives any one whom I send receives 20
me; and he who receives me receives him who sent me."

G Compare § 57 portion P
Compare § 78 portion G
Compare § 82 portion Q

H When Jesus had thus spoken, he was troubled in spirit, and testified, 21
"Truly, truly, I say to you, one of you will betray me." The disciples 22
looked at one another, uncertain of whom he spoke.

H Compare § 138 portion E
Compare § 138 portion K

---

1 Or *to the uttermost*   2 Some ancient authorities omit *except for his feet*   3 The Greek word for *you* here is plural
4 Greek *reclined again*   5 Or *slave*   6 Greek *an apostle*   7 Many ancient authorities read *his bread with me*   8 Or *I am*

HS references: John 13:18 = Psalm 41:9

E Compare § 211 portion H

MT-MK-LK   JOHN 13

I¹ One of his disciples, whom Jesus loved, was lying close to the breast of 23 Jesus; so Simon Peter beckoned to him and said, "Tell us who it is of whom 24 he speaks." So lying thus, close to the breast of Jesus, he said to him, 25 "Lord, who is it?"

J Compare § 138 portion E
   Compare § 138 portion F
With verse 27 compare Luke 22:3 in
§ 137 portion F

J Jesus answered, "It is he to whom I shall give this morsel when I have 26 dipped it." So when he had dipped the morsel, he gave it to Judas, the son of Simon Iscariot. Then after the morsel, Satan entered into him.   27

Kᴷ Jesus said to him, "What you are going to do, do quickly." Now no one 28 at the table knew why he said this to him. Some thought that, because Judas 29 had the money box, Jesus was telling him, "Buy what we need for the feast"; or, that he should give something to the poor. So, after receiving the 30 morsel, he immediately went out; and it was night.

L When he had gone out, Jesus said, "Now ¹is the Son of man glorified, 31 and in him God ¹is glorified; if God is glorified in him, God will also 32 glorify him in himself, and glorify him at once.

Mᴹ Little children, yet a little while I am with you. You will seek me; and 33 as I said to the Jews so now I say to you, 'Where I am going you cannot come.'

Nᴺ A new commandment I give to you, that you love one another; even as I 34 have loved you, that you also love one another. By this all men will know 35 that you are my disciples, if you have love for one another."

O Compare § 139 portion D

O Simon Peter said to him, "Lord, where are you going?" Jesus answered, 36 "Where I am going you cannot follow me now; but you shall follow afterward." Peter said to him, "Lord, why cannot I follow you now? I will 37 lay down my life for you." Jesus answered, "Will you lay down your life 38 for me? Truly, truly, I say to you, the cock will not crow, till you have denied me three times.

§ 210 Farewell Discourses of Jesus

JOHN 14:1-31

A "Let not your hearts be troubled; ²believe in God, believe also in me. In 1 my Father's house are many ³rooms; if it were not so, would I have told 2 you that I go to prepare a place for you? And when I go and prepare a place 3 for you, I will come again and will take you to myself, that where I am you may be also.

Bᴮ And ⁴you know the way where I am going." Thomas said to him, "Lord, 4 we do not know where you are going; how can we know the way?" Jesus 5 said to him, "I am the way, and the truth, and the life; no one comes to the 6 Father, but by me.

---

1 Or *was*   2 Or *you believe*   3 Or *abiding-places*   4 Other ancient authorities read *where I am going you know, and the way you know*

HS references: John 13:34 = Leviticus 19:18

I For other references to the disciple whom Jesus loved, compare § 217 E, § 219 B, § 222 AC and § 223 A
K Compare § 204 portion D
M Compare § 189 portion D
N Compare § 211 portion E

B Compare § 211 portion L

C If you had known me, you would have known my Father also; henceforth 7 you know him and have seen him." Philip said to him, "Lord, show us the 8 Father, and we shall be satisfied." Jesus said to him, "Have I been with you 9 so long, and yet you do not know me, Philip? He who has seen me has seen the Father; how can you say, 'Show us the Father'? Do you not believe that 10 I am in the Father and the Father in me? The words that I say to you I do not speak on my own authority; but the Father who dwells in me does his works. Believe me that I am in the Father and the Father in me; or else 11 believe me for the sake of the works themselves.

D "Truly, truly, I say to you, he who believes in me will also do the works 12 that I do; and greater works than these will he do, because I go to the Father.

E Whatever you ask in my name, I will do it, that the Father may be 13 glorified in the Son; if you ask¹ anything in my name, I will do it. 14

E   Compare § 78 portion U
Compare § 127 portion D

F "If you love me, you will keep my commandments. And I will ²pray the 15 Father, and he will give you another ³Counselor, to be with you for ever, 16 even the Spirit of truth, whom the world cannot receive, because it neither 17 sees him nor knows him; you know him, for he dwells with you, and will be in you.

G "I will not leave you ⁴desolate; I will come to you. Yet a little while, and 18 the world will see me no more, but you will see me; because I live, you 19 will live also. In that day you will know that I am in my Father, and you in 20 me, and I in you.

H He who has my commandments and keeps them, he it is who loves me; 21 and he who loves me will be loved by my Father, and I will love him and manifest myself to him." Judas (not Iscariot) said to him, "Lord, how is it 22 that you will manifest yourself to us, and not to the world?" Jesus answered 23 him, "If a man loves me, he will keep my word, and my Father will love him, and we will come to him and make our home with him. He who does 24 not love me does not keep my words; and the word which you hear is not mine but the Father's who sent me.

H   With verse 23b compare verse 20 in § 78 portion U and verse 20b in § 151 portion C

I "These things I have spoken to you, while I am still with you. But the 25 ³Counselor, the Holy Spirit, whom the Father will send in my name, he will 26 teach you all things, and bring to your remembrance all that I have said to you.

I   Compare § 57 portion C
Compare § 91 portion I
Compare § 134 portion I

J Peace I leave with you; my peace I give to you; not as the world gives do 27 I give to you. Let not your hearts be troubled, neither let them be afraid. You heard me say to you, 'I go away, and I will come to you.' If you loved 28 me, you would have rejoiced, because I go to the Father; for the Father is greater than I.

K And now I have told you before it takes place, so that when it does take 29 place, you may believe. I will no longer talk much with you, for the ruler of 30 this world is coming. He has no power over me; but I do as the Father has 31 commanded me, so that the world may know that I love the Father. Rise, let us go hence.

K   With the last sentence in verse 31, compare § 139 A and the last verse in § 140 G.

1 Other ancient authorities add *me*   2 Greek *make request of*   3 Or *Advocate* or *Helper*; Greek *Paraclete*   4 Or *orphans*

§ 211 Farewell Discourses of Jesus (*concluded*)

MT-MK-LK   JOHN 15:1-16:33

A "I am the true vine, and my Father is the vinedresser. Every branch of 1 mine that bears no fruit, he takes away, and every branch that does bear 2 fruit he prunes, that it may bear more fruit. You are already made clean by 3 the word which I have spoken to you.

B Abide in me, and I in you. As the branch cannot bear fruit by itself, 4 unless it abides in the vine, neither can you, unless you abide in me. I am 5 the vine, you are the branches. He who abides in me, and I in him, he it is that bears much fruit, for apart from me you can do nothing. If a man does 6 not abide in me, he is cast forth as a branch and withers; and the branches are gathered, thrown into the fire and burned.

C *Compare § 78 portion U*
Compare § 127 portion D

C If you abide in me, and my words abide in you, ask whatever you will, 7 and it shall be done for you. By this my Father [1]is glorified, that you bear 8 much fruit, and [2]so prove to be my disciples.

D As the Father has loved me, so have I loved you; abide in my love. If 9 you keep my commandments, you will abide in my love, just as I have kept 10 my Father's commandments and abide in his love. These things I have 11 spoken to you, that my joy may be in you, and that your joy may be full.

E *With verse 14 compare § 46 E and*
§ 49 E and § 87

E[E] "This is my commandment, that you love one another as I have loved 12 you. Greater love has no man than this, that a man lay down his life for his 13 friends. You are my friends if you do what I command you. No longer do I 14 call you [3]servants, for the [4]servant does not know what his master is doing; 15 but I have called you friends, for all that I have heard from my Father I have made known to you.

F *Compare § 35 portion B*
Compare the references under
portion C above

F You did not choose me, but I chose you and appointed you that you 16 should go and bear fruit and that your fruit should abide; so that whatever you ask the Father in my name, he may give it to you. This I command 17 you, to love one another.

G *Compare § 36 portions HI*
Compare § 57 E and § 134 K

G "If the world hates you, know that it has hated me before it hated you. If 18 you were of the world, the world would love its own; but because you are 19 not of the world, but I chose you out of the world, therefore the world hates you.

H *With verse 20a compare § 38 H*
and § 57 G
With verses 20b-21 compare § 36 HI,
§ 57 A and § 134 G

H[H] Remember the word that I said to you, 'A [4]servant is not greater than his 20 master.' If they persecuted me, they will persecute you; if they kept my word, they will keep yours also. But all this they will do to you on my 21 account, because they do not know him who sent me.

---

1 Or *was*   2 Many ancient authorities omit *so prove to*   3 Or *slaves*   4 Or *slave*

HS references: John 15:1 = Isaiah 5:1-7 and Jeremiah 2:21 and Ezekiel 19:10-14

E Compare § 209 portion N
H Compare § 209 portion E

JOHN 15-16

MT-MK-LK

I If I had not come and spoken to them, they would not have sin; but now 22 they have no excuse for their sin. He who hates me hates my Father also. If 23 I had not done among them the works which no one else did, they would 24 not have sin; but now they have seen and hated both me and my Father. It 25 is to fulfil the word that is written in their law, 'They hated me without a cause.'

J But when the ¹Counselor comes, whom I shall send to you from the 26 Father, even the Spirit of truth, who ²proceeds from the Father, he will bear witness to me; and you also are witnesses, because you have been with me 27 from the beginning.

K "I have said all this to you to keep you from falling away. They will put 16: you out of the synagogues; indeed, the hour is coming when whoever kills 1 you will think he is offering service to God. And they will do this because 2 they have not known the Father, nor me. But I have said these things to 3 you, that when their hour comes you may remember that I told you of them. 4

Lᴸ "I did not say these things to you from the beginning, because I was with you. But now I am going to him who sent me; yet none of you asks me, 5 'Where are you going?' But because I have said these things to you, sorrow 6 has filled your hearts.

M Nevertheless I tell you the truth: it is to your advantage that I go away, 7 for if I do not go away, the ¹Counselor will not come to you; but if I go, I will send him to you. And when he comes, he will ³convince the world 8 concerning sin and righteousness and judgment: concerning sin, because they 9 do not believe in me; concerning righteousness, because I go to the Father, 10 and you will see me no more; concerning judgment, because the ruler of 11 this world is judged.

N "I have yet many things to say to you, but you cannot bear them now. 12 When the Spirit of truth comes, he will guide you into all the truth; for he 13 will not speak on his own authority, but whatever he hears he will speak, and he will declare to you the things that are to come. He will glorify me, 14 for he will take what is mine and declare it to you. All that the Father has is 15 mine; therefore I said that he will take what is mine and declare it to you.

O "A little while, and you will see me no more; again a little while, and 16 you will see me." Some of his disciples said to one another, "What is this 17 that he says to us, 'A little while, and you will not see me, and again a little while, and you will see me'; and, 'because I go to the Father'?" They said, 18 "What does he mean by 'a little while'? We do not know what he means." Jesus knew that they wanted to ask him; so he said to them, "Is this what 19 you are asking yourselves, what I meant by saying, 'A little while, and you will not see me, and again a little while, and you will see me'?

I *With verse 23 compare § 82 portion Q*

J *Compare § 150 portion E Compare § 151 portion C*

K *Compare § 57 portion D Compare § 134 portion J With verses 1 and 4 compare the last verse of § 135 portion B*

M *With verse 11 compare verse 18 of § 82 R*

N *With verse 15 compare § 41 Q and § 82 T and § 151 B*

O *Compare § 139 portion C Compare § 147 portion F*

---

1 Or *Advocate* or *Helper;* Greek *Paraclete*   2 Or *goes forth from*   3 Or *convict*

HS references: John 15:25 = Psalms 35:19 and 69:4   John 16:2 = Isaiah 66:5

L Compare § 210 portion B

MT-MK-LK	JOHN 16

P *With verse 22 compare the references under portion O above*

P Truly, truly, I say to you, you will weep and lament, but the world will 20 rejoice; you will be sorrowful, but your sorrow will turn into joy. When a 21 woman is in travail she has sorrow, because her hour has come; but when she is delivered of the child, she no longer remembers the anguish, for joy that [1]a child is born into the world. So you have sorrow now, but I will see 22 you again and your hearts will rejoice, and no one will take your joy from you.

Q *Compare § 78 portion U*
Compare § 127 portion D

Q In that day you will [2]ask nothing of me. Truly, truly, I say to you, if you 23 ask anything of the Father, he will give it to you in my name. Hitherto you 24 have asked nothing in my name; ask, and you will receive, that your joy may be full.

R "I have said this to you in [3]figures; the hour is coming when I shall no 25 longer speak to you in [3]figures but tell you plainly of the Father.

S In that day you will ask in my name; and I do not say to you that I shall 26 [4]pray the Father for you; for the Father himself loves you, because you have 27 loved me and have believed that I came from the Father.

T I came from the Father and have come into the world; again, I am leaving 28 the world and going to the Father." His disciples said, "Ah, now you are 29 speaking plainly, not in any [5]figure! Now we know that you know all things, 30 and need none to question you; by this we believe that you came from God."

U *Compare § 139 portion B*

U Jesus answered them, "Do you now believe? The hour is coming, indeed 31 it has come, when you will be scattered, every man to his home, and will 32 leave me alone; yet I am not alone, for the Father is with me.

V I have said this to you, that in me you may have peace. In the world you 33 have tribulation; but be of good cheer, I have overcome the world."

§ 212 Farewell Prayer of Jesus

JOHN 17:1-26

A When Jesus had spoken these words, he lifted up his eyes to heaven and 1 said, "Father, the hour has come; glorify thy Son that the Son may glorify thee,

B *With verse 2a compare § 41 Q and § 82 T and § 151 B*

B since thou hast given him power over all flesh, to give eternal life to all 2 whom thou hast given him. And this is eternal life, that they know thee the 3 only true God, and Jesus Christ whom thou hast sent.

C I glorified thee on earth, having accomplished the work which thou gavest 4 me to do; and now, Father, glorify thou me in thy own presence with the 5 glory which I had with thee before the world was made.

D "I have manifested thy name to the men whom thou gavest me out of the 6 world; thine they were, and thou gavest them to me, and they have kept thy word. Now they know that everything that thou hast given me is from thee; 7

---

1 Greek *a human being*   2 Or *ask me no question*   3 Or *parables*   4 Greek *make request of*   5 Or *parable*

HS references: John 16:21 = Isaiah 13:8   John 16:22 = Isaiah 66:14   John 16:32 = Zechariah 13:7

JOHN 17   MT-MK-LK

for I have given them the words which thou gavest me, and they have 8
received them and know in truth that I came from thee; and they have
believed that thou didst send me.

E I ¹am praying for them; I ¹am not praying for the world but for those 9
whom thou hast given me, for they are thine; all mine are thine, and thine 10
are mine, and I am glorified in them. And now I am no more in the world, 11
but they are in the world, and I am coming to thee.

E *With verse 10a compare the references under portion B above*

F Holy Father, keep them in thy name, which thou hast given me, that they
may be one, even as we are one. While I was with them, I kept them in thy 12
name, which thou hast given me; I have guarded them, and none of them is
lost but the son of perdition, that the scripture might be fulfilled. But now I 13
am coming to thee; and these things I speak in the world, that they may
have my joy fulfilled in themselves.

G I have given them thy word; and the world has hated them because they 14
are not of the world, even as I am not of the world. I do not ¹pray that thou 15
shouldst take them out of the world, but that thou shouldst keep them ²from
³the evil one. They are not of the world, even as I am not of the world.   16

H Sanctify them in the truth; thy word is truth. As thou didst send me into 17
the world, so I have sent them into the world. And for their sake I 18
consecrate myself, that they also may be consecrated in truth.   19

H *With verse 18 compare § 56 C and § 82 A*

I "I do not ¹pray for these only, but also for those who believe in me 20
through their word, that they may all be one; even as thou, Father, art in 21
me, and I in thee, that they also may be in us, so that the world may believe
that thou hast sent me.

J The glory which thou hast given me I have given to them, that they may 22
be one even as we are one, I in them and thou in me, that they may become 23
perfectly one, so that the world may know that thou hast sent me and hast
loved them even as thou hast loved me.

K Father, I desire that they also, whom thou hast given me, may be with 24
me where I am, to behold my glory which thou hast given me in thy love
for me before the foundation of the world.

L O righteous Father, the world has not known thee, but I have known thee; 25
and these know that thou hast sent me. I made known to them thy name, 26
and I will make it known, that the love with which thou hast loved me may
be in them, and I in them."

L *Compare the second half of § 41 Q and § 82 T*

§ 213 At the Place Named Gethsemane

JOHN 18:1-2

When Jesus had spoken these words, he went forth with his disciples across 1
the Kidron valley, where there was a garden, which he and his disciples
entered. Now Judas, who betrayed him, also knew the place; for Jesus often 2
met there with his disciples.

Compare § 139 A and § 140 A
Compare § 140 portion B

---

1 Greek *make request*   2 Greek *out of*   3 Or *evil*

HS references: John 17:12 = Psalm 41:9   John 18:1 = II Samuel 15:23

§ 214 Betrayal and Arrest of Jesus

MT-MK-LK   JOHN 18:3-11

A *Compare § 141 portion A*

A So Judas, procuring a band of soldiers and some officers from the chief 3 priests and the Pharisees, went there with lanterns and torches and weapons.

B Then Jesus, knowing all that was to befall him, came forward and said to 4 them, "Whom do you seek?" They answered him, "Jesus of Nazareth." 5 Jesus said to them, "I am he." Judas, who betrayed him, was standing with them. When he said to them, "I am he," they drew back and fell to the 6 ground. Again he asked them, "Whom do you seek?" And they said, "Jesus 7 of Nazareth." Jesus answered, "I told you that I am he; so, if you seek me, 8 let these men go." This was to fulfil the word which he had spoken, "Of 9 those whom thou gavest me I lost not one."

C *Compare § 141 portion D*

C Then Simon Peter, having a sword, drew it and struck the high priest's 10 slave and cut off his right ear. The slave's name was Malchus.

D *Compare § 141 portion F*
Compare § 120 portion C
Compare § 140 portion C

D Jesus said to Peter, "Put your sword into its sheath; shall I not drink the 11 cup which the Father has given me?"

Chapter XV

JUDICIAL TRIALS AND CRUCIFIXION

§ 215 Trial before the Jewish Authorities

JOHN 18:12-27

MT-MK-LK

A^A So the band of soldiers and their [1]captain and the officers of the Jews 12 seized Jesus and bound him. First they led him to Annas; for he was the 13 father-in-law of Ca'iaphas, who was high priest that year. It was Ca'iaphas 14 who had given counsel to the Jews that it was expedient that one man should die for the people.

A Compare § 142 portion A

B Simon Peter followed Jesus, and so did another disciple. As this disciple 15 was known to the high priest, he entered the court of the high priest along with Jesus, while Peter stood outside at the door. So the other disciple, who 16 was known to the high priest, went out and spoke to the maid who kept the door, and brought Peter in.

C The maid who kept the door said to Peter, "Are not you also one of this 17 man's disciples?" He said, "I am not."

C Compare § 142 portion H

D Now the [2]servants and officers had made a charcoal fire, because it was 18 cold, and they were standing and warming themselves; Peter also was with them, standing and warming himself.

D Compare § 142 portion B

E The high priest then questioned Jesus about his disciples and his teaching. 19 Jesus answered him, "I have spoken openly to the world; I have always 20 taught in [3]synagogues and in the temple, where all Jews come together; I have said nothing secretly. Why do you ask me? Ask those who have heard 21 me, what I said to them; they know what I said." When he had said this, 22 one of the officers standing by struck Jesus [4]with his hand, saying, "Is that how you answer the high priest?" Jesus answered him, "If I have spoken 23 wrongly, bear witness to the wrong; but if I have spoken rightly, why do you strike me?"

E Compare § 142 portion D
With verse 20 compare § 141 G

F Annas then sent him bound to Ca'iaphas the high priest.   24

F Compare § 142 portion M

G Now Simon Peter was standing and warming himself. They said to him, 25 "Are not you also one of his disciples?" He denied it and said, "I am not."

G Compare § 142 portion I

H One of the [2]servants of the high priest, a kinsman of the man whose ear 26 Peter had cut off, asked, "Did I not see you in the garden with him?" Peter 27 again denied it; and at once the cock crowed.

H Compare § 142 portion J
Compare § 142 portion K

§ 216 Trial before the Roman Authorities

JOHN 18:28-19:16

A Then they led Jesus from the house of Ca'iaphas to the praetorium. It was 28 early. They themselves did not enter the praetorium, so that they might not be defiled, but might eat the passover.

A Compare § 142 portion M
Compare § 143 portion A

B So Pilate went out to them and said, "What accusation do you bring 29 against this man?" They answered him, "If this man were not an evildoer,   30

---

1 Or *military tribune*; Greek *chiliarch*   2 Or *slaves*   3 Greek *synagogue*   4 Or *with a rod*

A Compare § 202 portion C

MT-MK-LK	JOHN **18-19**

we would not have handed him over." Pilate said to them, "Take him 31 yourselves and judge him by your own law." The Jews said to him, "It is not lawful for us to put any man to death." This was to fulfil the word 32 which Jesus had spoken to show by what death he was to die.

C *Compare § 143 portion D*

C Pilate entered the praetorium again and called Jesus, and said to him, 33 "Are you the King of the Jews?"

D *Compare § 143 portion E*

D Jesus answered, "Do you say this of your own accord, or did others say 34 it to you about me?" Pilate answered, "Am I a Jew? Your own nation and 35 the chief priests have handed you over to me; what have you done?" Jesus 36 answered, "My kingship is not of this world; if my kingship were of this world, my ¹servants would fight, that I might not be handed over to the Jews; but my kingship is not from the world."

E *Compare § 143 portion D*

E Pilate said to him, "So you are a king?" Jesus answered, "²You say that I 37 am a king.

F *Compare § 143 portion E*

F For this I was born, and for this I have come into the world, to bear witness to the truth. Every one who is of the truth hears my voice." Pilate 38 said to him, "What is truth?"

G *Compare § 143 portion F*

G After he had said this, he went out to the Jews again, and told them, "I find no crime in him.

H *Compare § 143 portion I*

H But you have a custom that I should release one man for you at the 39 Passover; will you have me release for you the King of the Jews?"

I *Compare § 143 portion K*

I They cried out again, "Not this man, but Barab'bas!" Now Barab'bas was 40 a robber.

J *Compare § 143 portion M*

J Then Pilate took Jesus and scourged him.   19:1

K *Compare verse 11 of § 143 G*
Compare § 143 portion N

K And the soldiers plaited a crown of thorns, and put it on his head, and 2 arrayed him in a purple robe; they came up to him, saying, "Hail, King of 3 the Jews!" and struck him ³with their hands.

L *Compare § 143 portion H*

L Pilate went out again, and said to them, "See, I am bringing him out to 4 you, that you may know that I find no crime in him." So Jesus came out, 5 wearing the crown of thorns and the purple robe.

M *Compare § 143 portion K*

M Pilate said to them, "Behold the man!" When the chief priests and the 6 officers saw him, they cried out, "Crucify him, crucify him!" Pilate said to them, "Take him yourselves and crucify him, for I find no crime in him."

N The Jews answered him, "We have a law, and by that law he ought to 7 die, because he has made himself the Son of God." When Pilate heard these 8 words, he was the more afraid; he entered the praetorium again and said to 9 Jesus, "Where are you from?" But Jesus gave no answer. Pilate therefore 10

---

1 Or *officers*: as in verses 3, 12, 18, 22   2 Or *You say it, because I am a king*   3 Or *with rods*

HS references: John 19:7 = Leviticus 24:16

JOHN 19   MT-MK-LK

said to him, "You will not speak to me? Do you not know that I have
[1]power to release you, and [1]power to crucify you?" Jesus answered him, 11
"You would have no [1]power over me unless it had been given you from
above; therefore he who delivered me to you has the greater sin."

O Upon this Pilate sought to release him, but the Jews cried out, "If you 12
release this man, you are not Caesar's friend; every one who makes himself
a king sets himself against Caesar." When Pilate heard these words, he 13
brought Jesus out and sat down on the judgment seat at a place called The
Pavement, and in Hebrew, Gab'batha. Now it was the day of Preparation of 14
the Passover; it was about the sixth hour. He said to the Jews, "Behold your
King!" They cried out, "Away with him, away with him, crucify him!" 15
Pilate said to them, "Shall I crucify your King?" The chief priests answered,
"We have no king but Caesar." Then he handed him over to them to be 16
crucified.

O *On the charge of making himself a*
king, compare § 143 C
With verse 16 compare § 143 M

§ 217 The Crucifixion of Jesus

JOHN 19:17-30

A So they took Jesus, and he went out, bearing his own cross,   17

A *Compare § 144 portion A*

B to the place called the place of a skull, which is called in Hebrew
Gol'gotha. There they crucified him, and with him two others, one on either 18
side, and Jesus between them. Pilate also wrote a title and put it on the 19
cross; it read, "Jesus of Nazareth, the King of the Jews."

B *Compare § 144 portion C*

C Many of the Jews read this title, [2]for the place where Jesus was crucified 20
was near the city; and it was written in Hebrew, in Latin, and in Greek.
The chief priests of the Jews then said to Pilate, "Do not write, 'The King 21
of the Jews,' but, 'This man said, I am King of the Jews.'" Pilate answered, 22
"What I have written I have written."

D When the soldiers had crucified Jesus they took his garments and made 23
four parts, one for each soldier; also his tunic. But the tunic was without
seam, woven from top to bottom; so they said to one another, "Let us not 24
tear it, but cast lots for it to see whose it shall be." This was to fulfil the
scripture,

D *Compare § 144 portion C*

>   "They parted my garments among them,
>   and for my clothing they cast lots."
So the soldiers did this.   25

E[E] But standing by the cross of Jesus were his mother, and his mother's
sister, Mary the wife of Clopas, and Mary Mag'dalene. When Jesus saw his 26
mother, and the disciple whom he loved standing near, he said to his
mother, "Woman, behold, your son!" Then he said to the disciple, "Behold, 27
your mother!" And from that hour the disciple took her to his own home.

E *Compare § 144 portion L*

F After this Jesus, knowing that all was now finished, said (to fulfil the 28
scripture), "I thirst." A bowl full of vinegar stood there; so they put a 29
sponge full of the vinegar on hyssop and held it to his mouth.

F *Compare § 144 portion G*

---

1 Or *authority*   2 Or *for the place of the city where Jesus was crucified was near at hand*

HS references: John 19:24 = Psalm 22:18   John 19:28-29 = Psalm 69:21

E For other references to the disciple whom Jesus loved, compare § 209 I, § 219 B, § 222 AC, and § 223 A

MT-MK-LK	JOHN 19

G *Compare § 144 portion H*

G When Jesus had received the vinegar, he said, "It is finished"; and he 30 bowed his head and gave up his spirit.

§ 218 The Burial of Jesus

JOHN 19:31-42

A *Compare § 145 portion A*

A Since it was the day of Preparation, in order to prevent the bodies from 31 remaining on the cross on the sabbath (for that sabbath was a high day),

B the Jews asked Pilate that their legs might be broken, and that they might be taken away. So the soldiers came and broke the legs of the first, and of 32 the other who had been crucified with him; but when they came to Jesus and 33 saw that he was already dead, they did not break his legs. But one of the 34 soldiers pierced his side with a spear, and at once there came out blood and water.

C He who saw it has borne witness--his testimony is true, and he knows that 35 he tells the truth--that you also may believe. For these things took place that 36 the scripture might be fulfilled, "Not a bone of him shall be [1]broken." And again another scripture says, "They shall look on him whom they have 37 pierced."

D *Compare § 145 portion B*

D After this Joseph of Arimathe'a, who was a disciple of Jesus, but 38 secretly, for fear of the Jews, asked Pilate that he might take away the body of Jesus, and Pilate gave him leave. So he came and took away his body.

E[E] Nicode'mus also, who had at first come to him by night, came bringing a 39 [2]mixture of myrrh and aloes, about a hundred pounds' weight.

F *Compare § 145 portion D*

F They took the body of Jesus, and bound it in linen cloths with the spices, 40 as is the burial custom of the Jews. Now in the place where he was 41 crucified there was a garden, and in the garden a new tomb where no one had ever been laid. So because of the Jewish day of Preparation, as the 42 tomb was close at hand, they laid Jesus there.

---

1 Or *crushed*   2 Some ancient authorities read *roll*

HS references: John 19:36 = Exodus 12:46 and Numbers 9:12 and Psalm 34:20   John 19:37 = Zechariah 12:10

E For other references to Nicodemus, compare § 161 A and § 189 H

Chapter XVI

SUBSEQUENT TO THE DEATH OF JESUS

§ 219 The Visits to the Sepulchre

JOHN 20:1-18   MT-MK-LK

A Now on the first day of the week Mary Mag'dalene came to the tomb 1 early, while it was still dark, and saw that the stone had been taken away from the tomb.

A *Compare § 147 portions ABC*

B[B] So she ran, and went to Simon Peter and the other disciple, the one 2 whom Jesus loved, and said to them, "They have taken the Lord out of the tomb, and we do not know where they have laid him."

B *Compare § 147 portion G*
Compare § 147 portion I
Compare § 149 portion C

C Peter then came out with the other disciple, and they went toward the 3 tomb. They both ran, but the other disciple outran Peter and reached the 4 tomb first; and stooping to look in, he saw the linen cloths lying there, but 5 he did not go in. Then Simon Peter came, following him, and went into the 6 tomb; he saw the linen cloths lying, and the napkin, which had been on his 7 head, not lying with the linen cloths but rolled up in a place by itself. Then 8 the other disciple, who reached the tomb first, also went in, and he saw and believed; for as yet they did not know the scripture, that he must rise from 9 the dead. Then the disciples went back to their homes.   10

C *Compare § 147 portion J*
Compare § 149 portion D

D But Mary stood weeping outside the tomb, and as she wept she stooped to 11 look into the tomb; and she saw two angels in white, sitting where the body 12 of Jesus had lain, one at the head and one at the feet. They said to her, 13 "Woman, why are you weeping?" She said to them, "Because they have taken away my Lord, and I do not know where they have laid him."

D *Compare § 147 portion D*
Compare § 149 portion C

E Saying this, she turned round and saw Jesus standing, but she did not 14 know that it was Jesus. Jesus said to her, "Woman, why are you weeping? 15 Whom do you seek?" Supposing him to be the gardener, she said to him, "Sir, if you have carried him away, tell me where you have laid him, and I will take him away." Jesus said to her, "Mary." She turned and said to him 16 in Hebrew, "Rab-bo'ni!" (which means Teacher). Jesus said to her, "Do not 17 hold me, for I have not yet ascended to the Father; but go to my brethren and say to them, I am ascending to my Father and your Father, to my God and your God." Mary Mag'dalene went and said to the disciples, "I have 18 seen the Lord"; and she told them that he had said these things to her.

E *Compare § 147 portion H*
For the record of the ascension here promised, compare § 150 portion F

§ 220 With the Disciples in Jerusalem

JOHN 20:19-29

A On the evening of that day, the first day of the week, the doors being 19 shut where the disciples were, for fear of the Jews, Jesus came and stood among them and said to them, "Peace be with you." When he had said this, 20 he showed them his hands and his side. Then the disciples were glad when they saw the Lord.

A *Compare § 150 portion B*

B For other references to the disciple whom Jesus loved, compare § 209 I, § 217 E, § 222 AC, and § 223 A

MT-MK-LK   **JOHN 20**

B *Compare § 150 portion E*
Compare § 151 portion C

C *Compare § 71 portion F*
Compare § 78 portion T

B Jesus said to them again, "Peace be with you. As the Father has sent me, 21 even so I send you."

C And when he had said this, he breathed on them, and said to them, 22 "Receive the Holy Spirit. If you forgive the sins of any, they are forgiven; 23 if you retain the sins of any, they are retained."

D Now Thomas, one of the twelve, called the Twin, was not with them 24 when Jesus came. So the other disciples told him, "We have seen the Lord." 25 But he said to them, "Unless I see in his hands the print of the nails, and place my finger in the mark of the nails, and place my hand in his side, I will not believe."

E Eight days later, his disciples were again in the house, and Thomas was 26 with them. The doors were shut, but Jesus came and stood among them, and said, "Peace be with you." Then he said to Thomas, "Put your finger here, 27 and see my hands; and put out your hand, and place it in my side; do not be faithless, but believing." Thomas answered him, "My Lord and my God!" 28 Jesus said to him, "Have you believed because you have seen me? Blessed 29 are those who have not seen and yet believe."

§ 221 Purpose of the Record of John

JOHN 20:30-31

Now Jesus did many other signs in the presence of the disciples, which are 30 not written in this book; but these are written that you may believe that 31 Jesus is the Christ, the Son of God, and that believing you may have life in his name.

§ 222 With the Disciples at the Sea of Tiberias

JOHN 21:1-23

A *For an account in the Mt-Mk-Lk record having some elements in common with this narrative, compare § 27 (Luke)*

A[A] After this Jesus revealed himself again to the disciples by the Sea of 1 Tibe'ri-as; and he revealed himself in this way. Simon Peter, Thomas called 2 the Twin, Nathan'a-el of Cana in Galilee, the sons of Zeb'edee, and two others of his disciples were together. Simon Peter said to them, "I am going 3 fishing." They said to him, "We will go with you." They went out and got into the boat; but that night they caught nothing.

Just as day was breaking, Jesus stood on the beach; yet the disciples did not 4 know that it was Jesus. Jesus said to them, "Children, have you any fish?" 5 They answered him,"No." He said to them, "Cast the net on the right side 6 of the boat, and you will find some." So they cast it, and now they were not able to haul it in, for the quantity of fish. That disciple whom Jesus loved 7 said to Peter, "It is the Lord!" When Simon Peter heard that it was the Lord, he put on his clothes, for he was stripped for work, and sprang into the sea. But the other disciples came in the boat, dragging the net full of 8 fish, for they were not far from the land, but about [1]a hundred yards off.

When they got out on land, they saw a charcoal fire there, with [2]fish lying 9 on it, and bread. Jesus said to them, "Bring some of the fish that you have 10 just caught." So Simon Peter went aboard and hauled the net ashore, full of 11 large fish, a hundred and fifty-three of them; and although there

---

1 Greek *two hundred cubits*   2 Or *a fish*

A For other references to the disciple whom Jesus loved, compare § 209 I, § 217 E, § 219 B, and § 223 A.

were so many, the net was not torn. Jesus said to them, "Come and have 12 breakfast." Now none of the disciples dared ask him, "Who are you?" They knew it was the Lord. Jesus came and took the [1]bread and gave it to them, 13 and so with the fish. This was now the third time that Jesus was revealed to 14 the disciples after he was raised from the dead.

B When they had finished breakfast, Jesus said to Simon Peter, "Simon, son 15 of [2]John, do you [3]love me more than these?" He said to him, "Yes, Lord; you know that I [4]love you." He said to him, "Feed my lambs." A second 16 time he said to him, "Simon, son of [2]John, do you [3]love me?" He said to him, "Yes, Lord; you know that I [4]love you." He said to him, "Tend my sheep." He said to him the third time, "Simon, son of [2]John, do you [4]love 17 me?" Peter was grieved because he said to him the third time, "Do you [4]love me?" And he said to him, "Lord, you know everything; you [5]know that I [4]love you." Jesus said to him, "Feed my sheep.

C[C] Truly, truly, I say to you, when you were young, you girded yourself 18 and walked where you would; but when you are old, you will stretch out your hands, and another will gird you and carry you where you do not wish to go." (This he said to show by what death he was to glorify God.) And 19 after this he said to him, "Follow me."
 Peter turned and saw following them the disciple whom Jesus loved, who had lain close to his breast at the supper and had said, "Lord, who is it that 20 is going to betray you?" When Peter saw him, he said to Jesus, "Lord, what about this man?" Jesus said to him, "If it is my will that he remain until I 21 come, what is that to you? Follow me!" The saying spread abroad among 22 the brethren that this disciple was not to die; yet Jesus did not say to him 23 that he was not to die, but, "If it is my will that he remain until I come, what is that to you?"

§ 223 Conclusion of the Record of John

JOHN 21:24-25

A[A] This is the disciple who is bearing witness to these things, and who has 24 written these things; and we know that his testimony is true.

B But there are also many other things which Jesus did; were every one of 25 them to be written, I suppose that the world itself could not contain the books that would be written.

---

1 Or *a loaf*   2 Greek *Joanes*: called in Matthew 16:17 *Jonah*   3 Greek *agape*   4 Greek *phileo*   5 Or *perceive*

C Compare § 222A and attached references

A Compare § 222A and attached references

EXHIBIT OF THE RELATIONS BETWEEN THE RECORD
OF MT-MK-LK AND THE RECORD OF JOHN

IN THE ORDER OF MT-MK-LK

§ 11C . . . . § 189F	§ 45Q . . . . § 182B	§ 71E . . . . § 155B
§ 17 . . . . § 152B	§ 46E . . . . § 211E	§ 71F . . . . § 220C
§ 17D-F. . . . . . § 153C	§ 47J . . . . § 207B	§ 73AB . . . . . . § 206C
§ 17O . . . . § 153A	§ 49E . . . . § 211E	§ 74C . . . . § 152D
§ 17P . . . . § 152E	§ 53B . . . . § 188A	§ 74M . . . . § 153B
§ 17P . . . . § 153E	§ 53B . . . . § 193D	§ 76A . . . . § 184
§ 17P . . . . § 154A	§ 53B . . . . § 193E	§ 78B . . . . § 209D
§ 17R . . . . § 164	§ 53B . . . . § 197G	§ 78D . . . . § 161C
§ 18B . . . . § 154B	§ 54C . . . . § 187A	§ 78E . . . . § 209D
§ 18B . . . . § 154D	§ 54D . . . . § 182F	§ 78G . . . . § 176B
§ 18C . . . . § 154C	§ 54H . . . . § 172B	§ 78G . . . . § 208A
§ 18C . . . . § 154D	§ 54J. . . . . . . § 185B	§ 78G . . . . § 209G
§ 20G . . . . § 156B	§ 56B . . . . § 170D	§ 78H . . . . § 209D
§ 21A . . . . § 167	§ 56C . . . . § 212H	§ 78T . . . . § 220C
§ 21A . . . . § 172A	§ 56D . . . . § 155B	§ 78U . . . . § 210E
§ 21B . . . . § 158	§ 56D . . . . § 156A	§ 78U . . . . § 210H
§ 22C . . . . § 187A	§ 57A . . . . § 211H	§ 78U . . . . § 211C
§ 22D . . . . § 182F	§ 57C . . . . § 210I	§ 78U . . . . § 211F
§ 22H . . . . § 172B	§ 57D . . . . § 211K	§ 78U . . . . § 211Q
§ 23 . . . . § 155A	§ 57E . . . . § 211G	§ 82A. . . . . . . § 212H
§ 24A . . . . § 158	§ 57G . . . . § 209E	§ 82B. . . . . . . § 170D
§ 24B . . . . § 189G	§ 57G . . . . § 211H	§ 82Q. . . . . . . § 176B
§ 24E . . . . § 189G	§ 57NO . . . . . § 206C	§ 82Q. . . . . . . § 208A
§ 27 . . . . § 155A	§ 57P . . . . § 176B	§ 82Q. . . . . . . § 209G
§ 27 . . . . § 222A	§ 57P . . . . § 208A	§ 82Q. . . . . . . § 211I
§ 29GH . . . . . . § 174C	§ 57P . . . . § 209G	§ 82R. . . . . . . § 206E
§ 32 . . . . § 195B	§ 58BC. . . . . . § 153B	§ 82R. . . . . . . § 211M
§ 32B . . . . § 175A	§ 58D . . . . . . § 164	§ 82T. . . . . . . § 166B
§ 33 . . . . § 195B	§ 60A . . . . § 178A	§ 82T. . . . . . . § 182H
§ 33G . . . . § 175C	§ 60B . . . . § 178B	§ 82T. . . . . . . § 189B
§ 35B . . . . § 183D	§ 60C . . . . § 178C	§ 82T. . . . . . . § 197D
§ 35B . . . . § 211F	§ 60D . . . . § 178D	§ 82T. . . . . . . § 209B
§ 35C . . . . § 155B	§ 60F . . . . § 178E	§ 82T. . . . . . . § 211N
§ 35C . . . . § 156A	§ 60G . . . . § 178G	§ 82T. . . . . . . § 212B
§ 36HI. . . . . . § 211G	§ 60H . . . . § 178H	§ 82T. . . . . . . § 212E
§ 36HI. . . . . . § 211H	§ 60I . . . . § 178F	§ 82T. . . . . . . § 212L
§ 38H . . . . § 209E	§ 60J . . . . § 180A	§ 84 . . . . § 200A
§ 38H . . . . § 211H	§ 60K . . . . § 179B	§ 84 . . . . § 204A
§ 38X . . . . § 189G	§ 61A . . . . § 180B	§ 86C. . . . . . . § 188A
§ 39 . . . . § 173B	§ 61B . . . . § 180C	§ 86C. . . . . . . § 193D
§ 41E . . . . § 153C	§ 61D . . . . § 180D	§ 86C. . . . . . . § 193E
§ 41G . . . . § 153B	§ 62A . . . . § 180D	§ 86C. . . . . . . § 197G
§ 41Q . . . . § 166B	§ 65 . . . . § 178A	§ 86D. . . . . . . § 182B
§ 41Q . . . . § 182H	§ 66A . . . . § 194C	§ 87 . . . . § 211E
§ 41Q . . . . § 189B	§ 67A . . . . § 178B	§ 91I . . . . § 210I
§ 41Q . . . . § 197D	§ 67C . . . . § 178C	§ 94A . . . . § 209B
§ 41Q . . . . § 209B	§ 67D . . . . § 178D	§ 95A. . . . . . . § 206D
§ 41Q . . . . § 211N	§ 67E . . . . § 178E	§ 98 . . . . § 195B
§ 41Q . . . . § 212B	§ 67F . . . . § 178G	§ 102 . . . . § 195B
§ 41Q . . . . § 212E	§ 67H . . . . § 178H	§ 104C . . . . . . § 206C
§ 41Q . . . . § 212L	§ 67I . . . . § 178F	§ 112J . . . . . . § 206C
§ 42A . . . . § 204B	§ 67J . . . . § 180A	§ 116C . . . . . . § 161C
§ 44 . . . . § 185B	§ 68A . . . . § 182B	§ 120C . . . . . . § 214D
§ 45C . . . . § 188A	§ 70A . . . . § 194C	§ 120J . . . . . . § 209D
§ 45C . . . . § 193D	§ 71A . . . . § 179B	§ 124C . . . . . . § 205D
§ 45C . . . . § 193E	§ 71C . . . . § 153B	§ 124E . . . . . . § 205C
§ 45C . . . . § 197G	§ 71D . . . . § 183C	§ 124F . . . . . . § 205A

LOCATION OF PASSAGES IN THE RECORDS